Apt

Dr

Turkey > P.S.L.
Stuff

Salad > Nickus
Rolls

Potatoes >
liquor > Brian

desserts > Steve + Amy

The
Only
Cookbook
you'll ever need

The Only Cookbook

you'll ever need

Zoë Camrass

RAND M^cNALLY & COMPANY
New York   Chicago   San Francisco
in association with
Mitchell Beazley Publishers Limited
London

The Only Cookbook You'll Ever Need was edited and
designed by Mitchell Beazley Publishers Limited,
Mill House, 87–89 Shaftesbury Avenue,
London W1V 7AD

Editor
Rachel Grenfell

Art Editors
Mike Rose
Celia Welcomme

Assistant Editors
Corine Plough
Gillian Abrahams

Researchers
Ursula Whyte
Marsha Lloyd
Mary-Jane Sinclair

Design Assistant
Jackie Whelan

Editorial Assistant
Margaret Little

Production
Hugh Stancliffe

Indexer
Susan Wilson

Publisher
Bruce Marshall

Art Director
John Bigg

Consultant
Glorya Hale

Photographer
Roger Phillips

Stylist
Lucy Su

Home economist
Caroline Ellwood

Reference photography
Simon de Courcy-Wheeler

Props
David Mellor; Divertimenti;
Elizabeth David Ltd

Artists
Tamara Blake; Ray Burrows and
Corinne Clarke; Chris Forsey;
Julia Fryer; Vana Haggerty;
Clive Hayball; Hayward and
Martin Ltd; Ingrid Jacob; Sally
Launder; Kevin Maddison; Lucy
Su; Michael J. Woods

The publishers gratefully
acknowledge the assistance of
the following:
W. Fenn Ltd; Richards (Soho)
Ltd; Slater and Cooke, Bisney
and Jones Ltd

Published 1977 in the United States of America
by Rand McNally & Company, P.O. Box 7600,
Chicago, Illinois, 60680
Printed in U.S.A.

Library of Congress Catalog Card Number:
77-77528

SBN 528-81001-4

Introduction and contents

As a child I lived on a farm in Yorkshire, England, where almost everything we ate was homegrown and full of flavor. We ate simply, but wonderfully well. The milk, cream and butter came from our own cows and at a very early age I learned how to milk a cow and churn the butter. We ate our own poultry and cured our own bacon, then hung the hams from the oak beams in the kitchen.

When my mother wasn't making bread, cakes or pies, which were baked in the oven that was heated by the flames of the open wood fire, she was busy making cream cheese, preserving our own fruit or blackberries we had picked from the hedges or making apple jelly or jam in our old copper preserving pan—I liked the jam days best of all for the sweet smell, in spite of the constant buzzing of the wasps.

Watching my mother cook I learned to bake and knead and mix ingredients at about the time I was learning to read. I couldn't have had a better teacher, for my mother had the most important asset any cook can have—she loved food. She was also an inventive cook. My father would bring in a hare or pheasant that he had shot and my mother, who always had the imagination to adapt a recipe, would make it into a superb dish.

In *The Only Cookbook You'll Ever Need* I try to show how easy it is to prepare the raw ingredients and to cook them in the most suitable way. Each cooking method—boiling and steaming, stewing and casseroling, broiling, frying and sautéing, roasting and baking—is described in detail, and each of these sections is preceded by a contents list in the form of a chart.

On the charts the recipes are divided into first courses, main courses, light lunch or supper dishes, accompaniments and desserts, and there are suggestions wherever necessary for what to serve with each dish. There is also a miscellaneous section, which includes cakes, pastries, breads, snacks and such breakfast dishes as porridge.

Once you understand the reasons behind the basic cooking techniques you should be able to tackle any recipe, however complicated, for even the elaborate dishes of the haute cuisine are just a combination of a number of simple operations.

The Only Cookbook You'll Ever Need will be, I hope, a springboard to start you off on a lifetime of good, exciting and creative cooking.

Kitchen equipment 8
Illustrations and text on the basic kitchen equipment you need for cooking.

Buying and storing 10
How to select the best foods, and how long you can keep them.

Freezing 14
Preparing food for freezing, and a guide to freezer storage life for the basic foods.

Basic preparation 16
Step-by-step illustrations show you how to prepare different types of food.

The heart of good cooking 54
Recipes and information about stocks, soups and sauces.

The methods 70
Full explanations of all the basic cooking methods, with recipes as examples.

The cold table 206
Additional cold dishes, ranging from pâtés to salads and desserts.

Glossary and index 218
Glossary of the cooking terms used, and a fully cross-referenced index.

	Basic preparation 16	Boiling and steaming 72	Stewing and casseroling 104	Broiling 124	Frying and sautéing 136	Roasting and baking 164
Fish and shellfish	18	74	106	126	138	166
Poultry and game birds	26	82	110	130	142	170
Meat and game	30	86	114	132	146	174
Vegetables	40	90	120	134	150	180
Fruit	46	94		134	154	184
Cereals (pastry, pasta, cakes and breads)	48	97	122		156	188
Eggs and dairy products	53	100		134	160	202

Kitchen equipment

The choice of cooking equipment is enormous and the less experienced cook can be forgiven for not knowing quite what to buy. Although the following list is basic, there may be items in it that are irrelevant to your style of cooking. If, for example, you rarely bake cakes and cookies there will be no need for you to buy such a wide range of baking pans. Specialist utensils, such as those required for making sauces or steaming (for example a vegetable steamer) are described in the appropriate sections.

It is more economical in the long run to buy the best-quality kitchen equipment, for only such equipment can be expected to survive high temperatures, constant cleaning and hard wear.

For cutting, stirring and beating

Good kitchen knives are a sound investment, and those made of carbon steel are still the best because they can be kept very sharp. Stainless steel, however, is easier to keep clean.

Keep knives away from other cutlery—for example on a knife rack—for safety and to prevent them from being blunted on other implements. Wash carbon steel knives immediately after use and rub them lightly with soap-filled steel-wool pads to keep them bright and shiny. If knives become discolored, rub them with a damp cloth and scouring powder, then rinse and dry them immediately or they will rust.

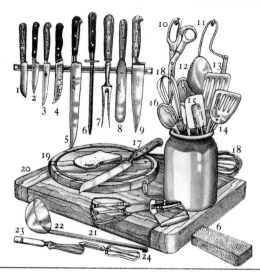

1 Paring knife for peeling vegetables, preparing garnishes or boning fish. 2 Chef's knife. 3 Filleting knife with flexible blade. 4 Small, stainless steel serrated knife. 5 Carving knife. 6 Sharpening steel. 7 Carving fork with guard. 8 Spatula. 9 Chopping knife. 10 Kitchen scissors. 11 Meat saw. 12 Long-handled kitchen spoon. 13 Large pancake turner. 14 Small pancake turner. 15 Rubber spatula. 16 Wooden spoons. 17 Serrated bread knife. 18 Wire whisks in graduated sizes. 19 Bread board. 20 Chopping board. 21 Rotary beater. 22 Ladle. 23 Stainless steel apple corer. 24 Vegetable peeler.

Pots and pans

Good pans are designed for utility rather than for appearance. They are made from high-quality metals that conduct heat evenly. The inexpensive and more decorative pans that abound in many hardware stores are a waste of money because inferior metals conduct heat poorly. This causes the base of the pan to overheat—burned milk and ruined sauces too often confirm this.

Aluminum pans with heavy bases last a lifetime, but they discolor when they are used for boiling water. Add a little vinegar to the pan or bring back the shine by using soap-filled steel-wool pads. Stainless steel pans are equally durable and always stay shiny.

Among the other types of pans available, the heavy enameled ones are excellent for making casseroles but are too heavy for general use. Take care not to chip the enamel, because once damaged, the lining cannot be replaced. Nonstick pans are useful for heating milk and for making scrambled eggs, but the coating wears off eventually.

You can also buy handsome copper pans, but they need relining from time to time. To clean a copper crêpe pan, just wipe it with paper towels. Other copper pans can be cleaned with soap-filled steel-wool pads.

Store all pans without their lids on to prevent them from smelling musty.

1 Copper crêpe pan. 2 Cast-iron or aluminum frying pans of different sizes. 3 Cast-iron omelet pan. 4 Poaching kettle with rack and lid—useful for fish, puddings, hams, galantines. 5 Nonstick saucepan. 6 Stainless steel or aluminum saucepans of various sizes, with lids. 7 Large, deep aluminum pan (good for cooking shellfish and pasta). 8 Double boiler. 9 Sauté pan, a straight-sided, heavy-based pan with lid. 10 Pressure cooker. 11 Enameled casseroles of various sizes with well-fitting lids.

How to season a new cast-iron omelet or crêpe pan

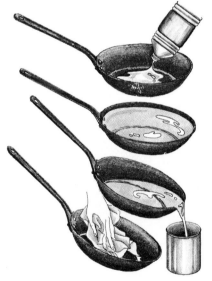

Fill the pan with oil and heat it slightly. Turn the heat off and allow the oil-filled pan to stand for twenty-four hours. Pour off the oil and wipe the pan with paper towels to remove any excess grease. Never wash the inside of the pan—just wipe it with paper towels. If the pan becomes very dirty, rub it all over with salt, wipe with a damp cloth and then oil lightly. Wash the underside of the pan after use to prevent dirt from accumulating.

Baking utensils and molds

1 Muffin tins. 2 Baking sheets to fit oven.
3 Cooling rack. 4 Oval ovenproof dishes of
different sizes. 5 Rectangular hinged pan.
6 Pie plates of different sizes. 7 Fluted
cookie cutters. 8 Three-way springform
cake pan. 9 Plain cookie cutters. 10 Plain
flan rings of various sizes. 11 Mousse or
jelly molds. 12 Bombe mold. 13 Small tart
pans. 14 Flan case with removable base for
tarts and fruit flans. 15 Porcelain crinkle-
edged flan dishes. 16 Soufflé dishes of
various sizes. 17 Oval ovenproof casseroles.
18 Jelly roll pans of different sizes. 19
Roasting pans to fit oven. 20 Charlotte
mold. 21 Earthenware lidded pot.
22 Individual soufflé or ramekin dishes.
23 Layer cake pans of different sizes. 24 Pie pans of different sizes. 25 Loaf pans.

Other useful equipment

1 Vegetable slicer. 2 Conical strainer.
3 Corkscrew. 4 Wire sieves in different
sizes. 5 Wire salad basket. 6 Potato masher.
7 Garlic press. 8 Can opener. 9 Food
grinder. 10 Colander. 11 Pestle and mortar.
12 Citrus fruit juicer. 13 Rotary grater.
14 Four-sided grater. 15 Sugar sifter.
16 Food mill. 17 Candy thermometer.
18 Metal skewers. 19 Trussing needle.
20 Weighing scales. 21 Measuring cup.
22 Copper bowl for beating egg whites. 23 Set
of measuring spoons. 24 Flour sifter.
25 Funnel. 26 Pastry brush. 27 Pudding
molds in various sizes. 28 Set of graduated
mixing bowls. 29 Basting syringe. 30 Rolling
pin. 31 Large pastry tube with nozzles.
32 Marble slab or pastry board. You will
also need : aluminum foil in two sizes ;
waxed paper ; clear plastic wrap ; paper
towels ; parchment paper ; cheesecloth ;
string ; rubber bands and a roll of plastic
bags with fasteners.

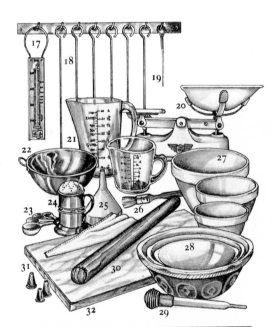

Electrical equipment

Of all the electrical gadgets available the
only really essential one is the blender.
It eliminates many tedious kitchen
chores such as crumbing bread and
puréeing vegetables and fruit, and it
saves time when making hollandaise
sauce or mayonnaise.

The portable electric beater is useful for mixtures that need to be beaten
over hot water or ice for a long time.

A coffee grinder is necessary if you
wish to serve really fresh coffee. If you
keep the grinder very clean and free of
ground coffee, it can also be used for
grinding nuts and making bread crumbs
in small quantities.

Although it is possible to have all
these gadgets incorporated in one large
all-purpose electric mixer, the convenience of the portable beater cannot be
matched by the electric mixer.

1 Blender. 2 Coffee grinder. 3 All-purpose
electric mixer. 4 Portable electric beater.

Buying and storing

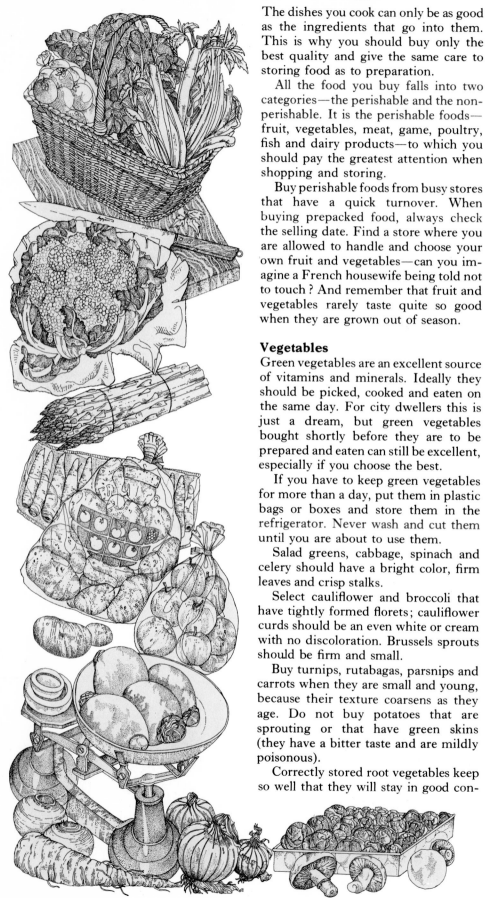

The dishes you cook can only be as good as the ingredients that go into them. This is why you should buy only the best quality and give the same care to storing food as to preparation.

All the food you buy falls into two categories—the perishable and the non-perishable. It is the perishable foods—fruit, vegetables, meat, game, poultry, fish and dairy products—to which you should pay the greatest attention when shopping and storing.

Buy perishable foods from busy stores that have a quick turnover. When buying prepacked food, always check the selling date. Find a store where you are allowed to handle and choose your own fruit and vegetables—can you imagine a French housewife being told not to touch? And remember that fruit and vegetables rarely taste quite so good when they are grown out of season.

Vegetables

Green vegetables are an excellent source of vitamins and minerals. Ideally they should be picked, cooked and eaten on the same day. For city dwellers this is just a dream, but green vegetables bought shortly before they are to be prepared and eaten can still be excellent, especially if you choose the best.

If you have to keep green vegetables for more than a day, put them in plastic bags or boxes and store them in the refrigerator. Never wash and cut them until you are about to use them.

Salad greens, cabbage, spinach and celery should have a bright color, firm leaves and crisp stalks.

Select cauliflower and broccoli that have tightly formed florets; cauliflower curds should be an even white or cream with no discoloration. Brussels sprouts should be firm and small.

Buy turnips, rutabagas, parsnips and carrots when they are small and young, because their texture coarsens as they age. Do not buy potatoes that are sprouting or that have green skins (they have a bitter taste and are mildly poisonous).

Correctly stored root vegetables keep so well that they will stay in good con-dition from one season to the next. Because they require cool, dry condi-tions a cellar is the best place to store them. If you grow your own vege-tables you may keep potatoes and turnips outdoors packed in earth "pies"—the vegetables neatly stacked, covered with straw and then with soil. In the same way carrots can be layered in sand in a clean trash can or similar container. In the kitchen, root vegetables keep better on a vegetable rack than in the refrig-erator.

Buy asparagus that has tightly closed tips and fleshy stalks. The stalks vary in size and color from the large, pale, mauve-tipped asparagus to the slimmer, green, delicately flavored variety. Green asparagus is generally preferred—it is an early spring crop which is cut when the young stalks reach to about eight inches (20 cm) above the ground.

An artichoke should have firm, green, overlapping, fleshy leaves in a tight rosette. If the leaves have spread and are discolored the artichoke will be tough.

It is often difficult to find ripe avo-cados on the day you want them, so to avoid disappointment buy them in ad-vance, slightly underripe, and let them ripen in a warm kitchen. To test for ripeness, gently press the stalk end; if it gives slightly it is ripe.

Of all the vegetables that fall into the category of pods and seeds, corn is the one that deteriorates fastest after harvesting. Young corn is naturally sweet, but shortly after the cob is cut off the stalk the sugar begins to convert into starch, so cook corn as soon as you can after buying it.

Fresh young peas taste best—they are sweet, not starchy, and have smooth, well-filled pods. Green beans should be bright green and so fresh that they break with a snap when you bend them.

The vegetable fruit—squash, zuc-chini, cucumbers, eggplants, peppers and tomatoes—should be firm, smooth-skinned and bright. If they are in good condition when you buy them they will keep well in the refrigerator for at least three to four days.

The most delicious mushrooms are the wild ones, which you pick yourself in fields and woods or buy in a few special shops. The variety most com-monly sold, however, is the commer-cially grown white mushroom. There is usually a choice between small or large mushrooms. Small mushrooms look attractive in casseroles, but the large mushrooms have a better flavor. Mushy, decayed mushrooms are dangerous to eat. Wild mushrooms in particular do not keep well.

Buy onions that are firm and without shoots. They keep well on a vegetable rack or hung in a dry, cool cellar. If your kitchen is small and warm, refrigerate onions; humidity and warmth will make them sprout. Use scallions within a day or two of purchase or, if you want to keep them longer, put them in a plastic bag and refrigerate. Garlic bulbs keep best strung up like onions in a cool cellar, but if you have to keep them in the kitchen for any length of time they should be stored in the refrigerator. Leeks are best when they have long, slender stems, more white than green. They should be eaten fresh, but can be stored for up to two days in the refrigerator.

Use fresh herbs during the short season when they are available; they are incomparably superior to the dried or frozen ones. Buy fresh herbs in small quantities for use that day, and make sure they are truly fresh; limp, discolored leaves mean loss of flavor. If you have bought more than you can use, put them in plastic bags in the refrigerator, where their freshness will be preserved a few days longer. They can also be dried successfully. Such herbs as mint and rosemary will survive a day or two in a cool place if the stems are kept in water.

Fruit
When buying fruit remember that, generally speaking, small is delicious; overgrown fruit is often tasteless. Keep unripe fruit in a brown paper bag at room temperature. Look at them every day and when they are ripe use them immediately or put them in the refrigerator.

Apples and pears that are firm and free from bruises will keep well in a cool cellar or in a refrigerator.

Select grapefruit, oranges and lemons that have smooth skins and are heavy for their size. Green patches indicate that they are not ripe and, therefore, may be sour. Lemons with thin skins are usually the most juicy. All citrus fruit can be refrigerated for a few weeks.

Buy bananas that are yellow, not those that are turning black. Do not refrigerate them or they will darken. Bananas ripen quickly so use them within a few days of purchase.

Although the sweetest melons are those that are ripened on the vine, you can buy underripe ones that will mature well in the kitchen. If necessary you can store ripe melons for up to a week in the refrigerator. Avoid buying melons at the end of their season, because they may rot before they ripen. When a melon is ripe it smells fragrant and "gives" at the stalk end. Chill it whole and only cut it just before serving. Once a melon has been cut, wrap it in clear plastic or enclose it in a plastic bag, and keep it in the refrigerator.

Soft fruit—berries and currants—are best when eaten or cooked within two days of picking, so if you buy them from a store, use them as quickly as possible. Do not wash soft fruit until just before you use it.

When buying peaches, nectarines, plums and cherries, choose unblemished fruit. If the salesperson insists on selecting your fruit for you, tell him when you want to eat it and be warned that, as often as not, any fruit he says is ready for eating will probably need to be ripened for a further day or two.

Green figs are not unripe purple figs —they are a different variety. All figs sold in stores are ready to eat, because they must always ripen on the tree.

Grapes should be plump and covered with a bloom (a light powdery deposit). Eat ripe grapes immediately or store them for up to twenty-four hours in the refrigerator. Wash grapes in cold water just before eating them.

Pineapples are sold in various stages of ripeness. A ripe pineapple will have a strong fragrance and well-rounded "eyes," and if a leaf in the crown is tugged it will come out easily. Keep an unripe pineapple in a warm kitchen, away from sunlight, for a few days until it ripens.

Buying and storing

Dairy products

Before you buy milk, cream, buttermilk, yogurt and sour cream, check the selling date stamped on the container. Unfortunately this precaution does not necessarily guarantee freshness, because some stores do not display dairy products correctly, so check milk bottle tops and the lids on yogurt and cream cartons. If they bulge, the contents are probably past their prime.

Cheese should be stored and sold by someone who understands how to handle it. It should not be overchilled, for example, because it is a living organism and the extreme cold will destroy its character and flavor. This may be why the refrigerated Bries and Camemberts sold in supermarkets never taste quite the same as they do in their native regions.

There is a cheese expert in Paris, M. Androuët, who has a famous cheese shop where he keeps and ripens to perfection many types of French cheese. Before he sells a cheese, you must tell him which day you wish to eat it, as well as the hour of the day. He will then select for you the cheese which is at just the right stage of ripeness. With a little effort, however, you can learn to judge for yourself whether or not a cheese is ripe.

Hard cheeses are best when they are cut from the wheel. Blue or green cheeses should be creamy in color with the veins evenly distributed and reaching almost to the edge. If they are either yellow or "weepy," they are overripe and will smell of ammonia. Some English farms keep their Stilton wrapped in cheesecloth wrung in beer. If you have to store small pieces of blue or green cheese, put them in a plastic bag or a plastic box in the refrigerator.

Camembert and Brie should be soft but not runny inside, and should not smell of ammonia; it is better to buy these delicate cheeses on the day you want to eat them. If you do have to store

them, keep them wrapped in several layers of cheesecloth in a cool place.

Keep such crumbly cheeses as Cheshire and Caerphilly wrapped in foil. Plastic bags make cheese sweat. Grated Parmesan cheese will keep for a week or two in a screw-top jar. The hard cheeses and cream cheeses can be successfully refrigerated.

Keep butter in its wrapper or in a covered dish in the refrigerator away from other foods because it absorbs strong flavors. If you leave it in a warm place for any length of time, it will turn rancid. Butter freezes well.

Whenever possible buy eggs directly from a farm or from a supplier who stamps the cartons with a date before which the eggs must be sold. If you are doubtful about the freshness of an egg, place it in a bowl of water. The egg will sink to the bottom if it is sound; if it sits right up, or floats, discard it. Never store a dirty egg because the dirt will be absorbed through the porous shell. Keep eggs in the refrigerator or in a cool cellar and bring them out an hour or two before they are to be used for cooking. Eggs used for frying, however, may be taken straight from the refrigerator.

Fish and shellfish

If you do not get fish fresh from the ocean or a river, buy from a fish dealer who receives a daily supply. Fish is so good when it is fresh but so objectionable when it is not that it is better to buy frozen fish rather than "fresh" fish of uncertain age.

Fresh fish has clear, bright, bulging eyes and shiny, tight scales. If the fish smells strongly and its scales are falling off, then it is not fresh. Look for red-pink gills and flesh that is resilient to the touch. Never buy a fish about which you have any doubts. Do not, for example, buy a sea bass with sunken eyes just because you have decided to serve bass for dinner.

When buying smoked fish, be sure that it is firm, dry, glossy-skinned and sweet-smelling. Smoked fish can be kept in an airtight container and refrigerated for up to a week.

Although it is best to buy fresh fish the day it is to be eaten, it will keep for a day or two if promptly gutted, sprinkled with salt, wrapped in foil or in clear plastic and refrigerated. Oily fish, such as herring, deteriorates more quickly than lean fish, so cook it at once.

Mollusks must be bought alive and cooked on the same day. Clams, mussels, oysters and scallops should have tightly closed shells. Scallops can also be bought prepared for cooking—they should have very white flesh and a bright orange roe.

Among the crustaceans, fresh crabs should have rough shells and lobsters springy tails and uncluttered shells—encrustations are a sign of age. Shrimp should be dry and firm to the touch.

Meat

Beef and lamb should be firm, odorless, medium-red in color and well marbled—this shows that the fat content is high and, therefore, the meat will be tender. Veal should be very pale pink and odorless. High-grade pork is close grained, pale pink and odorless.

To store meat, wrap it loosely and keep it in the refrigerator. A large piece will keep for five days. For longer periods seal it in aluminium foil and keep it in the freezing compartment.

Poultry

Such poultry as chicken, turkey and goose should have white, unwrinkled skin, a plump, firm breast and clear, bulging eyes. The feathers, if they have not been plucked, should be soft and full. The feet should also be soft and flexible.

Remember fresh poultry that is cut into pieces perishes more quickly than whole birds. Buy poultry in airtight wrappings and cook within eight to twenty-four hours.

The underbill of a fresh, young duck is flexible and soft. There should be plenty of flesh on the breast and the skin should be thin. Duck can be stored in the refrigerator for up to three days.

When you buy prewrapped, oven-ready poultry, remove the wrapping, then store the giblets and the bird separately in the refrigerator.

Although guinea hen is now bred for the table it was once a game bird. It is available oven-ready and frozen from many shops. Squabs or Cornish hens and pigeons can also be bought oven-ready and frozen as well.

Game birds

Game birds can only be bought in season, although frozen birds are sometimes available from special stores out of season. The most commonly available in stores are pheasant, quail and grouse. Choose birds with feathers and feet intact so that you can judge their age. This is important for determining the method of cooking. A young bird has pliable, soft feet, hardly formed spurs, pointed wing feathers and a supple breastbone. An old bird has scaly legs, fully formed spurs, rounded wing feathers and a firm breastbone.

Young game birds can be cooked by a variety of dry heat methods, while older birds are tastier if cooked with a moist heat method. If you are doubtful about the age of a game bird, then it is best to cook it in milk or marinate it for a few hours to tenderize the meat.

Game

Skin and clean rabbits soon after killing. Use a young rabbit for roasting and an old one for stewing. To test for age, hold the ear of the rabbit with both hands and twist. If the ear tears, the animal is young.

Only a young hare is worth eating, so test it for age as you would a rabbit. Skin and clean the hare and cut into pieces, saving as much blood as possible for cooking. Use immediately or refrigerate for no longer than two days.

When you buy venison from a good butcher, it will have been hung and will be ready for cooking. If you receive a gift of venison, ask your butcher to prepare it for you.

Moose, elk and calf elk are other kinds of game that you can buy ready prepared or a butcher will hang and prepare it for you. Cook moose like pork, elk like beef and calf elk in the same manner as veal.

It is interesting to note that an animal taken by surprise is more tender than one that has been chased. The violent exercise makes the flesh tough.

Venison, particularly an older animal, requires marinating for one to four days before it is cooked and is best stewed; roast only very young animals.

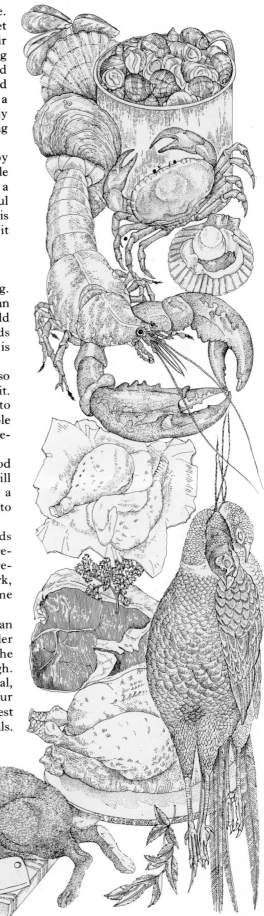

Freezing

Home freezing is one of the simplest and most convenient ways of preserving food. The home freezer will safely store whole meals prepared at leisure, leftovers that would otherwise be wasted, stocks, sauces and soups useful for quick meals, inexpensive seasonal fruit and vegetables and meat, game and poultry bargains.

To get the best out of your freezer, however, you must put in the best—good-quality food, well prepared and correctly wrapped.

Food must be packed in airtight, moistureproof wrappings or it will become dry and lose its flavor. Worse still, it will pick up the flavors of other foods. Some foods, such as small fish and various fruit and vegetables, may be tray frozen before they are packed. Spread them out on a tray, without touching each other, freeze, then pack and seal in airtight containers. They can then be removed from the containers individually.

Heavy-duty plastic bags are suitable for most foods. Use a straw to suck all the air out of the bag, then seal it quickly with wire fasteners or special freezer sealing tape.

Heavily waxed cartons and plastic boxes are excellent for fruit, vegetables, cooked foods, sauces and liquids. Allow about half an inch (1 cm) in a two-and-a-half-cup (575-ml) container for the expansion of liquids.

Pastry, pies, desserts and any dishes that will be reheated in the oven can be frozen in aluminum foil dishes.

For such dishes as lasagne or goulash, line a baking dish with freezer foil, allowing enough foil to cover the food completely. Place the food in the dish, freeze it, then remove the food from the dish, cover the top with foil and return it to the freezer. To reheat, peel off the foil and put the frozen block back into the original container.

Freezer foil is particularly useful for wrapping such awkwardly shaped food as chops or a leg of lamb.

Always keep an up-to-date record of the contents of your freezer and label anything that goes into it. Using a soft wax marking pencil and special low-temperature adhesive labels, state the contents of each package and the number of servings. Remember to include the date on the label because all food will deteriorate or lose flavor if kept too long in the freezer.

Fish and shellfish

Only freeze really fresh seafood. Tray freeze small fish and shellfish. Cut larger fish into steaks—wrap each piece separately before packing in boxes, bags or foil. Cook such shellfish as lobster and crab before freezing. Do not, however, cook shrimp before freezing them because they become tough. Shell oysters, clams and scallops, then pack them in their own liquid.

The maximum storage life for	
White fish	6 months
Oily fish, shellfish	3 months
Mollusks	6 months
Cooked fish dishes	3 months

Meat and poultry

To freeze veal scallops, lamb chops, steaks, hamburgers or any other individual pieces of meat, wrap the pieces singly in double layers of foil or waxed paper. The thawing time for individual servings is usually one to two hours. Large pieces of raw meat should be thawed in the refrigerator for twenty-four hours. If poultry is frozen whole, remove the giblets and wrap them separately in moistureproof wrapping before putting them back inside the bird. Do not stuff a bird before freezing it. To save space, halve or joint a bird.

The maximum storage life for	
Beef, lamb	6–9 months
Pork, veal	3–4 months
Variety meats	1–2 months
Ground meat, sausages	1–2 months
Poultry	9 months
Hare, rabbit, venison	6 months
Cooked dishes	2–3 months

Vegetables

According to some experts almost all vegetables should be blanched prior to freezing to retard enzyme activity, which causes loss of nutrition and flavor. Others say that for such vegetables as lima beans, peas and corn on the cob, blanching is unnecessary as long as they are absolutely fresh. Try both methods and see which you prefer. Such vegetables as Brussels sprouts, cauliflower florets and artichoke hearts can be tray frozen.

To freeze fresh herbs, wash and dry them, tie into bundles and freeze in sealed, airtight plastic bags.

The maximum storage life for	
Vegetables	12 months

Fruit

Discard fruit that have bruises, or any that are underripe or overripe. Such fruit as berries can be frozen in dry sugar, in syrup, or as a purée. They can also be tray frozen, without sugar. Large fruit must be pitted or cored and pared and the stalks removed before freezing.

The maximum storage life for	
Fruit with sugar	12 months
Fruit with no sugar, and purées	6 months

Dairy products

Heavy cream (but only to be used for beating or for making ice cream), butter, margarine and cooking fats freeze well. Hard and semi-hard cheeses freeze well, but not soft cheeses.

Eggs cannot be frozen in their shells. Break them and beat them lightly, adding half a teaspoon of salt or one teaspoon of sugar to two eggs. Or store the whites and yolks separately, adding salt or sugar only to the yolks.

The maximum storage life for	
Eggs, sweet butter	6 months
Heavy cream, salted butter, ice cream	3 months
Cheese (whole or grated)	6 months

Bread dough and pastry

Knead unrisen yeast dough once, then put it in a large, greased plastic bag, tie loosely and freeze.

Unbaked yeast dough for rolls should be allowed to rise then knocked down, rekneaded and shaped into rolls. Grease the rolls, tray freeze then pack in a plastic bag. Tray freeze unbaked cookies then pack.

Pastry with a high fat content freezes well. If you are making a filled pie, brush the pastry shell with egg white and the top crust with fat. Slit the top crust just before baking. Unbaked frozen pies taste better than pies baked prior to freezing.

The maximum storage life for	
Bread dough	10 days
Bread dough for rolls	7 days
Unbaked cookies	2 months
Baked pastry	6 months
Pastry dough	9 months
Uncooked fruit pie	4–6 months

Bread, cakes and cookies

Freshly baked bread should be cooled for three hours prior to freezing. It will keep for six months in the freezer, but begins to lose its flavor after two months. Wrap cakes in plastic or waxed paper then pack them in cartons. Frosted cakes can be frozen provided the frosting is made with butter and confectioners' sugar. Freeze the cake before wrapping it.

Tray freeze baked cookies then pack in plastic bags.

The maximum storage life for	
Baked bread	2–6 months
Cakes	2–6 months
Frosted cakes	2 months
Baked cookies	3 months

Stocks, sauces and soups

Chill stocks, sauces and soups quickly over ice water, then skim off any fat. Leave room in the storage container for expansion. Add such ingredients as cream and final seasonings to soups and sauces just before serving. Because you often require only a little stock to flavor a sauce or stew, freeze in ice cube trays first, then transfer the cubes to a bag.

The maximum storage life for	
Stocks, sauces, soups	4 months

Stews

When freezing stews, use salt, pepper, herbs and spices sparingly because seasonings often intensify or change in flavor during freezing.

Remove any bay leaves or a bouquet garni from a dish before freezing it. Remember to slightly undercook any dish that will require heating before serving.

Foods to be reheated straight from the freezer should be put in the oven for twice the normal reheating time, at 350°F (180°C) or reheated in a double boiler on the top of the stove.

The maximum storage life for	
Stews	2 months

Foods that do not freeze well

The foods that can never be frozen successfully include salad vegetables—lettuce, cucumber, Belgian endive, curly endive, celery and tomato (except in stews and casseroles or as a purée)—uncooked potatoes and other root vegetables, squash and other vegetable fruit.

The fruit that do not freeze well are avocados and bananas, which turn black, and pears, which lose their delicate flavor and texture.

Fresh milk, cream, sour cream and yogurt separate if frozen; custards also tend to separate. Cottage cheese becomes rubbery.

Mayonnaise and other egg-based sauces do not freeze well because the oil separates from the egg yolk.

It is not a good idea to freeze fried foods—they become tough and dry.

The whites of hard-cooked eggs become leathery in the freezer, and clear jellies lose their texture.

Carbonated drinks may explode at low temperatures.

Thawing

All foods, with the exception of raw vegetables, should be thawed slowly, either at room temperature or in the lower part of the refrigerator. Stews and casseroles, pies and such dishes as cauliflower au gratin can go straight from the freezer into the oven.

Basic preparation

What would be your reaction if you were presented with a duck—bill, feathers and all—by a proud hunter who wanted it for dinner? Or, even more alarming, if you were given a lively, wriggling eel? You may well be a good cook, but the chances are you do not have the first idea how to deal with such foods in their natural state.

Today most people buy fish and meat that has been pre-packaged, frozen or prepared at the fish market or by the butcher, and are helpless on the rare occasions when they are confronted by the "real thing." This may also be true of some fruit and vegetables; others are so common that we all know how to prepare them, although it may not always be in the quickest and simplest way.

The squeamish may find some aspects of basic preparation unpleasant, especially where game and poultry are concerned. It is true, however, that the more experienced you become at drawing a chicken or skinning a rabbit, for example, the quicker the whole operation becomes.

This section will teach you how to handle anything—from a live crab to a green bean—and to know how to have it ready for cooking in the minimum time, with the least effort and waste.

Fish

One of the greatest delights is the sight of a well-arranged fish dealer's slab. The variety of shapes, sizes, colors and markings of the many kinds of fish is overwhelming.

Although it is possible to have almost any fish prepared by your fish dealer, it is well worth learning how to deal with a fish that has just been caught. You never know when you might receive a gift of freshly caught trout, or, if you are lucky, a salmon. And the flavor of a fresh fish is incomparably better than that of any fish you might find in a market.

If you are baking or broiling a whole fish, it can be stuffed after it has been gutted. Put the stuffing in the stomach cavity of a round fish and use toothpicks to keep the slit closed. To stuff a flatfish use a sharp knife to make a slit down the middle of the back, then tuck the stuffing between the fillets and the backbone. It is also possible to stuff fillets. Those taken from flatfish are simply folded around a roll of stuffing. Fillets of round fish may be sandwiched together with the stuffing mixture.

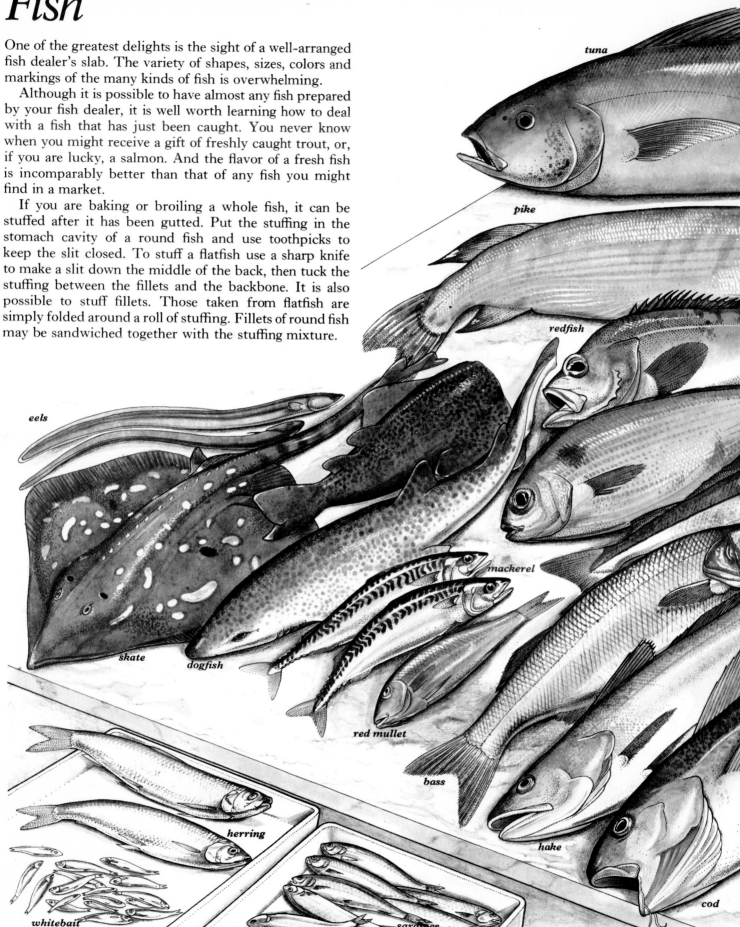

tuna

pike

redfish

eels

skate

dogfish

mackerel

red mullet

bass

herring

hake

whitebait

sardines

cod

salmon

salmon trout

bream

trout

whiting

sole

brill

flounder

turbot

dab

Dover sole

Fish

For preparation, fish are usually divided into two groups —flatfish, for example flounder and sole, and round fish, of which cod, mackerel and herring are the most common. Fish within a group can generally be prepared in the same way, with the obvious exception of eel, a round but otherwise unique fish.

Many fish are smoked, salted, pickled or dried. Dried salt cod must be soaked in cold water for two days. The water should be changed regularly—about three times a day. At the end of the soaking time the fish will have swollen to twice its size and is then ready for cooking.

Such smoked fish as trout and mackerel need only to be skinned. No other preparation is required.

Round fish

To scale the fish, hold it by the tail and scrape toward the head with the back of a knife.

Lift the gill flap and slit the skin underneath. With the point of a knife, scrape out the gills.

Using sharp scissors, snip off the fins as close to the skin surface as possible.

Now hold the fish firmly and slit the stomach. Using a teaspoon, scrape out the entrails.

Turn the fish around and slit it right along the backbone, from the gill flap to the tail end.

Keeping the knife flat against the backbone, cut out the fillet with clean, sweeping strokes.

Turn the fish over and cut out the other fillet. Reserve the bones, head and tail for stock.

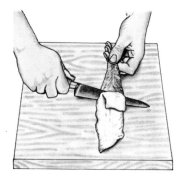

To skin the fillet, hold one end firmly and run the knifeblade between the skin and flesh.

Small round fish

Small round fish come in the category of oily fish. They include smelts, sardines (Pacific sardines are twice the size of the smaller Atlantic sardines), herring and anchovies. Anchovies are almost always bought filleted and canned. Pick out any bad or damaged ones. Because small round fish have such small scales they require very little preparation : just wipe them over with a damp cloth, cut the heads off, squeeze out the entrails, and leave on the tail.

Cut the head off below the gills and squeeze the body until all the entrails come out.

Herring

Herring is a round fish that also comes into the category of oily fish. It is available fresh and smoked. When a herring is smoked it is called a kipper. Herring are full of tiny bones, and only some of these can be removed before cooking or smoking. The bones are a nuisance, but the flavor of the fish more than compensates for this. Fresh herring is the fish that is most often pickled in many European cuisines.

Slit the fish down its belly and lay it down skin side up. Press down on its back to open it out.

Cut the backbone just above the tail. Using the point of the knife, gently loosen the bone.

You should now be able to pull the backbone out easily, then lift out the side bones.

Eel

Although the eel is categorized as a round fish it is different from all other fish in shape and method of preparation. An eel must be alive when you buy it and killed and skinned only hours before you cook it. Once the eel has been killed it will keep on wriggling until you have almost finished preparing it. The skin should peel off easily in one piece, but the eel is slippery and slimy, so dip your hand into salt or wrap the part you are holding in newspaper to get a firm grip.

Hold the eel firmly just below the head and cut the head off with a clean, sharp movement.

With the point of a sharp knife, make a small cut at the neck end of the eel to loosen the skin.

Grasp the neck skin firmly with pincers and tug hard—it should come away in one piece.

Flatfish

A flatfish is easily recognizable because it has a flattened body and both eyes are on the same side of its head. Flatfish include brill, turbot, flounder, halibut and the various types of sole. They all have fairly similar shapes and are therefore cleaned, gutted, skinned and filleted in the same way. Skate is also a flatfish, but it is different from other flatfish because the body part is inedible and only the wings are eaten.

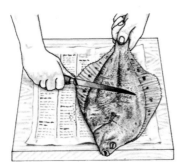

To scale a flatfish, grasp it by the tail and run the back of a knife from the tail to the head.

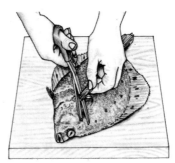

With a sharp pair of kitchen scissors, snip off the dorsal fins on each side of the body.

Now cut off the side fins, which surround the body. Follow the contours of the fish's shape.

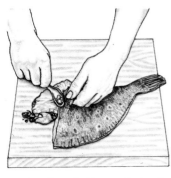

With a sharp knife, cut the head off and then scoop out the gills with a teaspoon.

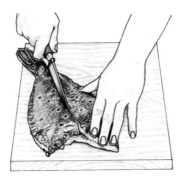

Hold the fish down flat with one hand and make a slit down the backbone from top to tail.

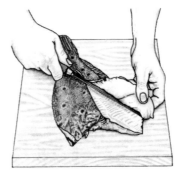

Keeping the knife flat against the bones, work the flesh away from the bones to make a fillet.

Hold the tail end of one fillet firmly and scrape the flesh away from the skin.

Sole

Sole is a flatfish with an oval-shaped body. The flesh is white and the skin varies in color from light sand to muddy brown. There are two main types of sole—lemon sole and Dover sole. Dover sole is considered the best of the two, and is said to have the finest flavor of any white fish. For this reason it should be cooked simply and served with subtle sauces and plain vegetables to enhance its delicate flavor.

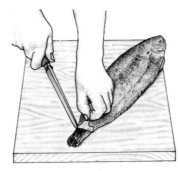

One method of skinning Dover sole is to make a small nick in the tail end of the skin.

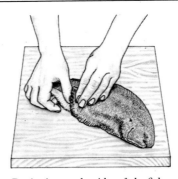

Beginning at the sides of the fish, start carefully easing the skin away from the flesh.

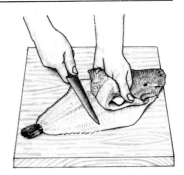

When the side skin has been eased away, pull the skin off sharply from the tail end.

Shellfish/mollusks

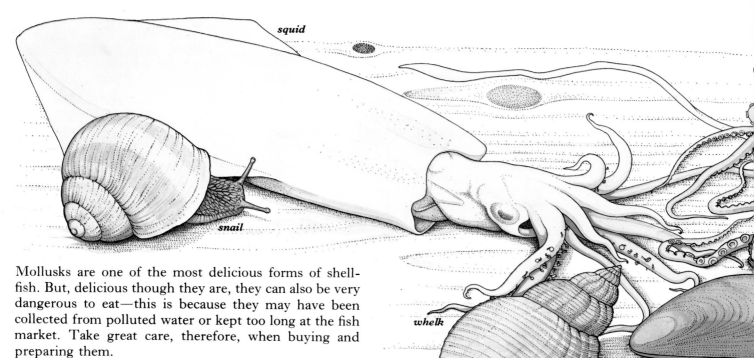

Mollusks are one of the most delicious forms of shell-fish. But, delicious though they are, they can also be very dangerous to eat—this is because they may have been collected from polluted water or kept too long at the fish market. Take great care, therefore, when buying and preparing them.

Most bivalve mollusks (those, such as the mussel and oyster, that have a hinged shell) must be bought alive and absolutely fresh. The shells must be tightly closed or should close immediately when given a sharp tap.

To prepare mollusks, scrub them thoroughly under cold running water. They should open during the cooking period; discard any that remain closed.

Univalve mollusks, such as periwinkles, have one shell, which is open at the base. They can often be bought cooked, but if you buy them uncooked they must be alive. To test them, gently prod the flesh through the open end. If the periwinkle retreats into its shell, it is alive; if it remains inert, it is dead and should be discarded. Soak periwinkles in water for several minutes, rinse, then put them into a pan containing boiling salted water for twenty minutes. Use a needle to remove them from their shells.

Snails are univalve land mollusks, and they too can be dangerous to eat because they quite happily feed off plants that are poisonous to us. If you can obtain live snails, gather them during the winter, when they are hibernating. Or, at other times of the year, starve them for up to ten days before cooking them.

To prepare snails for cooking, soak them in a bowl of salted water for four hours, changing the water every half hour. While the snails are soaking, make a court bouillon with equal quantities of wine and water. Strain the court bouillon into another saucepan and let it cool.

Put the snails into the court bouillon and bring it to a boil. Simmer for three hours. Remove the snails from the pan and ease them from their shells, using a needle or a sharp-pointed knife. Cut off the membrane and the black part of each snail.

Octopus and squid are mollusks with a small internal shell and are prepared in a totally different way.

Scrub the oyster shell thoroughly to remove all the grit. Insert an oyster knife into the hinged part of the shell and pry it open.

When the two shells have come apart, cut the oyster flesh off the flat shell, making sure you do not waste any flesh.

Mussels must be scrubbed very thoroughly. The small "beard" coming out of one side must be cut off before cooking.

If any mussels remain open after washing, tap them sharply. This should make them close; discard any that do not.

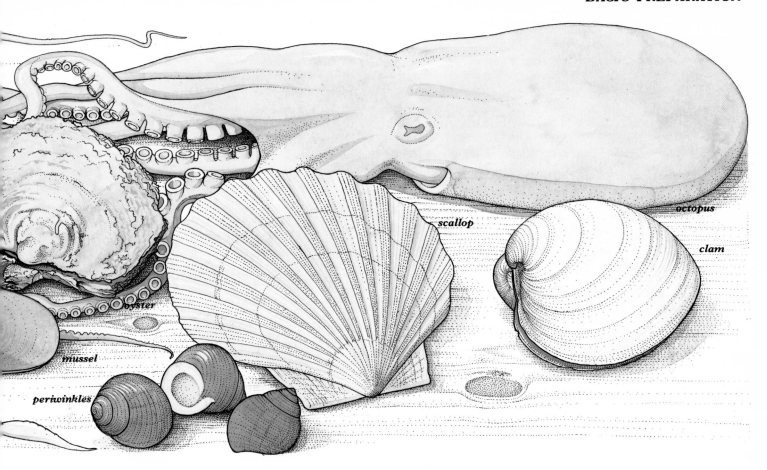

octopus

scallop

clam

oyster

mussel

periwinkles

Lay the scrubbed scallops on a baking sheet, not touching each other, and heat in a low oven for 2 minutes or until they open.

Cut through the hinge with a sharp knife and pull the shells apart. Cut the scallop flesh from the flat shell.

With a small, sharp knife, cut off the inedible parts from the scallop flesh—the beardlike fringe and the intestinal cord.

Scrub the clam shells thoroughly with a stiff brush. Open them through the hinge with a knife and remove the flesh.

Hold the squid's body and pull the head end out. Most of the gut—a milky substance—will come out easily with it.

Wash the body under cold running water. Insert your fingers into the body and carefully remove the coral and ink sac.

The squid has only one bone, and that will pull out easily. Cut the tentacles off below the eyes and discard the head and bone.

The periwinkle is very small, so nothing larger than a pin should be used to pry it out of the shell.

Shellfish/crustaceans

The term crustacean is applied to shellfish that have jointed shells, rather like suits of armor. They include crab, lobster and shrimp.

In their natural state crustaceans vary in color from pale gray to blackish-blue—ideal camouflage in their habitat, the sea. But once cooked their color undergoes a dramatic change, ranging from pale pink to deep coral.

Like mollusks, crustaceans can be dangerous to eat; the only way you can ensure that they will do you no harm is to buy from a reliable market that sells only the freshest seafood. Most crustaceans can be bought either cooked or alive.

The killing of crab, lobster and spiny lobster (which is prepared in the same way as lobster) is worth a mention, for it is thought that they are more sensitive to pain than other shellfish. It is believed that the most painless way of killing a crab is to drive a sharp instrument through the nerve center. The most practical method for the cook is to drop the live crab or lobster into briskly boiling water, but if the lobster is to be broiled, the point of a sharp knife must be driven through its head—the exact spot is conveniently marked by a cross—and death is instantaneous.

The stomach sac and intestine of lobster and crab must be discarded. The red coral and the greenish-colored liver of lobster are edible.

Crayfish are sometimes gutted before they are cooked.

Wash them thoroughly under cold running water, then twist off the central tail fins—the intestines will come away with them. Have a pan of briskly boiling water ready, drop in the crayfish, cover and boil for about seven minutes. Alternatively, after the crayfish have been cooked, pry open the tail shell, lift out the meat and remove the dark, string-like intestine. To extract the meat from the claws, cut off the movable claws and with a sharp knife loosen and remove the meat.

Shrimp or prawns are often sold already frozen and ready to cook. If they are alive, however, cook them, like crayfish, in boiling water. Shrimp and prawns will be ready in five minutes; jumbo shrimp require fifteen minutes. To prepare shrimp, twist and pull off the tail, snap off the head, then peel off the shell.

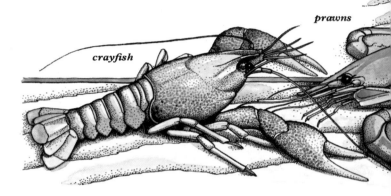

prawns

crayfish

Preparing hard-shell crab

To kill a crab, lay it on a wooden board with the underside facing upward. Drive a knife between the eyes and through the brain.

The flesh is removed after the crab has been boiled. Begin by twisting off all the legs and the two large claws.

Using the back of a knife or a small hammer, crack the claws in several places. Remove the meat and discard the shell.

Lay the crab on its back. Hold it with both hands. Press the body upward with your thumbs until it comes away from the shell.

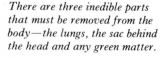

There are three inedible parts that must be removed from the body—the lungs, the sac behind the head and any green matter.

Using a teaspoon, scrape the meat out of the main part of the body into a bowl. Keep the white and brown meat in separate bowls.

With the teaspoon, scrape all the brown meat out of the shell. Wash the shell under cold running water and pat it dry.

Using a small hammer, lightly break off the rough edges and trim the edge of the shell into a uniform shape.

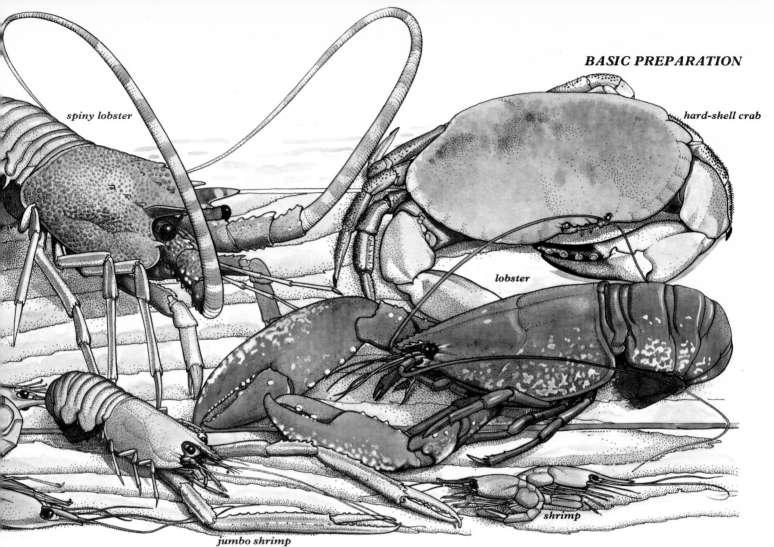

spiny lobster

hard-shell crab

lobster

shrimp

jumbo shrimp

Preparing lobster

To kill a lobster, drive the point of a knife through the brain, which lies under the cross where the body meets the head.

Hold the lobster firmly by the body and twist off the two large claws and small pincers. Remove the meat from these first.

Using a hammer or a lobster cracker, crack the large claw shells. Remove any small shell particles before taking out the meat.

Extract the meat from the claws, using the point of a knife if it does not come out easily. Then remove the membrane.

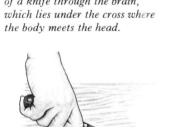

Lay the main body of the lobster on its stomach. Using a very sharp knife, split the lobster in half down the center of the back.

Separate the two halves; remove and discard the black intestinal cord, the gills and the stomach sac. The greenish liver is edible.

Preparing shrimp

To shell shrimp, twist the tails and pull them off. Open up the body shells, to which the legs are attached, and peel them off.

Preparing crayfish

Crayfish may be gutted before being cooked. Grip the middle tail fin, twist and pull to remove the gut. Drop into boiling water.

Poultry and game birds

All poultry and game birds, unless they are bought oven-ready, must be hung, plucked and drawn before they are cooked.

Poultry—chicken, duck, turkey, goose and guinea hen—is traditionally plucked before it is hung by its feet. Game birds—pheasant, partridge, squab, grouse, quail, snipe, mallard, teal and woodcock—are hung by their necks unplucked.

Hanging times vary according to the bird, its age and the weather. A young chicken should be hung for one day only. A duck or goose needs two days, and a turkey or guinea hen must be hung for about three to five days.

Game is nearly always hung until the flesh is "high" and has developed a strong flavor. If after about three days the feathers above the bird's tail come out easily when pulled, it is, according to most tastes, ready for cooking.

In warm weather hang all birds for shorter periods, but remember that an older bird must be hung for longer than a young one or the flesh will not be tender.

Poultry and game birds are plucked in the same way. Any stubborn feathers can be singed off and the quill ends removed with tweezers.

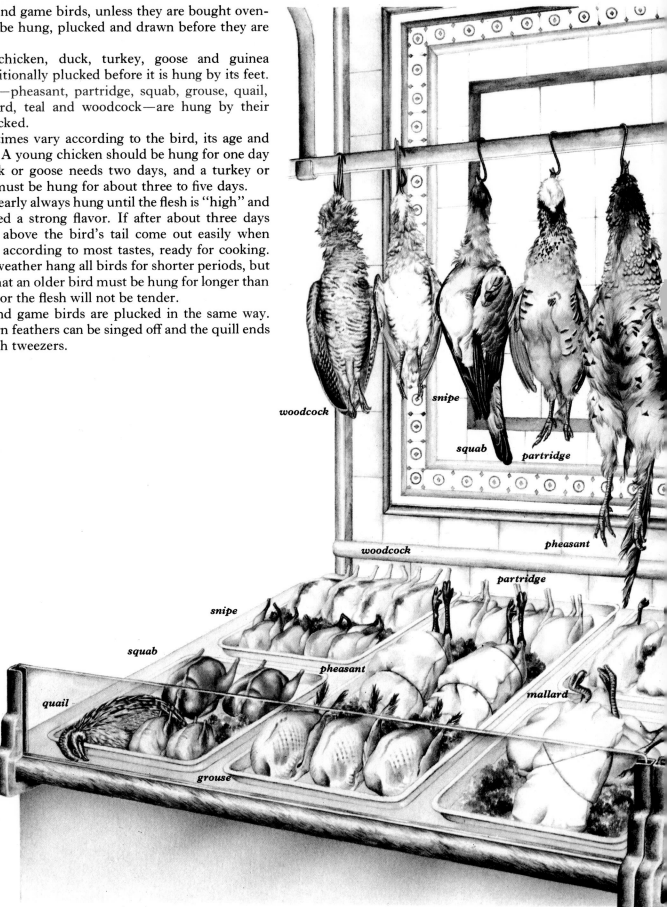

woodcock

snipe

squab · partridge

pheasant

woodcock

partridge

snipe

squab · pheasant

quail · mallard

grouse

teal

grouse

mallard

guinea hen

chicken

duck

goose

turkey

teal

guinea hen

chicken

duck

goose

turkey

Poultry and game birds

Drawing a bird is not a complicated process—it is just a matter of cutting off its head and feet and removing its entrails. (If a game bird is to be roasted, however, the feet are usually left on.) The bird's intestines are discarded, but the heart, gizzard and neck are kept for making stock or gravy. The liver is not used in stock but can be mixed into the stuffing. Before using the liver the gall bladder must be cut away from it. If the gall bladder breaks while you are doing this, discard the whole liver because it will taste unpleasantly bitter. The leg tendons are removed by making a slit in the side of the leg, just below the drumstick. Use a skewer to pull out the four or five tendons. Scald the feet, scrape off the skin and use for stock.

Plucking a bird

Plucking is done in the same way for all poultry and game birds. Lay the bird down on a table with the feet pointing toward you. Hold the bird firmly by the feet and begin plucking from under the wing toward the breast. Pull the feathers away from the direction of growth. If the bird is old, it can be plunged into boiling water for one minute (no more) to facilitate plucking : but if you do this the bird must be cooked at once or it will decompose.

Cleaning a bird

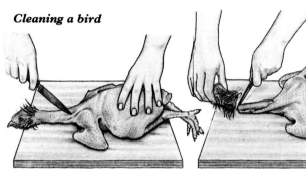

Using a small, very sharp knife, make a slit from the base of the neck to the base of the head and open up the slit.

Stretch the neck slightly by pulling the head. With a sharp movement, cut off the head cleanly at the top of the neck.

Pull the neck skin right back and scrape off the fat. Pull the neck and cut it off at the base. Reserve it for making stock.

Hold the bird firmly and pull out the windpipe, crop and any fat from inside the neck cavity.

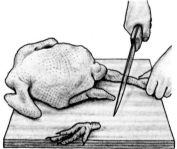

Turn the bird around and cut the skin around the base of the knee joint. Twist and pull off the lower part of the leg and tendons.

Make a short slit in the vent to increase the cavity opening. You can also make a slit above the vent to tuck the tail in later.

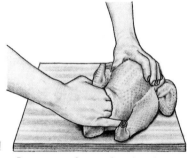

Insert your fingers, keeping them near the breastbone, and dislodge the entrails. Take great care not to break the gall bladder.

Carefully pull out all the entrails : the stomach, heart, intestines and liver. Cut the gall bladder away from the liver.

Cutting up a bird

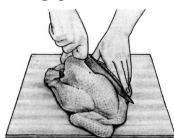

Using a very sharp carving knife, split the chicken through the breastbone right down the center.

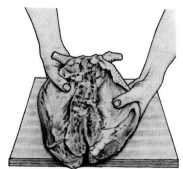

Open out the two halves and lay the chicken skin side down on the table. Cut through the backbone.

With a sharp knife, cut the thigh away from the wings and breast of the chicken.

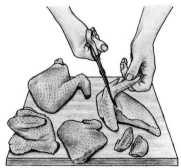

Use kitchen scissors to cut off the wings and cut the rest of the chicken into smaller pieces.

Trussing a bird

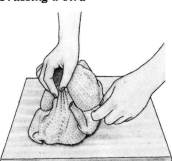

Place the bird on its breast and fold over the neck skin. Pull and stretch the skin over the back.

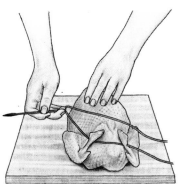

Bend the wings back to hold the neck skin in place and tie them with trussing string.

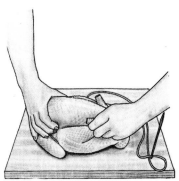

Turn the chicken over and push the legs together to plump up the breast.

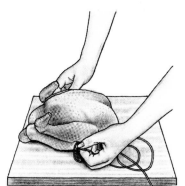

Push the threaded trussing needle into the fleshy part of one thigh and push it through the body.

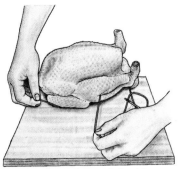

The needle and thread should come out of the other thigh in exactly the same place.

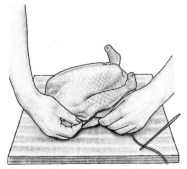

Pass the loose end of string from the other thigh under the body and tie with the other end.

Pass the threaded needle through just under the end of the back and pull the two ends together.

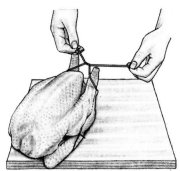

Use the two loose ends of string to tie the back legs together firmly in place.

Boning a bird

Lay the bird breast side down on the work surface. With a very sharp knife, make a cut along the backbone, piercing the skin.

Resting the knife against the bone and keeping it flat, work the flesh away from the backbone on both sides.

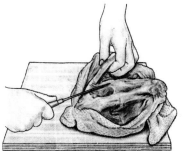

Trim the flesh away from the thighbone and lift out the thigh-bone. Be very careful not to pierce the flesh.

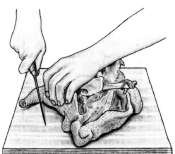

With a clean, sharp movement, chop the leg off at the knee joint. The wings are left intact to give the chicken a better shape.

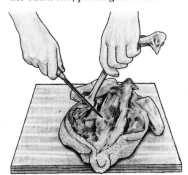

With the edge of the knife, scrape all the meat from the leg bone. Lift out the leg bone and reserve with the other bones for stock.

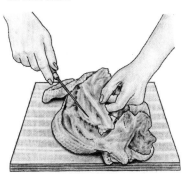

Very carefully scrape the meat off the rib cage. Great care must be taken at this stage as very little flesh covers this part.

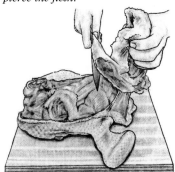

When all the meat has been scraped off, lift out the carcass. The chicken is now ready for stuffing.

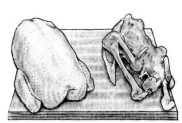

Stuff the bird, fold the sides over, tuck in the ends and sew into place. Plump the bird into shape; it can now be cooked.

Meat and game

A good butcher will do most of the preparation of meat for you. There will be occasions, however, when he may be too busy or when at the last moment you decide you want to bone and stuff a large piece of meat or turn a rack of lamb into a crown roast.

Some cuts of meat require little preparation, others much time-consuming trimming, cutting, beating or sewing. But whatever the task there is no doubt that practice will bring perfection.

Boning and rolling is one of the jobs that is much less complicated than it looks. Although meat cooked on the bone has more flavor, a boned and rolled cut has the advantage that it can be stuffed and is much easier to carve.

Other preparations that you can easily learn to do yourself include paunching and skinning a hare or rabbit, making noisettes of lamb or a crown roast from rib sections of two pork or lamb loins.

You can also learn to salt or pickle meat. Such pieces of beef as plate, brisket, flank and tongue are soaked (for several days or, in some cases, weeks) in a brine solution before being cooked, or they may be pickled in a similar solution to which such spices as mace, ginger and cloves are added. In the days before refrigeration, salting or pickling was a way of preserving meat. Today it is done purely for the delicious flavor it gives the meat.

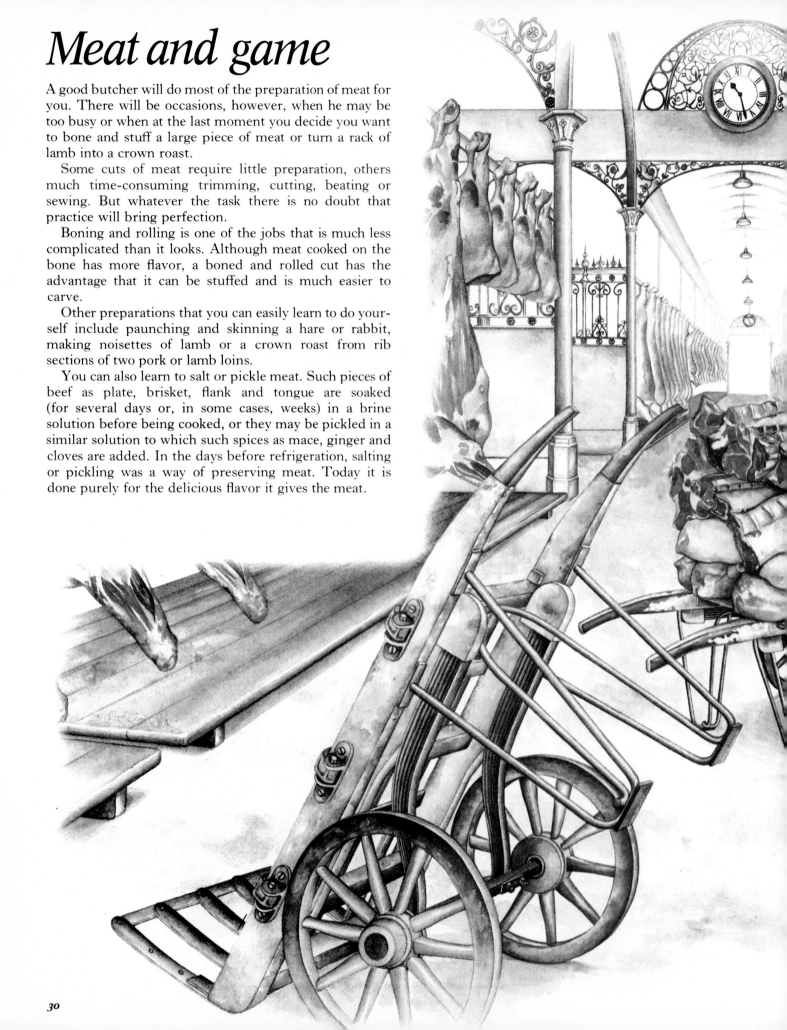

Ingrid Jacob

Beef and veal

Traditionally such cuts as sirloin of beef and shoulder of veal are boned and rolled before being roasted. To prevent a lean cut, such as fillet, from drying out, lard it with thin strips of fatback or fat bacon. Use a special larding needle and thread the fat through the surface of the meat.

To tenderize beef, marinate it in beer for up to twenty-four hours. For two pounds (900 g) of chuck steak use one and a half cups (375 ml) beer, half a cup (125 ml) corn oil, two tablespoons lemon juice mixed with salt, sugar, garlic and mustard to taste.

If you have a grinder, grind your own meat—it is the only way to balance the lean meat with fat. Once ground, the meat should not be kept for more than one day.

Larding a fillet

To lard a fillet of beef, take a piece of fatback and cut it into thin, even-sized strips. Clip one strip onto a larding needle.

Being very careful not to tear through the surface of the meat, thread the needle and fat in and out of the fillet.

Tournedos

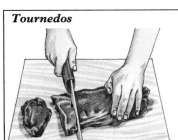 

To make tournedos, cut a beef fillet into thick steaks. Cut strips of fatback wide and long enough to fit around the steaks.

Shape each steak into a round and tie a piece of the fat securely around the steak, fastening it on with trussing string.

Veal scallops

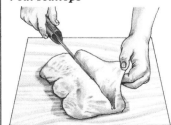 

With a long, very sharp meat knife, cut an even slice from a piece of veal fillet.

Place the slice of fillet between two sheets of waxed paper and beat it with a blunt object until it is paper thin.

Boning a sirloin

 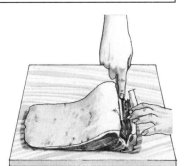 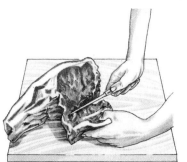 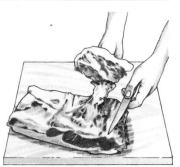

Take a wing rib of beef (a sirloin without the fillet) and lay it on its fatty side. Cut out the undercut.

Turn the meat over. Cut down the other side of the chine bone, pulling it away from the meat.

Turn the meat over on its side and cut away most of the flesh, keeping the blade of the knife flat against the bone.

Turn the meat over, laying it fat side down. Cut away the last pieces of meat and fat from the bone and pull the bone right off.

 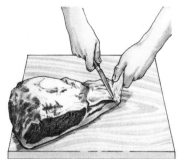  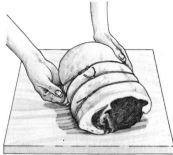

Depending on the size of the sirloin, there will be between three and four rib bones in the meat and these must be cut out.

Turn the meat around and cut and scrape the meat and fat from the rib bones as you pull them out.

When all the rib bones have been cut out, put the undercut on top of the meat and pack it in.

Roll up the boned sirloin and tie the roll in several places with trussing string.

Boning a veal breast

Lay the veal breast fat side down. Make a slit along the length of the skirt and pull it back.

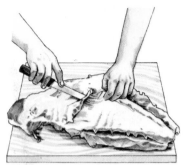

Trim the surplus fat from the surface of the meat.

Keeping the knife flat against the underside of the rib bones, begin slitting the meat through the middle.

Hold the meat on its side and continue slitting the meat down the middle, cutting right against the rib bones.

As you continue cutting down into the meat, the meat will fall to one side, leaving the ribs bare.

Continue cutting right down until the whole rib section can be pulled away from the meat.

Begin cutting through the middle of the meat as before, separating the meat from the fat. Remove excess fat.

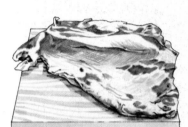

Stop cutting before you get to the other side of the meat. Open the meat out like a book. It can now be stuffed and then rolled.

Boning a veal loin

Cutting close to the bone, begin loosening the fillet away from the chine bone.

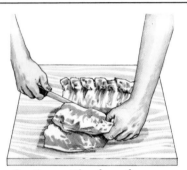

Continue cutting down the chine bone, pulling the fillet away gently as you cut.

Turn the meat over so the fatty side is up. Make a cut through the other side of the chine bone.

Hold the meat down and move the bone back and forth to loosen it from the meat.

Hold the bone firmly and cut it right away from the meat.

Trim off the back gristle and all surplus fat from the meat.

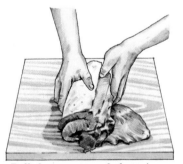

Roll the meat up and plump it into shape. The roll should be fairly tight.

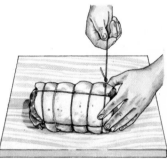

Tie the roll up in several places across and lengthwise.

Mutton and lamb

Lamb is the flesh of a sheep aged between about three and twelve months old. The flesh of an older animal is known as mutton. The most popular cuts of lamb for roasting or braising are the leg, shoulder and breast.

Loin, shoulder and rib chops may be fried or broiled, but before cooking score the fat that surrounds the meat so that the meat does not curl up as it cooks.

Two impressive dishes, crown roast and guard of honor, are prepared by sewing together the rib sections of two loins of lamb. Each piece of loin is made up of about eight chops or ribs. Scrape the fat and gristle from the narrow end of each bone to form the "prongs" of the crown and the "crossed swords" of the guard of honor.

Noisettes

To make noisettes, carefully cut the chine bone from a loin of lamb and reserve for stock.

Using a sharp knife, trim the fat from the thin end of the loin to make a thin, even layer.

Now pound the layer of fat with a blunt instrument, a rolling pin for example, to flatten it.

Roll the meat up tightly so that it is completely enclosed by the layer of fat.

Tie the roll up at regular intervals with trussing string or strong button thread.

With a very sharp knife, cut the meat in thick slices between the string to make the noisettes.

Crown roast and guard of honor

Lay the loin of lamb fat side down on a wooden board and saw either side of the chine bone with a meat saw to loosen it.

Bend the meat inward and, holding one end firmly, peel off the surface layer of skin. It should come away easily.

Cut out the loosened chine bone. Cut down the middle of the meat right to the other side and separate the two halves.

With a sharp-pointed knife, trim the fat and skin from the end of the rib bones. This is known as "French trimming."

Tie the two halves together by passing trussing string through the top and bottom of the end ribs and tying a knot.

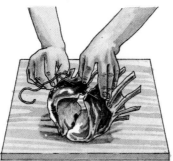

Bend the meat around to form a circle and sew it up with trussing string to keep the circle together.

Once the crown roast has been cooked, it is traditionally garnished with a paper frill on top of each rib bone.

Guard of honor is made in the same way except that the two halves are sewn and tied together with the bones crossing.

Boning a leg of lamb

Hold the leg of lamb at the shin end. With the point of a knife, loosen and lift out the bladebone.

Turn the leg around and, with the point of the knife, cut around the shinbone to loosen it.

Lift the whole shinbone out of the leg, cutting close to the bone as you pull it out.

Keeping the knife close against the bone, tunnel into the leg to loosen the middle bone.

Loosen the middle bone from the cavity left by the bladebone as well, and pull out from the leg.

Trim around the small bone at the shin end and pull it out. This is the last bone in the leg.

Push the shin end of the meat into the cavity left by the bone, tucking it in neatly.

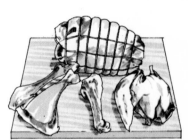

Plump the meat into shape and tie it securely at regular intervals with trussing string.

Boning a shoulder of lamb

Trim off the fat from the shoulder. Hold the meat by the shoulder bone and loosen the meat from the bone and joint.

With a very sharp knife, cut right through the joint and bend the shoulder bone back until the joint cracks.

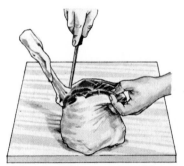

Slice through any meat and fat between the bone and the body of the meat and pull out the shoulder bone.

Being very careful not to break through the surface of the skin, loosen the meat all around the middle bone.

Cutting off the meat and fat as you go, pull out the middle bone.

Keeping the knife as close as possible to the bone, loosen the meat from the shoulder blade.

Hold one end of the shoulder-blade bone firmly and pull it out.

Roll up the meat, fat side out, and tie the roll with trussing string.

Pork

To prepare pork for roasting you must either remove the skin altogether or score it deeply and rub with salt and fat for deliciously crisp cracklings. When you are cooking a pork chop, make several nicks in the fat surrounding the meat to prevent it from curling up during cooking.

A country ham should be soaked in cold water for at least two to three hours and preferably overnight before cooking to reduce its saltiness. Remove the skin after boiling and, if you like, score the ham, stud it with cloves, cover it with brown sugar and bake it.

Bacon is sold either in one piece (slab bacon) or in slices. To insure crispness when frying bacon slices, pour away the grease as it accumulates in the pan.

Bacon rolls

To make bacon rolls, first trim off the fat with kitchen scissors and then cut away any gristle with a sharp knife.

Using a round-bladed knife and being careful not to tear the bacon, pull and stretch it, roll it up and fasten if necessary.

Pork scallops

Lay the pork tenderloin on a wooden board and slit it down the middle to the center.

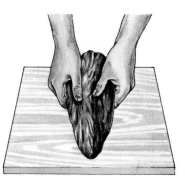

Open the tenderloin out like a book and lay it between two sheets of waxed paper.

Pound the tenderloin with a blunt instrument, a rolling pin, for example, until paper thin.

Remove and discard the waxed paper—the tenderloin is now ready to be cooked.

Ham

Put the ham skin side up on a wooden board and make a small cut to get a grip on the skin.

Grip the piece of cut skin firmly and pull, cutting it as you go, until it all comes off.

Using a sharp knife, score the surface of the fat diagonally in parallel lines.

Turn the ham around and score it the other way to make diamond shapes. Stud with cloves.

Pork chop

When a pork chop cooks, the fat surrounding it shrinks and the meat tends to curl up. Nick the fat all around to prevent this.

Cracklings

To make sure the cracklings will be crisp all the way through, score the surface of the skin in close parallel lines.

Suckling pig

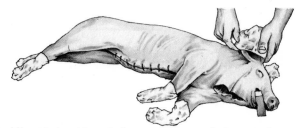

Suckling pig is sold ready for cooking. The entrails will have been removed, the feet cut off and the body cleaned. All you have to do is cover the ears and leg ends with foil to prevent them from burning and put a piece of wood into the mouth.

Game

Hare and rabbit are prepared in the same way, but a rabbit should be cooked as soon as possible after it has been killed. If you are cooking an older animal, choose a recipe which uses moist heat—stewing, simmering, braising, steaming, boiling or casseroling all bring out the flavor of older game, small or large.

When handling any wild meat, always be sure to wear rubber gloves to protect against the danger of tularemia infection. Do not rush the cooking of small game. The meat of wild animals should be thoroughly cooked.

There are two methods of skinning a hare or rabbit. You can either lay the animal on a table, where it may be skinned according to the instructions below, or you can push a meat hook through the animal's back legs and hang it up with a bowl under its head. Using a sharp knife, cut the skin down the back of each hind leg and around the thighs, and ease the skin away from the flesh. To remove the rest of the skin, pull it down over the animal's body and front legs. Cut off and discard the head with the skin.

Venison is very lean and dry and should be marinated, covered and refrigerated for up to 3 days. Then it should be larded or barded if it is to be roasted.

Hare and rabbit may also be marinated before cooking to give the meat better flavor and to insure that it will be tender. Use a deep dish so that the flesh can be completely submerged in the liquid.

Skinning and jointing rabbit

If the rabbit has not been paunched by the butcher, slit it along the stomach. Pull out the intestines and stomach.

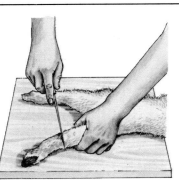
Slit the fur and skin all around halfway up the leg.

With the point of a sharp knife, make a small incision in the middle of the spine to get a firm grip on the fur.

Hold the head end of the rabbit with one hand. Take hold of the fur at the incision with the other and pull the skin off.

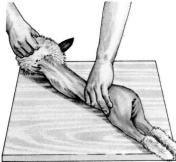
Turn the rabbit around and pull the fur off the upper part of the body in the same way. Pull right up to the end of the head.

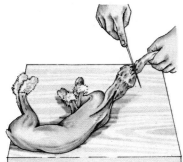
Cut through the skin attaching the fur to the head and pull the fur right off.

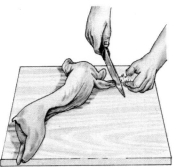
Cut off the head and then cut off the ends of the feet.

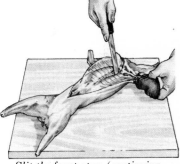
Slit the front open (continuing from the paunch slit) up to the neck, open up the body and remove the heart and lungs.

To joint the skinned rabbit, begin by cutting off the hind legs.

Cut off the forequarters—that is, the front legs and upper part of the body.

Split the forequarters in half down the middle.

Cut the saddle across into serving pieces.

Variety meats

All the edible parts that are left when an animal or poultry carcass has been divided into cuts are known as variety meats. Because they are extremely perishable, variety meats should always be eaten as soon as possible after the animal or bird has been killed.

Tripe, which is the lining of beef stomach, is nearly always sold blanched and ready for cooking.

Sweetbreads should be soaked in salted water and blanched after soaking. Brains and hearts should be soaked in salted or acidulated water (water to which a little vinegar or lemon juice has been added).

The best sweetbreads, brains and livers are those of calves, although chicken livers are also delicious. Calves and lambs both provide delicately flavored kidneys and the most tender hearts come from lambs.

Calves' and pigs' feet are cooked and eaten either hot or cold, or are used to make a highly concentrated stock. Lambs' and sheep's heads are also used for making stock, but pigs' and calves' heads are usually used for making head cheese. Calves' heads may also be boiled and eaten hot or cold. Before cooking a head, scrub it thoroughly and soak it in salted water for at least thirty minutes or preferably overnight.

Oxtail, which can be used to make a wonderfully rich casserole, cheek and tongue (a delicacy when pickled in brine) are also categorized as variety meats.

Liver

Lay the liver on a wooden board and clean it thoroughly by wiping it all over with a damp cloth.

Carefully peel off all the skin from the liver—it should come away quite easily.

With a sharp knife, cut off the fat, gristle and core.

Wash the liver in cold water then wipe dry. Cut the liver —the slices should be very thin for frying and broiling.

Kidney

 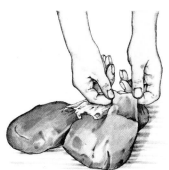  

Kidneys are surrounded by a layer of fat, which is usually removed before cooking : the fat is used as suet.

The next step is to remove the skin : insert the point of a knife between the skin and meat and loosen the skin at this point.

Pull the loosened piece of skin down toward the core and do the same on the other side of the kidney.

The skin will still be attached to the central core—pull it right to the edge of the core and cut it off.

Cut the kidneys across in half— this can be done with a pair of scissors or a knife.

Cut out every part of the central core with a pair of scissors.

The core of beef kidney is removed in the same way, usually with a pair of scissors.

When the preparation is finished, the kidneys should be neatly trimmed and have a hole where the core was removed.

Beef heart

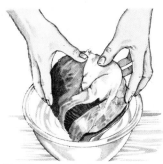

A beef heart is the largest edible heart sold by the butcher—it usually weighs about four pounds (2 kg).

Rinse the heart under cold running water and pat dry. With scissors, snip out the very tough artery stumps and tendons.

Beef heart is tough and needs to be stewed for several hours. Soak it overnight in acidulated water before cooking.

Drain the heart and pat it dry. It can now be stuffed, or cut into pieces and stewed, braised or casseroled.

Sweetbreads

Soak sweetbreads in a bowl of cold water for about 2 hours to remove all the blood.

Put the sweetbreads into a pan of cold salted water and bring to a boil. Drain off the water, repeat the process and drain.

When the sweetbreads are cool enough to handle, pull off all the skin, veins and membranes.

The prepared sweetbreads can now be cooked in stock for about 20 minutes and then finished off by frying.

Pigs' feet

Pigs' feet are sold cleaned by the butcher, and the usual serving is one per person. They can be boiled or stewed whole, or split in half. After cooking, they may be finished off by being dipped in egg and bread crumbs and fried. Pigs' feet can also be boned, stuffed and baked or broiled.

Because of their high gelatin content, pigs' feet are often used in stocks and to make head cheese and aspics.

Oxtail

Trim as much fat as possible from the oxtail and cut it into pieces. Generally, one whole oxtail will serve four people.

Oxtail is usually stewed or made into casseroles and soups. It requires long, slow cooking—anything from 3 to 5 hours.

Tripe

Tripe is the lining of beef stomach. It is always sold partially prepared by the butcher: that is, cleaned, blanched and half-cooked. In addition to this preparation, tripe should be cooked in milk (flavored with onions and herbs) for about 2 hours, depending on how long it was precooked by the butcher. After cooking, cut up the tripe and serve with a sauce.

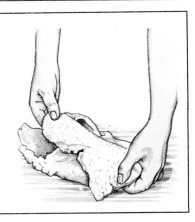

Brains

Brains must be soaked in cold salted or acidulated water for 3 to 4 hours before cooking.

Remove the brains from the water and pat them dry. Pull off all the skin and membranes.

Vegetables

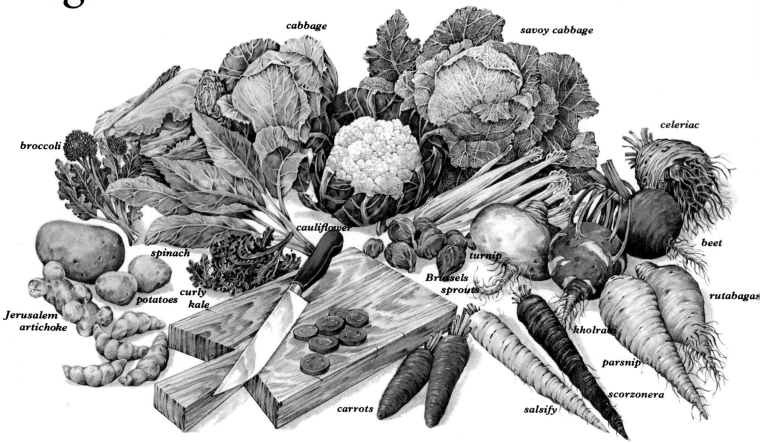

broccoli

cabbage

savoy cabbage

celeriac

cauliflower

spinach

curly kale

potatoes

turnip

Brussels sprouts

beet

Jerusalem artichoke

rutabagas

kholrabi

parsnip

scorzonera

carrots

salsify

All vegetables must be prepared in some way even if they are going to be eaten raw, but do not prepare them too far in advance, for once peeled or cut they quickly lose their freshness. The exceptions to this rule are vegetables that are marinated, dried pods and seeds that are soaked prior to cooking and such vegetables as eggplant and cucumber, which are degorged (sliced or chopped and layered with salt in a colander, left for about thirty minutes and then rinsed).

Many vegetables lose flavor and nutrients by being peeled and cut. So before preparing a vegetable consider whether that is really necessary. There is, for example, no reason to peel mushrooms, baby carrots or new potatoes.

Always wash vegetables, even if they appear to be clean, under cold running water, using a nylon pan scourer or nailbrush to scrub them if necessary. Vegetables you grow yourself must also be washed thoroughly; any soil clinging to the skin, even in minute particles, will give an unpleasant, gritty texture. Slugs, caterpillars and many other small insects are masterly at hide-and-seek, so swirl leaf vegetables vigorously in a bowl of cold, well-salted water.

There are a great many machines on the market to slice, shred, dice and even peel your vegetables for you, and although they save time you can manage perfectly well without them. All you really need is a sharp vegetable knife, a parer, a sturdy wooden chopping board, a grater and perhaps a vegetable slicer.

Tubers

A tuber is the natural swelling of an underground stem. The most important tuber is the potato, which, at its best, requires little preparation—a good scrub and it is ready to be boiled or steamed. The yam, or sweet potato, is easier to peel after it has been cooked, but is otherwise prepared and cooked in the same way as the potato. Another vegetable in this group is the Jerusalem artichoke. When young, it needs only to be scrubbed and any discolored patches scraped off.

To make potato chips, cut a potato into paper-thin slices, using a vegetable slicer.

Scrub Jerusalem artichokes in cold water, then scrape or peel away any discolored patches.

Put the prepared artichokes into a bowl of water with a little vinegar to retain color.

Brassicas

The most common brassicas are cabbage (green, red and white), Brussels sprouts, cauliflower, broccoli and kale. Chinese cabbage, a relative newcomer to Western markets, is becoming increasingly popular for its delicate flavor and lack of odor when it is cooked. All brassicas should have their stalks trimmed and the coarse outer leaves removed. Wash cauliflower and broccoli carefully and then soak in cold salted water for a few minutes to get rid of any grubs. Slit broccoli stalks before cooking.

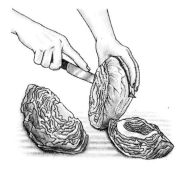

Remove the coarse outer leaves of a cabbage, then cut it into quarters and remove the core.

To shred cabbage, hold one quarter firmly and slice it thinly down its length.

To prepare Chinese cabbage, cut off the coarse outer leaves and slice it crosswise into shreds.

To make a whole cauliflower cook faster, remove a wedge from the core or cut a cross in the base.

To separate a cauliflower into florets, first cut it in half then break it apart.

To prepare green sprouting broccoli, trim the stem, then make a slit in the thicker end.

Remove the coarse outer leaves of Brussels sprouts. Trim and cut a cross in the center of the base.

Root vegetables

Such root vegetables as turnips, rutabagas and celeriac should be peeled thickly. To obtain the best flavor from salsify and scorzonera (the black-skinned salsify), do not peel or scrape until the vegetables are cooked. To prepare beets, cut off the top, leaving about one inch (2 cm) of stem, then wash with the utmost care—if the skin is pierced the beets will "bleed" during cooking.

Cook small root vegetables whole; larger ones are diced or cut into chunks or julienne strips.

Before slicing carrots, scrub them, then cut off the top end and trim the root end.

To make julienne strips, cut the carrot in half lengthwise, then cut each half into strips.

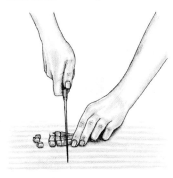

To dice carrots, cut them as for julienne strips, then slice the strips across.

Chop celeriac into manageable pieces, peel it thickly, then slice finely.

Peel the parsnip, cut off the pointed end and cut the thicker end in half before cooking.

Remove the leaves, stalk and tapering root end of kohlrabi before peeling thickly.

Ginger root should be peeled thinly with a very sharp knife, then sliced, chopped or grated.

Vegetables

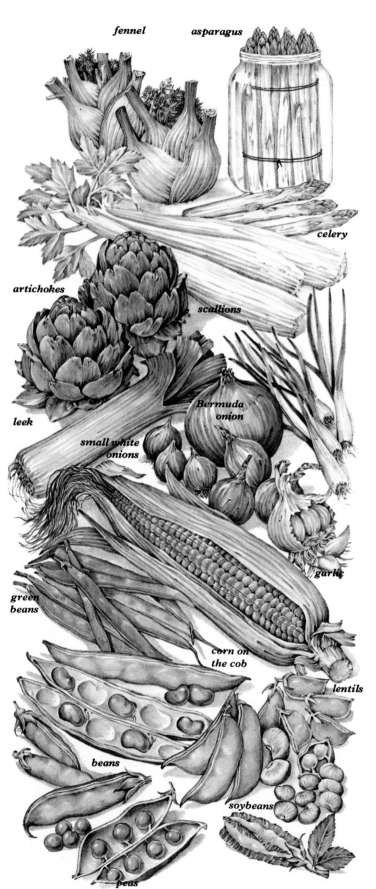

fennel

asparagus

celery

artichokes

scallions

leek

Bermuda onion

small white onions

garlic

green beans

corn on the cob

lentils

beans

soybeans

peas

Stalks and shoots

Celery, asparagus and artichokes are the best-known vegetables in this category. Others include fern shoots, fennel and cardoons. Cut fern shoots in the spring when they are still curled. Wash them, tie them in bundles and cook like asparagus. Trim the top stalks of Florence fennel and cut a slice from the base. Scrub it thoroughly before cooking. Cardoons are grown only for their leaf stems: discard the tough outer stalks and remove the "strings" from the remaining stalks.

Trim the root end and any damaged stalks from celery and remove the strings.

With a sharp knife, cut off the woody part at the base of the asparagus stalks.

Scrape the white part of the stalk, then tie the stalks in bundles for cooking.

Break off the tough outer leaves of the artichoke, then slice off the stalk and trim the base.

Cut off the top third of the artichoke, snip tops off the leaves and rub with lemon.

Hold the artichoke in one hand and pull out the prickly leaves surrounding the choke.

Using a metal teaspoon, scrape out the hairy choke. Sprinkle the inside with lemon juice.

The onion family

The onion family includes garlic, leeks, shallots, scallions and chives, as well as many other varieties. They are invaluable as flavorings —few spicy dishes would be complete without a touch of onion or garlic. If the onion has too strong a flavor, blanch it in boiling water for three minutes. Although a garlic press is an invaluable kitchen aid, perfectionists argue that it impairs the flavor of the garlic—they prefer instead to sprinkle a little salt on the garlic and crush it with a spoon or knife.

Slice off the root end and coarse green leaves of the leek. Slit lengthwise to the center.

Spread the leaves apart and wash thoroughly to remove all the dirt and grit.

Coarsely chop a garlic clove, sprinkle over a little salt and crush to a paste with a spoon.

To make onion rings, cut the onion across into thin slices and push out into rings.

To chop an onion, peel and halve it, retaining the root end. Slice horizontally up to the root end.

Turn the onion around and slice at right angles to the first cuts, up to the root end.

Turn the onion around once more and slice it across the previous cuts to make dice.

Pods and seeds

Pods and seeds is a category that covers a great many vegetables that are prepared in different ways. Some, such as lentils, split peas and dried beans, are bought dried and must be soaked before cooking. Others, for example peas and beans, must be removed from their pods, whereas sugar or snow peas and green or string beans are cooked and eaten pods and all. Unless they are dried, pods and seeds are best eaten young, when they are sweet and tender and before they become coarse.

Peel back the husks right down to the stalk end and cut them off. Tear off the silk.

To remove corn from the cob, cook the cob, then scrape the kernels off with a blunt knife.

Young snow peas need only be washed and trimmed; remove strings on older ones.

Press the pea pod gently to split it open. Run your thumb along the inside to dislodge the peas.

Tough beans usually have their skins peeled off. It is easier to do this after cooking.

Young green beans are very tender and need only to be trimmed before cooking.

To remove the strings from older, larger beans, cut through the stalk end and pull off the strings.

Vegetables

Mushrooms

Mushrooms are wild or cultivated, large or small, flat or round, and their color varies from black to the palest cream. They are used in soups and stews, as a vegetable accompaniment or garnish, or stuffed as a main dish. Remove the stalks from old, tough mushrooms, then peel the caps, if necessary. Young mushrooms keep their stalks; cook them whole and un-peeled. When mushrooms are cooked as part of a dish, remember that they give out a lot of juice, so reduce the cooking liquid accord-ingly.

To prepare mushrooms, wipe them clean, wash them only if necessary, trim stalks and slice.

Salad vegetables

The most popular salad vegetables are radish, Belgian endive, curly endive, watercress and lettuce—the crisp-hearted cabbage type, the long and crisp romaine type, and the soft, round cabbage type. Most salad vegetables are eaten raw, but some, for example curly endive and Belgian endive, may also be cooked. All salad vegetables are prepared in the same way: Trim the root end and any damaged or yellowing leaves, then wash the leaves in cold water and drain.

Trim off all but a short end of the leaf stalks, then slice off the root end.

Vegetable fruit

Some vegetables are classified as fruit but are cooked and eaten as vegetables. The one thing they have in common is seeds. Squash, peppers and pumpkin always have their seeds removed before cooking; chilies, tomatoes, cucumbers and zucchini are sometimes seeded, but eggplant never is. With the exception of chilies, all vegetable fruit can be stuffed and baked. Eggplant, zucchini, cucumbers and squash can be degorged to remove excess liquid. Rinse and pat dry before cooking or eating.

Wipe the eggplant clean with a damp cloth, then use a sharp knife to cut off the stalk end.

Chop or slice the eggplant, or halve it, according to the recipe. The seeds are edible.

Layer the eggplant with salt in a colander and weight down with a plate. Leave for 30 minutes.

One method of peeling a tomato is to dip it into boiling water to loosen the skin.

Another method is to spear the tomato on a fork and hold it over heat until the skin splits.

Cut carefully around the stem of the pepper. Remove the stem— the core should come away with it.

Cut off the stalk end and slit the chilies in half to take out the seeds (the hottest part).

To remove seeds from zucchini, cut in half lengthwise and run a teaspoon down the middle.

Or remove seeds by cutting zucchini into lengths and scooping them out with a knife.

Cut the pumpkin into manageable pieces, peel it and scoop out all the seeds and strings.

Cut the squash in half lengthwise and use a large metal spoon to scoop out all the seeds.

Fresh herbs need little preparation—just wash and dry them and remove any leaves that have become yellow. When adding herbs to a dish, chop them finely or use whole leaves or sprigs. Alternatively, for stocks, stews or casseroles, make a traditional bouquet garni by tying together a bunch of fresh or dried herbs—parsley, bay and thyme are the ones most commonly used, but such herbs as tarragon, savory, and chervil may also be included.

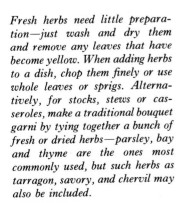

A quick way of chopping parsley is to use a small food mill.

Make a bouquet garni by tying a few herbs in a bunch, encasing

them in a split leek or in a small piece of cheesecloth.

Fruit

Wash fruit that is to be eaten unpeeled under running water, to insure that all traces of dirt or chemical sprays have been removed. Such soft fruit as strawberries, raspberries or currants, however, should be washed only if it is absolutely necessary.

Hull all berries before they are served and strip currants from their stalks—just run a fork down the length of each stalk and the currants will come away easily.

Some fruit, for example apples and bananas, discolor when they have been peeled and sliced. To prevent discoloration, sprinkle the cut fruit with a little lemon juice.

If grapes or peaches are difficult to peel, dip them in a bowl of boiling water for a minute or less. Then dip them in cold water and peel immediately.

Several kinds of nuts also have skins that are hard to remove. Shelled almonds and pistachios should be dropped into boiling water for a few minutes. The skins can then be rubbed off without any trouble.

To peel chestnuts, first cut a cross on the flat side of the nut or slit it at the pointed end. Put the nuts in a pan of cold water and boil them for two to three minutes. Use a spoon to lift a few nuts at a time out of the water and shell and peel them while they are still hot. Alternatively, slit the shells and bake the chestnuts in a 400°F (200°C) oven for ten minutes.

Toast shelled hazelnuts under a broiler, then rub them together in a paper bag. The skins will soon come off.

A mature coconut (the only kind available away from the tropics) has a hard, tough shell. To open it, puncture the three dark spots, or "eyes," with a skewer or any other strong, sharp instrument. Strain out the liquid and tap the coconut sharply with a hammer. It should break in half. If it does not break, put the coconut into a 400°F (200°C) oven for fifteen minutes. Then take it out, put it on a board and give it a sharp tap with a hammer. It will split in half and the flesh will come away from the shell. To grate the coconut, peel away the brown skin and use a hand grater.

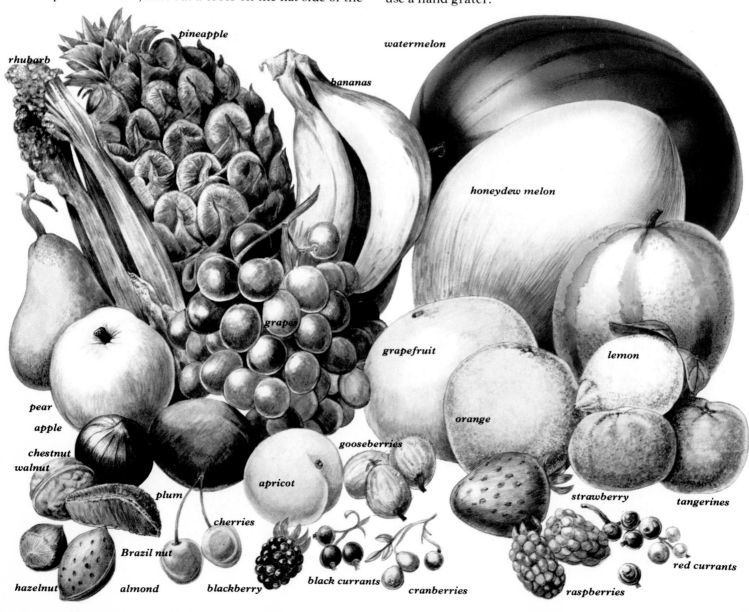

How to prepare fruit and nuts

To prepare fruit you need little equipment—just a few sharp knives of various sizes and a chopping board. Other pieces of equipment that are not essential but which you may wish to buy include a special scoop for making melon balls, and a cherry pitter, although cherry pits and grape seeds can be removed with a bobby pin.

Small hard-shelled nuts should be cracked open with nutcrackers, but to break a coconut you will need a hammer.

To peel an orange, turn the fruit while cutting away strips of peel and pith with a sharp knife.

Remove any remaining pith, then cut through the membranes to release the orange segments.

Cut the melon in half, remove the seeds, then use a special scoop to cut out the melon balls.

The best way to peel a pineapple is to cut it diagonally, removing the skin and the "eyes" together.

Cut the pineapple into slices, then use an apple corer to remove the hard center from each slice.

Another way to serve pineapple is to cut the fruit in half and remove all the flesh from both halves.

Cut the flesh into pieces and remove the core, then pile all the flesh into one of the empty shells.

To prepare a mango, cut it into three, keeping the knife as close as possible to the seed.

Slice an avocado pear in half, cutting around the central pit. Remove the pit and serve.

Insert a clean bobby pin into the stem end of a cherry, hook it around the pit and lift it out carefully.

To prepare a strawberry, pull the stalk and the soft central core will come away with it easily.

Use a pair of nutcrackers to shell such small nuts as almonds, hazelnuts, walnuts and Brazil nuts.

To release the liquid from a coconut, puncture the three "eyes" with a strong, sharp instrument.

Having strained out the liquid, crack open the coconut by tapping it sharply with a hammer.

Before peeling a chestnut cut a cross in the side, immerse in water and boil for a few minutes.

Cereals

Pastry making is an art and a science. The art lies in the lightness of your touch, and the science in the correct combination and proportion of ingredients. With a few exceptions pastry dough should be mixed as lightly as possible to introduce air into the mixture; too much handling or a "heavy" hand knocks out the air. (It is the air in the dough that expands with the heat of the oven and makes pastry light.)

The main types of pastry are: basic pie crust, rich pie crust, pâte sucrée (French flan pastry), puff, strudel, choux, hot-water crust and suet crust, an old-fashioned pastry using suet for the shortening.

There are a few basic rules for pastry making. If possible, always work in a cool kitchen with cool ingredients.

Use all-purpose flour unless otherwise instructed. Self-rising flour or the addition of baking powder to flour makes a spongy pastry, which is unsuitable for most purposes. When you are making a savory cheese dough, however, add a very small amount of baking powder to lighten the pastry.

Butter is the best fat to use for making a rich, light pastry, but hard margarine or a mixture of butter or hard margarine and shortening may be used instead. Pastry made entirely with lard, for example hot-water crust, is only suitable for meat pies.

The consistency of the fat is important; it should be kept at room temperature until it is cool and firm. If the fat is cold and hard, you will find it difficult to cut it into the flour evenly; if it is too warm and soft, the mixture will have the texture of a paste rather than of bread crumbs and the result will be uneven, unmanageable dough.

Use your fingertips to work the fat into the flour. Or, if the weather is warm, start by using a knife or pastry blender, then use your fingertips to bring the dough together after the water has been added.

Water is generally used to bind the dough, but milk or a mixture of milk and water may be used. Sprinkle the liquid, all at once, over the flour and fat mixture. If you pour it into the center your pastry may be streaky. The amount of water you add is important; if you use too little, the dough will crack and become difficult to roll out. The cracks let the air out when the dough is baked and this makes the pastry heavy. If too much water is added, the dough will be sticky and too soft to handle; add more flour to compensate for this and you will unbalance the proportion of fat to flour—the result will be pastry that is tough.

When the dough is ready, shape it into a ball and chill it in a covered bowl in the refrigerator for at least thirty minutes. The longer you chill it—up to twelve hours—the easier the pastry will be to handle. Remove the dough from the refrigerator one hour before using it if it has been chilled more than two hours.

Plain and rich pie pastry may be flavored with herbs, garlic, cheese, ground or finely chopped nuts and orange or lemon rind. A teaspoon of lemon juice added to pie or puff dough lightens the pastry.

Roll pastry dough on a lightly floured, cool, smooth surface. A marble slab or wooden board is ideal. Use a heavy rolling pin without handles and make light, short movements from the center out. Turn the dough but not the rolling pin. Rest the rolled-out dough for five minutes before using; this prevents shrinkage during baking.

Before baking pastry shells, chill them in the refrigerator for at least thirty minutes.

The oven must be heated to the required temperature before the pastry is baked. Initially, the oven is set to high because high heat causes the air trapped in the dough to expand rapidly making the pastry light.

Basic pie pastry
This amount of pastry will line one 9-inch (23-cm) pie pan.
1½ cups (175 g) all-purpose flour
Pinch salt
6 tablespoons butter
2 to 3 tablespoons ice water

Sift the flour and salt into a bowl and add the butter. Cut the butter into the flour, then lightly work it in with your fingertips until the mixture resembles coarse bread crumbs. Sprinkle in most of the water, then mix it in with a knife, adding a little more if necessary.

Give the dough a final mix with your fingertips to bring it together. Shape it into a ball, cover and chill.

Cut the butter into the flour.

Work it in with your fingertips.

Rich pie pastry
This amount of pastry will line one 11-inch (28-cm) pie pan.
2 cups (225 g) all-purpose flour
Pinch salt
¾ cup (175 g) butter
1 egg yolk mixed with 2 to 3 tablespoons ice water

Sift the flour and salt into a bowl and add the butter. Cut it into small pieces with a knife, and then lightly work it into the flour with your fingertips until the mixture resembles coarse bread crumbs. Add the egg and water mixture and mix it in, adding a little more water if necessary. Give the dough a quick, final mix with your fingertips. Shape into a ball, cover and chill.

Almond pastry
This is a difficult pastry to roll out. It is easier to press it into the pan with your fingertips.
1 cup (125 g) all-purpose flour
6 tablespoons butter, cut into small pieces
¼ cup (50 g) sugar
1 egg yolk
⅓ cup (50 g) ground almonds
Few drops almond extract

Sift the flour into a mixing bowl. Cut in the butter until the mixture resembles coarse bread crumbs. Mix in the remaining ingredients until the dough is smooth.

Shape the dough into a ball, wrap it in waxed paper and chill in the refrigerator for 1 hour.

Pâte sucrée

This amount of pastry will line one 11-inch (28-cm) pie pan. Pâte sucrée is sometimes called French flan pastry.

1½ cups (175 g) all-purpose flour
3 tablespoons softened butter,
1 tablespoon sugar
1 tablespoon confectioners' sugar
3 egg yolks
Vanilla extract

Sift the flour onto a marble slab or wooden board. Make a well in the center and put in the butter, sugar, egg yolks and a few drops of vanilla extract.

With the fingertips of one hand, mix the butter, sugar, yolks and vanilla together, gradually drawing in the flour. When all the flour has been drawn in, flatten the dough with the heel of your hand to make it smooth, then bring it together again. Repeat no more than six times.

Wrap the dough in waxed paper and let it rest for at least 40 minutes before using.

Mix the butter, eggs and sugar together, drawing in the flour.

Flatten the dough with the heel of your hand several times.

English flaky pastry

1½ cups (175 g) all-purpose flour
Pinch salt
4 tablespoons butter
4 tablespoons shortening
3 to 4 tablespoons ice water

Sift the flour and salt into a bowl. Cut half the butter into the flour then work it in with your fingertips. Mix in the water to make a dough, adding more if necessary. Chill.

Roll out the dough into a rectangle. Cut half the shortening into small pieces and dot it over two-thirds of the dough. Fold the unused one-third of dough upward, and the top third downward and over. Turn the dough so that the open end faces you and roll it out into a rectangle. Cut up the remaining butter, dot it over the dough and repeat the whole process. Cut up the remaining shortening and repeat the process.

If the dough looks too streaked, roll it out and fold it once more. Wrap the dough in waxed paper and chill for at least 1 hour before using.

Dot the butter over two-thirds of the rolled-out dough.

Fold the dough in three and seal the edges before rolling out.

Puff pastry

This amount of pastry will make about six 3-inch (8-cm) vol-au-vent cases.

1½ cups (175 g) flour with a high gluten content
Pinch salt
¾ cup (175 g) butter
1 teaspoon lemon juice
About ½ cup (125 ml) ice water

Sift the flour and salt into a bowl and add a walnut-sized piece of the butter. Cut it into small pieces then lightly work it into the flour with your fingertips. Mix in the lemon juice and most of the water to make a firm dough, adding a little more water if necessary. Turn the dough out onto a lightly floured slab or board and knead it very gently, for the shortest time possible, until the dough is smooth.

Roll the dough out into a square about ½ inch (1 cm) thick.

Place the remaining butter between two sheets of waxed paper and beat it (no more than two or three times) until it is pliable but not soft. Remove the paper and place the butter in the center of the dough. Wrap the dough like a parcel to enclose the butter. Wrap the parcel in waxed paper and chill for 15 minutes.

Remove the dough from the refrigerator, unwrap it and place it on the board or slab, the seam facing upward. Flatten it slightly with the rolling pin, then roll it out to a rectangle about ½ inch (1 cm) thick. Turn the dough so that the short end is facing you. Fold the bottom third over toward the middle. Bring the top third down over the folded third to make three layers of dough. Turn the dough around so that the open edges are facing you and seal the edges by pressing lightly with the rolling pin. Roll the dough out into a rectangle again and fold as before. Wrap the dough in waxed paper and chill for 15 minutes.

Repeat the rolling and folding process another four times. Chill the dough for at least 20 minutes before using.

Put the butter between sheets of paper and beat to flatten.

Put the butter on the rolled-out dough and fold in the sides.

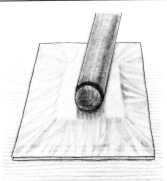

Fold the dough in three and turn the open edges toward you.

Roll the dough into a rectangle, fold and repeat four times.

Cereals/pastry

Pour the flour into the liquid.

Beat until smooth and glossy.

Choux pastry

This amount of pastry will make eighteen 4-inch (10-cm) éclairs.

1¼ cups (315 ml) water
½ cup (125 g) butter, cut into pieces
1 cup (125 g) plus 2 tablespoons all-purpose flour
3 eggs

Put the water and butter into a saucepan over moderate heat. When the butter has melted, bring the mixture to a boil. Remove the pan from the heat and let the bubbles subside. Add the flour all at once, stirring quickly until the dough is smooth and leaves the sides of the pan. Cool the dough slightly, then beat in the eggs one at a time. Continue beating vigorously until the dough is glossy. Use immediately.

Strudel pastry

This amount of pastry will make one 6-foot (2-meter) strudel. Once stuffed and rolled it may be cut to fit your baking sheets.

2½ cups (275 g) sifted all-purpose flour
Pinch of salt
1 egg, lightly beaten
¾ cup (175 ml) plus 2 tablespoons lukewarm water
2 tablespoons melted butter

Sift the flour and salt into a mixing bowl. In another mixing bowl, beat the egg, water and butter together with a fork. Stir the liquid into the flour with a wooden spoon to make a soft dough. Place the dough on a lightly floured board or slab and knead it well for about 10 to 15 minutes or until it is smooth and shiny.

The dough will stick to your fingers and be difficult to knead. The technique is to lift the dough with a twist and throw it onto the board, gather it up and throw it again. Continue doing this until the dough ceases to be sticky and becomes smooth and elastic. Shape the dough into a ball, place in a bowl, cover and set aside in a warm place for 30 minutes. Use immediately.

Useful baking equipment

Although a pastry blender results in a much lighter and crisper pastry, some people prefer to use their fingertips to blend the butter and flour together.

Fluted and plain cookie cutters and a pastry wheel make uniform shapes for cookies and scones, and a pastry brush is invaluable for glazing pastry, breads and scones.

A pie funnel placed under a pastry lid allows the steam to escape as the pie bakes and so avoids a soggy crust.

For other useful baking equipment, see page 9.

Hot-water crust

This amount of pastry will make one pie.

3 cups (350 g) all-purpose flour
Pinch of salt
¾ cup (175 ml) water
6 tablespoons lard, chopped

Sift the flour and salt into a bowl and make a well in the middle. Put the water and lard into a small saucepan over moderate heat. When the lard melts, bring the mixture to a boil. Take the pan off the heat and pour the contents into the middle of the flour. Working very quickly, mix the dough with a wooden spoon and then with your hands until it is smooth. It must be used while still warm or the lard will solidify and the dough will become brittle and impossible to mold.

Suet crust

This amount of suet crust will line and cover a 2½- to 3-pint (1¼- to 1½-liter) pudding bowl.

4 cups (450 g) self-rising flour
Pinch of salt
1 generous cup (150 g) fresh white bread crumbs
2½ cups (275 g) shredded suet
Ice water

Sift the flour and salt into a bowl and stir in the bread crumbs and suet. Very lightly work the suet into the flour mixture with your fingertips for just a few minutes. Using a spoon, mix to a spongy dough with a little water. Shape into a ball and use immediately.

Basic pasta dough

Pasta is the Italian name for a dough made with flour, water and eggs or just with flour and water. Spinach, which is sometimes added to the dough, gives it an interesting green color.

The dough is cut to whatever shape is required to make such dishes as ravioli and cannelloni.

4 cups (450 g) all-purpose flour or semolina
1 teaspoon salt
4 eggs
4 tablespoons water

Put the flour and salt on a pastry board or work surface and make a well in the center. In a bowl beat the eggs with the water then pour the mixture into the well. Using your hands, combine the flour with the egg mixture until a dough is formed. The dough should be stiff, so add more flour if necessary. Shape into a ball then knead for 10 minutes or until smooth and elastic.

Sour cream pastry

This pastry can be used to make savory meat loaves, to cover meat pies and to make savory turnovers. If you add a little sugar and grated lemon rind, you can also use it for sweet pies and tart shells. This amount will line one 9-inch (23-cm) pie pan.

1½ cups (175 g) all-purpose flour
Pinch of salt
6 tablespoons butter
1 small egg yolk
2 tablespoons sour cream
1 to 2 tablespoons ice water

Sift the flour and salt into a large mixing bowl. Add the butter and cut it into small pieces with a knife. Using a pastry blender, cut the butter into the flour until the mixture resembles fine bread crumbs.

In a small bowl, mix the egg yolk with the sour cream and a little of the water.

Make a well in the center of the flour mixture and add the egg-yolk mixture. Mix it into the flour with a knife, then knead the dough lightly, just enough to bring it together.

Shape the dough into a ball and wrap it in waxed paper. Chill the dough in the refrigerator for 40 minutes before using.

Cream cheese pastry

This amount of pastry will make about 40 small pies or tarts.

¾ cup (175 g) cream cheese
¾ cup (175 g) butter
1½ cups (175 g) self-rising flour
Salt

Cream the cheese in a bowl. Beat in the butter and mix in the flour and salt.

Knead the dough lightly, shape it into a ball with well-floured hands and chill in the refrigerator for 2 hours.

Cereals/bread

In the past everyone baked their own bread and thought nothing of it. Twentieth century housewives with less time on their hands have welcomed the store-bought loaf, however, and the art of bread making has almost been forgotten. For many people the smell and taste of homemade bread has almost become part of a nostalgic memory.

Today, an interest in healthy eating, a longing for the forgotten flavors of home baking and boredom with the tastelessness of manufactured bread is bringing the homemade loaf back into favor. Bread making is one of the most exciting and satisfying culinary experiences, yet it is not a complicated process. Simply follow the basic rules and work in a warm, draft-free room, using warm utensils and ingredients.

Yeast is a living organism which, given the right conditions, produces carbon dioxide, the gas that causes bread to rise. Warmth is required to activate yeast—between 75° and 85°F (24° and 29°C) is ideal. A little sugar—a quarter teaspoon for one cake compressed yeast or one envelope dry yeast—will quicken the process, but too much will slow it down.

Bread can be made from compressed or dry yeast. Compressed yeast should be an even gray-beige color; it should break with a clean edge and crumble easily. If it is streaky or sour-smelling, it is past its best and must be thrown away. Compressed yeast will keep in a plastic bag in the refrigerator for up to a week. Dry yeast will keep in a screw-top jar in a cool cupboard for up to six months.

Dissolve yeast in a little lukewarm water or milk with a quarter teaspoon of sugar and leave it in a warm, draft-free place for about fifteen minutes or until it is frothy and puffed up. For dry yeast this activation is necessary, but compressed yeast may be dissolved in lukewarm water and mixed into the flour without waiting for it to froth. If, however, you are not sure that the yeast is "live" this is a good way of finding out.

The plain and self-rising flours that are used to make cakes and cookies are unsuitable for making bread. This is because their gluten content is not sufficiently high; it is the gluten in the flour that makes the dough elastic and springy. All-purpose bread, whole wheat or graham, granary and rye are the main types of flour used for bread making. Rye, which has a low gluten content, makes a flatter, heavier loaf that is popular in such countries as Norway, Sweden and Germany.

Salt is added to the flour to bring out the flavor of the bread—use about one teaspoon to 4 cups (450 g) of flour. Never add salt directly to the yeast because it slows down its growth.

Use lukewarm water or milk or a mixture of both, to bind the flour into a dough. If the liquid is too hot it will kill the yeast. The amount of liquid required varies with the kind of flour used, because some flours absorb more than others.

Eggs are sometimes added to a white dough (for ex-ample brioche) to make it richer and to give it a yellow color.

Although butter or oil are not essential ingredients, they can be added to a bread dough to help it to expand more easily and to improve its flavor. The bread will also stay fresh longer. Rub the butter into the flour or melt it and add it with the liquid. Stir oil into the liquid before adding it to the flour.

Apart from the small amount of sugar that is "fed" to the yeast to help activate it, a certain amount can also be added to the flour to sweeten or to improve the flavor of the bread. Honey can be used instead of sugar; it improves the keeping quality of the bread.

Such additional ingredients as dried fruit, cheese, herbs, garlic and malt can be added to the dough to make sweet or savory breads. They are generally mixed in with the flour, with the exception of malt, which goes in with the liquid.

When all the ingredients have been mixed together, shape the dough into a ball, turn it out onto a floured board and knead it for at least ten minutes. Kneading is vital for two reasons: it distributes the ingredients evenly to make a smooth-textured, evenly risen bread, and it develops the gluten content in the flour. It also reduces the stickiness of the dough.

After kneading the dough, shape it into a ball and place it in a large, lightly greased bowl. Cover the bowl with plastic wrap or a damp cloth and set it aside for the dough to rise in a warm, draft-free place until it has doubled in bulk—it will take up to two hours. The time the dough takes to rise depends on the ingredients used and the weather. If, however, it rises too quickly the texture of the bread may be uneven.

As soon as the dough has doubled in bulk, turn it out of the bowl and punch it to knock out the air pockets, then knead it again for two to three minutes.

Bread dough can be baked in pans or shaped into rolls, a braid or a ball with a cross cut on top and baked on a baking sheet. Having shaped the dough or put it in a pan, leave it to rise for up to one hour. It must double in bulk, and, if it is in a bread pan it should rise to the top of the pan. Then brush the top lightly with salted water, egg yolk or milk or a mixture of both or with melted butter, and sprinkle over coarse salt, nuts, or poppy seeds. For how to bake bread and for bread recipes see page 198.

Yeast dough is also used to make flat bread or pitta. The ingredients are plain flour (white or whole wheat), yeast, water, salt and sometimes a little oil and the proportions and the preparation of the dough are the same as for ordinary bread. Punch the dough down, divide it into pieces, then roll out into circles. Dust with flour, cover and allow to prove. Set the oven at its highest. Heat lightly oiled baking sheets for ten minutes, slip the dough circles onto them and bake for six to ten minutes or until they are puffed up but not colored. Cool on a rack. The bread will collapse but a pocket will remain inside.

Cereals/bread

Basic bread dough

MAKES ONE LARGE LOAF

1 cake compressed yeast
1 tablespoon plus 1 pinch
   sugar
1¾ cups (425 ml) lukewarm
   water
6 cups (700 g) flour with a
   high gluten content
2 teaspoons salt
1 tablespoon butter

Mash the yeast with the pinch of sugar and 2 tablespoons of the water in a small bowl until smooth. Set aside in a warm, draft-free place for 15 minutes or until the mixture is puffed up and frothy.

Sift the flour and salt into a mixing bowl and work in the butter. Stir in the sugar and make a well in the center. Pour in the yeast mixture and the remaining water and mix to a dough. When the dough comes away from the sides of the bowl, turn it out onto a floured surface and knead for 10 minutes, or until it is smooth and elastic.

Put the dough into a lightly oiled bowl and cover with a damp cloth. Set aside in a warm, draft-free place for 1 to 1½ hours or until doubled in bulk.

Turn the dough out of the bowl and knead it for about 3 minutes. Either shape the dough and put it on a greased baking sheet or put it into a greased loaf pan. Set aside in a warm place for at least 30 minutes or until it has doubled in bulk or risen to the top of the pan. The dough can now be baked.

See page 198 for instructions on baking bread.

Let the yeast mixture rise.

Pour it into the flour mixture.

Mix to a dough with your hands.

Knead the dough for 10 minutes.

Let the dough double in bulk.

Shape it and let it rise again.

Bread crumbs, bread cases and croutons

Bread crumbs should always be made with bread that is at least one day old. Fresh white bread crumbs are used for making meat loaves, stuffings and bread sauce. To make bread crumbs, cut off the crusts, then rub the bread through a sieve, pull it apart with your fingers or a fork, or use a blender. Fresh bread crumbs will not keep and must be used immediately.

Dry white bread crumbs are used to coat food that is to be fried. Put fresh bread crumbs on a baking sheet and bake them in a very low oven, 250°F (130°C), until they are dried but not brown. Dried bread crumbs can be stored in a screw-top jar for several weeks.

Dry brown bread crumbs are used to cover a gratin. Take several crusts of bread and brown them in a 325°F (170°C) oven. Place the browned crusts on a breadboard and crush them with a rolling pin or in a blender. If the crumbs are not to be used immediately, store them in an airtight container.

Bread cases make unusual and delicious containers for all sorts of foods. To make them, follow the step-by-step instructions on this page.

Croutons are made from toasted or fried cubes or thin slices of bread. The smaller cubes are used as a garnish for soups or added to a dressed green salad just before serving. The larger slices are used to put under a steak or chop. To make fried croutons, trim the crusts, cut the bread into cubes and fry in butter, bacon fat or oil.

Cut a circle out of a very thick piece of bread with a round biscuit cutter.

Cut out a smaller circle, not quite to the bottom, or scrape the bread out with a knife.

To make large bread cases, cut the crust off a large oblong loaf and slice in half.

With a knife, scrape the insides out of each half to make two bread cases.

Eggs and dairy products

Eggs

Keep eggs at room temperature (70° to 75°F/21° to 24°C) for an hour or two before using them, except when they are needed for frying, when they may be taken straight from the refrigerator.

Although it is possible to buy a special gadget for separating egg whites from egg yolks, the three-bowl method is still the most successful. Have ready three bowls, one of which should be large and deep and in which the whites can be beaten. This bowl should be made of copper, glazed earthenware or glass, but not of plastic or aluminum, which have a detrimental effect on the color and volume of the beaten whites. Wash the whisk and bowls and dry thoroughly before using them. If you cannot be sure that every trace of grease has been removed, rub all around with a lemon slice or some vinegar, then rinse and dry.

To separate an egg, give it a sharp tap in the middle of its side against one of the smaller bowls. Then, holding the egg in both hands with the cracked side up and the wider end lower than the pointed end, ease the two halves of the shell apart. While you are doing this, some of the egg white will slip into the bowl. To finish separating the egg, tip the yolk from one half of the shell into the other until there is no white left in the shell. Tip the egg yolk into the bowl that has not yet been used, transfer the egg white into the larger, deep bowl, then begin the process again with another egg. This process may seem tedious, but it helps you to discover a bad egg before it taints the others in the bowl.

If, while you are separating an egg, the yolk breaks, try and remove any that has fallen into the white, using the broken eggshell to scoop it up. If this fails, tip the whole egg into an airtight container and store it in the refrigerator to be used for another purpose. The reason for this is that egg whites will not whip to several times their original volume if they come into contact with even a trace of the fat from the broken yolk.

The traditional way to beat egg whites, and one the purists say is the most effective, is to use a copper bowl and a wire whisk. If you do not have either a copper bowl or the endurance to use a wire whisk, an electric beater will do; the result may not be quite as good but it will be adequate.

To whip egg whites in the traditional way, take a thin wire whisk and with a relaxed wrist beat lightly and steadily until the whites become foamy. Increase the tempo and beat more vigorously until they stand in stiff, glossy peaks. Overbeating will make them dry and collapse.

Use three bowls when cracking eggs to prevent yolks mixing with whites.

Dairy products

Before beating whipping or heavy cream (light cream cannot be beaten), particularly in warm weather, chill the cream, the bowl in which it is to be beaten and the wire whisk (an electric beater may also be used). Then beat the cream until it forms soft, glossy peaks when you lift the beater. Check frequently to see if the cream is thick enough. If you overbeat cream it will turn into butter.

All eggs used in the recipes in this book are large eggs that weigh about two ounces (50 g) each.

Clarified butter

Butter is clarified to clear it of impurities, salt and milk solids. The result is a pure fat that, when heated, does not burn as easily as butter and is therefore more useful for frying at higher temperatures. Clarified butter is also used in such recipes as potted shrimp and *cervelles au beurre noir* (brains in black butter).

To clarify butter, put it into a pan over very low heat and let it melt. When it has melted, cook it for thirty seconds without coloring. Remove any scum from the surface, take the pan off the heat and strain the butter into a bowl through a sieve lined with cheesecloth. Put the bowl aside for a few minutes. Any sediment will settle at the bottom.

Then pour the butter into a clean bowl, leaving the sediment behind. The butter is now clarified and ready for use, or it can be stored in an airtight container in the refrigerator.

Butter curls and molds

To make butter curls, dip a butter curler into warm water then run it along the top of a stick of firm, but not frozen, butter. Butter molds must be dipped first in boiling water then in ice water before use. When using a mold, cut the butter into squares the same size as the mold.

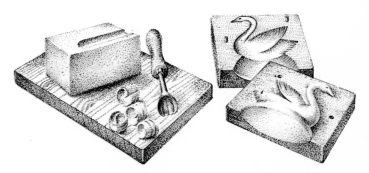

To present butter attractively, use a butter curler or butter molds.

The heart of good cooking

Stock is to the cook what foundations are to the builder, for so many of the great dishes of Western cooking are based on this simply made yet indispensable liquid.

There is something marvelously rewarding about making stock. You put a few bones into a pan of water, add some meat and vegetable trimmings and a few herbs and simmer until all the flavor of the ingredients has been extracted. Thus with very little effort you have created something valuable out of almost nothing.

Stock makes a plain soup seem luxurious. It is an essential part of all brown sauces and some white sauces. It is used in stews, casseroles and many dishes where the food is braised, poached or sautéed. As Mistress Margaret Dods, a nineteenth-century Scottish cook, wrote, stock is a "floating capital subservient to many purposes," and it does indeed give us much interest.

Stocks

It is a great pity that the art of making good stock has been abandoned by so many cooks in favor of the stock cube.

Homemade stock is so easy to make—bones, meat and vegetables (or vegetables alone) are simmered in water until all their flavor has been extracted. Strained, cooled and any fat skimmed off, the stock is then ready to be used as the base for countless soups, sauces and gravies, and for all kinds of casseroles, stews and savory pies. And, apart from the culinary considerations, making your own stock is an economy no cook can afford to ignore. So much of the debris of cooking—fish and meat bones, game bird and poultry carcasses and vegetable peelings—is there waiting to be turned into delicious stock. To throw it away is a wasteful and unnecessary extravagance.

The stockpot, however, should never be treated as a trash can for kitchen waste. You should give the same careful thought to choosing the ingredients for a stock as you would for a stew. And you should also take into consideration how the stock is going to be used. White stocks, for example, are used for making cream sauces, white stews and soups.

It is a good idea to freeze bones or poultry carcasses until there are enough of them to make the preparation of stock worthwhile. But if you need to make a stock and have no leftover bones, or not enough of them, you can buy them from the butcher; or you can use a piece of stewing meat such as flank, shin or brisket, rich in gelatin, which gives body to a stock.

A simple household stock can be made from the bones of cooked meat and chicken, bacon rinds, mushroom peelings and stalks, carrots, onions and celery. A small piece of beef shin or veal knuckle added to the pot will improve its flavor and color.

Only a little salt should be added to a basic stock because the stock will become unpleasantly salty if it has to be reduced in volume by boiling.

Stock can be kept in the refrigerator for about one week provided it is well covered.

Points to remember when making stock:

Never add cooked vegetables or gravies to the stockpot.

Use unpeeled onions for making brown stock, and peeled onions for light stock.

Always put the ingredients into cold water and bring it slowly to a boil, then simmer on a very low, even heat.

Remove as much scum as possible before the stock comes to a boil. Do not leave or store stock in a warm place because it will soon turn sour.

Household stock

MAKES 5 CUPS (1¼ LITERS)

3 lb (1½ kg) cooked meat bones
½ lb (225 g) stewing steak or beef or veal shin
Chicken carcass and giblets (but not the liver)
A few bacon rinds
10 cups (2½ liters) water
Mushroom peelings and stalks
2 onions, sliced
2 carrots, sliced
2 leeks, sliced
1 celery stalk, sliced
Bouquet garni

Saw the bones into short lengths. Put them into a pot and brown them slightly without adding any fat. Add the meat, chicken carcass, giblets and bacon rinds. Pour in the water and bring it slowly to a boil, skimming off the scum as it forms.

Add the vegetables and the bouquet garni. Partly cover the pan and simmer very gently for 3 hours.

Strain the stock into a large bowl through a sieve lined with wet cheesecloth. Discard the contents of the sieve. When the stock is cool, cover it and refrigerate.

Bone stock

MAKES ABOUT 8 CUPS (2 LITERS)

4 lb (2 kg) beef marrow bones, sawed into short lengths
15 cups (3¾ liters) water
1 lb (450 g) beef shin or veal knuckle and stewing veal
¼ lb (125 g) bacon trimmings
2 onions, sliced
2 carrots, sliced
1 celery stalk, sliced
Mushroom peelings and stalks
2 leeks, cut in half
Bouquet garni

Wrap the bones in cheesecloth to prevent the loss of the marrow and put them into a large pot. Pour in the water and bring it slowly to a boil. As it begins to boil, skim off the scum. Add the remaining ingredients, half cover the pot and simmer gently for 1 hour. Remove the vegetables, because all their flavor will have been extracted, and continue simmering for a further 2 hours.

Do not let the stock boil quickly or it will become cloudy. Strain the stock into a bowl through a colander lined with wet cheesecloth. When the stock is cool, cover it and refrigerate.

Other bone stocks:
Brown stock
Brown stock is made in the same way, except that the bones are browned in drippings in a roasting pan before being put into the stockpot.

White stock
Use veal bones and ½ pound (225 g) of veal knuckles instead of the beef.

Game bird or chicken stock
For stock made with only the carcass, proceed as for bone stock but cook for only 1 hour. The best chicken stock, however, is made from a cut-up boiling fowl, which should simmer for 3 hours. A good chicken stock can also be made from chicken wings, necks and backs.

Vegetable stock
MAKES ABOUT 8 CUPS (2 LITERS)
Vegetable stock is used for many delicately flavored soups and sauces.

2 tablespoons butter
1 lb (450 g) carrots, cut into large pieces
1 lb (450 g) onions, peeled and cut into large pieces
6 celery stalks, cut into large pieces
½ lb (225 g) turnips, peeled and cut into large pieces
1 leek, sliced (optional)
Bouquet garni
6 peppercorns
2 teaspoons salt
15 cups (3¾ liters) hot water

Melt the butter in a large pan or Dutch oven. Add the vegetables and cook them over low heat, stirring frequently, until they are brown. Add the remaining ingredients and the water and bring it to a boil. Partially cover the pan and simmer for 3 hours. The liquid should have reduced to about one-third of its original volume. Pour the stock into a bowl through a colander lined with wet cheesecloth. Cool the stock, then store it in the refrigerator.

Pot au feu

In most French households a pot au feu is cooked every week. This provides a stock that is full of body, as well as delicious boiled meat, which is served either hot or cold.

If the meat is to be served hot, remove some of the stock (it may require seasoning) to serve with it. The vegetables from the pot may be served with the meat along with jacket potatoes, horseradish, mustard, gherkins and a salad.

If the meat is to be served cold, let it cool in the stock and serve it sliced the next day with a potato salad dressed with a vinaigrette to which chopped capers, scallions and parsley have been added. Garnish the dish with quartered hard-cooked eggs. Serve it as a main course or as an hors d'oeuvre.

Traditionally a pot au feu is cooked in a deep earthenware crock, but an enamel or stainless-steel pot will do just as well.

SERVES SIX

2 lb (900 g) beef flank
½ lb (225 g) beef shin
1 lb (450 g) veal knuckle, cut into pieces
½ lb (225 g) beef liver
1 lb (450 g) oxtail, cut into pieces and soaked in cold water for 2 hours
15 cups (3¾ liters) cold water
2 onions, halved
2 leeks, halved
2 carrots
1 celery stalk
½ lb (225 g) turnips or parsnips, peeled
1 tomato, halved
Bouquet garni
2 teaspoons salt
4 peppercorns

Put all the meats into a pot. Pour in the water and very slowly bring it to a boil, skimming off the scum as it rises to the top. The scum will be quite thick and will continue to surface as the water begins to simmer. When the scum is sparse and white, add the vegetables and seasonings. Partly cover the pan and simmer very gently for 3 hours.

Remove the pan from the heat and take out all the vegetables and meat. Strain the stock into a bowl through a colander lined with wet cheesecloth. Skim the fat off the top using paper towels to absorb the grease or, if the stock is not to be used at once, let it cool, then refrigerate and remove the layer of solidified fat before reheating.

Stocks

Fish stock

Fish stock is used to make sauces that are required to coat a finished fish dish. This is suitable for sole, flounder, whiting and turbot. If the fish dealer is filleting fish for you, be sure to ask for the heads and bones—and some extra ones if you feel you will need them.

MAKES ABOUT 5 CUPS (1¼ LITERS)

1 lb (450 g) fish bones, from sole, flounder, turbot or whiting
1 onion, sliced
1 cup (15 g) chopped parsley or parsley stalks
2 tablespoons butter
Strips of lemon peel
¼ cup (65 ml) white wine
6 peppercorns
1 teaspoon salt
5 cups (1¼ liters) cold water

Break the bones into pieces and put them into a pan with all the other ingredients. Partly cover the pan and simmer the stock for 20 minutes. Pour the stock through a sieve. Cool the stock and then keep in the refrigerator until it is needed.

Court bouillon

This is basically a seasoned, acidic liquid in which such large whole fish as salmon and turbot are cooked. The simplest court bouillon is strained seawater to which vinegar or lemon juice has been added.

MAKES ABOUT 8 CUPS (2 LITERS)

½ cup (125 ml) white wine
10 cups (2½ liters) water
2 onions, peeled
½ lb (225 g) carrots, sliced
1 bay leaf
1 large thyme sprig
2 teaspoons salt
½ cup (125 ml) tarragon vinegar
2 cups (25 g) chopped parsley, with stalks
12 peppercorns

Put all the ingredients into a saucepan and bring to just under boiling point. Simmer gently for 1 hour. Strain, cool and refrigerate.

To clarify stock

Stock is clarified to make clear, sparkling aspics, consommés and chaud-froids. The ingredients used include a small amount of ground raw beef, which helps the clarification process and enriches the stock. A stock can be clarified without the beef, but it will be less tasty.

½ lb (225 g) stewing beef, ground
3½ cups (875 ml) cold stock
¼ cup (65 ml) sherry or wine (optional)
1 eggshell, broken up
1 egg white, beaten until frothy

Put the meat, stock, wine, if you are using it, and the eggshell into a large pan. Add the egg white and beat steadily. Stop beating when the stock comes to a boil. Without disturbing the crust that will have formed on the top, allow the stock to rise in the pan, then remove the pan from the heat. Line a colander with a piece of cheesecloth that has been scalded and then wrung out. Gently tip the crust into the strainer and pour the stock slowly through it.

Aspic

Make the stock for the aspic in the same way as bone stock, but use a calf's foot and a chicken carcass instead of the marrow bones. For a fish aspic make a strong fish stock using only sole bones.

MAKES ABOUT 5 CUPS (1¼ LITERS)

5 cups (1¼ liters) stock
¼ cup (65 ml) sherry
¼ cup (65 ml) white wine
2 tablespoons wine vinegar
3 tablespoons gelatin, dissolved in a little of the stock
2 egg whites, beaten until frothy

Put the stock, sherry, wine, vinegar and gelatin in a large pan. Add the egg whites and beat steadily. Stop when the stock boils and rises in the pan. Draw the pan aside, then return it to the heat and allow the stock to boil and rise in the pan again. Repeat this once more. Do not disturb the crust that will have formed on the top.

Remove the pan from the heat. Line a colander with a piece of cheesecloth that has been scalded and then wrung out. Gently tip the crust into the strainer and pour the stock slowly through it.

Let the aspic cool and use it when it is on the point of setting.

Soups

A soup can be delicious or dreadful, depending on the amount of care, time and effort you are prepared to devote to its preparation.

One of the nicest things about soups is their variety—they range from thin and delicate, like a consommé, to rich and creamy, like crème Crécy, and can be made from almost any ingredients that have enough flavor.

Soup is usually served as a first course, but a thick soup makes an excellent light lunch. Some soups, such as pot au feu, can be eaten as a complete meal, with the broth being served as the first course and the meat and vegetables as the main course.

There are many types of soups, but for convenience they can be divided into two groups—thin soups and thick soups. The thin soups include consommés and broths and the thick soups include creams, veloutés, purées and bisques. In addition, there are soups that do not fit into any category—fruit soup, beer soup and gazpacho. When you have mastered the techniques of making these soups, you can experiment with all kinds of ingredients to create soups in a variety of flavors and textures.

A garnish can alter the taste of a soup and add texture. It can make a thin soup more filling and a plain soup more fancy. The simplest garnishes are chopped fresh parsley, chives, basil, mint and watercress, slices of lemon or orange, grated cheese, croutons and whipped or sour cream. More elaborate garnishes are choux pastry puffs, quenelles, dumplings and tiny meatballs.

Clear, sparkling consommés are made from well-flavored stocks which have been clarified with egg whites and shells.

THIN SOUPS

Consommé madrilène

Serve this consommé hot or well chilled with lemon quarters. If the chicken stock is not strong enough to set, add 1 to 1½ teaspoons of gelatin to every 2 cups (500 ml) of stock.

SERVES FOUR

5 cups (1¼ liters) chicken stock, made from fresh chicken or from chicken wings and necks
¾ lb (350 g) ripe tomatoes, finely chopped
½ lb (225 g) ground beef
2 egg whites, beaten to a froth
Pinch cayenne pepper
Salt and pepper

Combine the cold stock, tomatoes, beef and egg whites in a large saucepan. Bring the mixture to a boil over moderate heat, beating constantly. Allow the soup to rise up the sides of the pan as it boils, then turn down the heat to low and simmer very, very gently for 30 minutes. Add the cayenne and season to taste.

Remove the pan from the heat and strain the soup through a sieve lined with wet cheesecloth. Serve the soup hot, or cool and then chill the consommé in the refrigerator before serving.

Consommé aux profiteroles

SERVES FOUR

Make this consommé in the same way as the madrilène, but add a little fresh tarragon with the other ingredients to the stock. After straining the soup, put it back into the saucepan, which has been rinsed out.

Meanwhile, make up half a recipe of choux pastry and stir in ¼ cup (25 g) of grated Parmesan cheese. Pipe or spoon the pastry into pea-sized balls onto a greased baking sheet and bake in a hot oven, 400°F (200°C), for 5 to 8 minutes or until golden. Serve the choux puffs separately with the hot consommé.

Game consommé

One pheasant or two quail or pigeons may be used to make this well-flavored consommé. Serve it with fried croutons.

SERVES SIX

2 tablespoons butter
1 onion, sliced
½ lb (225 g) stewing veal, cut into small cubes
1 onion, unpeeled and cut in half
3 carrots
1 celery stalk
Bouquet garni
1 teaspoon salt
8 peppercorns
1 stewing game bird
8 cups (2 liters) cold water

Melt the butter in a large saucepan. Add the sliced onion and fry, stirring, until golden. Add the veal and continue frying until it is slightly browned.

Stir in the rest of the vegetables, the bouquet garni, salt and peppercorns and the game bird. Pour over the water and bring it slowly to a boil. Skim off the scum, partly cover the pan and simmer very gently for 3 hours.

Strain the liquid through a sieve lined with wet cheesecloth. Cool and then chill the consommé. Remove any fat.

To serve, reheat the consommé, adjusting the seasoning if necessary.

Borscht

Chilled borscht makes a refreshing start to a summer meal. A few chopped chives sprinkled on the sour cream adds flavor and makes an attractive garnish.

SERVES FOUR

5 cups (1¼ liters) clarified beef stock
¾ lb (350 g) beets, peeled and grated
Salt and pepper
½ cup (125 ml) sour cream

Put the stock into a saucepan, add the beets and simmer gently for 30 minutes. Strain the soup through a sieve lined with wet cheesecloth. Season to taste. Chill the borscht and serve topped with sour cream.

Soups

Scotch broth

Broths are seldom thickened or clarified. They usually thicken naturally from being cooked with such ingredients as rice, pasta, potatoes, beans or barley.

SERVES SIX

2 lb (900 g) neck of mutton, trimmed of excess fat and cut into small pieces
8 cups (2 liters) water
2 tablespoons pearl barley, blanched for 1 minute and drained
2 leeks, diced
2 carrots, diced
2 small turnips, diced
1 onion, diced
2 celery stalks, diced
Salt and pepper
Chopped parsley

Put the meat into a large saucepan. Pour over the water and bring it to a boil, skimming off any scum as it rises. Add the barley and simmer for 20 minutes. Put in the vegetables and seasoning, cover the pan and simmer the broth for 1 hour.

Remove the meat from the pan. Take the meat from the bones and discard the bones. Skim off the fat from the surface of the broth with a metal spoon or by touching the surface of the soup with a paper towel. Return the meat to the pan. Serve hot, garnished with the parsley.

Minestrone

SERVES SIX

1 cup (225 g) dry white beans, soaked overnight in cold water and drained
8 cups (2 liters) beef stock
2 tablespoons olive oil
2 cups (225 g) chopped onions
1 cup (125 g) chopped celery
1 garlic clove, crushed
1 lb (450 g) canned tomatoes
2 cups (25 g) finely chopped parsley
½ small cabbage, finely chopped
2 zucchini, cut into small cubes
Salt and freshly ground black pepper
Grated Parmesan cheese

Place the beans in a large saucepan with the stock. Bring the stock to a boil, reduce the heat to low and simmer for 1 hour.

Heat the oil in a frying pan, add the onions and celery and fry them until the onions are transparent but not brown. Stir in the garlic and fry for a few seconds. Scrape the contents of the frying pan into the stock. Add the tomatoes and half the parsley and simmer for 15 minutes. Add the cabbage and zucchini and cook for a further 15 minutes.

Add the seasoning. Sprinkle the remaining parsley over the soup.

Serve the soup with the Parmesan cheese in a separate bowl.

Potage bonne femme

This soup may be served with a dish of fried croutons. A little cream may be stirred into the soup just before serving.

SERVES FOUR

¼ cup (50 g) butter
4 leeks, white part only, chopped
1 lb (450 g) potatoes, peeled and chopped
4 cups (1 liter) stock
Salt and pepper
½ teaspoon sugar
A few parsley sprigs

Melt the butter in a large saucepan and cook the leeks gently until they are softened. Add the potatoes, stock, salt, pepper and sugar. Bring the stock to a boil, skimming off any scum as it rises. Reduce the heat and simmer for 20 minutes.

Adjust the seasoning, if necessary, and add the parsley before serving.

Thin mushroom soup

SERVES FOUR

2 tablespoons butter
1 lb (450 g) mushrooms, very thinly sliced
1 garlic clove, crushed
4 cups (1 liter) chicken or veal stock
¼ cup (65 ml) dry sherry

Melt the butter in a large saucepan and add the mushrooms and garlic. Cook gently for a few minutes, stirring constantly, then add the stock. Bring the stock to simmering point and simmer for 1 minute. Remove the pan from the heat, add the sherry and serve.

French onion soup

SERVES FOUR

¼ cup (50 g) butter
3 large onions, peeled and thinly sliced
5 cups (1¼ liters) chicken or beef stock
Salt and pepper
12 French bread slices
1¼ cups (125 g) grated Gruyère cheese

Melt the butter in a large saucepan. Add the onions and fry them for about 15 minutes or until they are soft and lightly browned. Add the stock and salt and pepper to taste. Simmer very gently for 30 minutes.

Preheat the oven to 475°F (245°C). Place the bread slices on a baking sheet and bake until they are evenly browned on both sides.

Pour the soup into a casserole or into 4 individual ovenproof soup bowls. Float the toast on the top, sprinkle with the cheese and bake in the oven for about 10 minutes or until the cheese is golden brown on top.

Clam chowder

If fresh clams are not available, use two cans of minced clams. Measure the liquid in the cans and make it up to 1¼ cups (315 ml) with water to use in the recipe.

SERVES EIGHT

¼ lb (125 g) slab bacon or salt pork
2 large onions, peeled and chopped
1 lb (450 g) peeled potatoes, cut in ½-inch (1-cm) cubes
1¼ cups (315 ml) water
1 quart (2 lb/900 g) clams, chopped
2½ cups (625 ml) milk
2 tablespoons butter
Salt and pepper

Cut the fat into cubes and cook it in a casserole over low heat until it is rendered down. Be careful not to burn the fat.

Add the onions and fry them until they are soft and translucent. Add the potatoes and water and cook for 10 minutes. Add the clams, milk, butter and seasoning. Cook for 10 minutes more, or until the potatoes are tender.

Serve hot.

THICK SOUPS
Cream of watercress soup

This basic recipe can be used for such other leafy vegetables as lettuce (use 2 or 3 heads) and spinach (use 1 lb/450 g fresh spinach). Cream of watercress soup is particularly good served with fried croutons and lemon slices floated on top.

SERVES FOUR

3 tablespoons butter
1 onion, peeled and chopped
4 large bunches watercress, washed, shaken dry and chopped
1 tablespoon flour
5 cups (1¼ liters) milk
Salt and pepper
2 tablespoons arrowroot
½ cup (125 ml) cream

Melt the butter in a large saucepan. Add the onion and cook over low heat until soft but not brown. Add the watercress, cover the pan and cook gently for 5 minutes. Remove the pan from the heat and stir in the flour.

Scald the milk (bring it to just under boiling point) and pour it slowly into the pan, stirring constantly. Cook the soup for 15 minutes, stirring occasionally. Season to taste.

Remove the pan from the heat and blend the soup in a blender. Return the soup to the pan.

In a small bowl mix the arrowroot with the cream until smooth. Add a few spoonfuls of soup to the arrowroot and cream mixture, then stir it into the soup in the saucepan. Bring the soup to a boil, simmer for 1 minute and serve immediately.

Cream of fish soup Normandy

SERVES FOUR

½ lb (225 g) white fish (cod, haddock or whiting)
1 onion, peeled
1 celery stalk
2 tomatoes, peeled and seeded
½ cup (125 ml) dry white wine
Bouquet garni
4 cups (1 liter) water
2 cups (225 g) shelled shrimp
1 slice fresh white bread, crumbled
Salt and pepper
½ cup (125 ml) heavy cream
1 tablespoon chopped parsley

Put the fish, onion, celery, tomatoes, wine, bouquet garni and water into a large saucepan and bring to a boil. Reduce the heat and simmer for 30 minutes.

Strain the liquid into another saucepan. Remove all the bones from the fish. Blend the fish and vegetables with some of the liquid in a blender or rub the mixture through a sieve. Stir the mixture into the liquid in the saucepan. Add the shrimp, bread crumbs and seasoning and bring the soup to a boil. Remove the pan from the heat and stir in the cream. Garnish with the parsley and serve.

Cream of asparagus soup

This recipe can also be used with mushrooms (¾ lb/350 g), cauliflower (1 head) or celery (1 head). Because celery is so stringy, however, it cannot be blended. Either rub it through a sieve or use a food mill.

Cream of chicken soup can be made from the basic chicken stock using the same method but omitting both the asparagus and the onion.

This soup can be served chilled or hot.

SERVES FOUR

30 asparagus spears
5 cups (1¼ liters) chicken stock
1 small onion, peeled and chopped
3 tablespoons butter
2 tablespoons flour
Salt and pepper
½ cup (125 ml) cream

Cut the asparagus into small pieces and reserve a few of the best tips for the garnish. Put the stock, asparagus and onion in a large pan and simmer for 25 minutes.

Remove the pan from the heat and either blend the soup in a blender or rub it through a sieve.

Wash and dry the saucepan and return it to the heat. Put in the butter and when it has melted, remove the pan from the heat and stir in the flour. Gradually stir in the soup. Season to taste, return the pan to the heat and bring the soup to a boil, stirring constantly. Simmer for 2 minutes.

Meanwhile, cook the reserved asparagus tips in a little water until tender and add them to the soup with the cream just before serving.

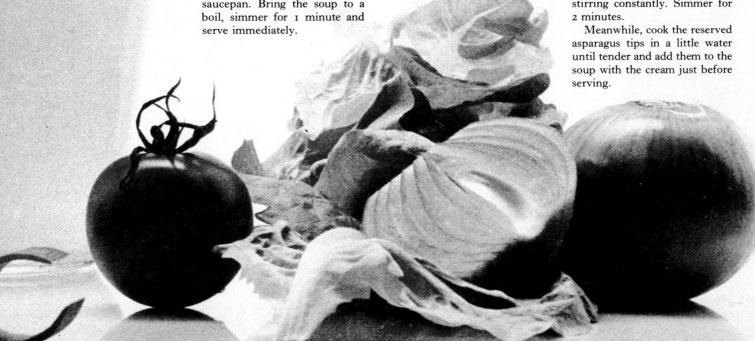

Soups

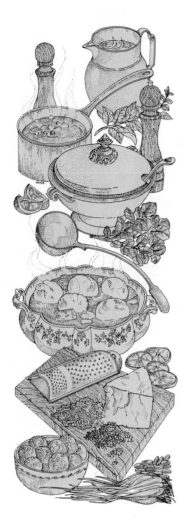

Cream of avocado soup

This soup is eaten cold, and because avocados discolor, it should be served soon after it is made.

SERVES SIX

3 ripe avocados
2 teaspoons lemon juice
5 cups (1¼ liters) chicken stock
½ cup (125 ml) cream
Salt and pepper
Cayenne pepper
1 tomato, skinned, seeded and diced

Cut the avocados in half and scoop out the flesh into a blender or sieve and sprinkle with the lemon juice. Add some of the stock and either blend in the blender or rub through the sieve.

Stir in the remaining stock, the cream and seasoning, adding just a pinch of cayenne. Garnish with the diced tomato.

Cream of cauliflower soup

This recipe can be used for carrots (Crème Crécy), celeriac, fennel, sorrel, Jerusalem artichokes, turnips and spinach.

SERVES FOUR

4 tablespoons butter
1 head of cauliflower, separated into florets
1 small onion, chopped
2½ cups (625 ml) white stock
1 cup (250 ml) béchamel sauce
½ cup (125 ml) cream
Salt and pepper

Melt the butter in a large pan. Add the cauliflower florets and the onion and cook for a few minutes until the onion is softened. Add the stock and simmer for about 15 minutes or until the cauliflower is tender. Remove the pan from the heat. Purée the soup in a blender or rub through a sieve.

Return the soup to the pan. Stir in the béchamel sauce, cream, and salt and pepper to taste. Reheat the soup and serve.

Chicken and mushroom velouté

Velouté is the French word for "velvety." It is the name of a sauce that is based on a roux but made with stock instead of milk. Cucumber, celery, chestnuts or white asparagus can be substituted for the mushrooms.

SERVES FOUR

2 cups (500 ml) chicken velouté
2 cups (500 ml) chicken stock
½ lb (225 g) white mushrooms, chopped
½ cup (125 ml) cream
Salt and white pepper
4 tablespoons diced cooked chicken
4 tablespoons diced cooked ham

Combine the velouté and stock in a large saucepan, add the mushrooms and bring to a boil. Reduce the heat and cook, stirring, for 10 minutes. Remove the pan from the heat and either blend the mixture in a blender or rub it through a sieve.

Return the soup to the pan, stir in the cream and season to taste. Reheat the soup gently. Garnish with chicken and ham.

Purée Saint Germain

Puréed soups are usually made from dried legumes, which thicken while cooking, or from puréed vegetables. They are often finished with an egg and cream liaison before serving, or thickened and enriched with the addition of beurre manié—a paste made from equal quantities of flour and butter—which is added a small piece at a time.

SERVES SIX

1 lb (450 g) split green peas
5 cups (1¼ liters) salted water
4 tablespoons diced fatty slab bacon or bacon fat
1 cup (250 ml) beef stock
Bouquet garni
Pepper
1 tablespoon beurre manié
Fried croutons

Soak the peas in cold water for 2 to 3 hours. Drain the peas and put them into a large saucepan with the salted water. Bring the water to a boil, skimming off any scum. Partly cover the pan and cook for 2 to 3 hours or until the peas are tender. Remove the pan from the heat and drain the peas. Blend the peas in an electric blender or rub them through a sieve.

In a large saucepan fry the fat until it is rendered down. Add the puréed peas, stock, bouquet garni and pepper and simmer for 15 minutes. Remove the bouquet garni, stir in the beurre manié, a small piece at a time, and serve at once with fried croutons.

Purée of lentil soup

Lentil soup is delicious on a cold day, and it is also rich in iron. Yellow split peas and white flageolets can be substituted for the lentils.

SERVES FOUR

½ lb (225 g) lentils, picked over and washed
5 cups (1¼ liters) stock
1 onion, peeled and stuck with 2 cloves
1 carrot
Bouquet garni
Salt and pepper
1 slice bacon, chopped
2 tablespoons butter

Put the lentils into a large saucepan with the stock and bring to a boil, skimming off any scum as it rises. Add the onion, carrot,

bouquet garni, seasoning and bacon and simmer gently, covered, for 1 hour.

Take the pan off the heat and remove and discard the bouquet garni, onion and carrot. Blend the soup in a blender or rub it through a sieve. Pour it back into the saucepan and bring to a boil. Add the seasoning, stir in the butter and serve.

Tomato soup

Canned tomatoes may be used for this recipe if fresh ones are not available.

If the soup does not taste strongly enough of tomato, add some tomato paste.

SERVES FOUR

2 lb (900 g) very ripe tomatoes, halved
1 onion, peeled and diced
2 teaspoons salt
2 teaspoons arrowroot
3½ cups (875 ml) milk or half milk, half stock
2 tablespoons butter
¼ teaspoon ground mace
1 teaspoon chopped fresh chervil or parsley

Put the tomatoes, onion and salt into a large saucepan. Cook, covered, for 10 minutes or until the onion is very soft. Remove the pan from the heat and either blend the mixture in a blender or rub it through a sieve. Return the purée to the pan.

Mix the arrowroot with a little of the milk. Stir it into the tomato mixture with the remaining milk. Cook, stirring, until the mixture is smooth. Stir in the butter, mace and chervil or parsley. When the soup is heated through, serve immediately.

Crème vichyssoise

SERVES FOUR

4 tablespoons butter
6 leeks, white part only, thinly sliced
3 potatoes, peeled and sliced
5 cups (1¼ liters) chicken stock
Salt and white pepper
½ cup (125 ml) cream
Chopped chives

Melt the butter in a large pan. Add the leeks, cover the pan and cook over moderate heat for about 15 minutes or until they are softened. Shake the pan gently from time to time to prevent the leeks from sticking. Be careful not to let them brown.

Add the potatoes and stock and bring to a boil, stirring. Reduce the heat and simmer for 30 minutes.

Remove the pan from the heat and either blend the soup in a blender or rub it through a sieve. Season to taste.

Cool the soup and stir in the cream. Put the soup into the refrigerator to chill. Serve very cold, garnished with chives.

Fresh green pea and lettuce soup

In the summer fresh peas and lettuce can make a very refreshing soup, especially if made with young peas from the garden.

SERVES FOUR

½ cup (125 g) butter
2 lb (900 g) green peas, shelled
1 crisp head lettuce, washed and shredded
Salt and pepper
1 teaspoon sugar
4 cups (1 liter) water

Melt the butter in a large saucepan and add the peas, lettuce, salt, pepper and sugar. Cover and cook gently for 5 minutes, shaking the pan. Add the water and cook for 15 minutes, stirring occasionally.

Remove the pan from the heat and either blend the soup in a blender or rub it through a sieve. Return the soup to the pan. Adjust the seasoning, reheat the soup and serve.

Soup normande

The thinly sliced potatoes disintegrate during the cooking period and thicken the soup.

SERVES SIX TO EIGHT

4 tablespoons butter
3 leeks, thinly sliced
2 small white turnips, peeled and thinly sliced
½ lb (225 g) potatoes, peeled and thinly sliced
8 cups (2 liters) beef stock
½ cup (125 g) dried lima beans, cooked, or 1 cup fresh lima beans
Salt and pepper
1 cup (250 ml) milk
2 tablespoons heavy cream

Melt the butter in a large saucepan. Add the leeks and turnips and fry very gently for 2 to 3 minutes without browning them. Add the potatoes and continue to cook until they are soft.

Add the stock and lima beans and season to taste. Bring the soup to a boil then add the milk. Simmer over low heat for 20 minutes or until the lima beans are tender. Stir in the cream and serve.

Lobster bisque

Add a little beurre manié if the soup is too thin.

SERVES SIX

1 lobster, killed but not cooked
1 tablespoon butter
1 tablespoon oil
¾ cup (125 g) diced carrots
1 cup (125 g) diced celery
1 cup (125 g) chopped onion
Bouquet garni
1 garlic clove
2 cups (500 ml) chicken stock
1 lb (450 g) canned tomatoes
1 cup (250 ml) dry white wine
2 tablespoons tomato paste
Salt and pepper
Cayenne pepper
½ cup (125 ml) heavy cream
2 tablespoons brandy

Break off the lobster's tail. Cut the body into quarters. Discard the sac near the eyes. Reserve any coral. Crack the claws.

In a heavy saucepan melt the butter with the oil. Add the lobster pieces, tail, claws and vegetables and fry, stirring, for 3 to 4 minutes. Add the bouquet garni, garlic, stock, canned tomatoes and wine and bring to a boil. Stir in the coral, if any, and the tomato paste. Cover the pan and simmer for 40 minutes.

Remove the claws and tail from the soup and set aside. Put the lobster carcass in a food mill and push through as much as you can, then blend in batches. Return the soup to the saucepan, season to taste, add the cream and bring to a boil.

Remove the tail and claw meat from the shells. Cut the lobster meat into cubes and add them to the bisque. Pour the brandy into a small saucepan and

heat it gently. Ignite it and when the flames have died down, stir it into the soup.

Serve immediately.

Clam bisque

If fresh clams are not available use 1½ cups canned clams, and add them to the soup with the clam juice, rice and tomatoes. Oysters and mussels may be prepared in exactly the same way. This is a very rich and delicious soup.

SERVES FOUR

12 clams
4 tablespoons butter
1 onion, peeled and chopped
1 garlic clove, chopped
1 teaspoon fresh thyme
2 teaspoons flour
1 lb (450 g) canned tomatoes
Salt and pepper
½ cup (125 ml) white wine
1 cup (250 ml) heavy cream

Open the clams over a bowl and reserve all the juice and meat.

Melt the butter in a large saucepan and add the onion, garlic and thyme. Fry, stirring, until the onion is soft, then add the clams and cook for 5 minutes. Stir in the flour, tomatoes, seasoning and clam juice. Bring to a boil. Remove the pan from the heat. Either blend the soup in a blender or rub it through a sieve. Put the soup back into the pan. Add the wine and cream, adjust the seasoning and heat thoroughly before serving.

Soupe à la bière

SERVES FOUR

5 cups (1¼ liters) hot beer
½ cup (100 g) sugar
4 egg yolks
3 tablespoons sour cream
Salt and pepper
Cinnamon
4 slices French bread

Put the beer and sugar into a large saucepan over moderate heat. Stir until the sugar dissolves and remove the pan from the heat.

In a small bowl beat the egg yolks with the sour cream and a little hot beer, then stir it into the rest of the beer. Add the salt, pepper and cinnamon to taste. Return the pan to a low heat.

Heat the soup thoroughly but do not let it boil.

Put one slice of bread into each soup bowl, pour the soup over the bread and serve.

Gazpacho

This is always a welcome summer soup. Serve with hot herb bread and black olives.

SERVES SIX

2 lb (900 g) tomatoes, peeled and chopped
1 cucumber, peeled and chopped
1 green pepper, cored, seeded and chopped
2 garlic cloves, chopped
1 cup (250 ml) water
5 tablespoons olive oil
½ cup (125 ml) wine vinegar
Salt
2 slices fresh white bread

Mix all the ingredients together in a bowl and either blend in a blender for a short period or rub through a fairly coarse sieve. Serve chilled.

Apricot soup

Fruit soups can be made with any fruit or combination of fruit. The fruit may be puréed or finely sliced and the soup may be served hot or well chilled.

SERVES FOUR

1½ lb (700 g) apricots, pitted and sliced
Rind and juice of 1 orange
2 teaspoons lemon juice
¼ cup (65 ml) white wine
3 cups (750 ml) water
2 level teaspoons arrowroot
Granulated sugar
4 tablespoons whipped cream
A few pistachio nuts, chopped

Put the apricots into a saucepan with a strip of orange rind, the orange and lemon juice, wine and water. Simmer the mixture for 8 to 10 minutes.

In a small cup mix the arrowroot with 2 tablespoons of water. Remove the pan from the heat and stir in the arrowroot. Return the pan to the heat and bring the soup to a boil, stirring.

Add the sugar to taste. Pour the soup into bowls, garnish with the cream and sprinkle the nuts on top. Serve immediately.

Sauces

Sauces are divided into two categories—savory and sweet. Among the savory sauces pride of place naturally goes to the classic sauces—brown (espagnole, Madeira), white (béchamel and velouté), butter (hollandaise and béarnaise) and cold (mayonnaise and vinaigrette)—and the sauces derived from them. Then there are the dessert sauces and those miscellaneous sauces that do not fit into any particular category.

Most sauces freeze well, including the sensitive butter sauces. A butter sauce should be thawed first and then reheated in a double boiler. While the sauce is reheating it must be stirred frequently to prevent curdling. Do not freeze mayonnaise as it will separate. Some sauces will keep for up to a week in the refrigerator, but those made with eggs, cream or milk should not be kept for more than three days.

The utensils and tools required for sauce making can usually be found or improvised in most kitchens. A bowl set over a pan of simmering water, for example, can be substituted for a double boiler, and a roasting pan filled with hot water makes an adequate bain-marie.

Useful tools for making sauces include a variety of beaters, a mortar and pestle, a conical strainer and, best of all, a blender.

For savory sauces the simplest ingredient is the residue—juices and scrapings—left in a pan after sautéing, broiling, frying or roasting poultry or meat.

Strong, well-flavored, degreased stocks are essential for certain sauces. They can be made in advance and kept in the refrigerator (remove the top layer of fat only just before using) for up to a week.

Wines and stronger liquors are useful flavorings, particularly when the stock is lacking in body and taste. And to enrich a sauce and improve its consistency there are egg yolks, butter and cream.

The consistency of a sauce varies, depending on how it is to be used; thin for pouring, thicker for coating and thicker still for binding.

One of the simplest ways of thickening a sauce is by reduction. The sauce is boiled or simmered, uncovered, until it is reduced by evaporation. Another common method of thickening is with a roux. Roux is flour cooked in fat, and depending on how long it is cooked and the color it acquires, it is called white, blond or brown. When making a roux remember that the amount of fat used should always be slightly more than the amount of flour.

Arrowroot and potato flour are often used to thicken sauces. Just over two tablespoons of flour will thicken two and a half cups (625 ml) of thin liquid. Mix the flour in two tablespoons of cold water, stir it into the boiling liquid and cook for a few seconds.

Beurre manié, or kneaded butter, is made from equal quantities of butter and flour kneaded together to make a paste. Form the paste into small balls and add them one by one to the simmering sauce, stirring constantly.

Four tablespoons of beurre manié thickens two and a half cups (625 ml) of thin liquid.

Egg yolks can be used on their own or in combination with butter or cream to thicken sauces. Combine the egg yolks with a little cold stock or milk, then mix in a few tablespoons of the hot sauce. Add the egg mixture to the hot sauce and, stirring constantly, cook it over very low heat until it thickens. If you allow the sauce to boil the eggs will curdle. The addition of a little flour to the egg yolks will help to prevent this. Three egg yolks will thicken two cups (500 ml) of liquid.

Egg yolks combined with butter thicken such sauces as hollandaise and béarnaise and, when combined with oil, thicken a mayonnaise.

Blood (from the animal that is being cooked) is used to thicken some sauces, mainly in game dishes. It is added just before the dish is served. Strain the blood into a bowl, mix in a few spoonfuls of hot sauce and then stir it into the casserole. Simmer (never boil) for two minutes and remove the casserole from the heat.

Although it is essential for a good cook to know how to make the grand sauces, they are not always suitable—for reasons of economy, time and health—for everyday cooking. Often the simple gravy made from pan juices and scrapings of roasted or fried meat is delicious.

To make a deglazed sauce, remove the meat or poultry

from the pan. Remove all the fat. Return the pan to the top of the stove and pour in between a quarter and half a cup (65 and 125 ml) of water. Stir and scrape the bottom of the pan and bring the gravy to a simmer. Season and serve. A little wine or stock can be used instead of water.

To make a gravy, remove the meat or poultry from the roasting pan. Tip off all but a tablespoon of the fat into a bowl. Return the pan to the heat on top of the stove. Stir in two teaspoons of flour and brown over medium heat. Add 1 cup (250 ml) of stock, or stock and the water in which the vegetables were cooked. Stir well, scraping the pan, and cook until thickened. Strain the gravy into a warmed gravy boat.

When the poured-off fat (drippings) from the meat has set in a bowl, separate it from any jellied stock or juices which are at the bottom. To these add any juice that is left after the meat has been carved. Save these juices to make any future gravies or sauces.

To keep a sauce hot, put it in a bain-marie or in a double boiler. The water should be hot, but on no account should it be allowed to simmer or boil.

To prevent a skin forming on the sauce, you can either stir it every few minutes or lay a piece of waxed paper or plastic wrap gently on the surface. If the sauce is very thick, rub the surface all over with a pat of butter.

Sauces that contain eggs sometimes curdle either because they have been brought to a boil, because they have been overbeaten, or because too much oil or butter has been added initially. If a hollandaise or béarnaise sauce curdles, start again with a clean bowl and another egg yolk. Begin beating the egg yolk and slowly blend in the curdled sauce a teaspoon at a time, increasing the amount as the sauce "takes" until it is all incorporated. A curdled mayonnaise can be revived in the same manner.

A curdled custard, if caught in time, can be stabilized by folding a little whipped cream into it. Or, if that fails, it can be resuscitated in the blender, but the sauce will not be quite as smooth and thick as it should be.

Sauces

The brown sauces

The most important of the brown sauces are sauce espagnole and sauce demi-glace. Both are made from a strong bone stock in which the bones have been previously browned. The stock must be strained, chilled and the fat removed before it is used.

Sauce espagnole

MAKES ABOUT 4 CUPS (1 LITER)
- **6 tablespoons drippings or butter**
- **1 cup (125 g) sliced onions**
- **¾ cup (125 g) sliced carrots**
- **4 slices bacon, chopped**
- **4 parsley sprigs, chopped**
- **3 tablespoons flour**
- **6 cups (1½ liters) brown bone stock**
- **2 teaspoons tomato paste**
- **1 cup (250 ml) white wine**
- **2 thyme sprigs**
- **1 bay leaf**
- **¼ cup (65 ml) sherry**
- **Salt and pepper**

Melt the fat in a large saucepan. Add the onions, carrots, bacon and parsley and cook, stirring, until the vegetables are softened.

Stir in the flour, reduce the heat to very low and cook, stirring, for 10 minutes or until the mixture is a rich brown.

Gradually pour in the stock, stirring constantly. Add the tomato paste and wine and, still stirring, bring the liquid to a boil. Add the herbs and simmer, uncovered, very gently for 2 hours or until the sauce is reduced by just over one-third. Using a metal spoon, skim the sauce frequently while it cooks.

Remove the pan from the heat and pour the sauce through a fine strainer. Let the sauce cool, cover it and then refrigerate.

When the sauce is cold, remove the fat from the top. The sauce is now ready to use as a base for other sauces. If you are going to use the sauce as it is, return it to a pan and bring it to a simmer. Stir in the sherry and add seasoning to taste.

Sauce demi-glace

MAKES ABOUT 1 CUP (250 ML)
- **1 cup (250 ml) sauce espagnole**
- **1 cup (250 ml) bone stock**
- **¼ cup (65 ml) Madeira**
- **Salt and pepper**

Put the sauce and stock into a saucepan and bring them to a boil. Lower the heat and simmer, uncovered, for 30 minutes or until the liquid is reduced by half. Pour in the wine and season to taste. Strain the sauce. The sauce is now ready to use. If you are using it as a base for another sauce, leave out the seasoning.

Madeira or red wine sauce

MAKES ABOUT 1½ CUPS (375 ML)
- **1 cup (250 ml) Madeira or red wine**
- **1 cup (250 ml) demi-glace sauce**
- **Salt and pepper**

In a small saucepan bring the wine to a boil and cook until it is reduced by half. Stir in the demi-glace and the seasoning to taste. Simmer for 10 minutes and serve.

Sauce bordelaise

This is another red wine sauce, traditionally served with steaks.

MAKES ABOUT ¾ CUP (175 ML)
- **1 tablespoon butter**
- **2 tablespoons chopped shallots**
- **½ cup (125 ml) red wine**
- **6 peppercorns**
- **1 thyme sprig**
- **½ cup (125 ml) demi-glace sauce**
- **4 tablespoons diced beef marrow**

Melt the butter in a small saucepan. Add the shallots and cook them until they are softened. Add the wine, peppercorns and thyme and continue cooking until the wine is reduced by half. Add the demi-glace and simmer for 15 minutes. Remove the pan from the heat. Skim off the fat and strain the sauce. Pour the sauce into the top part of a double boiler.

Add the marrow and stir to dissolve it over very low heat for 10 minutes.

Sauce bigarade

This is a red wine sauce suitable for serving with game birds.

MAKES ABOUT ¾ CUP (175 ML)
- **1 tablespoon butter**
- **2 tablespoons chopped shallots**
- **¼ cup (65 ml) red wine**
- **1 bay leaf**
- **Rind and juice of 1 orange**
- **½ cup (125 ml) demi-glace**
- **1 teaspoon red currant jelly**

Melt the butter in a small saucepan. Add the shallots and cook until they are softened. Add the wine and bay leaf and continue cooking until the wine is reduced by one-third. Add the juice and half the rind of the orange, and the demi-glace sauce. Simmer for 5 minutes.

Shred the remaining orange rind very thinly. Blanch it for 5 minutes and drain.

Strain the sauce and return it to the pan with the blanched orange rind and the red currant jelly. Bring to a boil, stirring until the jelly has dissolved.

Sauce Robert

MAKES ABOUT 1 CUP (250 ML)
- **1 tablespoon butter**
- **1 tablespoon chopped onion**
- **½ cup (125 ml) vinegar**
- **1 cup (250 ml) demi-glace sauce**
- **3 gherkins, finely chopped**
- **2 teaspoons French mustard**
- **1 teaspoon chopped parsley**

Melt the butter in a small saucepan. Add the onion and fry it gently until it is softened. Pour in the vinegar and continue cooking until it is reduced by half. Add the demi-glace sauce and simmer for 15 minutes. Stir in the rest of the ingredients.

The white sauces

The basic white sauces are béchamel and velouté. Béchamel is made with a white roux and milk and velouté is made with a golden roux and stock.

Sauce béchamel

MAKES ABOUT 1 CUP (250 ML)
- **1 cup (250 ml) milk**
- **1 mace blade**
- **Bouquet garni**
- **4 white peppercorns**
- **1 shallot, sliced**
- **1½ tablespoons butter**
- **1½ tablespoons flour**
- **Salt**

Put the milk, mace, bouquet garni, peppercorns and shallot into a small saucepan and place it over a very low heat for 5 minutes to infuse. Do not stir. Strain the milk and set aside.

Melt the butter in another small pan. Stir in the flour and remove from the heat. Gradually stir in the strained milk. Beat well to prevent lumps from forming, then cook, stirring constantly, over moderate heat until the sauce boils. Season to taste.

Cream sauce

To 1 cup (250 ml) of béchamel sauce add ¼ cup (65 ml) of cream and season with a squeeze of lemon juice and a pinch of cayenne pepper.

Sauce mornay

For a stronger flavor a pinch of cayenne pepper or a teaspoon of French mustard may be added to this sauce.

MAKES 1 CUP (250 ML)
- **1 cup (250 ml) béchamel sauce**
- **⅔ cup (50 g) grated Parmesan or Gruyère cheese**
- **¼ cup (65 ml) cream**

Heat the béchamel sauce in a small pan. Add the cheese and stir until it has dissolved. Stir in the cream and serve.

Mushroom sauce

MAKES ABOUT 1½ CUPS (375 ML)
- **2 tablespoons butter**
- **2 cups (125 g) sliced mushrooms**
- **Salt and pepper**
- **Cayenne pepper**
- **1 cup (250 ml) béchamel sauce**
- **¼ cup (65 ml) cream**

Melt the butter in a small frying pan. Add the mushrooms and fry quickly, shaking the pan, for 2 to

3 minutes. Season the mushrooms.

Keep the béchamel sauce hot in a saucepan. Remove the pan from the heat and add the mushrooms and their cooking liquid. Stir in the cream and serve.

Sauce velouté

MAKES ABOUT 4 CUPS (1 LITER)

6 tablespoons sweet butter
3 tablespoons flour
3¾ cups (925 ml) chicken stock
¼ cup (65 ml) cream
Salt and pepper
1 teaspoon lemon juice

Melt half the butter in a saucepan. Add the flour and mix it in to form a roux. Cook the roux, stirring constantly, over very low heat for 5 to 7 minutes until it becomes straw colored.

Add the stock gradually, stirring constantly. Bring the sauce to a boil, reduce the heat and simmer gently for 5 minutes. Stir in the cream and simmer for 2 minutes. Add seasoning to taste and the lemon juice. Stir in the butter and serve.

Sauce suprême

MAKES ABOUT 2½ CUPS (625 ML)

3 egg yolks
¼ cup (65 ml) heavy cream
2 cups (500 ml) velouté sauce
Salt and pepper

In a small bowl mix the yolks with the cream.

Heat the sauce in a double boiler. Remove the pan from the heat and add a few tablespoons of the sauce, a spoonful at a time, to the egg mixture. When well mixed, pour the egg mixture into the sauce and beat until it is smooth and velvety. Serve the sauce hot.

Sauce normande

MAKES ABOUT 1 CUP (250 ML)

1 cup (250 ml) velouté sauce
1 egg yolk
2 tablespoons butter, cut into small pieces
Lemon juice
Salt and pepper

Heat the velouté sauce in a double boiler. Put the egg yolk into a small bowl. Beat a little of the sauce, a spoonful at a time, into the egg. When well mixed, pour the egg mixture into the sauce and mix well. Beat in the butter, one piece at a time. Stir in the lemon juice and seasoning to taste.

Sauce poulette

MAKES ABOUT 1 CUP (250 ML)

1 cup (250 ml) velouté sauce
1 tablespoon chopped parsley
1 teaspoon lemon juice
1 egg yolk
2 tablespoons cream

Heat the velouté sauce in a double boiler. Stir in the parsley and lemon juice. In a small bowl combine the egg yolk with the cream. Beat a little of the hot sauce, a spoonful at a time, into the egg mixture. Beat the egg mixture into the sauce. Whisk until the sauce is thick and smooth.

The butter sauces

The basic butter sauces are hollandaise and béarnaise. Delicate and delicious, they can turn the simplest vegetable dish, poached fish or broiled steak into something special. They require care in making, however, and have the unhappy trait of curdling when you least expect it. Butter sauces must always be made in a double boiler as too much heat causes curdling.

Sauce hollandaise I

MAKES ¾ CUP (175 ML)

6 to 8 tablespoons butter
2 egg yolks
Salt and pepper
1 tablespoon white wine vinegar or lemon juice

Using a metal spatula, work the butter until it is slightly soft. In a small ovenproof bowl or in the top of a double boiler mix the egg yolks with a teaspoon of the softened butter and a pinch of salt and pepper. Add the vinegar or lemon juice. Place the bowl over a pan of water or set the pan over the bottom half of the double boiler. The water must be hot but not boiling. Stir the mixture with a whisk until it has thickened. Gradually add the butter, half a teaspoon at a time, stirring constantly. Season to taste. The sauce should be smooth and thick.

Sauce hollandaise II

This version is made in an electric blender.

MAKES ABOUT 1¼ CUPS (315 ML)

1 cup (225 g) butter
4 egg yolks
2 tablespoons lemon juice
¼ teaspoon salt

Melt the butter in a saucepan over low heat. Do not allow it to turn brown. Put the egg yolks, lemon juice and salt into the blender. Cover the container and blend at low speed for 20 seconds. Uncover and pour in the hot butter in a steady stream while the motor is running. Pour the sauce into the top of a double boiler and put it over a pan of hot water until ready to use.

Sauce mousseline

MAKES ABOUT 1½ CUPS (375 ML)

Prepare 1 cup (250 ml) of hollandaise sauce. Fold in 6 tablespoons of whipped cream.

Sauce maltaise

MAKES ABOUT 1 CUP (250 ML)

Prepare 1 cup (250 ml) of hollandaise sauce. Mix in the juice and finely grated rind of ½ orange.

Sauce béarnaise

MAKES ¾ CUP (175 ML)

4 tablespoons white wine
2 tablespoons white wine vinegar
1 bay leaf
1 mace blade
½ teaspoon dried thyme
1 shallot
4 peppercorns
2 egg yolks
½ cup (125 g) butter, softened
2 teaspoons chopped tarragon
Salt and pepper

Put the vinegar and wine, bay leaf, mace, shallot, thyme and peppercorns into a small pan. Bring to a boil and cook until it is reduced to 2 tablespoonfuls. Strain and set aside.

In the top of the double boiler or in a small bowl mix the egg yolks with 1 teaspoon of the butter and a pinch of salt. Pour the vinegar over the egg mixture and stir to mix. Place the double boiler, or bowl, over the heat —the water must be hot but not boiling—and beat the egg mixture until it has thickened.

Gradually add the rest of the butter in half teaspoonfuls, stirring constantly, until the sauce is like whipped cream. Add the chopped tarragon and seasoning.

Sauce batarde

MAKES ABOUT 1½ CUPS (375 ML)

½ cup (125 g) butter
2 tablespoons flour
1 cup (250 ml) boiling water
2 egg yolks mixed with 1 tablespoon cold water
1 to 2 teaspoons lemon juice
Salt

Melt 2 tablespoons of the butter in a small saucepan. Stir in the flour to make a roux. Pour in the water gradually, stirring constantly, to prevent lumps from forming. Remove the pan from the heat and beat in the egg yolk and water mixture. Add the remaining butter a small piece at a time. Stir in the lemon juice and salt.

Stand the saucepan in a pan of hot water.

Sauce ravigote

MAKES ABOUT 1 CUP (250 ML)

2 shallots, finely chopped
4 tablespoons vinegar
1 cup (250 ml) sauce bâtarde
1 teaspoon each of chopped parsley, chervil and tarragon
2 teaspoons chopped capers
2 teaspoons French mustard

In a small saucepan bring the shallots and the vinegar to a boil. Cook them until the vinegar is reduced by half. Set aside.

Put the sauce bâtarde into a bowl. Mix in the chopped herbs, capers and mustard. Strain the vinegar into the sauce and mix.

Sauces

White wine sauce

This sauce can also be made with red wine.

MAKES ABOUT 1 CUP (250 ML)

¼ cup (50 g) butter
1 tablespoon flour
½ cup (125 ml) well-flavored white stock (fish or chicken)
6 tablespoons dry white wine
½ cup (125 ml) cream
1 tablespoon lemon juice
Salt and pepper

In a small saucepan make a roux with 2 tablespoons of the butter and flour. Draw the pan off the heat and gradually stir in the stock and wine, taking care to avoid lumps. Bring to a boil, stirring constantly. Add the cream, lemon juice and seasoning. When the sauce has thickened, remove the pan from the heat and stir in the remaining butter in small pieces. Use at once or keep hot in a double boiler.

Beurre noir

This sauce is served with fish, eggs and vegetables. Lemon juice can be substituted for the vinegar.

MAKES ½ CUP (125 ML)

1 tablespoon vinegar
Salt and freshly ground black pepper
½ cup (125 g) sweet butter
1 tablespoon chopped parsley

In a small saucepan boil the vinegar and seasoning until it is reduced by half. In another small saucepan melt the butter and cook until it is dark brown but not black. Stir in the reduced vinegar and parsley and pour the sauce over the food.

Cold sauces

Sauce mayonnaise

If you wish to keep the mayonnaise for a few days, stir 2 tablespoons of boiling water into the finished sauce. This will prevent the mayonnaise from separating.

MAKES ABOUT 1 CUP (250 ML)

2 egg yolks
½ teaspoon salt
½ teaspoon French mustard
1 cup (250 ml) olive oil
2 teaspoons wine vinegar or the juice of ½ lemon

Using a wooden spoon, mix the egg yolks well with the salt and mustard in a mixing bowl. With the oil in a measuring cup begin pouring it onto the yolks, drop by drop, beating all the time. Continue pouring and beating, adding the oil more quickly as the mayonnaise thickens. When all the oil has been incorporated the sauce will be very thick and glossy. Carefully fold in the vinegar or lemon juice.

To make mayonnaise in a blender, first blend the egg yolks and salt together, then slowly, drop by drop, begin to add the oil, gradually pouring in a steady stream. Finally add vinegar or lemon juice and mustard.

Thousand island dressing

MAKES ABOUT 1½ CUPS (375 ML)

1 cup (250 ml) mayonnaise
4 tablespoons tomato catsup
2 tablespoons chopped green pepper
2 tablespoons chopped green olives
1 tablespoon chopped parsley
1 tablespoon finely chopped onion
1 hard-cooked egg, chopped

Combine all the ingredients well.

Aioli or garlic mayonnaise

MAKES ABOUT 1½ CUPS (375 ML)

4 to 6 garlic cloves
Salt
2 egg yolks
1½ cups (375 ml) olive oil
Pepper
Lemon juice

Crush the garlic with a little salt in a mortar. Beat in the egg yolks. Then, beating steadily, add the olive oil drop by drop. When the sauce thickens, add the oil a little faster. Season with pepper and lemon juice.

Mayonnaise for coating

MAKES 1½ CUPS (375 ML)

1½ teaspoons powdered gelatin
½ cup (125 ml) aspic, hot
1 cup (250 ml) mayonnaise

Dissolve the gelatin in the aspic and cool the mixture. Beat it into the mayonnaise. Use the mayonnaise as it begins to set.

Sauce tartar

MAKES ABOUT 1 CUP (250 ML)

¾ cup (175 ml) mayonnaise
¼ cup (65 ml) whipping cream, whipped until thick
2 teaspoons lemon juice
1 teaspoon chopped chives
1 tablespoon chopped capers
1 tablespoon chopped gherkins

Put all the ingredients into a small mixing bowl and beat well until they are well mixed.

Sauce verte

MAKES 1 CUP (250 ML)

10 watercress sprigs
4 parsley sprigs
4 tarragon sprigs
10 spinach leaves
Salt
1 cup (250 ml) mayonnaise

In a small saucepan boil the watercress, parsley, tarragon and spinach for 3 minutes in a little salted water. Drain the herbs and spinach, reserving 1 tablespoon of the liquor. Rub the greens through a sieve.

Mix the purée into the mayonnaise with the reserved tablespoon of cooking liquid.

Brown chaud-froid sauce

Brown chaud-froid sauce is used for coating duck and game.

MAKES ABOUT 2 CUPS (500 ML)

1½ cups (375 ml) demi-glace sauce
2 teaspoons gelatin
½ cup (125 ml) aspic jelly
¼ cup (65 ml) sherry or port

Warm the demi-glace. Dissolve the gelatin in the aspic jelly over low heat and add it to the demi-glace with the wine. Stir the sauce while it is cooling. When it begins to set it is ready.

White chaud-froid sauce

A white chaud-froid sauce is used for coating fish or chicken. Fawn chaud-froid sauce, made with a velouté instead of béchamel, is used to coat veal and lamb.

MAKES ABOUT 2 CUPS (500 ML)

2 teaspoons gelatin
¼ cup (65 ml) warm fish or chicken aspic
1½ cups (375 ml) béchamel sauce
¼ cup (65 ml) cream
Salt and pepper

Soften the gelatin in the warm aspic and add it to the bechamel with the cream. Season to taste. Stir frequently while the sauce is cooling to prevent a skin from forming. When the sauce is thick it is ready to be used.

Sauce vinaigrette or French dressing

The classic proportions of a vinaigrette are three parts oil to one of vinegar. The proportions, however, depend on the strength of the vinegar and may be altered.

Use a good-quality olive oil, or a groundnut oil or a combination of oils, and a wine, herb or cider vinegar or lemon juice. A finely chopped garlic clove, one teaspoon of French mustard and one tablespoon of chopped fresh tarragon, chives, thyme or parsley can also be added.

MAKES ½ CUP (125 ML)

2 tablespoons good wine vinegar or lemon juice
¼ teaspoon salt
Freshly ground pepper
6 tablespoons oil

Place the vinegar, salt and pepper into a salad bowl. Beat in the oil, add salad ingredients and toss.

English salad dressing

MAKES ABOUT ¾ CUP (175 ML)

Yolks of 2 hard-cooked eggs
Salt and pepper
2 tablespoons olive oil
2 teaspoons Worcestershire sauce
2 teaspoons vinegar
½ teaspoon dry mustard
2 scallions, finely chopped, or 2 teaspoons chopped chives
½ cup (125 ml) cream or yogurt

In a small bowl, crush the egg yolks well with a fork. Add the salt and pepper. Beat in the oil drop by drop, then the Worcestershire sauce, vinegar, mustard and the onions or chives. Then gradually beat in the cream.

Miscellaneous sauces

Tomato sauce

MAKES ABOUT 2 CUPS

1 tablespoon butter
1 tablespoon olive oil
2 onions, sliced
1½ lb (700 g) chopped tomatoes
1 teaspoon salt
1 teaspoon sugar
Parsley
1 garlic clove
2 basil sprigs, chopped
2 tablespoons tomato paste

Melt the butter with the olive oil in a wide, shallow pan. Cook the onions gently until they are soft and golden. Stir in the remainder of the ingredients and simmer over low heat for 30 minutes. Put the sauce through a food mill and adjust the seasoning.

Bread sauce

MAKES ABOUT 1½ CUPS (375 ML)

1 onion, peeled and studded with 2 cloves
½ bay leaf
1 mace blade
4 peppercorns
1¼ cups (315 ml) milk
6 tablespoons fresh white bread crumbs
Salt
1 tablespoon cream
1 tablespoon butter

Put the onion, bay leaf, mace blade, peppercorns and milk in a saucepan over low heat for 10 minutes. Strain the milk and return it to the pan. Increase the heat and bring the milk to a boil. Stir in the bread crumbs and simmer over low heat until the sauce becomes thick. Remove the pan from the heat. Season and stir in the cream and butter.

Mint sauce

MAKES ABOUT ½ CUP (125 ML)

1 large handful mint leaves
2 tablespoons boiling water
3 tablespoons wine vinegar
Salt
1 tablespoon sugar

Wash and dry the mint leaves. Chop them very finely or purée them in a mortar. Put the puréed mint into a bowl, pour in the boiling water to "set" the color. Stir in the vinegar, salt and sugar.

Applesauce

MAKES ABOUT 1 CUP (250 ML)

1 lb (450 g) tart apples, peeled and cored
2 strips orange peel
3 tablespoons water
1 to 2 tablespoons sugar
1 tablespoon butter

Put the apples in a saucepan with the orange peel and water. Cover the pan tightly and cook over low heat for about 15 minutes or until the apples are soft and fluffy. Stir in the sugar to taste and then add the butter.

Cumberland sauce

MAKES ABOUT 1½ CUPS (375 ML)

½ lb (225 g) red currant jelly
Rind and juice of 2 oranges
Rind and juice of 1 lemon
¼ cup (65 ml) port
1 tablespoon vinegar
1 teaspoon French mustard
2 teaspoons arrowroot

In a small saucepan, dissolve the red currant jelly with the fruit juice and rind. Bring the mixture to a boil, reduce the heat and simmer for 5 minutes. Stir in the port, vinegar and mustard.

Mix the arrowroot with a tablespoon of cold water and stir it into the sauce. Simmer for 2 seconds and serve cool.

Cranberry and orange sauce

MAKES ABOUT 3 CUPS (750 ML)

1 lb (450 g) cranberries
Rind and juice of 1 orange
1 cup (250 ml) water
1 cup (225 g) sugar

Put all the ingredients together in a deep saucepan. Cover and cook over very low heat for 10 minutes. Serve cool.

Dessert sauces

Chocolate sauce

MAKES 1 CUP (250 ML)

4 squares (100 g) unsweetened chocolate, broken into pieces
1 tablespoon vanilla sugar
1 teaspoon cocoa
1 cup (250 ml) water
Rum to taste (optional)

Break up the chocolate and put it into a saucepan with the sugar, cocoa and half the water. Stir over low heat until the chocolate has dissolved, then bring it to a boil. Reduce the heat and simmer for 2 minutes. Add the remaining water and simmer for 10 to 15 minutes or until the sauce is glossy and syrupy. Stir in the rum if you are using it.

Fruit sauce

MAKES 1 CUP (250 ML)

1 lb (450 g) fresh or frozen raspberries, strawberries, peaches or red currants
1 teaspoon lemon juice
½ cup (50 g) confectioners' sugar

Crush the fruit or purée it in a blender and then rub it through a sieve. Stir in the lemon juice and sugar to taste.

Butterscotch sauce

For a variation add 2 tablespoons of chopped walnuts to the sauce after you have taken it off the heat.

MAKES ABOUT 1 CUP (250 ML)

6 tablespoons butter
1¼ cups (225 g) brown sugar
1 tablespoon corn syrup (any commercial brand)
½ cup (125 ml) heavy cream

Melt the butter in a saucepan over low heat. Stir in the sugar, syrup and cream. When the sugar has dissolved, bring the mixture to a boil. Remove the pan from the heat. Cool slightly before serving.

Custard sauce

Custard sauce can be flavored with coffee, chocolate or flavor extracts.

Whipped cream can be added to the custard once it has cooled.

MAKES 1½ CUPS (375 ML)

2 egg yolks
2 teaspoons vanilla sugar
1¼ cups (315 ml) milk

In a small bowl, beat the egg yolks with a fork. Dissolve the sugar in the milk in the top of a double boiler. The water in the lower pan should be hot but not boiling. When the milk is hot, pour it onto the egg yolks. Mix well and return the mixture to the pan. Stir over the hot water until the custard thickens sufficiently to coat the back of a wooden spoon.

Sauce sabayon

If it is made with brandy or rum, sabayon sauce makes an excellent accompaniment to Christmas pudding and mince pies.

MAKES ABOUT ¾ CUP (175 ML)

3 egg yolks
2 tablespoons sugar
6 tablespoons sherry or Marsala

In the top of a double boiler, beat the egg yolks with the sugar until pale and frothy. Stir in the wine and bring the water in the lower pan to a boil, beating constantly until the sauce is thick. Serve the sauce at once, or cool it and then place the top part of the pan over ice and beat until it is cold.

Brandy butter

A teaspoon of finely grated orange rind gives brandy butter extra flavor and helps lighten the richness. For rum butter use a fine, dark brown sugar and a little grated lemon rind.

MAKES 2 CUPS (225 G)

½ cup (125 g) sweet butter
½ cup (125 g) sugar
4 tablespoons brandy

Have ingredients at room temperature. Cream the butter until white and fluffy. Gradually beat in the sugar and then the brandy, a little at a time. Spoon into a serving dish and stand in a cool place to set.

The methods

Boiling and steaming, stewing and casseroling, broiling, frying and sautéing, roasting and baking—these are the basic methods of cookery. Some types of food, such as most cakes or pastry, can be made only by one method—they need the enveloping heat of the oven. Most foods, however, may be cooked either in an oven or below or above the heat.

On the following pages each cookery method is described and recipes are given for cooking every type of food by that method. When a dish must be cooked by a combination of methods the recipe will be found under the method that forms the main part of the cooking.

All metric equivalents are approximate, and centigrade conversions have been made to the nearest round figure, except for deep-frying temperatures which are more accurately converted. Tablespoons and teaspoons are standard U.S. measure. Amounts given are for level spoonfuls.

Boiling and steaming

Boiling is such a traditional English method of preparing food that the French often attach the label *à l'anglaise*—the English way—to boiled dishes. The term boiling is not, however, a truly accurate description of what actually takes place, for most foods would fall to pieces and lose all their flavor were they to be cooked in fast-boiling liquid. Although the liquid is initially brought to a boil, the heat is then lowered and the food is simmered or poached—the liquid stays well under boiling point.

Fast boiling is recommended, however, when liquid is to be reduced and thickened, and for syrups and preserves.

Steaming, on the other hand, is one of the better ways of cooking such delicate foods as fish and vegetables as well as some grains, such as couscous and occasionally rice.

Although it is useful to have special equipment for steaming, you can improvise with a colander or strainer fitted over a saucepan and covered with a tight-fitting lid.

A steamer that opens like a flower and fits inside most saucepans is useful for cooking vegetables. A version of the double boiler with a perforated pan that fits on top is useful for steaming puddings and is available with a double tier for steaming more than one pudding at a time.

The Chinese use a many-tiered bamboo steamer. Rice is boiled in the bottom pan and the steam is used to cook a whole array of dishes in separate baskets, which fit one on top of the other.

Poaching kettles can also be fitted with a steaming rack, that holds fish above the water.

Always bring the water to a boil in the pan before fitting the perforated top in place, and remember that steamed vegetables need to cook for about four to five minutes longer than boiled vegetables.

Some vegetables—asparagus, cauliflower and broccoli, for example—may be steam-boiled (there is a special pan for asparagus). Bring a small amount of water to a boil in a saucepan. Stand the vegetables in the pan, cover with a lid and simmer—the stalks will boil in the water while the more delicate heads cook in the steam.

Fish and shellfish

Soused herring 77
Buttered granary bread 198

Bourride 78
French bread

Finnan haddie crêpes 78

Salmon mousse 78
Melba toast 81

Gefilte fish 78

Kipper pâté 79
Melba toast 81

Quenelles 79
Serve on croutons 158

Jellied eels 79
Buttered brown bread 198

Moules marinières 80
Garlic bread 189

Coquilles St. Jacques 80

Scallops à la provençale 80

Dressed crab 80
Salads: Green, Tomato 213

Potted shrimp 81
Melba toast 81,

Snails à la bourguignonne 81

Poached salmon 76
Poached salmon trout 76
Sauces: Hollandaise, Mousseline 67, Mayonnaise, Verte 68
Salads: Rice 212, Green 213
Boiled new potatoes 93

Sweet-sour pungent fish 77
Steamed sea bass 77
Serve as part of a Chinese meal or with Stir-fried bean sprouts 153

Salmon trout in aspic 77
Sauces: Mayonnaise, Verte 68
Salads: Tomato, Green 213

Trout in cider 77
Sauce hollandaise 67
Boiled fennel 92
Casseroled celery 120

Sole Véronique 77
Steamed Zucchini, Mashed potatoes 93

Fillets of sole florentine 78
Tomato salad 213

Steamed fish mold with anchovy sauce 79 Alternative sauces: Mornay, Mushroom 66, Boiled spinach 92, Peas 93, Baked potatoes 180

Crayfish with butter sauce 80

Lobster mayonnaise 81
Salads: Potato 93
Belgian endive, orange and watercress 213

Poultry and game

English boiled chicken 83
Glazed carrots 91, Brussels sprouts 92, Potato croquettes 151

Chicken à la king 84
Boiled rice 97, Croutons 158, Noodles 97

Chicken poached in wine 84
Deep-fried parsley 153, Potatoes à la dauphinoise 180, Green beans 92

Chicken fricassee 84
Boiled rice 97, Crusty noodles 158

Chicken with spicy mayonnaise 84

Chicken salad 84

Chicken and pineapple salad 84

Chicken chaud-froid 85
Salads: Rice 212, Celery, apple and walnut 213

Chicken florentine 85
Cottage fries 151

Duck galantine 85
Salads: Belgian endive, orange and watercress, Waldorf 213

Meat and game

Boiled (corned) beef and dumplings 86
Horseradish sauce 89, Mustard

Ham boiled in cider 86
Salads: Kidney bean 93, Avocado 213, Rice 212

English steak and kidney pudding 88
Bubble and squeak 152, Glazed carrots 91, Cabbage 92

Boiled shoulder of mutton 88

Boiled ham with lentils 88

Cold pressed tongue 89
Cumberland sauce 69 Salads: Zucchini 92, Russian, Spinach and mushroom 212

Cabbage dolmas 89
Cottage fries 151

Sweetbread vol-au-vents 89

Veal galantine 89
Sauces: Horseradish 89, Verte 68 Salads: Avocado, Tomato 213, Spinach and mushroom 212

Vegetables

Artichokes with shrimp-mushroom mayonnaise 91

Salad niçoise 92

Lima beans with garlic 93

Lima bean and mackerel salad 93

Steamed stuffed cabbage 91

Boiling and steaming chart 92-3

Brussels sprouts with curried almonds 91

Brussels sprouts with chestnuts 91

Petits pois à la française 91

Cauliflower salad 91

Belgian endive 91

Glazed carrots 91

Carrot and parsnip purée 91

Zucchini salad 92

Squash in caraway sauce 92

Spinach purée 92

Boiled fennel 92

Beet salad 92

Mashed potatoes 93

Potato salad 93

Kidney bean salad 93

Lentil salad 93

Fruit

Pommes aux fruits glacés 96

Red berry delight 96

Strawberry mousse 96 Cream, Macaroons 192

Fresh fruit compote 94 Custard sauce 69, Cream

Fresh peaches in vanilla syrup 94 Sauce sabayon 69

Pears in red wine 94 Whipped cream

Oranges in caramel 95

Cherries jubilee with vanilla ice cream 95

Rhubarb fool 95

Summer pudding 96 Cream

Danish apple cake 96 Cream

Black currant mousse 96 Butter cookies 191

Black currant kissel 96

Cereals

Spaghetti with pesto 97
Green salad 213

Noodles Alfredo 97
Green salad 213

Ravioli 97
Tomato sauce 69 Green salad 213

Gnocchi di semolina 98
Tomato sauce 69 Green salad 213

Polenta 98
Tomato sauce 69

Christmas pudding 98 Brandy or rum butter 69, Cream

Creamed rice pudding 99 Fresh fruit compote 94

Orange sponge pudding 99 Custard sauce 69

Boston steamed bread 99

Porridge 99 Cream

Eggs and dairy products

Eggs in crispy rolls 100
Sauce mornay 66

Eggs florentine with ham 100

Taramasalata eggs 100

Eggs in aspic 100

Swiss fondue 101

Curried eggs 101
Mint chutney 152 Sautéed bananas 154

Charlotte russe 101

Lemon mousse 101

Chocolate mousse 101 Cream

Crème brulée 102

Zabaglione 102

Bavarois 102

Jamaican rum custard 103

Oeufs à la neige 103

Austrian chocolate pudding 103 Chocolate sauce 69

First courses

Main courses

Light lunch-supper dishes

Accompaniments

Desserts

Miscellaneous

Fish

Boiling, or poaching, and steaming are the first stage in preparing many classic fish and shellfish dishes. The methods of boiling such shellfish as lobster and crab are given in the section on preparation, because in most cases this is part of their basic preparation.

There are two ways of poaching whole fish—on top of the stove or in the oven. Fish is poached in a poaching kettle or in a large pan deep enough to insure that it will be covered in liquid. If a pan is used, wrap the fish in cheesecloth, leaving enough cloth at both ends to make it easy to lift out the fish after it is cooked.

Cut a fish in half if it is too large for the pan and poach the two halves separately. Once cooked they can be put together on the serving dish, the seam covered with a sauce or a garnish.

To poach a whole fish, put it in enough court bouillon, salted water, fish stock or wine to barely cover it and bring it slowly to just under boiling point. Reduce the heat to low and simmer, allowing eight minutes per pound (450 g) for fish up to six pounds (3 kg) in weight and five to six minutes per pound (450 g) for fish up to twelve pounds ($5\frac{1}{2}$ kg) in weight.

Large pieces of such fish as turbot, skate and cod can be poached in the same way. The cooking time is the same as

for a whole fish. Small whole fish such as flounder, sole or whiting will take about ten minutes. Poach fish in the oven —the liquid must come to a simmer first—at a temperature of 350°F (180°C).

To test a fish to see if it is cooked, insert the point of a sharp knife into the flesh near the backbone. If the flesh lifts easily from the bone and is no longer translucent but quite white (or pink if the fish is salmon) and curdlike and flakes easily, the fish is cooked.

If the fish is to be skinned it is easier to do it while it is still hot.

Au bleu is an excellent way of cooking whole, delicate fish. Only freshwater fish are cooked *au bleu* and then only when they have been freshly caught and are still alive.

As soon as the fish is taken from the water, knock it on the head. Remove its gut through the smallest incision possible. Cut off the gills, but do not wash or scale the fish. Put the fish into a saucepan and sprinkle it with a little boiling vinegar. This sets the blue color of the skin. Pour in boiling court bouillon to cover and poach gently for eight to ten minutes. Fish, particularly trout, cooked in this way are usually served simply with steamed potatoes, melted butter and lemon wedges. They can also be served cold with a vinaigrette or mayonnaise dressing.

Fish

When cooking fish fillets and steaks, the cooking liquid should be boiling when the fish is put in so that the liquid seals the unprotected flesh. Then reduce the heat to very low so that the liquid barely simmers. When poaching such delicate fish as sole it is best to cook the fillets in the oven in a buttered shallow pan. The cooking time is the same whether you poach the fish in the oven or on top of the stove—eight to ten minutes for fillets; ten to fifteen minutes for steaks, depending on their size and thickness. Test the fish with the point of a knife—if the flesh flakes easily it is ready.

To steam fish fillets, place them in a buttered soup bowl. Season the fillets and sprinkle them with a little milk or lemon juice. Cover the fillets with waxed paper and place a second buttered bowl, upturned, over them. Put the bowls on top of a pan of simmering water and cook for fifteen minutes or until the fish is cooked and the flesh flakes easily.

Poached salmon I

This is a method of cooking salmon that is used by the fishermen in Scotland. If the salmon is being served hot it may be garnished with lemon wedges, parsley sprigs and thinly sliced cucumber that has been marinated in seasoned vinegar, and accompanied by a hollandaise sauce or melted butter.

To serve the salmon cold, lay thinly sliced cucumber in overlapping slices down the center of the fish. Cover lightly with almost-set aspic. When set, carefully transfer the fish onto a bed of watercress, parsley or lettuce. Serve with homemade mayonnaise.

To poach fish weighing up to 6 pounds (3 kg), bring the liquid very slowly to a boil and simmer for 12 minutes. Turn off the heat and leave the fish in the covered pan for 20 minutes.

1 salmon, about 12 pounds (6 kg), cleaned
About 15 cups (3¾ liters) court bouillon

Place the fish on the rack in a poaching kettle. Pour over enough cold court bouillon to cover the fish and bring it very slowly to a boil. Reduce the heat to low and simmer for 20 minutes. Turn off the heat and leave the fish in the covered pan for another 20 minutes (if it is to be served hot) or until it is room temperature.

Lift the fish carefully out of the kettle on the rack and slide it onto a serving dish. If it is to be served hot, remove the skin from the upper side of the fish—the fish will become cold if you turn it over to remove the skin from the underside—leaving the head and tail intact, and brush it all over with melted butter. Garnish.

If the salmon is to be served cold, remove the entire skin, leaving the head and tail intact. With a sharp knife, cut along the backbone, easing the flesh off the bone. Using a pair of scissors, snip the backbone just below the head and just above the tail. Carefully remove the backbone.

Poached salmon II

If the salmon is to be served cold, strain the cooking liquid and boil rapidly to reduce by half, then stir 2 tablespoons of it into 1 cup (250 ml) of mayonnaise to serve with the fish.

5-lb (2½-kg) salmon, cleaned, with the head and tail left on
3 lemons, sliced
6 black peppercorns
1 teaspoon dried dill
1 teaspoon salt
1 small onion, thinly sliced
1 bay leaf, crumbled
1 cup (250 ml) dry white wine

Lay the lemon slices over the bottom of a large, heavy ovenproof casserole to completely cover the base. Add the peppercorns, dill, salt, onion rings and bay leaf. Lay the salmon on top and pour the wine over it. Cover the casserole and bring the wine to a boil. Reduce the heat to very low and simmer for 40 minutes or until the flesh flakes easily when tested with the point of a sharp knife. Remove the casserole from the heat. Very carefully lift the salmon out of the casserole and peel off the skin. Place the salmon on a serving dish and allow it to cool completely before serving.

Poached salmon trout

Butter
3- to 4-lb (1½- to 2-kg) salmon trout, cleaned
1¾ cups (475 ml) white wine
Bouquet garni
Salt and pepper
2 tablespoons beurre manié
½ cup (125 ml) cream

Preheat the oven to 350°F (180°C).

Butter a baking dish, put the fish into it, curving it to fit. Pour the wine over the fish. Add the bouquet garni and seasoning. Cover the dish with buttered foil or waxed paper and place it in the oven.

Poach the fish, basting frequently, for 1 hour or until it is done. Test by inserting the point of a sharp knife into the flesh near the spine. If the flesh flakes easily, the fish is ready.

Coating fish with aspic

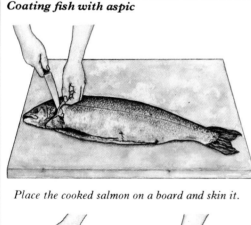

Place the cooked salmon on a board and skin it.

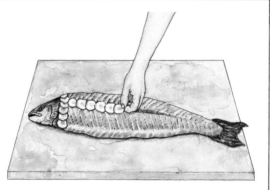

Decorate the skinned salmon with sliced cucumber.

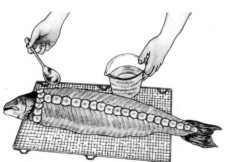

Spoon some cool aspic over the fish and garnish.

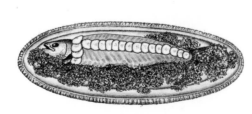

When the aspic has set, put the fish on a platter.

Remove the dish from the oven, lift out the fish carefully and place it on a heated serving dish. Keep it warm.

Strain the cooking liquid into a pan and bring it to a boil. Add the beurre manié, a little at a time, stirring constantly. Stir in the cream, adjust the seasoning if necessary and simmer for 1 minute. Serve immediately.

Salmon trout in aspic
SERVES FOUR TO SIX

3-lb (1½-kg) salmon trout, poached (see previous recipe), skinned, the backbone removed and chilled
3 cups (750 ml) fish aspic, cooled
1 cucumber, thinly sliced
6 shrimp, cooked
Fresh or dried dill weed
1 lemon, cut into slices
Mayonnaise or sauce verte

Place the salmon on a rack and carefully spoon a thin layer of cool aspic over it.

Pour a thin layer of aspic onto a serving platter and put it into the refrigerator to chill. When the aspic has set, lift the salmon trout onto it. Garnish the edges of the dish with the cucumber slices and spoon a little of the aspic over them. Return the dish to the refrigerator to chill.

Decorate the salmon with the shrimp, dill and lemon slices. Serve with the mayonnaise or sauce verte.

Trout in cider
SERVES FOUR

1 cup (250 ml) hard cider
1 tablespoon wine vinegar
Bouquet garni
1 onion, sliced
Salt and pepper
4 trout, cleaned and washed
1 cup (250 ml) hollandaise sauce

Put the cider, vinegar, bouquet garni, onion and the seasoning in a large frying pan and bring to a boil. Add the trout, reduce the heat, cover the pan and simmer gently for 10 minutes.

Lift the trout carefully onto a serving dish and serve immediately, with the hollandaise sauce in a separate bowl.

Sweet-sour pungent fish

Hoisin sauce is a thick, spicy sauce made from soybeans and spices. It is available in Chinese food stores and in some of the larger supermarkets.
SERVES FOUR

1 cucumber
2 carrots
1-inch (2-cm) piece ginger root
1 pickled gherkin
1 onion, finely grated
Salt
2 tablespoons sugar
½ cup (125 ml) wine vinegar
2 tablespoons plus 1 teaspoon cooking oil
3 lb (1½ kg) red snapper
1 tablespoon hoisin sauce
2 teaspoons cornstarch
2 garlic cloves, crushed
Pepper

Slice the cucumber in half lengthwise, remove the soft pulp and seeds and cut into 2-inch- (5-cm-) long matchsticks. Cut the carrots into matchsticks of the same size. Slice the ginger and gherkin into even finer strips and put them all into a bowl with the grated onion. Sprinkle with 1 teaspoon of salt and set aside for 10 minutes. Drain off the liquid. Mix the sugar, vinegar and ½ cup of water together and pour the mixture into the bowl. Let the vegetables marinate for 30 minutes.

Bring 10 cups of water to a boil in a poaching kettle. Add 2 tablespoons of salt and 2 tablespoons of oil. Place the fish carefully in the kettle. When the water comes back to a boil, cover and turn off the heat. Cook the fish in this way in the water for 30 minutes.

Meanwhile, drain the vegetables, reserving the marinade.

In a small bowl combine the marinade and the hoisin sauce. Mix the cornstarch with a tablespoon of cold water and stir it into the marinade mixture.

Heat the teaspoon of oil in a small saucepan. Add the garlic and fry for 1 minute. Add the marinade mixture and simmer, stirring, for 2 to 3 minutes.

Gently lift the fish onto a serving dish, sprinkle with salt and pepper, cover with the marinated vegetables and spoon the sauce over the top.

Serve immediately.

Steamed sea bass

The time taken to steam a whole 2-pound (1-kg) fish is about 15 minutes. A 4-pound (2-kg) fish will take about 20 to 25 minutes.
SERVES FOUR

1 sea bass, about 2 lb (1 kg), cleaned and scaled, with head and tail intact
1 tablespoon dry sherry
3 tablespoons vegetable oil
2 tablespoons finely shredded fresh ginger root
2 scallions, sliced
3 tablespoons soy sauce
1 teaspoon sugar
1 tablespoon chopped coriander leaves

Lay a piece of buttered waxed paper on the steaming tray of a poaching kettle and place the fish on top of it. Sprinkle the bass with sherry.

Bring the water in the kettle to a boil and fit in the tray. Be sure the fish is lying above the water and not in it. Reduce the heat to moderate and steam the fish for 15 minutes.

Meanwhile, heat a small frying pan over high heat for 15 seconds. Add the oil and swirl to coat the bottom of the pan. Add the ginger and cook for 1 minute. Add the scallions, soy sauce and sugar. Stir and cook for 1 minute.

Lift the fish out of the kettle and lay it on a heated serving dish. Pour the sauce over the fish and garnish with the coriander leaves.

Soused herring

All oily fish are suitable for sousing as the vinegar or lemon juice offsets the oiliness. Either wine or cider may be used instead of the water and such herbs as tarragon, dill or mace may be included in the marinade.
SERVES SIX

6 fresh herring, cleaned, with heads and tails removed
Salt
Pinch mace
4 allspice berries
1 small dried red chili
1 clove
6 black peppercorns
1 onion, sliced
1 bay leaf
½ cup (125 ml) wine vinegar
½ cup (125 ml) water

Preheat the oven to 300°F (150°C).

Split and bone the herring. Season lightly with the salt on the fleshy sides. Roll up the fish starting at the tail end, skin side out. Lay the rolls side by side in an ovenproof casserole. Add the spices, arrange the onion and bay leaf on top and pour over the vinegar and water, adding more if necessary, so that the herring is just covered. Cover the dish with foil and bake for 1½ hours.

Remove the dish from the oven and allow the herring to cool in the cooking liquid. Keep the dish in the refrigerator for 2 days before serving.

Sole Véronique
SERVES SIX

1½ lb (700 g) sole fillets, skinned and trimmed, bones reserved
Butter
¾ cup (175 ml) white wine
½ cup (125 ml) water
2 shallots, sliced
1 bay leaf
1¼ cups (315 ml) béchamel sauce
2 tablespoons heavy cream
Salt and pepper
½ lb (225 g) white grapes, peeled and seeded

Preheat the oven to 350°F (180°C).

Place the fish and fish bones in a buttered ovenproof casserole with the wine and water, shallots and bay leaf and put in the oven for 15 minutes or until cooked.

Remove the dish from the oven, take out the fillets and keep warm. Turn off the oven. Strain the cooking liquid into a small pan and bring it to a boil. Cook until the liquid is reduced to 3 tablespoonfuls.

Meanwhile, heat the béchamel sauce. Add the reduced fish liquid and the cream, and salt and pepper to taste. Stir to mix.

Wrap the grapes in foil and place them in the turned-off oven for 1 to 2 minutes or until they are warm.

Arrange the fish fillets on a heated serving dish, leaving a space down the center. Coat the fillets with the sauce and arrange the grapes in the middle.

Serve immediately.

Fish

Fillets of sole florentine

SERVES FOUR

1 lb (450 g) fresh or frozen spinach
1¼ cups (315 ml) mornay sauce
Grated nutmeg
Salt and pepper
8 sole fillets, skinned, washed and dried, bones reserved
½ cup (125 ml) dry white wine or cider
4 tablespoons grated Parmesan cheese

Preheat the oven to 350°F (180°C).

Wash the spinach thoroughly or thaw it slightly and cook it in a saucepan without any additional water. Press the spinach between two plates to drain thoroughly, then put it into a baking dish and mix in 4 tablespoons of the mornay sauce and a pinch of grated nutmeg. Season to taste. Set aside and keep warm.

Put the sole fillets into a buttered ovenproof casserole. Bring the wine or cider to a boil and pour it over the fillets. Cover with the reserved bones and poach in the oven for 15 minutes. Discard the bones and arrange the fillets on top of the spinach in the baking dish. Carefully drain the cooking liquid into a small saucepan and boil it until it has reduced by half. Stir the reduced liquid into the remaining mornay sauce. Cook the sauce for a few minutes to reduce it a little and season to taste. Pour the sauce over the fish, sprinkle the Parmesan cheese over the top and put under a broiler until the top is lightly browned.

Bourride

SERVES FOUR TO SIX

2 leeks, chopped
1 large onion, chopped
2 large tomatoes, chopped
3 lb (1½ kg) white fish, cut into steaks
3 garlic cloves
4 strips thinly pared orange rind
Bouquet garni
5 cups (1¼ liters) water
Salt and pepper
1 lb (450 g) potatoes, boiled
1 cup (250 ml) aioli sauce
8 to 12 slices French bread, fried in olive oil

Put the vegetables into a large saucepan. Put the fish on top. Add the garlic, orange rind, bouquet garni, water, salt and pepper—be careful with the seasoning because the stock will be much reduced later. Bring to a boil. Reduce the heat and simmer for 10 to 15 minutes or until the fish is cooked.

Transfer the fish to a warm tureen. Arrange the potatoes around the fish and keep warm.

Raise the heat and boil the ingredients remaining in the saucepan until about 2½ cups of liquid are left. Remove the pan from the heat and strain the liquid. Rinse out the pan.

Put half the aioli into a large mixing bowl. Pour in the hot liquid gradually, stirring to mix. Return the mixture to the clean pan and cook very gently, without letting the soup boil, for a few minutes or until it thickens slightly.

Put the fried bread into the tureen on top of the fish and pour in the soup.

Serve immediately with the remaining aioli sauce.

Finnan haddie crêpes

SERVES FOUR

1½ lb (700 g) finnan haddie
½ cup (125 ml) milk
¼ cup (65 ml) water
¼ cup (50 g) butter
2 cups (100 g) sliced mushrooms
2 tablespoons flour
¼ cup (65 ml) cream
Rind and juice of 1 lemon
1 tablespoon chopped parsley
8 thin crêpes, kept warm
1 lemon, cut into wedges

Poach the finnan haddie in the milk and water for 10 minutes. Strain off the liquid and reserve it. Flake the fish into a mixing bowl, discarding all the skin and bones.

Melt 2 tablespoons of the butter in a small saucepan and fry the mushrooms until soft. Add to the finnan haddie.

In another small saucepan melt the remaining butter, make a roux with the flour and stir in the reserved cooking liquid and cream. Cook the sauce, stirring constantly, until it has thickened. Add the lemon juice, rind and

the parsley. Mix into the fish.

Preheat the oven to 400 °F (200°C).

Lay the crêpes on your working surface. Place some of the fish mixture along one end of each crêpe and roll it up. Arrange the crêpe rolls in an ovenproof dish. Cover the dish with buttered foil and place it in the oven for 10 minutes to reheat. Serve with the lemon.

Salmon mousse

If the mousse is to be kept for a day or two, seal the top with a layer of aspic jelly.

SERVES FOUR

¾-lb (350-g) salmon steak, poached, skinned, boned and flaked
1¼ cups (315 ml) béchamel
½ teaspoon dried dill weed
Salt and pepper
2 level teaspoons gelatin
1 teaspoon lemon juice
½ cup (125 ml) whipping cream, beaten
2 egg whites, beaten until stiff
¼ cucumber, sliced thinly

Blend the salmon in a blender with the béchamel sauce until it is smooth. Scrape the mixture into a bowl, add the dill and season to taste.

In a cup, soften the gelatin in 2 tablespoons of water. Put the cup in a pan of simmering water until the gelatin dissolves. Stir the gelatin into the salmon mixture with the lemon juice. Fold in the cream and the egg whites.

Divide the mixture between 4 ramekin dishes or use a small soufflé dish. Chill the mousse until it has set. Garnish with cucumber slices.

Gefilte fish

Gefilte fish is a traditional Eastern European Jewish dish, served on feast days. Serve as a first course or as a main dish.

SERVES FIFTEEN TO TWENTY

6 lb (3 kg) fish fillets—a mixture of carp, whiting, whitefish or walleyed pike—heads, tails, bones and skin removed and reserved
4 onions, sliced, plus 2 onions, chopped
2 large carrots, thinly sliced

Soused herring is a dish made all over the world in various forms. Serve as a first course.

4 teaspoons sugar
Salt and pepper
3 eggs
2 tablespoons matzo meal
½ cup (125 ml) cold water

Grind the fish fillets very finely. Put the heads, tails, bones and skin into a saucepan and add the sliced onions, carrots, sugar, and plenty of salt and pepper. Just cover with water and bring to a boil. Reduce the heat to low.

Meanwhile, place the eggs and the remaining 2 onions in a blender and blend well. Fold them into the ground fish. Add the matzo meal and season well with salt and pepper. Fold in the cold water. Wet your hands and shape the mixture into balls. Drop the balls onto the fish trimmings and liquid and reduce the heat to very low. Cover the pan and simmer for 2 hours, removing the scum occasionally.

With a slotted spoon, remove the balls from the broth and arrange them on a serving dish. Garnish the balls with the sliced carrot. Strain the cooking liquid into a bowl. Put the balls and the strained broth into the refrigerator to chill.

Serve the gefilte fish with the jellied broth.

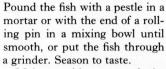

Pound the fish with a pestle in a mortar or with the end of a rolling pin in a mixing bowl until smooth, or put the fish through a grinder. Season to taste.

Melt 2 tablespoons of the butter in a saucepan, stir in the flour and gradually add the milk to make a panade, or thick paste. Set it aside to cool.

When the panade is cold, work in the fish then add the remaining butter, the whole egg and egg yolk. Beat the mixture thoroughly, using an electric beater. Beat in the cream a little at a time. Put the mixture into the refrigerator to chill for 1 hour.

Put the mixture into a pastry tube with an éclair or plain tip. Cut off 2-inch (5-cm) lengths with a knife. Arrange the quenelles in a buttered frying pan. Bring some salted water to a boil and gently pour in enough to cover the quenelles. Place the pan over low heat and simmer very gently for 10 minutes.

Lift out the quenelles with a slotted spoon. Drain on paper towels and serve.

Jellied eels

SERVES FOUR

2 lb (900 g) eels, prepared and cut into 2-inch (5-cm) pieces
2½ cups (625 ml) fish stock
1 teaspoon lemon juice
1 onion stuck with 1 clove
Bouquet garni
1 tablespoon chopped parsley
Salt and pepper

Put the eels into a large pan with the stock, lemon juice, onion and bouquet garni and bring to a boil. Reduce the heat, cover the pan and simmer for 30 minutes. Remove the pan from the heat and let the eels cool in the cooking liquid.

Lift the eel pieces out of the pan and arrange them in a large soufflé dish. Strain the cooking liquid, add the parsley, season to taste and pour it over the eels. Put the dish into the refrigerator to chill.

Remove the dish from the refrigerator. Run a knife around the edges of the dish to loosen the jelly and turn it out onto a platter. Cut the jelly into squares and serve.

Steamed fish mold with anchovy sauce

SERVES FOUR TO SIX

¾ lb (350 g) whiting or any other similar white fish
2 tablespoons butter
2 tablespoons flour
½ cup (125 ml) milk
4 eggs, beaten
Tabasco sauce
Salt
Lemon juice
Anchovy sauce, made with 1 cup (250 ml) velouté sauce and 2 teaspoons anchovy paste, kept hot

Skin the fish and grind or chop it finely. Melt the butter in a saucepan. Stir in the flour and cook for a few seconds. Add the milk, stirring, to make a thick paste, or panade. Remove the pan from the heat and set aside to cool.

When the panade is cool, beat in the fish. Beat in the eggs a little at a time. Push the mixture through a sieve or blend it in a blender until it is smooth. Add a few drops of Tabasco sauce, salt and lemon juice to taste.

Lightly grease a 7-inch (18-cm) ring mold. Put the fish mixture into the mold and cover it with a piece of waxed paper. Put the mold in a steamer or stand it on a rack in a large pan. Cover the pan and steam over gently boiling water for 45 minutes.

Lift out the mold and turn the mixture out onto a heated dish. Coat with the hot anchovy sauce and serve.

Kipper pâté

This is an easy-to-make and economical first course. Serve it with toast made with whole wheat or rye bread.

SERVES FOUR

2 kippers (or smoked mackerel), skinned and boned
½ cup (125 g) butter, softened
Juice and rind of 1 lemon
Pepper
1 hard-cooked egg, chopped

Put the kippers into a frying pan and pour over enough boiling water to cover them. Put the pan over very low heat for 10 minutes.

Drain the kippers and remove any small bones. Put the flesh into a blender with the butter, lemon juice and rind and a pinch of pepper and blend. When the mixture is well blended, add the hard-cooked egg and blend again just long enough to mix thoroughly.

Pack the pâté into ramekin dishes, cover with plastic wrap and put them into the refrigerator to chill for at least 1 hour before serving.

Quenelles

Quenelles are a kind of dumpling made from meat, poultry, game or seafood. Depending on the size, quenelles are used as a garnish or served as a first or main course.

Fish quenelles are traditionally made with pike, but whiting or cod can be used just as successfully. Serve the quenelles with 1 cup (250 ml) of velouté sauce to which ½ pound (225 g) of finely chopped shrimp has been added, or with a mornay sauce.

SERVES FOUR

½-lb (225-g) pike, skinned and boned
Salt and pepper
Grated nutmeg
½ cup (125 g) butter
1 tablespoon flour
¼ cup (65 ml) milk
1 whole egg plus 1 yolk
3 tablespoons heavy cream

Shellfish

Moules marinières

SERVES FOUR

3 quarts (3 liters) mussels,
    cleaned
2 shallots, finely chopped
Freshly ground black pepper
¾ cup (175 ml) dry white
    wine
Bouquet garni
1 tablespoon beurre manié
1 tablespoon chopped
    parsley

Put the mussels into a large saucepan with the shallots, pepper, wine and bouquet garni. Cover the pan and bring to a boil, shaking the pan occasionally. Reduce the heat and simmer for 5 minutes. Discard any mussels that do not open.

Remove the pan from the heat and strain the liquid into a saucepan. Put the mussels into a deep serving dish and keep warm. Put the saucepan on the heat, stir in the beurre manié, a little at a time, and bring the sauce to a boil.

Add the parsley. Pour the sauce over the mussels and serve.

Coquilles St. Jacques

If you want to serve Coquilles St. Jacques as a main course, use 8 large scallops to fill 4 large shells.

SERVES FOUR

6 scallops, prepared and
    removed from their shells
    (reserve 4 deep shells)
½ cup (125 ml) dry white
    wine
1 lemon slice
1 onion slice
6 white peppercorns
Salt
1 bay leaf
1 cup (250 ml) mornay sauce
    made with 1½ tablespoons
    each of Parmesan and
    Gruyère cheese

Put the scallops into a small pan with the wine, lemon, onion, peppercorns, salt and bay leaf and bring to a boil. Reduce the heat, cover the pan and simmer for 5 minutes.

Remove the scallops from the pan and set aside. Strain the liquid and return it to the pan. Return the pan to the heat and bring the liquid to a boil. Continue to boil until the liquid is reduced to 2 tablespoons. Stir the mornay sauce into the re-

duced liquid and adjust the seasoning.

Preheat the broiler to a medium heat.

Cut the scallops into quarters and place them in the reserved shells. Cover the scallops with the sauce and brown them lightly under the broiler.

Scallops à la provençale

SERVES FOUR

6 scallops, prepared and
    removed from their shells
    (reserve 4 deep shells)
¼ cup (65 ml) water
2 teaspoons lemon juice
1 onion slice
1 bay leaf
3 tablespoons butter
1 cup (50 g) sliced small
    mushrooms
1 tablespoon flour
¼ cup (65 ml) dry white
    wine
1 garlic clove
Salt and pepper
2 teaspoons tomato paste
2 tomatoes, peeled, seeded
    and chopped
1 lb (450 g) potatoes, boiled
    and puréed
2 tablespoons grated
    Gruyère cheese

Put the scallops into a small pan with the water, lemon juice, onion and bay leaf and bring to a boil. Reduce the heat, cover the pan and simmer for 5 minutes. Strain the contents of the pan; put the scallops into a bowl and reserve the liquid.

Melt the butter in another small saucepan. Add the mushrooms and fry them for 1 minute. Remove the mushrooms and set aside. Stir the flour into the butter and allow it to brown slightly. Stir in the white wine and the strained stock from the scallops. Crush the garlic with some salt and add it to the sauce with the tomato paste, tomatoes, mushrooms and seasoning. Simmer the sauce, stirring, for 5 minutes. Remove the pan from the heat and pour the sauce over the scallops.

Preheat the broiler to medium.

Put the mixture into the reserved shells. Pipe the potato purée around the edge of the shells. Sprinkle the cheese over the top and brown under the broiler.

Dressed crab

Serve dressed crab as a main dish with a variety of salads.

SERVES THREE TO FOUR

4-lb (2-kg) crab, cooked and
    prepared
Vinaigrette dressing
2 tablespoons fresh
    bread crumbs
1 to 2 tablespoons cream
Salt and pepper
Cayenne pepper
Lemon juice
1 hard-cooked egg yolk
1 tablespoon chopped
    parsley
Lettuce leaves, torn into
    pieces
1 cup (250 ml) tartar sauce

Wash the crab shell thoroughly and dry it well. Put all the white meat into a bowl, mix in a spoonful of vinaigrette and set aside.

In another bowl mix the claw meat with the bread crumbs, adding some of the cream if the mixture is too dry. Season to taste with salt, pepper, cayenne and a few drops of lemon juice.

Pile the white crabmeat into the middle of the shell. Arrange the claw meat on either side. Sieve the egg yolk and arrange it in 2 strips dividing the white

meat from the claw meat. Arrange the parsley in the same way. Lay the crab on lettuce leaves and serve with the sauce.

Crayfish with butter sauce

Crayfish has a very delicate flavor and is at its best when cooked very simply. The Scandinavians cook crayfish in a court bouillon and serve it piled up on a large platter with a bowl of melted butter flavored with dill.

Eat the crayfish with your fingers. Separate the tail from the body. Discard the body—the meat is in the tail. Use your hands to open the tail shell and lift out the meat.

SERVES FOUR

Court bouillon
48 crayfish, prepared
1 cup (225 g) butter
1 tablespoon chopped dill
    weed
Lemon juice
Salt
White pepper

Half fill a very large saucepan with court bouillon and bring to a boil. Add the crayfish, one or two at a time so as not to let the liquid fall below boiling point. Boil for 7 minutes.

Meanwhile, in a small saucepan melt the butter. Stir in the dill weed and the lemon juice. Add salt and pepper to taste. Pour the butter into a bowl.

Lift out the crayfish. Arrange them on a platter and serve with the butter.

Potted shrimp

Serve potted shrimp as a first course with lemon quarters and melba toast or thinly sliced, buttered brown bread. To make melba toast, slice white or brown bread very thinly, cut off the crusts and bake in a 250°F (130°C) oven until the bread is crisp and golden.

SERVES FOUR

¾ cup (175 g) butter, clarified
1 lb (450 g) shrimp, shelled
¼ teaspoon ground mace
½ teaspoon ground pepper
1 teaspoon paprika

Put 2 tablespoons of the clarified butter in a frying pan with the shrimp. Mix in the mace, pepper and paprika and heat for a minute. Spoon the mixture into 4 ramekin dishes. Press down the shrimp. Pour the rest of the butter over the shrimp so that they are completely covered. Put the ramekin dishes into the refrigerator. Serve chilled.

Lobster mayonnaise

SERVES FOUR

4 small or 2 large lobsters, boiled
1 head lettuce
1 bunch watercress
4 tomatoes, peeled and sliced
8 green olives, pitted
1 cup (250 ml) mayonnaise

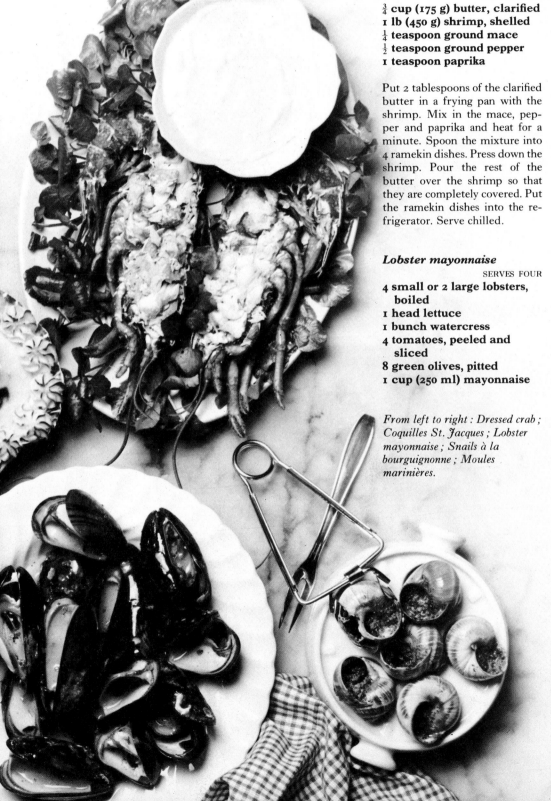

From left to right : Dressed crab; Coquilles St. Jacques; Lobster mayonnaise; Snails à la bourguignonne; Moules marinières.

Split the lobsters in half. Crack the claws. Lift out the tail meat and cut it into slices. Wipe the shells with a little oil to make them shiny.

Put the tail meat back into the shells, red side up. Place the claw meat in the top part of the shells. Arrange the lobster on a bed of lettuce and watercress. Garnish with sliced olives and tomatoes. Serve with the mayonnaise, well chilled.

Snails à la bourguignonne

There are special dishes for holding the snails for the final heating in the oven. These are dented so that the snails do not tip over and the butter does not run out.

SERVES FOUR

2 dozen snails, prepared
½ cup (125 ml) white wine
¼ cup (65 ml) stock
1 onion
1 carrot
Bouquet garni
Salt
¾ cup (175 g) sweet butter, softened
1 shallot, finely chopped
1 garlic clove, crushed
Freshly ground pepper
1 tablespoon chopped parsley

Put the snails into a saucepan with the wine, stock, onion, carrot, bouquet garni and salt and bring to a boil. Cover the pan and simmer for 3 hours. Cool the snails in the cooking liquid.

Remove the snails from their shells and cut off the membrane and black part. Boil the empty shells in water with ½ cup of salt for 30 minutes. Rinse the shells well and dry them with paper towels. Set aside.

In a small bowl combine the butter, shallot, garlic, pepper, salt and parsley. Shape the butter into a block or roll and put it into the refrigerator to chill for at least 30 minutes.

Preheat the oven to 400°F (200°C).

Put the snails in their shells and cover them with a piece of butter the size of a peanut or larger, stuffing it in until the butter is level with the rim of the shell.

Put the snails into a snail dish, open ends up, and heat in the oven for 5 to 6 minutes.

Poultry and game birds

Chicken and small turkeys are the kinds of poultry most often cooked by boiling or poaching, although duck is occasionally cooked in this manner. The Chinese and Japanese often steam chicken and duck, but this is not a feature of Western cooking. Game birds are rarely, if ever, boiled or steamed.

Poultry may be poached either on top of the stove or in the oven. Use a heavy kettle or Dutch oven with a tight-fitting lid. If you are using frozen poultry be sure that it is completely thawed before cooking—a large chicken can take up to a day and a half to thaw in the refrigerator, and a small or medium-sized turkey up to two days.

Today most chickens on the market are force-fed young birds and do not require boiling for a long time to make them tender. This is generally true whether the birds are fresh or frozen.

To poach a chicken or turkey, put the bird and its giblets into a heavy kettle or Dutch oven. Add two teaspoons of salt, two onions (halved or quartered), two carrots (halved), a bouquet garni or bay leaf and a few peppercorns. (These flavorings are sufficient for a medium to large chicken, but may of course be varied according to taste.) Pour in enough cold water to just cover the chicken—or use stock, wine or either of these mixed with water. Bring the liquid to a boil over high heat, skimming the fat and scum from the surface. Reduce the heat to low, cover the pan and simmer, allowing forty-five minutes for a two-and-a-half- to three-pound (1- to 1½-kg) chicken, one hour for a three- to four-pound (1½- to 2-kg) chicken and one and a quarter hours for a four- to six-pound (2- to 3-kg) chicken. A five- to six-pound (2½- to 3-kg) boiling fowl will take about two to three hours and a medium-sized turkey—ten to twelve pounds (4½ to 5½ kg)—will take about one and three-quarter hours. To test if the bird is cooked, pierce the plumpest part of the thigh with a sharp, pointed knife or fork; the juices that run out should be clear, not pink.

When the bird is cooked, lift it out of the pan. Strain the cooking liquid, skimming off any surface fat, and reserve it for stock.

To poach the bird in the oven, put it in a Dutch oven, cover it with cold water, add the flavorings and salt and bring to a boil over high heat. Cover the pot and put it into a 350°F (180°C) oven for the same amount of time as on top of the stove.

Chicken pieces can also be poached in the same way as a whole chicken. Allow about thirty to forty minutes for legs and about twenty to twenty-five minutes for breasts.

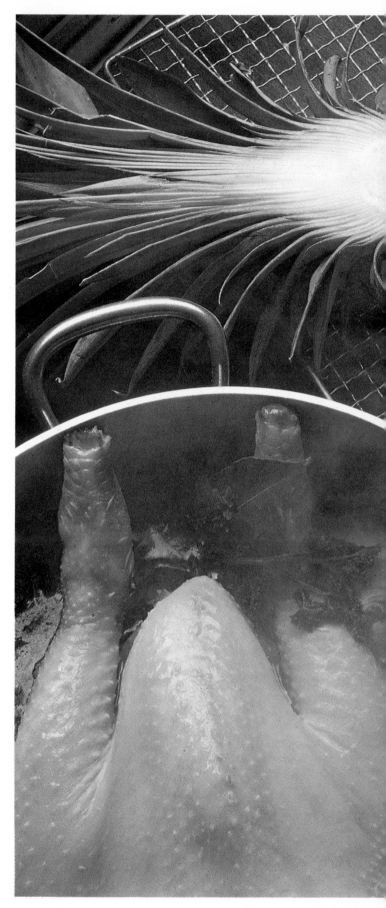

If you poach a chicken in the correct way it will be succulent and full of flavor, and can be used in a number of different dishes—for example, chicken à la king, chicken and pineapple salad and chicken chaud-froid.

English boiled chicken

This traditional English recipe can be varied by the addition of $\frac{1}{2}$ pound (225 g) of small mushrooms, which should be sautéed in butter for about 5 minutes. Drain and add them to the sauce at the same time as the parsley, cream and lemon rind.

This dish may also be served with plain boiled rice.

SERVES FOUR TO SIX

4- to 5-lb (2- to 2½-kg) chicken, poached, cooking liquid reserved
12 parsley sprigs
8 bacon slices
2 tablespoons butter
2 tablespoons flour
¼ cup (65 ml) cream
Grated rind of ½ lemon

Put $2\frac{1}{2}$ cups of the cooking liquid into a saucepan and bring to a boil over moderate heat. Boil briskly until the liquid has reduced to about 2 cups. Remove the pan from the heat and set aside.

Meanwhile, put the parsley sprigs into a small pan of boiling salted water and simmer for 5 minutes. Drain the parsley, then rub it through a strainer into a bowl to make a purée and set aside.

Roll the bacon slices and put on a skewer and set aside.

Melt the butter in a saucepan. Add the flour and mix it in to form a roux. Cook the roux, stirring constantly over very low heat, for 5 to 7 minutes, until it becomes straw-colored.

Remove the pan from the heat and gradually stir in the reduced cooking liquid. Return the pan to the heat and cook, stirring constantly, until the sauce thickens. Remove the pan from the heat and stir in the parsley purée, the cream and the lemon rind.

While you are making the sauce, preheat the broiler to moderately high and broil the rolled bacon slices, turning them occasionally, for 3 to 5 minutes or until they are cooked. Remove the bacon rolls from the skewer.

Carve the chicken into serving pieces and arrange them on a heated serving dish. Spoon over a little of the sauce and pour the rest into a gravy boat. Garnish with the broiled bacon rolls and serve immediately.

Poultry and game birds

Chicken à la king

This dish may be served on a bed of rice or on croutons or in hollowed-out baked bread cases or in rolls.

SERVES FOUR TO SIX

4-lb (2-kg) chicken, poached and cooled
$\frac{1}{4}$ cup (50 g) butter
2 green peppers, cored, seeded and finely sliced
$\frac{1}{2}$ lb (225 g) small mushrooms, finely sliced
2 tablespoons flour
$\frac{1}{2}$ teaspoon paprika
1 teaspoon salt
1$\frac{1}{4}$ cups (315 ml) poaching liquid, strained
$\frac{1}{2}$ cup (125 ml) cream
1 teaspoon lemon juice
2 tablespoons dry sherry

Skin the chicken. Remove the flesh from the bones and cut it into small pieces.

Melt the butter in a large saucepan. Add the green peppers and mushrooms and fry gently, stirring, until they are softened. Stir in the flour, paprika and salt. Gradually add the reserved poaching liquid and cream and bring the mixture to a boil, stirring constantly. Reduce the heat to low and cook the sauce for 2 to 3 minutes, stirring constantly until it has thickened.

Stir in the chicken pieces, lemon juice and sherry. Simmer over low heat, stirring occasionally, for about 5 minutes or until the chicken is heated through.

Chicken poached in wine

SERVES FOUR

3- to 3$\frac{1}{2}$-lb (1$\frac{1}{2}$-kg) chicken, cut up, or 4 chicken breasts
1$\frac{1}{4}$ cups (315 ml) dry white wine
1 small onion
3 peppercorns
3 tarragon sprigs
1 lb (450 g) apricots, halved
2 teaspoons cornstarch
$\frac{1}{2}$ cup (125 ml) cream
Lemon juice
Salt and pepper

Put the chicken into a saucepan. Add the wine, onion, peppercorns and tarragon sprigs. Set the pan over high heat and bring to a boil. Reduce the heat to low, cover the pan and simmer for 30 minutes.

Add the apricot halves to the saucepan, reserving about 8 for the garnish. Simmer the chicken for 10 minutes more or until it is cooked through. Remove the pan from the heat and transfer the chicken pieces and apricots to a warm serving dish.

Mix the cornstarch with the cream, then stir the mixture into the pan juices. Return the pan to moderate heat and bring to a boil, stirring constantly. Simmer for 1 minute, stirring. Strain the sauce over the chicken pieces, set the dish aside and keep hot.

Put the reserved apricots into a pan of boiling water to which a drop or two of lemon juice has been added. Blanch, drain and peel the apricots.

Garnish the dish with the blanched apricots and serve.

Chicken fricassee

Serve the fricassee with plain boiled rice or buttered noodles, and a mixed green salad.

SERVES FOUR

2 tablespoons butter
2 tablespoons flour
2 cups (500 ml) chicken stock or white wine and stock mixed
Salt and white pepper
Grated nutmeg
15 small onions
$\frac{1}{2}$ lb (225 g) small mushrooms
3 egg yolks
3 tablespoons cream
1 teaspoon lemon juice
3$\frac{1}{2}$- to 4-lb (1$\frac{1}{2}$- to 2-kg) chicken, poached, skinned, jointed and kept hot
Fried croutons
1 tablespoon chopped fresh parsley

Melt the butter in a saucepan. Stir in the flour to form a roux. Cook the roux, stirring constantly, over very low heat for 5 to 7 minutes or until it is straw-colored. Add the stock gradually, stirring constantly. Season with salt, pepper and a pinch of nutmeg.

Add the onions and simmer for 10 minutes, then add the mushrooms and simmer for 10 minutes more.

Combine the egg yolks, cream and lemon juice in a small bowl. Stir in a little of the hot sauce,

then pour the mixture into the saucepan, stirring constantly. Cook over very low heat, stirring, without letting the sauce boil. Check the seasoning.

Arrange the chicken pieces on a heated platter. Pour over the sauce, garnish with croutons and chopped parsley and serve.

Chicken with spicy mayonnaise

SERVES FOUR TO SIX

4-lb (2-kg) chicken, poached and cooled, cut up into small pieces
1$\frac{1}{4}$ cups (315 ml) mayonnaise, well seasoned with salt, pepper and mustard
2 teaspoons curry powder
2 tablespoons whipped cream
2 tablespoons apricot preserve, strained
2 teaspoons lemon juice
1$\frac{1}{4}$ cups (225 g) long-grain rice, cooked and cooled
4 tablespoons slivered almonds, toasted
2 pickled gherkins, finely chopped
1 red pepper, cored, seeded and finely shredded
1 cucumber, finely sliced
2 tablespoons vinegar

Skin the chicken. Remove the flesh from the bones and cut it into small pieces.

Mix the mayonnaise, curry powder, cream, preserve and lemon juice together in a large bowl. Stir in the chicken pieces until they are well coated.

Arrange the cold rice in a layer on a serving platter. (If you prefer, make a rice mold by pressing the hot cooked rice into a 9-inch/23-cm ring mold, refrigerating it until chilled, then unmolding it onto a platter.)

Arrange the chicken-mayonnaise mixture over the rice or in the center of the rice ring and scatter the toasted almonds, chopped gherkins and shredded pepper on top.

Put the cucumber slices into a pan of boiling water and blanch them for 1 minute. Drain them, then mix them with the vinegar. Set aside for 10 minutes. Drain off the vinegar, and arrange the cucumber slices around the rice. Chill for 30 minutes before serving.

Chicken salad

SERVES SIX

4- to 5-lb (2- to 2$\frac{1}{2}$-kg) chicken, poached and cooled
3 hard-cooked eggs, separated
4 tablespoons diced Cheddar
1 head celery, chopped
2 large oranges, peeled and sliced
1 green apple, cored, diced and mixed with 1 teaspoon lemon juice
4 tablespoons chopped walnuts
$\frac{1}{2}$ cup (125 ml) vinaigrette dressing
6 large radishes, sliced
1 bunch watercress

Skin the chicken, dice the meat into cubes and put them into a mixing bowl. Chop the egg whites and add to the bowl.

Add the cheese, celery, oranges, apple and walnuts to the chicken. Mash the egg yolks to a paste in a small bowl, gradually incorporating the vinaigrette. Pour the dressing over the chicken and toss the salad.

Arrange the salad decoratively in a serving dish. Garnish with the radish slices and watercress.

Serve slightly chilled.

Chicken and pineapple salad

SERVES SIX

4- to 5-lb (2- to 2$\frac{1}{2}$-kg) chicken, poached and cooled
1 large fresh pineapple
$\frac{1}{2}$ cup (125 ml) mayonnaise
$\frac{1}{2}$ cup (125 ml) sour cream
Rind and juice of $\frac{1}{2}$ lemon
2 celery stalks, diced
Salt and freshly ground black pepper
Walnuts or blanched almonds

Skin the chicken, cut the meat into neat, bite-sized pieces and put them in a large bowl.

Halve the pineapple. Using a serrated knife, remove the flesh from the skin, leaving the shell intact. Remove the core and chop the flesh into bite-sized pieces and add them to the chicken.

Mix the mayonnaise, sour cream and lemon rind and juice together. Add 6 tablespoons of the mayonnaise mixture and the celery to the chicken and pineapple in the bowl. Season to taste and mix well.

Pile the mixture into the pineapple shells and arrange the shells on a serving platter. Spoon over the remaining mayonnaise mixture and garnish with the walnuts or almonds.

Chicken chaud-froid

SERVES SIX TO EIGHT

8 large chicken breasts, skinned, boned, poached and cooled in the cooking liquid
1¼ cups (315 ml) chaud-froid sauce, cooled
2½ tablespoons gelatin, softened in 6 tablespoons hot water
5 cups (1¼ liters) reserved cooking liquid, degreased and clarified
Cucumber peel, cut into strips
Lemon juice
4 stuffed olives, sliced
Lemon wedges
Watercress sprigs

Put the chicken breasts on a rack over a plate and spoon the cool chaud-froid sauce over them. Refrigerate until the sauce sets.

Stir the softened gelatin into the clarified cooking liquid. Pour half of the liquid into a jelly roll pan and refrigerate until the aspic has set. Reserve the remaining liquid aspic and keep it cool so that it sets very lightly.

Decorate the chicken breasts with the cucumber peel and olives, then coat them with some of the reserved, lightly set aspic. Return the rack to the refrigerator until the aspic sets.

Arrange the chicken breasts on a serving dish. Chop the aspic in the jelly roll pan and decorate the dish with it. Garnish with lemon wedges and watercress.

Chicken florentine

SERVES FOUR

3- to 3½-lb (1½-kg) chicken, jointed, or 4 chicken breasts
1 tablespoon lemon juice
½ cup (125 ml) chicken stock
¼ cup (65 ml) dry white wine
Salt and pepper

1 lb (450 g) fresh leaf spinach, washed thoroughly and trimmed
3 tablespoons butter
½ cup (50 g) flour
1 cup (250 ml) milk
4 tablespoons cream
Grated nutmeg
1¼ cups (125 g) grated Gruyère
2 tablespoons fresh white bread crumbs

Put the chicken, lemon juice, stock, wine and seasoning into a saucepan over high heat and bring to a boil. Reduce the heat to low, cover the pan and simmer for 30 to 40 minutes or until the chicken is cooked.

Meanwhile, put the spinach into a large pan, add salt to taste and cook covered, without adding any water (there is enough trapped in the leaves after washing), over moderately high heat for 5 to 6 minutes. Remove the pan from the heat and drain the spinach thoroughly, using two plates to squeeze out excess moisture. Spread the spinach over the bottom of a medium-sized ovenproof casserole. Set aside and keep hot.

When the chicken pieces are cooked, remove the pan from the heat. Lift out the chicken pieces, skin them and arrange them on top of the spinach. Strain the cooking liquid into a bowl.

Preheat the oven to 350°F (180°C).

Melt the butter in a saucepan. Add the flour and mix it in to form a roux. Cook the roux, stirring constantly, over very low heat for 5 to 7 minutes or until it becomes straw-colored.

Gradually stir in the milk and bring to a boil. Cook for 1 to 2 minutes, stirring constantly, until the sauce thickens. Stir in the reserved cooking liquid, cream and a little nutmeg. Stir in ⅔ cup of the grated cheese and simmer gently until it melts. Season to taste and pour the sauce over the chicken.

Sprinkle the remaining grated cheese and the bread crumbs over the sauce. Bake in the oven for 15 minutes.

Meanwhile, preheat the broiler to moderately high. Remove the dish from the oven and place it under the broiler for 2 to 3 minutes or until the top is golden and bubbling.

Duck galantine

Chicken can be used instead of the duck, using marjoram instead of sage.

SERVES SIX TO EIGHT

1 duck, about 6 lb (3 kg), boned, with the wings and legs intact
1 lb (450 g) cooked tongue
1 lb (450 g) cooked ham
6 to 7 black olives, pitted and chopped
1 tablespoon pistachio nuts, blanched
¾ cup (175 ml) warm meat aspic

STUFFING
2 tablespoons butter
2 onions, chopped
1 lb (450 g) ground veal
⅔ cup (75 g) fresh white bread crumbs
2 teaspoons dried sage
1 egg
½ cup (125 ml) heavy cream
Salt and pepper

First prepare the stuffing. Melt the butter in a frying pan. Add the onions and fry them until they are softened. Remove the pan from the heat and transfer the onions to a large bowl. Combine the remaining stuffing ingredients with the onions until they are thoroughly mixed.

Lay the duck on a board, skin side down and open it out flat. Spread the stuffing over the duck, to within about 1 inch (2 cm) of the edges. Cut the tongue and ham into strips and arrange them over the stuffing with the olives and nuts.

Bring the outside edges of the duck's skin to the center and reform into the original shape. Sew up securely, using a trussing needle and strong thread. Enclose the duck in waxed paper, then in cheesecloth, tying each end securely with string and sewing up the seam.

Put the duck into a large pan or poaching kettle of boiling salted water. Cover the pan and simmer for 1½ to 2 hours.

Remove the duck from the pan and set it aside to cool, still in the cheesecloth wrapping. When cool, refrigerate until very cold before unwrapping.

Brush the duck with the aspic, applying 2 or 3 coats and allowing one coat to set before applying the next one. Serve cold.

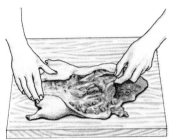

Duck galantine

Lay the duck on a board, skin side down, and open it out.

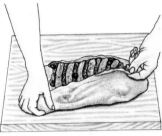

Spread with the stuffing, ham, tongue, olives and nuts.

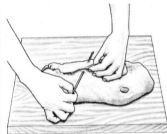

Bring the edges together, reshape the duck and sew it up.

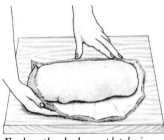

Enclose the duck completely in waxed paper and cheesecloth.

Tie the ends of the parcel up and sew up the center seam.

Meat and game

Boiling is not a method of cooking that is immediately associated with meat: yet some of the most delicious meat dishes are cooked by boiling. There are some famous examples from many countries: bollito from Italy, pot au feu from France, Boston boiled dinner from the United States, Wiener tafelspitz from Austria and boiled (corned) beef and dumplings from England.

Steaming meat, on the other hand, is unusual outside Chinese and Japanese cuisines. There are, however, a very few exceptions—the most common one is English steak and kidney pudding.

Game is rarely boiled or steamed.

Both salted and unsalted meat can be boiled. The minimum cooking time is twenty-five minutes per pound (450 g) plus twenty-five minutes for salted meat and twenty minutes per pound (450 g) plus twenty minutes for unsalted meat. But some cuts of meat may need up to double that time if the meat is to be really tender. Test the meat to see if it is done by piercing it with a sharp pointed knife. The knife should penetrate to the center easily.

To boil meat, put the piece into a large saucepan and pour in enough cold water to cover it. Bring the water slowly to a boil, skimming the scum as it rises. Add some onion, root vegetables (see the recipes that follow) and a bouquet garni. Cover the pan and simmer very gently until the meat is tender. Fill up with boiling water from time to time, if necessary.

Boiled (corned) beef and dumplings

Serve hot mustard or piquant horseradish sauce with this dish.

Boiled beef may also be served cold. Let the meat cool in the cooking liquid then remove it from the pan. Cover the meat and chill it in the refrigerator. Slice the beef thinly and serve it with a variety of salads.

SERVES SIX TO EIGHT

4 lb (2 kg) piece of beef, brisket, flank or plate
Bouquet garni
6 peppercorns
½ recipe suet crust, with 2 teaspoons chopped fresh herbs mixed in
6 onions, halved
6 carrots, halved
½ lb (225 g) turnips, cubed

Put the beef into a large saucepan, just cover with cold water and set over moderate heat. Bring to a boil, skimming the scum from the surface. Add the bouquet garni and peppercorns to the pan. Reduce the heat to low, cover the pan and simmer very gently for 2 hours, adding more boiling water if necessary.

Meanwhile, form the suet crust into small walnut-sized dumplings and set them aside.

Remove the bouquet garni from the pan and skim any fat or scum from the surface. Add the vegetables, cover the pan and simmer for 15 minutes more. Add the dumplings, cover the pan and cook for a final 20 minutes or until the meat and dumplings are cooked.

Remove the meat from the pan and put it on a warm serving dish. Surround it with the vegetables and dumplings. Skim the fat from the surface of the cooking liquid, strain it and serve separately in a gravy boat.

Ham boiled in cider

Hams are usually boiled, even if they are to be finished by baking or glazing in the oven. If you are using a home-cured salted ham, it must be soaked overnight in water before cooking.

SERVES FOUR TO SIX

3-lb (1½-kg) ham
5 cups (1¼ liters) hard cider
1 onion, halved
1 carrot, halved
4 tablespoons bread crumbs, toasted

Put the ham, cider, onion and carrot into a large saucepan over moderate heat. Bring to a boil, skimming the fat and scum from the surface. Reduce the heat to low, cover the pan and simmer for 1¼ hours (or allow 25 minutes per pound), until the ham is cooked. Remove the pan from the heat and let the ham cool in the cooking liquid. When the liquid is cold, transfer the ham to a board.

Skin the ham, then press the bread crumbs into the skinned side. It is now ready to be served.

To corn beef or tongue	To pickle beef or tongue
20 cups (5 liters) water	½ lb (225 g) salt
2 lb (900 g) salt	2 tablespoons saltpeter
1 tablespoon saltpeter	2 tablespoons brown sugar
2 tablespoons brown sugar	1 teaspoon ground mace
4 to 6 lb (2 to 3 kg) tongue or piece of beef	1 teaspoon ground ginger
	½ teaspoon ground cloves
	½ teaspoon black pepper
	½ teaspoon ground cinnamon
	4 to 6 lb (2 to 3 kg) tongue or piece of beef

Put the water into a large pan, add the salt, saltpeter and sugar and boil for 30 minutes. Skim, then allow to cool completely. Put the tongue or beef into a large, deep bowl or casserole and cover with the brine. Leave for 4 to 5 weeks for a tongue, 1 to 2 weeks for beef. Turn every 2 days. Remove the meat from the brine and rinse. The meat is now ready to be cooked.

In a bowl mix together the salt, saltpeter, sugar and spices. Put the tongue or meat on a large serving dish and rub the mixture in well all over. Turn the meat each day: tongue can be left for 2 weeks, beef for 6 days.

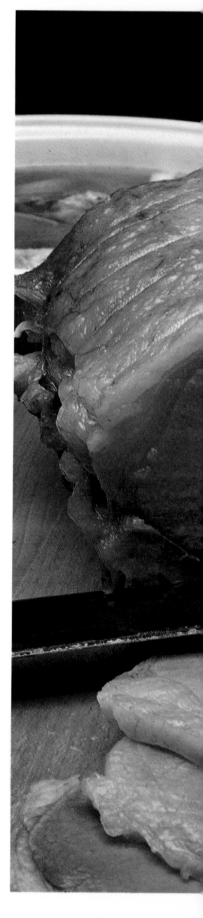

Boiled (corned) beef and dumplings, dolmas and English steak and kidney pudding.

Meat and game

English steak and kidney pudding

SERVES FOUR

Suet crust for a double crust
1½ lb (700 g) lean stewing beef, cut into cubes
½ lb (225 g) kidney, cubed
1 onion, finely chopped
¼ cup (25 g) flour, seasoned with salt, pepper and paprika
1 teaspoon dried mixed herbs or 2 teaspoons chopped fresh herbs
1 tablespoon Worcestershire sauce
½ cup (125 ml) beef stock

Roll out the pastry dough on a floured surface to a circle about 10 inches (25 cm) in diameter. Cut out a right-angled segment from the circle and set it aside. Moisten the cut edges of the dough circle with water, press them together then lift the dough and put it into a 1 quart (1 liter) pudding mold. Press it down lightly and trim with a sharp knife. Reserve the trimmings.

Toss the beef, kidney and onion in the seasoned flour and put them into the mold. Sprinkle the herbs over the meat and pour in the Worcestershire sauce and stock (the stock should come halfway up the sides of the mold, so add more stock if necessary).

Lightly knead the remaining dough segment and trimmings and roll out to a circle large enough to cover the mold. Dampen the edges of the dough in the mold, then carefully place the circle over the top, trimming off any excess dough. Press the edges of the dough together to seal the pie.

Dip a large piece of cloth in boiling water, wring it out and sprinkle it lightly with flour. Tie the cloth over the mold, making a 1-inch (2-cm) pleat in the center of the top to allow for expansion during cooking. Tie the cloth in place with string. (Aluminum foil can be used instead of cloth, if you prefer.)

Put the mold into a large kettle of boiling water—the water must come halfway up the side of the mold. Reduce the heat to moderately low, cover the kettle tightly and steam steadily for 4 hours. Add more boiling water to the kettle as it evaporates. Alternatively, use a steamer.

Remove the mold from the kettle and take off the cloth. Tie a clean napkin around the mold and transfer it to a warm serving dish. Serve immediately.

Boiled shoulder of mutton

Mutton is out of favor these days, which is sad because it is far more tasty than lamb.

SERVES FOUR TO SIX

4 lb (2 kg) boned and rolled shoulder of mutton
Salt and pepper
2 onions
2 carrots
2 celery stalks, halved
Bouquet garni
½ lb (225 g) turnips, chopped
½ cup (125 g) dried lima beans, soaked overnight in cold water and drained
2 teaspoons cornstarch
½ cup (125 ml) yogurt
2 tablespoons red currant jelly

Put the mutton into a large saucepan, add cold salted water to cover and bring to a boil, skimming off any scum as it rises to the surface.

Add the onions, carrots, celery and bouquet garni. Reduce the heat to low, cover the pan and simmer very gently for 1 hour. Season to taste and add the turnips and beans. Simmer, covered, for 40 to 45 minutes more.

Remove the pan from the heat and transfer the meat to a warm serving dish. Arrange the cooked vegetables around it and keep hot.

Strain the cooking liquid into a small saucepan. Set the pan over high heat and boil briskly until the liquid has reduced to about 1 cup, skimming the fat from the surface.

Mix the cornstarch, yogurt and red currant jelly together, then stir the mixture into the liquid. Bring to a boil, stirring, and cook for 1 to 2 minutes.

Pour a little of the sauce over the mutton. Serve the remainder in a warm gravy boat.

Boiled ham with lentils

SERVES SIX

1 small ham shank or butt, soaked in cold water overnight and drained
2 tablespoons drippings
2 onions, chopped
Pepper
1 lb (450 g) brown lentils, soaked in cold water for 1 hour and drained
1 carrot
1 celery stalk
2 garlic cloves
Bouquet garni
2 tablespoons butter, melted
2 tablespoons chopped parsley

Put the ham into a saucepan and add cold water to cover. Set the pan over high heat and bring the water to a boil, skimming the fat and scum from the surface. Remove the pan from the heat, drain the ham then rinse it in cold water.

Melt the drippings in a large saucepan. Add the onions and fry them, stirring, until they are golden. Put the ham into the pan and add pepper, the lentils, vegetables, garlic, bouquet garni and enough cold water to cover. Cover the pan and cook over low heat for 2 hours.

Remove the pan from the heat. Transfer the ham to a plate and remove the outer skin and fat. Discard the carrot, celery, garlic and bouquet garni. Strain the remaining contents of the pan and reserve the lentils. Discard the cooking stock. Toss the lentil mixture in the butter and transfer to a warm serving dish. Slice the ham and arrange around the lentils. Sprinkle with parsley and serve.

English steak and kidney pudding

Cut a segment from the circle.

Ease the dough into the mold.

Press the cut edges together.

Pour the stock over the meat.

Use the segment to make a lid.

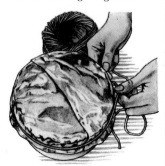
Tie on the covering with string.

Cold pressed tongue

SERVES EIGHT TO TEN

4- to 6-lb (2- to 3-kg) salted beef tongue, soaked in cold water for 24 hours and drained
2 carrots, halved
2 onions, halved
1 celery stalk, cut into short lengths
Bouquet garni
8 peppercorns

Wash the tongue and put it into a large saucepan. Cover completely with cold water and bring to a boil slowly, skimming the fat and scum from the surface. Add the vegetables, bouquet garni and peppercorns, cover the pan and simmer very gently for about 4 hours or until the tongue is cooked and the small bones at the root can be pulled out easily. If they do not come out easily, simmer the tongue for 30 minutes more and check again.

Remove the pan from the heat and cool the tongue in the cooking liquid. Drain and transfer the tongue to a board. Discard the cooking liquid. Skin the tongue, trim the root and remove all the gristle and bones.

Roll up the tongue and fit it into a deep 8-inch (20-cm) round cake pan (it should be a tight fit, so squeeze it in). Cover the tongue with a plate and put a heavy weight on top (use a pan full of water if you do not have

any other heavy object). Set aside in a cool place for 12 hours or overnight.

Run a knife around the edge of the pan to loosen the tongue, then invert it onto a serving plate. Serve thinly sliced.

Cabbage dolmas

SERVES SIX

1 medium-sized cabbage, washed and trimmed
1 tablespoon butter
1 onion, finely chopped
2 lb (900 g) ground lamb
½ cup (50 g) cooked rice
2 tablespoons pinenuts, blanched and chopped
1 tablespoon chopped fresh mint
2 cups (500 ml) beef stock
Salt and pepper
4 tablespoons flour
2 cups (250 ml) tomato sauce

Put the cabbage into a pan of boiling salted water and blanch for 3 minutes. Remove the pan from the heat and drain the cabbage. Carefully remove the leaves, one by one. (If they are difficult to remove, blanch the cabbage again.) Discard the hard core and tough stalk.

Meanwhile, melt the butter in a small saucepan and fry the onion until it is golden. Remove the pan from the heat.

Mix the meat, fried onion, rice, nuts, mint and three table-

spoons of the stock together in a bowl and season well.

Put a tablespoon of the meat mixture on each cabbage leaf at the stalk end. Fold the sides inward and then roll the leaf up to enclose the filling completely. Gently coat the rolls in the flour, then arrange them in a Dutch oven as tightly packed as possible to prevent them from unwinding. Pour over the remaining stock (the rolls should be covered, so add more if necessary). Set the Dutch oven over high heat on top of the stove and bring to a boil. Reduce the heat to low, cover the pot and simmer for 40 minutes.

Preheat the oven to 350°F (180°C).

Using a slotted spoon, transfer the dolmas to an ovenproof dish and pour over the tomato sauce. Put the dish into the oven and bake for 20 minutes.

Sweetbread vol-au-vents

SERVES FOUR

1 lb (450 g) sweetbreads, blanched for 10 minutes
1¼ cups (315 ml) stock
1 teaspoon lemon juice
1 bay leaf
2 tablespoons butter
¼ lb (125 g) mushrooms, chopped
1 tablespoon flour
6 black olives, pitted and sliced
3 tablespoons cream
Salt and pepper
8 small vol-au-vent cases, baked and kept hot

Cut the sweetbreads into pieces and put them into a large saucepan. Add the stock, lemon juice and bay leaf and bring to a boil. Reduce the heat to low, cover the pan and simmer for 10 minutes. Remove the pan from the heat and transfer the sweetbreads to a plate. Strain the stock.

Melt the butter in a saucepan. Add the mushrooms and cook, stirring, for 2 minutes. Stir in the flour. Add half the reserved stock gradually, stirring constantly, and bring to a boil. Cook the sauce for 2 to 3 minutes or until it thickens. Stir in the sweetbreads, olives and cream and season to taste. Simmer gently over low heat until the sweetbreads are heated through.

Spoon the mixture into the hot vol-au-vent cases and serve.

Veal galantine

Serve the galantine thinly sliced with horseradish sauce, or sauce verte, and pickles. To make horseradish sauce, mix 1 tablespoon of freshly grated horseradish into ½ cup (125 ml) stiffly whipped cream. Mix in 1 teaspoon of lemon juice and season with salt, pepper and sugar to taste.

SERVES SIX TO EIGHT

3 lb (1½ kg) breast of veal, boned and fat trimmed
Salt and pepper
1 onion, finely chopped
½ lb (225 g) sausage meat
½ lb (225 g) ground ham
1 teaspoon chopped parsley
1 teaspoon chopped basil
½ teaspoon chopped oregano
2 tablespoons brandy
1 tablespoon pistachio nuts, chopped
3 thick slices ham
10 cups (2¼ liters) stock
½ cup (125 ml) meat aspic

Lay the veal out flat on a board, fat side down. Season well.

Mix the onion, sausage meat, ground ham, the salt and pepper, herbs and brandy together in a bowl until they are well blended. Spread the stuffing over the veal to within ½ inch (1 cm) of the edges. Sprinkle the pistachio nuts over the stuffing. Lay the ham slices on top down the length of the meat. Roll up tightly and tie securely with string. Enclose the veal in waxed paper, then in cheesecloth, tying each end securely with string and sewing up the center seam.

Put the veal into a large pan and pour in the stock, cover the pan and simmer over low heat for 2 hours.

Remove the veal from the pan and set it aside to cool. Tighten and retie the cloth and put the veal on a board. Cover it with another board, put a heavy weight on top and leave it overnight. Then chill it in the refrigerator.

Unwrap the veal and remove the string. Brush the veal with aspic, applying 2 or 3 coats and allowing one coat to set before applying the next one. Allow the final coat to set before serving.

Pressed tongue

Trim off the root end and all the fat, bones and gristle.

Hold the tongue by the root end and peel off all the skin.

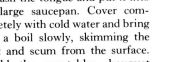

Curl the tongue into a cake pan—it should be a tight fit.

Cover the pan with a plate and put a heavy weight on top.

Vegetables

Vegetables, particularly those that grow above ground, require careful cooking if their goodness is not to be lost. Boiling has one great disadvantage—the vitamins and flavors contained in vegetables are often cooked out completely and thrown away with the water; so steam vegetables whenever it is practical.

There are two ways of steaming vegetables: you can use a French steamer, which is specially designed for vegetables, or a saucepan with a steamer attachment. Be sure that the water is boiling before putting the vegetables into the steamer.

If you have to boil a vegetable use as little water as possible, bring it to a boil, then reduce the heat and simmer. Choose a saucepan with a tight-fitting lid, although greens usually retain their color better if cooked uncovered. To keep such vegetables as cauliflower and Belgian endive white, add a few drops of lemon juice to the water. Always keep the cooking liquid; you can use it for making stocks and soups.

Most vegetables should be slightly undercooked—they are at their most delicious when they are slightly crisp; there is nothing more distasteful than limp, soggy vegetables.

Because cooking times are affected by such variables as the age and size of the vegetables, and whether they are cut or whole, the times given in the chart on pages 92–3 are only approximate.

Artichokes with shrimp and mushroom mayonnaise, lentil salad and steamed stuffed cabbage

Brussels sprouts with curried almonds

SERVES FOUR TO SIX

4 tablespoons butter
6 tablespoons slivered
   almonds
1 teaspoon curry powder
2 lb (900 g) Brussels sprouts,
   boiled and drained

Melt the butter in a large frying pan and add the almonds. Fry, stirring constantly, until they are golden. Add the curry powder and stir well. Add the sprouts to the pan, stir well to coat with the almond mixture and serve.

Brussels sprouts with chestnuts

SERVES FOUR TO SIX

1 lb (450 g) chestnuts,
   blanched and peeled
2½ cups (575 ml) vegetable
   stock
1 celery stalk
1 teaspoon sugar
2 tablespoons butter
2 lb (900 g) Brussels sprouts,
   steamed and kept warm
Salt and pepper

Put the chestnuts into a saucepan with the vegetable stock, celery and sugar and simmer for 35 to 40 minutes or until tender.

Drain the chestnuts and discard the celery stalk. Add the butter to the pan and melt it over low heat. Return the chestnuts to the pan, add the sprouts and seasoning to taste and serve.

Petits pois à la française

SERVES FOUR

6 tablespoons water
6 tablespoons butter
3 lb (1½ kg) peas, shelled
12 scallions, chopped
1 medium-sized crisp
   lettuce heart, shredded
2 teaspoons sugar
½ teaspoon salt
¼ teaspoon black pepper
Bouquet garni
2 teaspoons beurre manié

Put the water and butter in a large saucepan over moderate heat. When the butter has melted, add all the remaining ingredients except the beurre manié. Cover the pan with a tight-fitting lid and cook for about 10 minutes or until the peas are tender. Shake the pan occasionally.

If there is too much liquid left in the pan, add the beurre manié, a little at a time, until it thickens. Remove the bouquet garni before serving.

Cauliflower salad

SERVES FOUR

1 cauliflower, boiled in
   florets with 2 sprigs of
   rosemary and drained
½ cup (125 ml) vinaigrette
2 tomatoes, skinned, seeded
   and chopped

Put the cauliflower florets into a salad bowl and toss with the vinaigrette dressing and tomatoes. Serve hot or cold.

Steamed stuffed cabbage

SERVES FOUR

1 white cabbage, boiled for
   10 minutes and drained

STUFFING

4 tablespoons butter
1 large onion, chopped
½ lb (225 g) mushrooms,
   chopped
1 lb (450 g) ham, finely
   chopped
6 tablespoons cooked rice
Salt and pepper
Grated nutmeg
½ cup (125 ml) chicken
   stock
1¼ cups (315 ml) tomato
   sauce

Cut out the center of the cabbage in a circle and scoop out the center to form a cavity.

Melt the butter in a saucepan and fry the onion until soft. Add the mushrooms and cook for 4 minutes. Add the ham, rice and seasonings, moisten with chicken stock and mix well to combine.

Spoon the stuffing into the cavity. Place the cabbage in a buttered ovenproof bowl, cover with foil and steam over boiling water in a covered pan for 45 minutes.

Remove the pan from the heat. Lift out the cabbage, put it on a heated serving dish and serve with the tomato sauce.

Boiled Belgian endive

SERVES FOUR

1¼ cups (315 ml) water
1 teaspoon sugar
½ teaspoon salt
8 heads Belgian endive,
   washed and trimmed
4 tablespoons butter
Juice of ½ lemon
2 tablespoons chopped
   parsley

Bring the water to a boil in a large saucepan with the sugar and salt. Add the endive, butter and lemon juice, cover and cook for 15 to 20 minutes or until the endive is tender. Drain thoroughly, reserving the cooking liquid. Arrange the endive in a heated serving dish and keep hot.

Put the cooking liquid back into the pan and boil to reduce by half. Pour the liquid over the endive, sprinkle with the parsley and serve.

Artichokes with shrimp and mushroom mayonnaise

SERVES FOUR

1¼ cups (315 ml) sauce verte
½ lb (225 g) shelled cooked
   and diced shrimp
¼ lb (125 g) small
   mushrooms, quartered
4 artichokes, chokes re-
   moved, cooked and cooled

Put the sauce in a bowl. Stir in the shrimp and mushrooms and adjust the seasoning. Pile the mixture into the center of each artichoke.

To eat, dip the outer leaves in the sauce in the center of the artichokes, then eat the tender core at the bottom with a knife and fork.

Glazed carrots

SERVES FOUR

1½ lb (700 g) small carrots,
   trimmed
½ cup (125 ml) water
2 tablespoons butter
1 teaspoon sugar
Salt and pepper
1 tablespoon chopped
   parsley

Put the carrots into a saucepan with the water, butter, sugar and salt and pepper to taste. Cut out a circle of waxed paper to fit inside the saucepan. Grease the paper with a teaspoon of butter and place, waxed side down, over the carrots. Cover the saucepan with a tight-fitting lid and simmer for 20 minutes. Turn the carrots out into a serving dish, sprinkle with the parsley and serve.

Carrot and parsnip purée

SERVES FOUR

1 lb (450 g) mature carrots,
   peeled, boiled, drained
   and mashed
1 lb (450 g) parsnips, peeled,
   boiled, drained and
   mashed
Salt and pepper
1 egg yolk
4 tablespoons butter, melted
¼ teaspoon grated nutmeg

Beat all the ingredients together to form a smooth purée. Pile into a serving dish and serve at once or brown quickly under a hot broiler before serving.

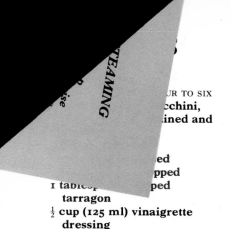

...UR TO SIX

...cchini,
...ined and

...ed
...pped

1 table... ...ped
tarragon
¼ cup (125 ml) vinaigrette
dressing

Put all the ingredients into a
salad bowl, toss well and serve.

Squash in caraway sauce

SERVES FOUR

1 squash, peeled, seeded
and cut into large cubes
Salt
2 tablespoons butter
1 tablespoon flour
1 cup (250 ml) chicken or
veal stock
2 teaspoons caraway seeds
1 tablespoon white wine
vinegar
Pepper

Put the squash cubes into a
colander, sprinkle with 2 tablespoons of salt and set aside for 15
minutes. Rinse off the salt and
drain the squash well.

Melt the butter in a large
saucepan and stir in the flour to
make a roux. Gradually stir in
the stock and cook, stirring, until
the sauce has thickened. Add the
caraway seeds, vinegar, squash
and seasoning to taste. Cover the
pan and simmer over very low
heat for 20 minutes.

Spinach purée

This spinach purée can be served
as a vegetable accompaniment or
used as a filling for pancakes,
with a cheese sauce poured over
the pancakes.

SERVES FOUR

2½ lb (1 kg) spinach,
prepared, cooked and
drained
2 tablespoons butter
2 tablespoons cream
Grated nutmeg
Salt and pepper

Chop the spinach finely or purée
it in a blender. Put it in a saucepan, stir in the butter, cream,
nutmeg and seasoning to taste.
Heat thoroughly and serve.

Boiled fennel

SERVES FOUR

4 heads of fennel, cut into
quarters, boiled in
acidulated water and
drained
¼ cup (50 g) butter
¼ cup (25 g) grated Parmesan
cheese
Salt and pepper

Place the fennel in a large saucepan and add the butter, cheese
and seasoning. Cook over low
heat for 5 to 6 minutes.

Beet salad

SERVES FOUR

4 tablespoons sour cream
1 tablespoon mayonnaise
1 tablespoon lemon juice
1 teaspoon horseradish
sauce
Salt and freshly ground
black pepper
1 tablespoon chopped fresh
chives
1 lb (450 g) cooked beets,
skinned and cut into large
dice
2 hard-cooked eggs, chopped

Put the sour cream, mayonnaise,
lemon juice, horseradish, salt,
pepper and chives in a salad
bowl. Beat with a wooden spoon
until thoroughly mixed. Add the
beets and toss gently to coat.
Sprinkle over the chopped egg
and serve.

Salad niçoise

SERVES FOUR TO SIX

1 lettuce heart, torn into
pieces
1 Spanish onion, finely
sliced
½ lb (225 g) green beans,
cooked whole
3 tomatoes, quartered
1 red pepper, thinly sliced
1 green pepper, thinly sliced
2 hard-cooked eggs, sliced
8 black olives, pitted and
halved
4 anchovy fillets, chopped
½ cup (125 ml) vinaigrette
flavored with garlic

Put the lettuce, onion, beans,
tomatoes, peppers and eggs in a
large salad bowl. Scatter the
olives and anchovies on top. Pour
the dressing over the salad just
before serving.

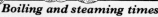

Boiling and steaming times

Belgian or French endive

Endive is always boiled, never
steamed. Plunge in a pan of boiling
water to which 2 teaspoons of sugar
and 1 teaspoon of lemon juice have
been added. Should be tender but
still firm—test through the base.
Boiling   15–20 min

Cauliflower

Use no more than 1 inch (2 cm) of
water in the pan when boiling
cauliflower florets.

A whole cauliflower should be
steamed. Use a vegetable steamer
or trim the base so it will stand in
the saucepan and pour in 1 inch
(2 cm) of boiling water, adding more
as it steams away.
Boiling   10–25 min
Steaming   15–25 min

Broccoli

Separate the stalks and use very
little water as the vegetable tends to
become waterlogged.
Boiling   10–15 min
Steaming   15–20 min

Cabbage, Kale

Cabbages are usually quartered,
sliced or shredded before cooking.
They should be slightly crisp at
the end of the cooking time. Add
1 tablespoon of vinegar or lemon
juice to the water when boiling red
cabbage. Red cabbage and kale are
not usually steamed.
Red, quartered
Boiling   35–40 min
Green and white, quartered, and kale
Boiling   10–15 min
Steaming   15–20 min

Brussels sprouts

Boil Brussels sprouts whole in very
little salted water.
Boiling   10 min
Steaming   15 min

Spinach

Spinach is never steamed. Boil it
in plenty of salted water, then drain
and press. Or cook it without water;
there is enough trapped in the leaves
after washing. Shake the washed
spinach gently and put it into the pan
with a little salt, cover the pan tightly
and cook over moderate heat.
Boiling   7–10 min

Asparagus

Tie stalks in bundles of 10 to 12. To
boil, prop upright with foil in a saucepan, fill with boiling water to just
below tips and cover. The water
must not touch the tips. To steam,
use a steamer or asparagus pan or

place in a glass jar, fill half with boiling water and cover with perforated
foil. Stand jar in saucepan of boiling
water. The stalks should be tender
but not limp. Test in the middle of
the stalk.
Boiling   10–15 min
Steaming   15–20 min

Globe artichoke

Cook whole or remove choke first
and halve the cooking times. The
leaves should pull out easily. The
water must be boiling before the
artichokes are put in the pan.
Boiling   35–40 min
Steaming   40–45 min

Celery, Fennel

Celery and fennel stalks are usually
cut into lengths and the hearts
quartered before being cooked. Use
plenty of salt when boiling. When
cooked, they should be tender but
not limp.
Boiling   10–20 min
Steaming   20 min

Bean sprouts

Steam bean sprouts or simmer them
in a very little salted water, but for
only 2 minutes or they will lose their
crunchy texture.
Boiling   2 min
Steaming   2 min

Shell beans

Very young shell beans are usually
boiled or steamed in their pods.
Shell mature beans first, add 10
minutes to the cooking time and
remove the skin after cooking if
tough. The beans should be tender.
Boiling   10–20 min
Steaming   15–25 min

Lima and other dried beans

Depending on age (old beans are
soaked for a longer period), soak
dried beans in a pan or bowl of
boiling water for between 1 and 3
hours, or soak them overnight in cold
water. Then boil them in salted
water until they are tender.
Boiling   40–180 min

Lentils, Split peas

Lentils and split peas do not have
to be soaked, but it shortens the
cooking time considerably.
Boiling   60 min

Green beans

Cook older beans 5 minutes longer
than young beans because they are
tougher. Cook them whole or sliced.
Boiling   5–10 min
Steaming   10–15 min

Snow peas

Boil snow peas in salted water or steam with a little butter. They should be slightly crisp when cooked.
Boiling　4–5 min
Steaming　5–6 min

Peas

Boil peas in lightly salted water to which a teaspoon of sugar and a few mint leaves may be added.
Boiling　5–10 min

Corn

Corn is not usually steamed. Plunge into a large pan of briskly boiling water to which a little salt (never salt as this toughens the kernels) has been added.
Boiling　5–6 min

Leeks

Leeks can be boiled or steamed whole, halved, split lengthwise down the middle or cut into lengths or rings. Cook until tender.
Boiling　10–20 min
Steaming　15–25 min

Onions

Boil or steam onions until they are very tender. The cooking times are for whole onions. Halve the times for small onions, scallions and shallots.
Boiling　20–30 min
Steaming　30–40 min

Beets

Boil or steam beets whole, and skin after cooking. Do not trim the root end until after cooking or the beets will "bleed" into the cooking liquid. Cook until very tender.
Boiling　90–120 min
Steaming　120 min

Carrot

Cook carrots whole or sliced, and, unless very old, do not peel them before cooking. They should be just tender. Add a little sugar with the salt to the water.
Boiling　15–30 min
Steaming　20–40 min

Celeriac

Peel and dice celeriac or cut into strips and add at least 2 teaspoons of lemon juice to the water.
Boiling　10–30 min
Steaming　35–40 min

Kohlrabi

Peel kohlrabi and cook whole when small; otherwise slice or dice.
Boiling　20–25 min

Parsnip

Cook whole or in thick slices. If old, cut out tough central core.
Boiling　20–35 min
Steaming　35–40 min

Salsify, Scorzonera

Peel and cook whole, or cut into lengths before cooking.
Boiling　15–20 min
Steaming　20–30 min

Rutabaga

Peel rutabagas and cut into cubes or dice; boil until very tender.
Boiling　30–40 min

Turnips

Turnips are always peeled before cooking, and can be boiled or steamed whole or sliced.
Boiling　15–25 min
Steaming　20–30 min

Potato

Cut large potatoes into quarters or small pieces; boil new potatoes whole. Scrub, or peel before or after cooking. Add the potatoes to a pan of cold salted water and bring to a boil slowly.
Boiling　20–40 min

Jerusalem artichoke

Peel after cooking. Boil in water or in milk and water. Should be just tender when cooked.
Boiling　15–20 min
Steaming　20 min

Zucchini, Squash, Cucumber

Cook zucchini unpeeled unless old with tough skins; cook whole or sliced. Overboiling makes them soggy.
　Halve squash or cut into pieces. Cook peeled or unpeeled. Add between 10 and 20 minutes to the cooking times shown. Cucumber, although more generally eaten raw, can be boiled or steamed in the same way as zucchini.
Boiling　10–15 min
Steaming　10–20 min

Mushrooms

Not usually boiled, mushrooms are often steamed for garnishes.
Steaming　15–20 min

Mashed potatoes

There are many different flavorings you can add to mashed potatoes to make them more interesting: grated nutmeg; finely chopped scallions; grated orange rind or grated cheese.

SERVES FOUR

1½ lb (700 g) potatoes, cut into quarters, cooked, peeled and drained
3 tablespoons butter
½ cup (125 ml) hot milk or cream
Salt and pepper

Put the potatoes in a large saucepan and put the pan over moderate heat. Shake the pan over the heat for a few minutes to dry the potatoes out. Mash the potatoes in the pan, gradually adding the butter and the milk. Season to taste and finish off by beating the potatoes with a wooden spoon.

Potato salad

This salad is delicious served with cold meats.

SERVES FOUR

1½ lb (700 g) boiled potatoes, cut into cubes and kept hot
6 scallions or a bunch of chives, chopped
½ cup (125 ml) vinaigrette dressing
1 tablespoon French mustard
Salt and freshly ground pepper

Put the hot potatoes into a salad bowl. Mix the remaining ingredients in a small bowl and pour the dressing over the potatoes. Toss and serve hot or cold.

Lima beans with garlic

SERVES FOUR

1 lb (450 g) lima beans, cooked and drained
2 tablespoons butter, melted
2 garlic cloves, crushed
1 teaspoon salt
1 tablespoon chopped parsley
1 teaspoon lemon juice
Freshly ground pepper

Put the beans into a saucepan over low heat. Add the butter, garlic, salt, parsley, lemon juice and pepper. Stir until the mixture is hot and serve at once.

Kidney bean salad

SERVES SIX

1 lb (450 g) kidney beans, cooked and drained
1 onion, very thinly sliced
6 tablespoons vinaigrette dressing
1 teaspoon French mustard

Put the beans and onion in a salad bowl. Mix the vinaigrette dressing with the mustard and spoon it over the vegetables. Toss well before serving.

Lentil salad

Serve lentil salad as a first course with brown bread and butter or as a winter salad.

SERVES FOUR

½ lb (225 g) green or orange lentils, cooked, puréed and cooled
1 garlic clove, crushed
4 tablespoons vinaigrette dressing
1 tablespoon lemon juice
Salt and pepper
1 onion, very finely chopped
3 gherkins, finely chopped
2 tomatoes, thinly sliced
2 hard-cooked eggs, thinly sliced
10 black olives, pitted

Mix the lentil purée with the garlic, vinaigrette, lemon juice, salt and lots of pepper. Add the onion and gherkins. Place in a serving dish and garnish with the tomato and egg slices and black olives.

Lima bean and mackerel salad

SERVES FOUR

½ cup (125 ml) sour cream
2 teaspoons lemon juice
2 teaspoons paprika
Salt and freshly ground black pepper
2 teaspoons finely grated orange rind
2 shallots, very finely sliced
½ lb (225 g) cooked lima beans
1 smoked mackerel, skinned, boned and flaked

Put the sour cream, lemon juice, paprika, salt, pepper and orange rind in a salad bowl and stir well. Add the remaining ingredients, toss gently but thoroughly and serve.

Fruit

Fruit makes some of the most delightful and refreshing desserts from the simplest compotes to the most elaborate charlottes. In midsummer, during the height of the soft fruit season, less-than-perfect fruit may be used to make compotes, water ices and purées for the freezer. A dried fruit compote can be made at any time of the year. A mixture of dried fruit and apples or pears is also delicious. For four servings, soak one pound (450 g) dried fruit in wine, wine and brandy or rum mixed, or in water overnight. Simmer in the soaking liquid for twenty minutes or until the fruit is soft. Add sugar if you prefer a sweeter dessert. Chill the compote well and serve it with cream.

Fresh fruit compote

Serve the compote well chilled with cream or custard sauce.

SERVES FOUR

¾ cup (175 g) sugar
1 cup (250 ml) water
2 lb (900 g) fresh mixed fruit (plums, cherries, blueberries, apricots, red currants and black currants), pitted and prepared
2-inch (5-cm) piece stick cinnamon
1 level teaspoon arrowroot
¼ cup (65 ml) white wine

Put the sugar and water in a saucepan, stir to dissolve the sugar, and boil for 5 minutes. Add the fruit to the syrup with the cinnamon and simmer gently for 5 minutes. Using a slotted spoon, remove the fruit to a serving dish.

Blend the arrowroot with the wine in a cup and stir it into the syrup. Increase the heat and boil for 1 minute. Remove the pan from the heat and let the syrup cool. Strain the syrup over the fruit.

Fresh peaches in vanilla syrup

Apricots may be substituted for the peaches. Use 2 pounds (900 g) of apricots, 1½ cups (350 g) of vanilla sugar and 3¾ cups (900 ml) of water.

Serve well chilled with cream.

SERVES SIX

6 large peaches
1 cup (225 g) vanilla sugar
2¼ cups (575 ml) water

Put the peaches into a large bowl and cover with boiling water. Leave for 2 minutes, then drain and peel. Cut the peaches in half and remove and discard the pits.

Dissolve the sugar in the water in a large saucepan. Add the peach halves, cover the pan and simmer gently for 5 minutes or until the peaches are just tender. Using a slotted spoon, remove the peaches from the syrup and arrange them on a serving dish. Increase the heat and boil the syrup rapidly until it reduces and thickens a little, then pour it over the fruit.

Serve cold.

Pears in red wine

Serve the pears chilled with whipped cream.

SERVES SIX

1 cup (225 g) sugar
½ cup (125 ml) water
2 cups (500 ml) red wine
1-inch (2-cm) piece stick cinnamon
6 firm pears
1 lemon

Dissolve the sugar in the water over low heat. Add the wine and cinnamon and bring to a boil. Reduce the heat and simmer for 10 minutes.

Meanwhile, peel the pears, leaving the stalks attached and making sure the bases are flat enough for them to stand upright. Rub the pears all over with the lemon to prevent them from discoloring. Place the pears close together, upright, in a large saucepan. Pour in the simmering wine syrup. Cover the pan and poach gently, basting occasionally, for 30 to 90 minutes or until the pears are tender.

Using a slotted spoon, lift the pears from the pan and arrange

them, standing upright, in a serving dish.

Remove and discard the cinnamon. Increase the heat and boil the syrup until it is reduced and has the consistency of a fairly heavy syrup.

Spoon the syrup over the pears. Put the pears in the refrigerator to chill, basting the fruit with the syrup occasionally.

Oranges in caramel
SERVES FOUR

5 large oranges
½ cup (125 g) sugar

Peel 4 oranges, taking great care to remove the pith as well. Shred the peel of 1 orange finely and set aside. Slice the oranges, removing the seeds, and put the slices together again in their original shape. Arrange them in a serving dish.

Put the sugar into a small, heavy saucepan and stir over low heat until it has melted and is caramel in color. Initially the sugar will be lumpy, but it will become smooth as it turns into a syrup.

Draw the pan off the heat and stir in ¼ cup of water. Return the pan to the heat and stir until the caramel is dissolved in the water. Remove the pan from the heat and stir in the juice from the remaining orange and the shredded peel. Let the syrup cool before pouring it over the oranges. Serve chilled.

Cherries jubilee with vanilla ice cream
SERVES SIX

1 cup (225 g) sugar
2½ cups (575 ml) water
Salt
1½ lb (700 g) cherries, pitted
2 teaspoons cornstarch
Vanilla ice cream
Up to ½ cup (125 ml) brandy

Dissolve the sugar in the water over low heat. Add a pinch of salt

Refreshing, colorful and simple, these fruit desserts are the perfect ending to a meal. On the top: oranges in caramel and cherries jubilee. Below: pears in red wine.

and bring to a boil. Add the cherries, reduce the heat to low, cover the pan and simmer gently for 8 to 10 minutes or until they are tender. Drain the cherries. Return the syrup to the pan and boil it rapidly until it is reduced to 1¼ cups.

Combine the cornstarch with a little cold water and add it to the syrup very gradually. Simmer, stirring, for 2 minutes. Add the cherries and remove the pan from the heat.

Spoon the ice cream into a bowl or into individual serving dishes.

Warm the brandy in a ladle or in a small pan, pour it over the cherry mixture and ignite with a match. Pour the flaming cherries over the ice cream.

Serve at once.

Rhubarb fool

All fruit fools are made in the same way, but some fruit require no preliminary cooking before they are puréed. The purée may be smooth or, if you prefer a coarser texture, crush the fruit with a fork instead of pushing it through a nylon strainer. Use granulated sugar except for rhubarb fool and, if you prefer it, use a custard sauce instead of the cream.

Garnish rhubarb fool with toasted almonds or freshly grated lemon rind and serve it with plain crisp cookies or ladyfingers.

SERVES SIX

2 lb (900 g) rhubarb
2 tablespoons water
Grated rind of 1 small
**   orange**
Dark brown sugar
1¼ cups (315 ml) whipping
**   cream, lightly whipped**

Wash the rhubarb and cut into pieces. Put it in a saucepan with the water and grated orange rind. Cover the pan and simmer gently for about 5 minutes or until the rhubarb is tender.

Drain the rhubarb and rub it through a sieve or put it in a blender. If the purée is too stiff, add a little of the cooking liquid. Add sugar to taste and leave the purée to cool completely before folding in the cream. Taste the fool and add more sugar if necessary. Spoon into individual dishes and chill.

Fruit

Summer pudding

Black currants or red currants, raspberries, blackberries and mulberries are all suitable for this pudding.

SERVES SIX

2 tablespoons sugar
1 cup (250 ml) water
2 apples, peeled, cored and sliced
1½ lb (700 g) mixed berries, washed
1 loaf stale white bread
Butter
1 teaspoon arrowroot

Put the sugar and water into a saucepan and stir over low heat until the sugar dissolves. Boil rapidly for 5 minutes. Add the fruit, cover the pan and simmer for about 10 minutes.

Strain the fruit, reserving the juice. Rub the fruit through a strainer to make a purée. Add half the reserved juice to the purée. Taste the purée, adding more sugar if necessary.

Slice the bread thinly, removing the crusts. Grease a 1-quart (1-liter) pudding mold with a little butter. Line the mold with overlapping slices of bread. Spoon over enough purée to cover the bottom of the mold. Put a layer of bread on top. Repeat this layering of bread and purée until the mold is full. Finish with a layer of bread. Cover the mold with a plate and weigh it down with a heavy weight and leave overnight.

Mix the arrowroot with a little of the reserved juice. Put the rest of the juice into a saucepan and bring to a boil. Add the arrowroot mixture, stirring well, and continue stirring until the sauce has thickened. Remove the pan from the heat. Cool and then chill the sauce.

Turn the pudding out onto a serving dish. Pour some of the sauce over the pudding and serve the rest separately.

Danish apple cake

SERVES SIX

½ cup (125 g) butter
1½ lb (700 g) apples, peeled, cored and sliced
Peel of ½ lemon
2 tablespoons sugar
2 cups (225 g) coarse fresh white bread crumbs
1 cup (250 ml) cream

Melt 1 tablespoon of the butter in a heavy saucepan and coat the bottom of the pan with it. Add the apples, lemon peel and sugar. Cover the pan and cook gently until the apples are transparent but still keep their shape. Remove the pan from the heat and discard the peel.

Melt the remaining butter in a frying pan and fry the bread crumbs until they are golden.

Arrange half the apples in a layer in a medium-sized dish. Use half the crumbs for the next layer, then the rest of the apples, and finally another layer of crumbs. Cover the dish with foil or plastic wrap and put it in the refrigerator to chill.

Serve cold with the cream.

Pommes aux fruits glacés

This jellied apple dessert requires no gelatin as the pectin in the fruit sets naturally.

SERVES FOUR TO SIX

⅓ cup (50 g) candied orange and lemon peel, coarsely chopped
4 tablespoons rum
2 cups (450 g) sugar
½ cup (125 ml) water
Rind and juice of 1 lemon
3 lb (1½ kg) tart cooking apples
½ cup (50 g) walnuts, coarsely chopped
¼ pint (125 ml) whipping cream, whipped

Put the candied orange and lemon peel in a cup with the rum to soak.

Dissolve the sugar in the water in a pan over very low heat. Add the lemon rind and juice.

Peel, core and thinly slice the apples. Add to the syrup. Increase the heat to high and boil rapidly, stirring constantly, for 20 minutes. If the mixture is still too liquid, boil it for 5 minutes longer. Be careful not to let the apples stick or burn. Remove the pan from the heat.

Sieve the apples. Stir in the walnuts and the candied peel and rum. Pour the apple mixture into a lightly oiled 1½-pint (900-ml) mold. Cover the mold and put it in the refrigerator for at least 6 hours or overnight.

Turn the jellied apple out onto a serving dish. Decorate with the whipped cream and serve.

Red berry delight

This traditional Danish dessert is made with any red berry or a combination of red berries.

SERVES SIX

½ lb (225 g) each red currants, raspberries, cranberries and strawberries
Sugar
Arrowroot
1 tablespoon sliced almonds
1 cup (250 ml) cream

Put the berries in a saucepan with 3 tablespoons of water. Bring to a simmer and cook until the skins burst and the juice runs out.

Push the fruit through a fine sieve, measure the purée and return it to the saucepan. Add sugar to taste.

To every 2 cups of the fruit purée measure 2 teaspoons of arrowroot. Mix the arrowroot with 2 tablespoons of water and stir into the purée. Bring the mixture to a simmer and cook for 30 seconds or until the purée thickens. Remove the pan from the heat.

Pour the mixture into a serving dish. Scatter the almonds over the top. Cover the dish and put it into the refrigerator to chill well. Serve with the cream.

Black currant mousse

Raspberries may be used instead of black currants or the two can be used in combination with excellent results.

SERVES SIX

1 lb (450 g) black currants, stripped off their stalks and washed
3 to 4 tablespoons sugar
1 tablespoon gelatin
2 tablespoons orange juice
1 cup (250 ml) whipping cream, whipped until thick but not stiff
3 egg whites, stiffly beaten

Put the black currants and the sugar—use the lesser amount adding more if necessary—in a saucepan and cook for a few minutes, stirring until the juice runs from the fruit and the sugar dissolves. Press the fruit through a sieve to make a purée and set aside to cool completely.

Dissolve the gelatin in the orange juice over low heat and stir it into the black currant purée. When the purée begins to thicken, gently fold in half of the whipped cream and then the stiffly beaten egg whites. Turn the mixture into a medium-sized soufflé dish, cover the top with plastic wrap and put it in the refrigerator to set.

Decorate the mousse with the remaining whipped cream and serve.

Strawberry mousse

Serve strawberry mousse with small macaroons or lady fingers.

SERVES SIX

1 tablespoon gelatin
2 lb (900 g) strawberries
1 cup (250 ml) whipping cream
4 tablespoons fine granulated sugar
4 eggs, separated
2 tablespoons Kirsch

Dissolve the gelatin in 2 tablespoons of water over low heat. Crush the berries in a bowl.

Put the cream, sugar and egg yolks in the top of a double boiler and beat over barely simmering water until the custard is smooth and thick. Stir in the gelatin, strawberries and Kirsch. Taste the mixture and add more sugar if necessary. Set aside to cool, stirring occasionally.

Whip the egg whites until they are stiff and fold them into the strawberry mixture. Pour the mousse into a glass bowl and refrigerate until well chilled and set.

Black currant kissel

SERVES FOUR

1 lb (450 g) black currants
Grated rind of ½ lemon
1½ cups (375 ml) white wine
½ cup (125 g) sugar
2 tablespoons arrowroot

Simmer the black currants and lemon rind in half the wine for 20 minutes. Purée the fruit, stir in the sugar and return the mixture to the pan.

Mix the arrowroot with 3 tablespoons of the remaining wine. Stir it into the fruit purée with the rest of the wine and cook, stirring, until the kissel thickens. Serve warm or cold.

Cereals

Most of the rice that is available in the West is either long-grain or short-grain. Such long-grain varieties as Basmati or Patna are served with curries or used to make pilaffs. Short-grain rice, for example Arborio, which comes from Italy, is used to make risottos. Although it is long-grained, Carolina rice is usually reserved for making desserts.

All rice, except Italian rice, should be rinsed under cold running water until the water runs clear. After washing, soak long-grain rice for about thirty minutes in cold water. The longer the rice soaks, the less time it will take to cook.

Preprocessed rice should be prepared and cooked according to the instructions on the package.

To boil long-grain rice, use two cups (500 ml) of water for every cup (175 g) of rice. The juice of half a lemon added to the water will keep the rice perfectly white. Put the rice, the water and a teaspoon of salt into the saucepan and bring to a fast boil. Cover the pan, reduce the heat to very low and simmer for fifteen to twenty minutes or until the rice is cooked and all the water has been absorbed.

Pasta should be cooked in large quantities of boiling, salted water. Bring the water to a fast boil, add the pasta gradually so that the water does not stop boiling and cook for five to six minutes if the pasta is homemade. Store-bought pasta should be cooked for about eleven minutes or the time recommended on the package. When cooked, pasta should be tender and what the Italians call *al dente*, or resistant to the bite. Drain the cooked pasta, then toss it in butter and serve with a sauce or with plenty of freshly grated Parmesan cheese.

Spaghetti with pesto

Pesto is a famous Genovese sauce that is eaten with many kinds of pasta and is the traditional flavoring for Genovese minestrone. The dish may be served with grated Parmesan cheese.

SERVES FOUR

1 handful fresh basil, washed and chopped
½ cup (125 ml) blanched pine nuts
2 garlic cloves
½ cup (50 g) Parmesan cheese
½ cup (125 ml) olive oil
1 lb (450 g) spaghetti
4 tablespoons butter

Blend the basil, nuts and garlic in a blender to form a smooth paste. Or use a mortar and pestle. Add the cheese and then, with the blender at low speed, drip the oil in very slowly, making sure that it is binding with the paste before adding more.

Cook the spaghetti, drain it and transfer it to a hot serving dish. Toss the spaghetti with the butter and the pesto sauce and serve immediately.

Noodles Alfredo

SERVES FOUR

½ cup (125 g) butter
1 lb (450 g) fresh noodles, cooked and kept hot
Freshly ground black pepper
½ cup (125 ml) cream
4 slices prosciutto ham, cut into strips
1 cup (125 g) Parmesan cheese, grated

Melt the butter in a saucepan over low heat. Add the noodles, black pepper, cream and ham and toss well over the heat until the mixture is heated through and well blended. Serve immediately with the grated cheese.

Ravioli

Both the fillings are enough for this amount of pasta dough.

Serve the ravioli with melted butter, grated Parmesan cheese, or with hot tomato sauce.

SERVES FOUR TO SIX

½ recipe pasta dough
Veal or cheese filling
2 tablespoons butter
1 cup Parmesan cheese, grated

Divide the dough in half (or in quarters if your board is not large enough). Roll out the dough on a floured board as thinly as possible. Put the rolled-out dough on a clean cloth and cover it with another cloth while rolling out the remaining dough.

Using one sheet of dough as the base of the ravioli, put a teaspoonful of filling at regular intervals, about 1½ inches (3 cm) apart. Moisten with water around the filling. Lift the other (slightly larger) sheet of dough and put it on top—this should lie loosely over the filling. Using a wheel or sharp knife, cut between the rows of filling, separating each ravioli. Make sure that the edges are well pressed together so that no filling can escape. Put the prepared ravioli on a floured surface until ready for use—but do not stack them—and cover with a floured cloth if they are not to be cooked at once. They will keep for up to a day.

Bring plenty of salted water to a gentle boil in a large pan. Slip the ravioli in and cook for 6 to 8 minutes or until they rise in the pan. Using a slotted spoon, lift the ravioli out of the water and put into a heated dish. Serve with the butter and cheese.

VEAL FILLING

1 tablespoon butter
1 lb (450 g) ground veal
Salt and pepper
1 garlic clove, crushed
1 teaspoon mixed chopped sage and rosemary

Melt the butter in a saucepan. Add the veal and fry, stirring with a fork, until it is lightly browned. Season well and add the garlic and herbs. Reduce the heat, cover the pan and cook for about 40 minutes, stirring occasionally. Cool before using.

CHEESE FILLING

1 cup (125 g) grated Parmesan cheese
1½ cups (175 g) grated Provolone cheese
¼ cup (50 ml) milk
3 eggs, beaten
Nutmeg
Marjoram
Salt and pepper

Mix all the ingredients together.

To make ravioli

Roll out two thin pasta sheets. Spoon filling over one sheet.

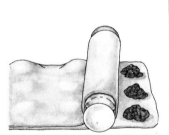

Lift the second sheet of dough over to cover the filling.

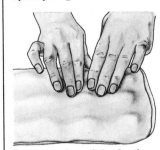

Press the edges of the dough together around the filling.

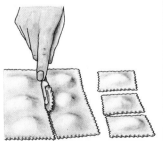

Using a wheel or sharp knife, cut the ravioli into squares.

Cereals

Gnocchi di semolina

SERVES FOUR

2½ cups (575 ml) milk
¾ cup (125 g) semolina
Salt and pepper
Nutmeg
1 cup (125 g) grated
  Parmesan
4 slices ham, chopped
2 eggs, beaten
¼ cup (50 g) butter

Pour the milk into the top part of a double boiler and place over moderate heat. When the milk is almost boiling, add the semolina and salt, pepper and nutmeg to taste. Reduce the heat to fairly low and cook, stirring, for about 40 minutes or until the mixture is very thick and stiff.

Remove the pan from the heat and stir in ¾ cup of the cheese, the ham and eggs. Pour the mixture into a shallow greased pan. Cool and chill briefly. When the gnocchi is quite cold, cut it into circles, using a cookie cutter.

Overlap the circles in a casserole. Dot with the butter and brown under a hot broiler. Sprinkle with the remaining grated cheese and serve at once.

Polenta

Polenta can be bought either coarsely or finely ground. It may be used to make gnocchi or it can be boiled, sliced, fried and served with tomato sauce.

SERVES SIX

5 cups (1¼ liters) water
Salt
1½ cups (225 g) cornmeal
  (polenta)
½ cup (50 g) grated Parmesan
½ teaspoon paprika
¼ cup (50 g) butter

Put 1 cup of cold salted water in a bowl and stir in the cornmeal.

Bring 4 cups of water to a boil in a saucepan. Stir in the cornmeal and cook for about 10 minutes, stirring frequently. Pour the mixture into a loaf pan and set aside to cool. When it is cool, chill in the refrigerator for 2 hours.

Turn the polenta out and cut it into fairly thick slices. Arrange the slices, overlapping, in a buttered shallow casserole. Sprinkle the cheese and paprika over the top. Dot with the butter and broil until browned.

Christmas pudding

MAKES THREE PUDDINGS

1 tablespoon butter
4 cups (450 g) bread crumbs
  from a homemade whole
  wheat loaf
3½ cups (400 g) sifted flour
1½ cups (350 g) golden raisins
1½ cups (350 g) raisins
3 cups (450 g) currants
¾ lb (350 g) grated suet
1½ cups (225 g) candied peel
1½ cups (225 g) candied
  cherries
1½ cups (350 g) dark brown
  sugar
2 tart apples, grated
4 carrots, grated
⅔ cup (125 g) blanched
  almonds, chopped
1 tablespoon grated nutmeg
1 tablespoon molasses
7 eggs, beaten
2½ cups (575 ml) beer
½ cup (125 ml) brandy
1 teaspoon salt

Using the tablespoon of butter, grease three 1-quart (1-liter) pudding molds.

Mix all the ingredients together in a large mixing bowl, using a wooden spoon. Divide the mixture between the pudding molds and smooth the tops down with the back of the spoon. Cover each mold with waxed paper and floured cheesecloth with a 1-inch (2-cm) fold in the center. Tie the cloths firmly around the rims of the molds.

Use a steamer or put the pudding molds into a deep kettle (steam the puddings separately unless you have a very large kettle) and pour enough boiling water into the kettle to come halfway up the sides of the mold. Put the kettle over moderate heat. Cover tightly and steam for 6 hours, adding more boiling water to the kettle from time to time.

When the puddings have been cooked, store them for at least 6 months in an airtight container in a cool, damp-free place.

At serving time, repeat the steaming process for 3 hours and remove them from the molds.

From left to right : orange sponge pudding, spaghetti with pesto, and cooked, filled ravioli.

Boston steamed bread

MAKES ONE LOAF

1 cup (125 g) whole wheat flour
1¼ cups (125 g) rye flour
¾ cup (125 g) cornmeal
1 level teaspoon soda
½ teaspoon salt
½ cup (125 g) dark raisins
½ cup (125 ml) blackstrap molasses
1¼ cups (315 ml) buttermilk

Mix the dry ingredients together. Make a well in the center and pour in the molasses and buttermilk. Using a wooden spoon, mix the liquids together and gradually add the flour mixture. Continue stirring until all ingredients are well combined.

Grease a 1-quart (1-liter) pudding mold. Pour in the mixture. Cover the mold with greased foil and tie it tightly under the rim.

Put the pudding mold in a kettle containing 1 inch (2 cm) of boiling water. Cover the kettle and cook for 3 hours, adding more water as it evaporates.

Serve the bread hot or cold.

Porridge

Serve with salt, sugar or syrup and milk or cream.

SERVES FOUR

2½ cups (575 ml) water
1 rounded teaspoon salt
⅔ cup (125 g) oatmeal

Bring the water to a boil and add the salt. Add the oatmeal gradually, keeping the water at a boil and stirring continuously with a wooden spoon to mix the oatmeal thoroughly. Simmer gently for 15 minutes, stirring occasionally.

Creamed rice pudding

SERVES FOUR

3 tablespoons rice, washed and drained
2½ cups (575 ml) milk
Vanilla bean
1 tablespoon sugar
½ cup (125 ml) whipping cream

Put the rice in the top of a double boiler with the milk and vanilla bean. Cook gently, stirring occasionally, for 1½ hours or until the rice is soft and creamy. Stir in the sugar. Remove the pan from the heat. Remove the vanilla bean and cool the rice. When the rice is cold, fold in the whipped cream. Chill for at least 1 hour before serving.

Orange sponge pudding

This sponge pudding can be made with other flavorings. Add 2 tablespoons of preserved ginger and 1 teaspoon of ground ginger. Or put 4 tablespoons of corn syrup into the pudding mold before pouring in the sponge mixture.

SERVES FOUR TO SIX

½ cup (125 g) butter
½ cup (125 g) sugar
2 eggs
1 cup (125 g) sifted self-rising flour
Juice and finely grated rind of 1 large orange
Milk

Cream the butter and sugar together in a mixing bowl. Beat in the eggs one by one, adding 1 tablespoon of the flour with each egg. Fold in the remaining flour with the orange rind and juice. The batter should drop easily from the spoon, so stir in a little milk if necessary.

Pour the mixture into a greased 1½-pint (900-ml) pudding mold. Cover the top with a piece of aluminum foil with a 1-inch (2-cm) fold in the center. Tie down securely with string. Put the pudding in a large kettle and pour enough boiling water into the kettle to come halfway up the sides of the mold. Cover the kettle and steam the pudding for 1½ to 2 hours. Add more boiling water to the kettle if necessary.

Eggs and dairy products

Boiling eggs is not usually considered to be one of the more demanding kitchen tasks. Even this, however, can be done in more than one way. The most usual method is as follows:

Fill a saucepan with enough water to cover the eggs and bring to a boil. Lower the eggs into the water with a spoon; if they have been kept at room temperature for about an hour, they are less likely to crack. In three and a half to four minutes the eggs will be soft cooked—the yolks will be runny and the whites fairly soft. In about another minute the whites will firm up. At this stage they are what the French call *oeufs mollets*, which can be substituted, often with advantage, for poached eggs. In seven to ten minutes the eggs will be hard cooked. Very fresh eggs take about one minute longer to cook.

Another method is to put the eggs in a pan, cover with boiling water and leave them, away from the heat, for about ten minutes, when they will be lightly cooked. Alternatively, they may be put into a pan of cold water (a good method if you keep your eggs in the refrigerator) and brought to a boil slowly, by which time they will be lightly cooked. For a firm white, either continue simmering for half a minute or turn off the heat and leave the eggs covered for another minute. For hard-cooked eggs cook for five minutes after the water has come to a simmer. Eggs cooked by either of these methods have more tender whites than those cooked by the first method.

If you are hard-boiling eggs, put them into cold water as soon as they are cooked. This will prevent an unappetizing gray rim appearing between the yolk and the white, and also makes it easier to shell the eggs. If they are not to be used immediately, keep them in a bowl of cold water until needed.

Technically, poached eggs are also cooked by immersion in boiling, or more usually barely simmering, water, but without their shells. Egg poachers actually steam the eggs rather than poach them and the results are tougher and not so light as true poached eggs.

To poach an egg, bring a pan (preferably a frying pan) of water to a boil. Add one tablespoon of wine vinegar—this helps to coagulate the whites. Some people also add a tablespoon of salt. Break each egg separately into a cup and slide it into the water. (It is difficult to poach more than two eggs at a time.) When the water comes back to a boil, remove the pan from the heat, cover it and leave for three and a half to four minutes. Use a slotted spoon to lift the eggs out of the water, then drain them on paper towels. Trim off any straggly pieces of white. If the eggs are not needed immediately, they can be kept in a bowl of cold water for a few hours. To reheat put the eggs in hot water.

If the eggs are boiled for just one minute before being shelled, this will help to prevent the whites from spreading out when the eggs are dropped into the poaching water. In this case they will be cooked in two and a half to three minutes after coming back to a boil.

Eggs in crispy rolls

These eggs may be served with béarnaise sauce.

SERVES FOUR

4 eggs
6 tablespoons butter, melted
1 garlic clove, crushed
Salt and pepper
2 teaspoons chopped fresh tarragon or chives
4 soft round rolls

Preheat the oven to 425°F (220°C).

Bring a pan of water to a boil, lower the eggs into the water, let the water return to a boil and cook for about 5 minutes. Remove the eggs from the pan and plunge them into cold water. Leave for 10 minutes before removing the shells.

Meanwhile, mix the melted butter, garlic, salt, pepper and herbs together in a cup.

Cut the tops off the rolls and scoop out their centers. Brush the insides of the rolls generously with some of the butter mixture and then bake for about 5 minutes or until the rolls are crisp.

Heat the eggs for 30 seconds in a pan of hot salted water. Drain the eggs and put one into each roll. Spoon the remaining butter mixture over the eggs. Serve at once.

Eggs Florentine with ham

SERVES SIX

6 eggs
1¾ cups (425 ml) béchamel sauce
6 tablespoons grated Gruyère cheese
6 slices ham
2 lb (900 g) fresh spinach, cooked, drained and kept warm in an ovenproof dish

Boil the eggs and shell them as in the preceding recipe. Heat the béchamel sauce in a saucepan and stir in half of the cheese. If necessary, reheat the eggs by immersing them in hot water for 30 seconds. Wrap each egg in a slice of ham and then place them on the spinach and coat them with the sauce.

Sprinkle the remaining cheese on the top of the sauce and brown under the broiler.

Serve at once.

Taramasalata eggs

Serve the eggs on a bed of wilted cucumber. To make wilted cucumber, slice the cucumber thinly and layer it in a bowl with salt. Put a weighted plate on top and leave it in the refrigerator for 2 hours. Drain, rinse and dry the cucumber.

SERVES SIX

6 eggs, hard-cooked
¼ lb (125 g) smoked cod's roe
2 slices crustless white bread, soaked in milk
1 garlic clove, crushed
2 tablespoons olive oil
2 teaspoons lemon juice
Pepper

Cut the eggs in half lengthwise, using a knife that has been dipped into water. Scoop out the yolks and rub them through a strainer.

Remove the skin from the cod's roe and squeeze out the milk from the bread. Beat the roe, bread and garlic together in a bowl, gradually mixing in the oil and lemon juice, until the paste is perfectly smooth. Or put the ingredients into a blender. Season with pepper. Stir in the egg yolks. Pipe or spoon the mixture into the egg whites.

Eggs in aspic

Chopped ham or chopped smoked salmon may be used instead of the crabmeat.

SERVES SIX

1¼ cups (315 ml) aspic
1 cup (125 g) crabmeat
6 eggs, poached, cooled and drained
2 pieces canned pimiento
2 to 3 scallions

Cool the aspic slightly. Arrange the crabmeat in 6 individual soufflé dishes or ramekins, spoon a thin layer of aspic over the crabmeat and put the dishes in the refrigerator to set. When the aspic is firm, put an egg into each ramekin.

Cut the green tops of the scallions into leaf shapes and the pieces of pimiento into flowers or other decorative shapes. Warm the aspic slightly and dip the leaves and flowers into it and arrange them on top of the eggs. Spoon over the remaining aspic carefully. Chill in the refrigerator before serving.

Swiss fondue

SERVES FOUR TO SIX

1 garlic clove
1½ cups (375 ml) white wine
¾ lb (350 g) Emmenthal cheese, grated
¾ lb (350 g) Gruyère cheese, grated
1 teaspoon cornstarch
3 tablespoons Kirsch
French bread, cut into 1-inch (2-cm) cubes

Rub an earthenware casserole or cast-iron pan with the garlic. Pour in the wine and set it over low heat. As the wine begins to heat, stir in the cheese, a handful at a time. Continue stirring until all the cheese has been added and the mixture is creamy. Mix the cornstarch with the Kirsch and add it to the fondue.

Put the casserole over an alcohol burner (with the flame turned down to low) on the dinner table. Serve with cubes of bread.

Curried eggs

SERVES FOUR

¼ cup (50 g) clarified butter
1 large onion, sliced
1 to 2 tablespoons curry powder mixed with a little water
1 tablespoon flour
1¾ cups (425 ml) chicken stock
1 tablespoon mango chutney
1 tablespoon raisins
2 teaspoons lemon juice
Salt and pepper
Scant 2 cups (350 g) rice, cooked
6 eggs, hard-cooked

Preheat the oven to 350°F (180°C).

Melt the butter in a saucepan. Add the onion and fry until golden and transparent. Add the curry paste and fry, stirring constantly, for 1 minute. Stir in the flour. Gradually add the stock and bring to a boil, stirring to prevent lumps. Reduce the heat and simmer for 15 minutes. Stir in the chutney, raisins, lemon juice and seasoning. Cover and remove from the heat.

Cut the eggs in half lengthwise. Put the rice into a shallow ovenproof serving dish. Arrange the eggs on top. Pour the sauce over the eggs, cover the dish and put it in the oven for 15 minutes.

Charlotte russe

You can alter the flavor of the custard: for example try 4 tablespoons of sherry instead of the lemon juice and rind.

SERVES SIX

½ cup (125 ml) lemon-flavored gelatin
6 candied lemon slices
24 ladyfingers
1 cup (250 ml) milk
4 egg yolks
⅓ to ½ cup (65 to 125 g) sugar
Salt
1 teaspoon cornstarch
2 teaspoons unflavored gelatin
2 tablespoons hot water
¼ cup (65 ml) lemon juice
Grated rind of 1 lemon
1½ cups (375 ml) whipping cream

Lightly oil the bottom of a 1-quart (1-liter) charlotte mold. Pour a thin layer of the lemon gelatin into the mold. When the gelatin is nearly set, arrange the candied lemon slices on top. Pour another thin layer of the gelatin on top. Arrange the ladyfingers upright around the sides of the mold, pushing the ends into the gelatin. Trim them to fit and chill in the refrigerator.

Scald the milk by bringing it to just below boiling point. Mix the egg yolks, sugar to taste, pinch of salt and the cornstarch in a bowl. Pour in a little hot milk and beat well. Gradually add the rest of the milk. Pour the egg and milk mixture into the top half of a double boiler and cook over low heat, stirring constantly, until the mixture is smooth and slightly thickened. Do not let the custard boil. Remove the pan from the heat.

Dissolve the unflavored gelatin in 2 tablespoons of hot water and pour it into the custard, stirring until it is well mixed. Let it cool. When the custard is cool, stir in the lemon juice and grated lemon rind. Pour the custard into a bowl and put it in the refrigerator until it is quite cold and very nearly set.

Whip the cream until it is thick but not stiff and fold two-thirds of it into the custard. Pour the mixture into the lined mold. Chill the charlotte for 2 to 3 hours or until it has set. Unmold the charlotte onto a serving platter and decorate with the remaining whipped cream.

Charlotte russe

Arrange the ladyfingers around the sides of the mold.

Carefully trim the ladyfingers to fit the mold.

Spoon the nearly set custard into the lined mold.

Unmold the charlotte and decorate it with whipped cream.

Lemon mousse

SERVES FOUR

4 eggs, separated
3 tablespoons sugar
Grated rind and juice of 2 large lemons
2 teaspoons gelatin
1¾ cups (425 ml) whipping cream, whipped
2 tablespoons almonds, blanched, toasted and finely chopped

Put the egg yolks, sugar, lemon rind and juice into a bowl and beat over hot water until thick and mousse-like.

Put the gelatin in a cup with 2 tablespoons of cold water and stand the cup in hot water, away from the heat, to dissolve the gelatin. Mix the gelatin into the egg and lemon mixture.

Put the bowl on ice and continue beating from time to time, until the mixture is cold but not completely set.

Fold in most of the cream. Beat the egg whites until stiff and fold them into the lemon mixture. Put the mousse into a serving bowl or into a small soufflé dish with a paper collar. Put the mousse into the refrigerator to chill thoroughly.

Before serving, remove the paper collar and decorate the mousse with the almonds and the remaining whipped cream.

Chocolate mousse

SERVES FOUR TO SIX

8 squares (225 g) semisweet chocolate
6 tablespoons water or coffee
2 tablespoons butter
2 tablespoons rum
4 eggs, separated

Melt the chocolate in the water over very low heat. Remove the pan from the heat and beat in the butter and the rum. Beat in the egg yolks one at a time.

Beat the egg whites until they are stiff and mix them into the chocolate mixture. Spoon the mousse into small crème pots, cover the pots and refrigerate for up to 24 hours before serving.

Preparing a soufflé dish

Tie a band of waxed paper around a soufflé dish to support a mousse until it sets or to make a raised soufflé.

Eggs and dairy products

Crème brulée

SERVES FOUR

4 egg yolks, well beaten
Fine sugar
2 cups (500 ml) whipping cream
1-inch (2-cm) piece of vanilla bean or 1 teaspoon (5 ml) vanilla extract

Combine the egg yolks with 1 tablespoon of sugar in a bowl.

Put the cream and vanilla bean into a saucepan, bring slowly to boiling point and boil for one minute exactly. Remove the pan from the heat, lift out the vanilla bean and pour the cream over the egg yolks and sugar, stirring all the time with a spoon. Strain the mixture into the top of a double boiler and cook, stirring constantly, for 25 minutes or until the custard is thick enough to coat the back of a wooden spoon. Pour the custard into a buttered, ovenproof serving dish, allow it to cool then chill in the refrigerator.

Sprinkle a layer of fine sugar to a depth of $\frac{1}{3}$ inch (1 cm) over the surface of the custard. Put the dish under a very hot broiler until the sugar melts and turns golden brown. Return the custard to the refrigerator for 2 to 3 hours before serving.

Zabaglione

A richer variation of this classic dessert, called zabaglione à la créole, is made in the same way with 2 tablespoons of rum and $\frac{1}{2}$ cup (125 ml) of whipped cream added when the mixture has cooled. The mixture must be whisked as it cools and then chilled in glasses before serving.

SERVES FOUR TO SIX

6 egg yolks
6 tablespoons sugar
2 teaspoons very finely grated orange or lemon rind
6 tablespoons Marsala or sweet white wine

Put the egg yolks, sugar and rind in an ovenproof mixing bowl and beat until the mixture becomes frothy. Stir in the Marsala or wine and set the bowl over a saucepan half filled with barely simmering water. Beat the mixture over low heat until it thickens and rises.

Remove the pan from the heat, divide the mixture between six glasses and serve immediately.

Bavarois

This classic dessert is a mixture of custard, gelatin, cream and flavoring. You can add any flavoring to the basic recipe. For example, for a coffee flavor add $\frac{1}{2}$ cup (125 ml) of strong black coffee or 2 tablespoons of instant coffee. For a chocolate flavor dissolve 4 squares (125 g) of unsweetened chocolate in the milk. For an orange flavor use the juice and finely grated rind or zest of 1 large orange. To extract the zest, rub the orange all over with 2 sugar cubes until they are completely impregnated with the oil in the skin. Then crush the sugar cubes and mix them in with the other sugar.

SERVES SIX

2 cups (500 ml) milk
1 vanilla bean or 1 teaspoon vanilla extract
4 egg yolks
$\frac{1}{4}$ cup (50 g) sugar
1 tablespoon gelatin
2 tablespoons water
$\frac{1}{2}$ cup (125 ml) whipping cream, whipped

Put the milk and the vanilla bean in a saucepan and heat gently. Remove the pan from the heat and allow the milk to infuse.

Beat the egg yolks with the sugar in the top of a double boiler. Remove the vanilla bean from the milk. Pour the milk over the egg yolk and sugar mixture in a steady stream, beating all the time. Put the top of the double boiler over barely simmering water and cook the custard, stirring gently, until it is thick and coats the back of the spoon.

Dissolve the gelatin in the water over low heat and stir it into the custard. Strain the custard into a bowl. Set the bowl on ice and stir until the custard thickens. Fold in half of the whipped cream and pour it into a lightly oiled or wet charlotte or jelly mold. Cover the mold and put it in the refrigerator for 4 hours.

Dip the bottom of the mold into hot water for 1 second, then turn the bavarois out onto a serving dish. Decorate the bavarois with the remaining cream.

Three delicious dishes based on eggs and dairy products : a luxurious, creamy dessert called bavarois, the traditional Swiss fondue and a light supper snack, eggs florentine with ham.

Jamaican rum custard

SERVES FOUR

5 egg yolks plus 1 egg white
¼ cup (50 g) dark brown sugar
1 tablespoon cornstarch
2½ cups (625 ml) milk
½ cup (125 ml) dark rum
½ cup (125 ml) whipping cream, whipped

Combine the eggs, sugar and cornstarch in a mixing bowl.

Scald the milk and stir a little of it into the egg mixture. Strain the mixture back into the pan of hot milk, beating constantly. Cook the custard, stirring continuously, until it is thick. Do not let the custard boil. Remove the pan from the heat and stir in the rum. Pour the custard into parfait glasses and serve chilled, decorated with whipped cream.

Austrian chocolate pudding

SERVES SIX

6 squares (175 g) semisweet chocolate
1¼ cups (315 ml) milk
8 slices crustless fresh white bread, cubed
¾ cup (175 g) butter, softened
¾ cup (175 g) sugar
6 eggs, separated
4 tablespoons ground almonds
Grated rind of ½ orange
2 tablespoons crushed macaroons
1 cup (250 ml) whipping cream or chocolate sauce

Melt the chocolate in a little of the milk over low heat. Soak the bread in the remaining milk for 5 minutes.

Cream the butter and sugar together in a mixing bowl. Beat in the egg yolks one at a time. Beat in the melted chocolate. Beat the soaked bread with the milk to form a smooth mixture and stir it into the chocolate mixture with the ground almonds.

Beat the egg whites until they form stiff peaks and carefully fold them into the chocolate mixture.

Generously butter a 2-quart (2-liter) pudding mold. Mix the orange rind and macaroons together and sprinkle the mixture over the bottom of the pudding mold. Pour in the chocolate mixture. Cover the mold with aluminum foil with a 1-inch (2-cm) pleat down the center. and tie down with string.

Fit a rack into a large kettle and place the mold on it. Pour in enough boiling water to come halfway up the side of the mold. Cover the kettle and steam for 1 hour.

Unmold the pudding while hot. Serve with the cream or chocolate sauce.

Oeufs à la neige

SERVES FOUR

1 cup (250 ml) milk
1 cup (250 ml) cream
3 egg whites
Salt
3 tablespoons sugar
4 egg yolks
3 tablespoons vanilla sugar

Scald the milk and the cream together in a saucepan and quickly remove the pan from the heat.

Beat the egg whites with a pinch of salt until they stand in peaks. Beat in the sugar, a little at a time, until the egg whites are stiff and glossy. Using a tablespoon, scoop out egg-shaped portions of the meringue mixture and drop a few of them at a time into the hot milk. Return the pan to low heat and poach the meringues gently (do not let the milk and cream mixture boil) for 2 or 3 minutes or until they are firm, turning them over once.

With a slotted spoon, lift out the meringues and drain on paper towels.

Beat the egg yolks with the vanilla sugar in the top of a double boiler until well mixed. Add the hot milk and cream in a steady stream, stirring continually. Cook over very low heat, for about 15 minutes or until the custard coats the back of a wooden spoon.

Pour the custard into a serving bowl. When the custard is cool, arrange the snow eggs on top. Put in the refrigerator to chill before serving.

Stewing and casseroling

Stewing and casseroling are methods of cooking meat, game, poultry, fish, vegetables or cereals very slowly, over a low heat or in an oven set at a low temperature. Bouillabaisse and other similar fish stews are the exceptions to the rule—they are cooked rapidly over high heat.

Basically there are two kinds of meat stews. White stews are made with veal, lamb, chicken or rabbit, which is sometimes soaked in cold, salted water for several hours or overnight to whiten the meat and to make the flavor more subtle. Rabbit and neck of lamb are the meats most commonly soaked.

Brown stews are made with beef, mutton or such variety meats as oxtail, heart or kidney. Before the cooking liquid is added the meat is browned in hot fat or oil.

Stewed or casseroled meat or poultry is cut into pieces before it is cooked. For pot roasting, however, the meat or poultry is left in one piece.

Pot roasting is a good way of cooking small pieces of meat or birds, which tend to become dry if cooked in the oven. Simply brown the meat or poultry in a little fat, reduce the heat, add a little more fat or a little wine or stock if necessary, then cover with a lid and cook until tender.

Braising is a method of cooking meat, game, fish and vegetables first on top of the stove and then in the oven. To braise meat, heat a little fat or oil in an ovenproof casserole, then brown the meat over moderate heat. Remove the meat from the pan and keep it warm. In the hot fat cook about half to one pound (225 to 450 g) of diced or sliced root vegetables until they are tender. A couple of slices of bacon, diced or left whole, may also be added to this mixture, which is called mirepoix.

When the vegetables are cooked, lay the meat on top, add a little liquid and some herbs and seasonings, then transfer the casserole to a preheated oven. Cook until tender. The mirepoix will have lost all its flavor by the end of the cooking time, so it is discarded. The cooking liquid, however, is strained and served with the meat.

Fish is braised in the same way as meat except that it is not browned before it is laid on the mirepoix. Such vegetables as celery and onions are excellent braised, but they should first be blanched to shorten the cooking time.

Pans used for stewing, pot roasting and braising should have thick bases and tight-fitting lids.

Fish and shellfish

Lobster à l'americaine 108
Green salad 213

Matelote 109
Garlic bread 189

Cioppino 109
Green salad 213,
Garlic bread 189

Mussel stew 109
Boiled fennel 92,
Broiled mushrooms 134

Squid casserole 109
Spinach and mushroom salad 212,
Boiled rice 97

Bouillabaisse 106

Fillets of haddock dieppoise 106
Cottage fries 151,
Spinach 92

Zarzuela de pescado 106
Aioli sauce 68

Fish casserole with peppers 108
Garlic bread 189

Psari plaki 108
Garlic mashed potatoes 180

Belgian fish stew 108
Belgian endive 91,
Soufflé potatoes 150

Portuguese salt cod 108

Eels stewed in white wine 108
Steamed broccoli 92
Mashed potatoes 93

Poultry and game birds

Coq au vin 110
Soufflé potatoes 150,
Petits pois à la française 91

Chicken in cider 110
Crusty noodles 158,
Deep-fried mushrooms 152,
Squash in caraway sauce 92

Duck with olives 112
Mushroom and herb casserole 121,
Mashed potatoes 93

Duck with cherries 112
Potato croquettes 151,
Belgian endive 91

Duck with turnips 112
Garlic mashed potatoes 180

Grouse casserole 112
Garlic mashed potatoes 180 or Potato chips 150,
Red cabbage with apples 120

Grouse en cocotte 112
Shoestring potatoes 150,
Green beans 92

Casseroled pheasant with cranberries and cream 113
Potato chips 150,
Spinach purée 92

Pheasant with Calvados 113

Guinea hen and celery casserole 113
Lima beans with garlic, Mashed potatoes 93

Meat and game

Squab with prunes and port 113
Potato croquettes 151, Green salad 213

Boeuf à la mode 114
Steamed broccoli 92, Boiled noodles 97

Kidneys braised in red wine 117
Cottage fries 151, Boiled peas 93, Deep-fried mushrooms 152

Carbonnade de boeuf à la flamande 114
Green salad 213, Garlic bread 189

Red-cooked pork 117
Boiled rice 97, Stir-fried bean sprouts 153

Boeuf à la bourguignonne 114
Steamed cauliflower 92, Parisienne potatoes 151

Cassoulet 117
Green salad 213

Boeuf en daube 115
Boiled noodles 97, Steamed leeks 93

Lancashire hot pot 117
Cabbage or spinach 92, Peas 93

Hungarian goulash 115
Green salad 213

Navarin printanier 118
Potato croquettes or Lyonnaise potatoes 151

Pot roast with prunes 116
Potato croquettes 151, Steamed broccoli 92

Jugged hare 118
Spinach 92

Beef olives 116
Garlic mashed potatoes 180, Belgian endive, orange and watercress salad 213

Rabbit stew 119
Leeks provençal 120, Mashed potatoes 93

Oxtail stew 116
Crusty noodles 158

Braised venison with juniper berries and sour cream 119
Carrot and parsnip purée 91, Green beans 92

Osso buco 116
Risotto alla Milanese 122 or Mashed potatoes, Boiled snow peas 93

Blanquette de veau 116
Boiled new potatoes 93, Glazed carrots, Petits pois à la française 91

Vegetables

Ratatouille 121

Peperonata 121

Caponata 121

Braised lettuce 120

Chestnuts with Chinese cabbage 120
Boiled noodles or rice 97, Stir-fried bean sprouts 153

Red cabbage with apples 120

Casseroled celery 120

Buttered Belgian endive 120

Braised onions 120

Leeks provençal 120

Sauerkraut 121

Mushroom and herb casserole 121
Boiled rice 97 or Crusty noodles 158

Stuffed peppers 121
Green salad 213, Peas 93

Cereals

Creole jambalaya 122
Green salad 213

Risotto alla Milanese 122
Green salad 213

Paella Valenciana 123

Biryani 123
Yogurt, Cucumber

Barley and vegetable casserole 123

Bulghur pilaff 122

Tomato rice 122
Avocado salad 213

Legend:
- First courses
- Main courses
- Light lunch-supper dishes
- Accompaniments
- Desserts
- Miscellaneous

Fish and shellfish

The most famous fish stews come from around the Mediterranean. Bouillabaisse, for example, is so well loved in the south of France that poems have been written about it and its invention has been attributed to Venus. The secret of its success lies in boiling the stew over a high heat to amalgamate the oil and water.

Although in Marseilles bouillabaisse is made with such fish as the rascasse, or scorpion fish, wonderful stews can be made in other parts of the world using many different saltwater fish—pollack, porgy, cod, haddock, whiting and skate, for example—and such shellfish as cockles, mussels, shrimp and scallops.

Bouillabaisse

It is always difficult to know whether to classify this dish as a soup or as a stew—really it is both, as the liquid is often served as a soup, separately from the fish itself. A true bouillabaisse, they say, cannot be made away from the Mediterranean, one possible reason is that one of the most traditional ingredients, the rascasse, or scorpion fish, is not found elsewhere. For this version of bouillabaisse use a selection of available fish—the more varied the better.

SERVES SIX

4 large tomatoes, peeled and chopped
2 onions, chopped
4 garlic cloves, chopped
⅔ cup (150 ml) olive oil
3 parsley sprigs
1 fennel sprig
1 bay leaf
Large pinch saffron
Salt and pepper
5 lb (2½ kg) fish—porgy, conger eel, red snapper, grunt, Boston scrod, whiting, lobster cut into chunks; and shrimp
12 slices French bread
1 cup (250 ml) aioli sauce

Put the tomatoes, onions and garlic into a large, heavy-bottomed pan with the oil. Add the herbs and the saffron and season well. Put the firmer fish (porgy and conger eel) on top and cover with boiling water. Cook over high heat for 5 minutes. Then add the more tender fish (whiting, lobster, shrimp and so on) and continue boiling hard for another 10 minutes.

Meanwhile, toast the bread in a hot oven (400°F/200°C), without letting it brown.

Transfer the fish to a serving dish and keep hot. Continue to boil the broth for 2 minutes longer and check the seasoning. Strain the broth. Put two slices of toasted bread into each soup bowl and pour in just enough broth to moisten the bread well. Serve with the fish and the aioli.

Fillets of haddock dieppoise

SERVES FOUR

2 lb (900 g) haddock fillets, skinned
Small bay leaf
2 teaspoons lemon juice
Salt and pepper
½ cup (125 ml) white wine.
1¼ cups (315 ml) milk
2 tablespoons butter
2 tablespoons flour
½ lb (225 g) shelled shrimp
½ cup (125 ml) cream

Preheat the oven to 350°F (180°C).

Wash the fish and put it in a buttered ovenproof dish. Add the bay leaf and lemon juice, season well, pour over the wine and cover with foil. Bake in the center of the oven for 20 minutes.

Meanwhile, bring the milk to just below boiling point. Melt the butter in a small pan. Stir in the flour to make a roux. Cook for 30 seconds then pour in the milk gradually and bring to a boil, stirring briskly. Reduce the heat and simmer for 5 minutes. Take the pan off the heat and stir in half the shrimp, the cream and seasoning.

Remove the fish from the oven. Lift out the fish and arrange the fillets on a warm serving dish. Strain the cooking liquid and stir it into the sauce. Pour over the fish and garnish with the remaining shrimp.

Zarzuela de pescado (Spanish stewed fish)

SERVES SIX

2 quarts (4 lb/2 kg) mussels
1 cup (250 ml) dry white wine
½ cup (125 ml) olive oil
2 large onions, chopped
1 lb (450 g) squid, sliced
6 large tomatoes, chopped
1 lb (450 g) cod fillets, skinned and cut into large pieces
¾ lb (350 g) shelled shrimp, 6 reserved unshelled
Salt and pepper
Large pinch saffron threads, soaked in 1 tablespoon boiling water for 5 minutes
2 large garlic cloves
2 tablespoons ground almonds
2 tablespoons chopped fresh parsley
12 slices French bread, fried

Put the mussels in a large frying pan with half the wine. Cover the pan and cook for about 8 minutes over high heat, shaking the pan frequently. Drain the mussels and reserve the liquid. Shell the mussels, reserving a few in their shells and discarding any that have not opened.

Heat the olive oil in a large saucepan, add the onions and fry gently until they are golden. Add the squid, tomatoes and the remaining wine and cook for 2 to 3 minutes. Add the cod and shelled shrimp and season to taste. Pour in the reserved cooking liquid and the saffron mixture. Cover the pan and simmer for 7 to 10 minutes or until the fish is cooked.

Put the garlic, ground almonds, parsley and 2 tablespoons of the cooking liquid into a small bowl and mix to a smooth paste. Stir the paste into the stew. Add the mussels. Ladle the stew into a large serving dish.

Garnish with the reserved shrimp and mussels. Arrange the slices of fried bread around the dish.

Bouillabaisse, almost a religion in the south of France, is made with a variety of Mediterranean fish and flavored with saffron, garlic and herbs.

Fish and shellfish

Fish casserole with peppers
SERVES FOUR

4 tablespoons butter
2 garlic cloves, chopped
4 leeks, cut into chunks
1 green pepper, seeded and
  thinly sliced
¼ lb (125 g) mushrooms,
  whole or cut in half if
  large
4 ripe tomatoes, peeled and
  chopped
Salt and pepper
2 lb (900 g) cod or haddock
  steaks
1 tablespoon tomato paste
1 cup (250 ml) well-flavored
  fish stock
Chopped parsley

Preheat the oven to 375°F
(190°C).

Melt the butter in a Dutch
oven. Add the garlic, leeks and
green pepper and cook gently for
10 minutes or until soft. Add the
mushrooms and tomatoes and
season well: Put the fish on top.
Blend the tomato paste with the
fish stock and pour it over the
fish. Cover the Dutch oven and
bake for 20 minutes.

Remove the Dutch oven from
the oven, sprinkle the parsley
on top and serve at once.

Psari plaki (Greek fish stew)
SERVES FOUR TO SIX

4 lb (2 kg) carp, sole or
  turbot (a whole fish or
  large piece), cleaned
1 tablespoon lemon juice
Salt and pepper
2 tablespoons olive oil
3 large onions, sliced
2 garlic cloves, chopped
4 tablespoons chopped
  parsley
¼ cup (65 ml) water
½ cup (125 ml) white wine
1 lemon, thinly sliced
1 lb (450 g) tomatoes, peeled
  and sliced

Preheat the oven to 350°F
(180°C).

Arrange the fish in a buttered
baking dish and sprinkle with
the lemon juice and seasoning.

Heat the oil in a frying pan
and fry the onions, garlic and
parsley gently until soft. Stir
in the water and the wine and
simmer for 1 minute. Pour this
mixture over the fish. Arrange
the lemon slices and tomatoes on

top. Put the dish in the oven for
45 minutes or until the fish is
cooked. Serve immediately.

Belgian fish stew
SERVES FOUR TO SIX

2 tablespoons butter
3 lb (1½ kg) carp or pike
  steaks
2 celery stalks, with the
  leaves
Salt and pepper
3 egg yolks
¼ cup (65 ml) cream
1 tablespoon chopped
  parsley

Melt the butter in a large Dutch
oven. Put in the fish and the celery
and enough water to cover.
Season lightly, bring to a boil
and cook over high heat for 10
minutes.

Lift out the fish and keep hot
on a serving dish. Remove and
discard the celery. Bring the
cooking liquid to a boil again
and boil hard until it is reduced
to a scant 2 cups.

Beat the egg yolks and cream
together in a small bowl. Blend
in a little of the hot cooking liquid
and add this mixture to the
liquid in the pot. Reduce the
heat to very low and cook,
stirring, until the sauce has thickened, but do not let it boil.
Pour the sauce over the fish,
sprinkle the parsley over the
top and serve.

Portuguese salt cod
SERVES SIX

2 lb (900 g) dried salt cod
2 lb (900 g) potatoes, peeled
  and sliced
½ cup (125 ml) olive oil
4 medium-sized onions,
  sliced
2 garlic cloves, crushed
4 tomatoes, peeled and
  sliced
12 black olives, pitted
4 hard-cooked eggs, sliced
1 tablespoon chopped
  parsley

Soak the cod overnight. Rinse
well, drain and put the cod into
a saucepan with just enough
fresh cold water to cover. Bring

to a boil, reduce the heat and
simmer for 30 minutes. Add the
potatoes and simmer for 20
minutes or until they are tender
and the fish is cooked.

Preheat the oven to 350°F
(180°C).

Lift out the fish, remove the
skin and bones and cut the
flesh into 2-inch (5-cm) pieces.
Drain the potatoes.

Heat 4 tablespoons of the
olive oil in a frying pan. Add
the onions and garlic and fry
gently until soft.

Arrange the potatoes, onions
and garlic, tomatoes, cod and
olives in layers in a deep
casserole. Pour the remaining oil
over the top. Cover the casserole
and put it in the oven for 20
minutes or until it is heated
through.

Remove the casserole from the
oven. Arrange the hard-cooked
eggs on top. Sprinkle the parsley
over the eggs and serve.

Eels stewed in white wine
SERVES FOUR

2 tablespoons olive oil
1 tablespoon butter
2 lb (900 g) eels, skinned and
  cut into pieces
1 small onion, thinly sliced
2 garlic cloves, crushed
4 large tomatoes, peeled and
  chopped
1 tablespoon chopped basil
1¼ cups (315 ml) white wine
1 teaspoon salt
Freshly ground black pepper
Beurre manié

Heat the olive oil with the butter
in a large Dutch oven. When the
fat is hot, add the eel pieces and
the onion and fry, stirring constantly, for 5 minutes. Add the
remaining ingredients, except
the beurre manié, and bring to
a boil, stirring.

Reduce the heat to very low,
cover the Dutch oven and simmer for 25 to 30 minutes or until
the eel is tender.

Remove the Dutch oven from

the heat. With a slotted spoon,
lift out the eel pieces and put
them into a warm serving dish.
Keep hot.

Return the Dutch oven to the
heat. Stir in the beurre manié, a
few pieces at a time, until the
sauce has thickened. Pour the
sauce over the eels and serve.

Lobster à l'américaine
SERVES TWO

1 tablespoon olive oil
¼ cup (50 g) butter
2-lb (900-g) uncooked lobster,
  cut into pieces (reserving
  the coral)
1 onion, peeled and chopped
1 garlic clove, finely
  chopped
Bouquet garni
2 tomatoes, peeled,
  quartered and seeded
1 tablespoon water
2 tablespoons brandy
1 cup (250 ml) white wine
2 tablespoons flour
1 teaspoon lemon juice
Cayenne pepper
Salt and pepper
1 tablespoon chopped
  parsley (or parsley and
  tarragon)

Heat the oil and half of the
butter together in a frying pan.
Add the lobster and fry over
fairly high heat for 2 to 3
minutes on each side or until
the shell turns red. Remove the
lobster. Add the onion, garlic,

bouquet garni and tomatoes to the pan with the tablespoon of water and simmer gently for a few minutes. Put the lobster pieces on top, pour over the brandy and ignite. When the flames die down, add the wine and, if necessary, enough water to just cover the lobster. Cover and simmer for 15 to 20 minutes.

Meanwhile, blend the coral with the remaining butter and the flour. Lift out the lobster, arrange the pieces on a warm serving dish and keep hot. Stir the butter and flour mixture into the sauce in the pan, add the lemon juice, a pinch of cayenne and season to taste. Strain the sauce over the lobster, sprinkle the herbs over the top and serve.

Matelote

In France, matelote usually refers to a stew of freshwater fish (eel, carp, pike or perch), but matelote à la normande, of which this is a version, uses saltwater fish.

SERVES SIX

1 quart (1 liter) mussels, scrubbed
1 cup (250 ml) court bouillon
2 lb (900 g) assorted fish (eel, sole or flounder, whiting) cleaned and cut into 2-inch (5-cm) chunks
2 cups (500 ml) hard cider or white wine
Bouquet garni

Salt and pepper
2 tablespoons butter
1 tablespoon flour
½ lb (225 g) small mushrooms
12 slices French bread, fried until golden

Put the mussels into a large frying pan. Pour in the court bouillon and bring to a boil, shaking the pan occasionally. Cover the pan and cook for 5 minutes. Lift out the mussels, discarding any that have not opened, and keep warm. Strain and reserve the cooking liquid.

Put the fish into a Dutch oven, pour in the cider or wine, together with the cooking liquid from the mussels, add the bouquet garni and seasoning. Cover the Dutch oven and simmer for 15 minutes.

Remove the fish from the pot and set it aside. Discard the bouquet garni, increase the heat and boil rapidly for 10 minutes. Reduce the heat to low. Mix 1 tablespoon of the butter with the flour to make beurre manié. Divide the beurre manié into small pieces and add them, one at a time, to the simmering liquid, stirring until the sauce thickens.

Return the fish to the Dutch oven; cook until heated through.

Gently fry the mushrooms in the remaining butter.

Ladle the fish and sauce into a serving dish. Garnish with the mushrooms, mussels and bread.

Cioppino

This seafood stew is popular in San Francisco, where many of the early fishermen came from Italy.

SERVES EIGHT

4 tablespoons olive oil
1 onion, chopped
2 celery stalks, chopped
1 carrot, chopped
2 lb (900 g) tomatoes, peeled and chopped
3 garlic cloves, chopped
1 tablespoon tomato paste
1 cup (250 ml) dry white wine (or a mixture of wine and fish stock made from the trimmings of the fish)
2 lb (900 g) white fish (hake, haddock, cod)
1 quart (1 liter) clams or oysters, well scrubbed
2 uncooked lobsters, chopped
1 lb (450 g) uncooked shrimp, shelled
Salt and pepper

Put the olive oil in a large, heavy-bottomed saucepan with the chopped vegetables and garlic. Dilute the tomato paste in a little water and stir it into the pan. Cover the pan and simmer gently for 30 minutes.

Add the wine, the white fish, clams or oysters and lobsters and stir well. Cook, covered, for 10 minutes. Add the shrimp and seasoning and cook for a further 10 minutes. Discard any clams or oysters that have not opened and serve.

Mussel stew

SERVES FOUR

1 quart (1 liter) mussels, scrubbed
1 cup (250 ml) white wine
¼ cup (50 g) butter
2 shallots, finely chopped
2 leeks, white part only, finely chopped
2 tomatoes, peeled and chopped
2 garlic cloves, chopped
2 tablespoons flour

2 cups (500 ml) milk
1 tablespoon anise-flavored liqueur
2 egg yolks
½ cup (125 ml) heavy cream
Salt and pepper

Put the mussels into a large frying pan with the wine. Cover the pan and cook over high heat for 5 minutes. Transfer the mussels to a deep serving dish, discarding any that have not opened, and keep warm. Strain the cooking liquid.

Melt the butter in a saucepan. Add the shallots, leeks, tomatoes and garlic and fry gently, stirring, until soft. Stir in the flour. Pour in the mussel liquid and the milk gradually, stirring constantly to insure there are no lumps. Continue cooking until the sauce thickens slightly. Add the liqueur and continue simmering gently for a few minutes.

Beat the egg yolks with the cream in a small bowl. Stir in a little of the hot sauce. Remove the pan off the heat and pour in the egg and cream mixture, stirring constantly. Adjust the seasoning, return the sauce to a low heat for a few seconds. Pour the sauce over the mussels and serve immediately.

Squid casserole

SERVES FOUR

½ cup (125 ml) olive oil
2 squid, cleaned and coarsely chopped
2 onions, thinly sliced
3 garlic cloves, crushed
1½ lb (700 g) tomatoes, chopped
1 tablespoon fresh rubbed thyme
Salt and freshly ground black pepper
½ cup (125 ml) dry white wine
10 black olives, pitted

Heat the olive oil in a medium saucepan. Add the squid and onions and fry, stirring, until the onions are golden.

Stir in the remaining ingredients, except the olives, and bring to a boil. Reduce the heat to low and simmer, uncovered, for 30 minutes, stirring occasionally. Add the olives and cook 5 minutes more. Transfer to a serving dish and serve.

Poultry and game birds

Stewing and casseroling are excellent methods of cooking poultry and game birds that are no longer young, for even a rather tough old bird, if it is cooked slowly in a well-flavored liquid, can arrive at the table tender and tasting delicious.

Pot roasting, on the other hand, is a suitable method of cooking both young and old birds.

Use fresh poultry and game birds whenever possible. If you have to use a frozen bird, be sure that it has thawed out completely before you start cooking.

Coq au vin

SERVES FOUR

4 slices bacon, chopped
3 tablespoons butter
12 small onions
4½- to 5-lb (2- to 2½-kg) roasting chicken, cut into serving pieces
2 tablespoons brandy
2 cups (500 ml) red wine (Burgundy or Beaujolais)
½ cup (125 ml) chicken stock
Bouquet garni
2 garlic cloves, finely chopped
Salt and freshly ground black pepper
¼ lb (125 g) mushrooms
2 tablespoons beurre manié

Put the bacon in a large Dutch oven over moderate heat and fry, stirring constantly, until it has rendered its fat.

Add 1 tablespoon of the butter and the onions and fry until they are golden. Transfer the onions and bacon to a plate and set aside.

Brown the chicken pieces on all sides in the fat, then pour the brandy over and ignite it. Shake the pan while the brandy is flaming. When the flames have subsided, pour in the wine and stock and add the bouquet garni, garlic and seasoning. Once the liquid is simmering, return the onions and bacon to the pan. Cover the pan, reduce the heat to low and simmer very gently for at least 1 hour or until the chicken is tender.

Melt the remaining butter in a small frying pan and fry the mushrooms for 2 to 3 minutes. Add them to the other ingredients in the Dutch oven.

When the chicken is cooked, add the beurre manié in small pieces, stirring constantly, until the sauce has thickened. Serve immediately.

Chicken in cider

SERVES FOUR TO SIX

¼ cup (50 g) butter
2 chickens, 2½ lb (1 kg) each, cut into quarters
Salt and pepper
2 onions, thinly sliced
3 apples, peeled, cored and sliced (reserve 1 apple in acidulated water for use as garnish)
8 small new carrots, scrubbed
1 bay leaf
Pinch thyme
1 cup (250 ml) hard cider or apple wine
¼ cup (65 ml) whipping cream
1 egg yolk

Melt the butter in a Dutch oven. Add the chicken pieces and brown them on all sides. Season well with salt and pepper. Add the onions, 2 apples, the carrots, bay leaf and thyme. Cook for one minute before adding the cider. Bring the cider to a boil, cover the pan and simmer gently for 35 minutes or until the chicken is tender. Transfer the chicken pieces to a serving dish, cover and keep warm in a low oven.

Boil the cooking liquid until it has reduced by half. Remove and discard the bay leaf.

Combine the cream with the egg yolk in a small bowl. Stir in 2 to 3 spoonfuls of the hot liquid and pour it into the pot, stirring until the sauce has thickened. Do not let the sauce boil.

Pour the sauce over the chicken. Garnish with the reserved apple.

Three superb dishes fit for any dinner party : braised duck with cherries, pheasant with Calvados and the classic coq au vin.

Poultry and game birds

Duck with olives

SERVES FOUR

¼ cup (50 g) butter
5-lb (2½-kg) duck, quartered
½ cup (125 ml) dry vermouth
Salt and pepper
Bouquet garni
1 cup (250 ml) veal stock
2 tablespoons tomato paste
2 tablespoons beurre manié
16 stuffed green olives
2 tablespoons olive oil
4 slices bread, cut into
    triangles

Preheat the oven to 350°F (180°C). Melt the butter in a Dutch oven. Add the duck quarters and fry them until they are well browned on all sides. Pour over the vermouth, season to taste and add the bouquet garni. Cover the pot and bake in the oven for 40 minutes.

Remove the duck from the Dutch oven and transfer it to a warm serving dish. Cover with foil and keep hot.

Pour the stock into the Dutch oven and bring it to a boil over moderate heat, scraping any sediment from the bottom of the pot. Remove and discard the bouquet garni. Reduce the heat to low, and when the sauce is barely simmering, stir in the tomato paste and then the beurre manié in small pieces, stirring constantly, until the sauce is thick. Add the olives and simmer for 3 minutes. Pour over the duck and keep hot.

Heat the olive oil in a large frying pan over moderate heat. Add the bread triangles and fry them on both sides until they are golden brown and crisp. Drain them well on paper towels and arrange them around the duck. Serve immediately.

Duck with cherries

SERVES THREE TO FOUR

5-lb (2½-kg) duck, trussed
Salt and pepper
¼ cup (50 g) butter
½ cup (125 ml) Madeira
1 tablespoon sugar
Juice and grated rind of 1
    orange
½ cup (125 ml) chicken stock
24 red cherries, pitted
1 teaspoon cornstarch

Rub the duck all over with the salt and pepper. Melt the butter

in a Dutch oven and brown the duck on all sides. Pour in the Madeira. Cover the Dutch oven, reduce the heat to low and cook for about 50 to 60 minutes or until the duck is cooked. Remove the duck from the Dutch oven and transfer it to a warm serving dish. Keep the duck hot in the oven.

Add the sugar, orange juice and rind and chicken stock to the Dutch oven. Bring to a boil and simmer for 10 minutes. Skim off the fat and strain the liquid.

Return the liquid to the pot and add the cherries. Mix the cornstarch with a tablespoon of water, stir in a little of the sauce and then pour the mixture into the pot. Cook for 3 minutes.

Taste and adjust seasoning if necessary. Pour a little sauce over the duck. Spoon some of the cherries around the duck and serve the rest of the sauce and cherries separately in a gravy boat.

Duck with turnips

SERVES THREE TO FOUR

1 large duck, trussed
3 tablespoons seasoned flour
6 tablespoons butter
1 lb (450 g) small turnips,
    peeled and halved
2 tablespoons sugar
8 small onions, peeled
2½ cups (625 ml) veal stock

Preheat the oven to 350°F (180°C).

Coat the duck all over with half the seasoned flour. Melt the butter in a Dutch oven and brown the duck on all sides.

Remove the duck and add the turnips. Sprinkle with the sugar. Cook over low heat until the turnips are golden brown. Add the onions and cook for 3 minutes more. Remove the vegetables and set aside.

Stir in the rest of the flour and gradually add the stock, stirring constantly. Return the duck to the Dutch oven, cover and put it in the oven for 40 minutes.

Add the turnips and onions and cook for 30 minutes.

Remove the duck from the Dutch oven and put it on a hot serving plate. Remove the trussing string and arrange the tur-

nips and onions around the duck.

Skim the fat off the sauce and boil over high heat for a few minutes. Strain the sauce over the duck and serve.

Grouse casserole

SERVES TWO

2 grouse, trussed
Salt and pepper
6 tablespoons butter
1 onion, chopped
2 cups (125 g) chopped
    mushrooms
2 carrots, peeled and
    diced
1 celery stalk, diced
2 tablespoons Scotch whisky
1¼ cups (315 ml) chicken
    stock
1 tablespoon red currant
    jelly
6 bacon slices, rolled,
    skewered, broiled and
    kept hot

Preheat the oven to 350°F (180°C).

Season the grouse well with salt and pepper. Heat the butter in a Dutch oven and brown the birds on all sides. Remove the grouse from the Dutch oven. Add the onion, mushrooms, carrots and celery. Cook over low heat, stirring, until the vegetables are soft but not browned.

Return the grouse to the pan, pour over the whisky and ignite it. Shake the pan until the flames die down. Add the stock, cover and bake in the oven for 1¼ hours.

When the grouse are cooked, cut them in half with poultry shears and place on a warm serving dish.

Strain the sauce into another pan and boil until it has thickened slightly. Stir in the red currant jelly. Spoon the sauce over the grouse and garnish with the bacon rolls, skewers removed.

Grouse en cocotte

SERVES TWO

2 grouse, halved
2 tablespoons olive oil
6 tablespoons red wine
1 tablespoon red wine
    vinegar
4 juniper berries
Strip lemon rind
1 teaspoon lemon juice
Salt and pepper
2 tablespoons butter
4 slices bacon
6 small onions
4 celery stalks, chopped
1 bay leaf
½ cup (125 ml) chicken stock
1 tablespoon red currant jelly
1 teaspoon arrowroot mixed
    with 1 tablespoon water

Prick the grouse all over with a fork. Mix the oil, wine, vinegar, berries, lemon rind and juice and seasoning together in

a large dish. Add the grouse and baste them well with the marinade. Marinate in a cool place for 24 hours, turning the grouse from time to time. Lift out the grouse and dry them with paper towels. Reserve the marinade.

Preheat the oven to 325°F (170°C).

Melt the butter in a Dutch oven and gently fry the bacon and onions for 5 minutes. Add the grouse, celery, bay leaf, stock and reserved marinade. Cover the Dutch oven and cook in the oven for 1¼ to 1½ hours or until the grouse are tender. Remove the Dutch oven from the oven. Transfer the grouse and onions to a warm serving dish.

Stir the red currant jelly and arrowroot mixture into the pot and set over moderate heat. Cook, stirring, for 1 to 2 minutes or until the liquid has thickened. Strain the sauce over the grouse and serve.

Casseroled pheasant with cranberries and cream

SERVES TWO

1 pheasant, trussed
Salt and pepper
4 bacon slices, chopped
2 tablespoons butter
¼ cup (65 ml) brandy
Juice of 1 orange
½ cup (125 ml) cream
2 teaspoons arrowroot
½ cup (125 ml) cranberry sauce

Season the pheasant well with salt and pepper. Fry the bacon in a Dutch oven over moderate heat until it has rendered its fat. Add the butter and brown the bird on all sides. Pour over the brandy and orange juice. Cover the pot, reduce the heat and simmer gently for 1 hour or until the pheasant is tender.

Transfer the pheasant from the pot to a warm platter and keep hot. Mix the cream with the arrowroot and stir it into the cooking liquid with the cranberry sauce. Cook over low heat until the sauce is thickened.

Carve the bird and arrange the meat on a warm serving dish, pour over some of the sauce and serve the rest separately.

Pheasant with Calvados

SERVES FOUR

2 pheasant, trussed
Salt and pepper
½ cup (125 g) butter
4 bacon slices, cut in pieces
1 teaspoon marjoram
3 tart apples, peeled, cored and sliced (reserve a few slices in water, with vinegar added, for garnish)
Rind and juice of 1 lemon
3 tablespoons Calvados or apple brandy
1 cup (250 ml) chicken stock
½ cup (125 ml) sour cream

Preheat the oven to 350°F (180°C).

Rub the pheasant all over with salt and pepper.

Melt half the butter in a Dutch oven and brown the birds on all sides. Add the bacon and marjoram and cook gently for 5 minutes. Remove the birds and bacon and set aside.

Melt the remaining butter in the pot and fry the apples until golden. Add the lemon juice and rind and the bacon. Place the pheasant on top of the apples, pour in the Calvados and ignite. When the flames die down, add the stock and bring to a boil. Cover the pot and bake for 1 hour or until the pheasant are tender.

Stir in the sour cream and cook for a further 10 minutes. Garnish with the apple slices.

Guinea hen and celery casserole

SERVES FOUR

2 guinea hens
Salt and pepper
¼ cup (50 g) butter
1 Spanish onion, chopped
1 large head celery, cut into 1-inch (2-cm) lengths, blanched for 1 minute and drained
1 teaspoon thyme
1 teaspoon marjoram
6 bacon slices
1 cup (250 ml) dry white wine
2 teaspoons arrowroot mixed with 4 tablespoons cream

Preheat the oven to 325°F (170°C).

Rub the guinea hens all over with the salt and pepper. Melt the butter in a large Dutch oven. Put in the guinea hens and brown them all over. Lift out the birds and set aside. Add the onion to the pot and fry until it is soft but not browned. Add the celery and herbs. Put the guinea hens on top of the celery and lay the bacon on the birds' breasts. Pour in the wine and bring to a boil. Cover the Dutch oven and put it in the oven for 50 to 60 minutes or until the birds are tender.

Remove the Dutch oven from the oven. Transfer the guinea hens to a warm serving dish and keep hot.

Strain the sauce into a saucepan and set over moderate heat. Stir in the arrowroot mixture and cook until the sauce has thickened. Pour the sauce over the guinea hens and serve.

Squab with prunes and port

Serve with garlic mashed potatoes and a green salad.

SERVES FOUR

3 tablespoons butter
2 squab, trussed
8 small onions
¼ cup (65 ml) port wine
½ cup (125 ml) beef stock
Salt and pepper
12 dried prunes, soaked for 4 hours in lukewarm water, drained and pitted
1 teaspoon arrowroot mixed with 1 tablespoon stock

Preheat the oven to 325°F (170°C).

Melt the butter in a Dutch oven, add the squab and brown on all sides. Lift out the squab. Add the onions to the pan and cook until golden. Return the squab to the pan, pour in the wine and stock and add the seasoning. Cover the pot and bake for 30 minutes.

Add the prunes and cook for another 30 minutes or until the squab are done.

Remove the pot from the oven. Transfer the squab and prunes to a warm serving dish and keep hot.

Strain the cooking liquid into a saucepan and set over moderate heat. Stir in the arrowroot mixture and cook the sauce until it has thickened. Pour the sauce over the squab and serve immediately.

Meat and game

Stewing, casseroling, braising and pot roasting are the best ways of dealing with the tougher cuts of meat, which become tender only if they are cooked very slowly over low heat. The long cooking time also enables the flavors of the meat and the herbs, spices and vegetables that are cooked with it to develop and blend. Stews improve in flavor if they are kept for a day or two before eating.

Onions, tomatoes and such root vegetables as carrots and turnips are especially valuable for flavoring meat stews. Peppers are popular in Hungary and okra are often used in Egypt.

Fruit can also complement meat. Apples and dried fruit go into a Danish pot roast of pork and also into the German *sauerbraten*, which is flavored with cloves and allspice. Fruit and spices are also used in the North African *tajine* and in many Middle Eastern stews.

Tough cuts of meat, and game such as venison, also benefit from being soaked in a marinade for anything from two hours to two days. The marinade is usually made from a mixture of olive oil, wine or vinegar, herbs and spices, and in the Middle East yogurt is often used. Once the meat has been removed, the marinade may be strained and added to the stock in which the meat is to be cooked.

Boeuf à la mode
This dish may also be served cold.

SERVES TEN

5 lb (2½ kg) rump roast of
  beef, in one piece, boned,
  larded and tied
Salt and pepper
2 garlic cloves, crushed
3 tablespoons olive oil
3 onions, sliced
2 tablespoons brandy
1 cup (250 ml) wine
1 calf's foot, blanched
Piece of pork rind about the
  size of your hand,
  blanched
Beef stock or water
Bouquet garni
15 small onions
2 lb (900 g) carrots, sliced

Rub the meat with salt, pepper and garlic. Heat the oil in a large Dutch oven and fry the onions until golden. Add the meat and brown it on all sides. Heat the brandy in a ladle, set it afire and pour it over the meat. When the flames die down, add the wine, the calf's foot, pork rind and enough stock or water to cover. Season well, add the bouquet garni, cover and simmer over very low heat or in a very slow oven for at least 4 to 5 hours.

Drain the beef, remove and discard the calf's foot, pork rind and bouquet garni. Return the cooking liquid to the pot and carefully skim as much fat as possible off the top. The liquid should be fairly thick; if it is not, reduce it a little by boiling. Return the meat to the pot, add the onions and carrots and simmer for about 20 minutes.

Carbonnade de boeuf à la flamande
SERVES SIX TO EIGHT

3 lb (1½ kg) beef, chuck or
  rump roast
Salt and pepper
6 tablespoons drippings or
  lard
6 small onions, thinly sliced
2 tablespoons flour
2½ cups (625 ml) dark beer
½ cup (125 ml) beef stock
1 tablespoon vinegar
1 teaspoon brown sugar
Bouquet garni

Cut the beef into thin slices and season well. Melt the drippings or lard in a large frying pan. Add the beef, a few slices at a time, and fry quickly over high heat until browned on both sides. Lift out the meat and set aside.

Reduce the heat, add the onions to the frying pan and fry, stirring, until browned. Using a slotted spoon, lift out the onions. Layer the meat and onions in an ovenproof casserole.

Stir the flour into the fat in the frying pan. Pour in the beer and stock and stir and scrape to mix to a smooth sauce. Stir in the vinegar and sugar and season well. Pour the sauce over the meat and onions and put in the bouquet garni.

Cover the casserole and cook gently over low heat or in a 325°F (170°C) oven for 1½ to 2 hours or until the meat is tender. Skim off any excess fat and serve.

Boeuf à la bourguignonne
This is a good dish for the cheaper cuts of beef because the long marinating time makes the meat more tender.

SERVES SIX

3 lb (1½ kg) beef, chuck or
  rump roast
2 tablespoons beef drippings
  or butter
½ lb (225 g) slab bacon, cut
  into strips ¼ inch (½ cm)
  thick
12 small onions
2 tablespoons flour
1¼ cups (315 ml) beef stock
2 garlic cloves, crushed
Bouquet garni
2 tablespoons butter
12 small mushrooms
1 tablespoon chopped
  parsley

MARINADE
1 tablespoon olive oil
2½ cups (625 ml) red wine or
  wine and water
1 onion, sliced
1 bay leaf
Salt and pepper

Cut the beef into 1½-inch (3-cm) cubes and put them in a bowl. Mix the ingredients for the marinade together and pour it over the meat. Marinate for at least 6 hours or overnight. Drain the beef and dry the cubes on paper towels. Strain and reserve the marinade.

Melt the drippings in a large, heavy saucepan. Add the bacon and fry, stirring, until the fat begins to run. Add the small onions and brown them over low heat. Using a slotted spoon, remove the onions and bacon

from the pan and set aside. Add the beef and brown quickly. Sprinkle the flour over the meat and cook for 2 minutes, stirring. Pour in the marinade and enough stock to cover the meat. Add the garlic and the bouquet garni. Cover the pan and simmer for 2 to 2½ hours.

Remove the pan from the heat.

Two French beef dishes, boeuf à la bourguignonne and boeuf à la mode.

4 carrots, sliced
2 garlic cloves, chopped
Bouquet garni
Salt and pepper
1¼ cups (315 ml) red wine
½ lb (225 g) black olives,
    pitted

Preheat the oven to 275°F (140°C).

Cut the beef into cubes. Heat the oil in a Dutch oven. Add the salt pork and fry, stirring, until brown. Add the beef and fry, turning the pieces frequently until brown all over. Add the onions, celery, carrots, garlic and bouquet garni. Season, but remember the saltiness of the pork, and pour in the wine. Cover the Dutch oven and bake in the oven for 4 hours or until the meat is very tender.

Thirty minutes before the end of the cooking time skim any excess fat from the top of the daube and add the olives.

Hungarian goulash
SERVES FOUR

2 tablespoons butter
2 tablespoons olive oil
2 lb (900 g) stewing beef,
    cut into cubes
4 medium-sized onions,
    sliced
4 medium-sized potatoes,
    sliced
2 garlic cloves, crushed
1 large bay leaf
2 tablespoons paprika
Salt and freshly ground
    black pepper
4 tablespoons tomato paste
¾ cup (175 ml) well-flavored
    beef stock
1 cup (250 ml) sour cream

Melt the butter with the olive oil in a large Dutch oven. Add the beef and onions and fry them for 6 to 8 minutes or until they are lightly browned.

Stir in the remaining ingredients and bring to a boil, stirring. Reduce the heat to very low, cover the Dutch oven and simmer for 2½ to 3 hours or until the meat is very tender and the onions and potatoes have almost melted away and thickened the liquid.

Discard the herbs. When the stew is cold, skim off the fat.

Melt the butter in a small frying pan. Add the mushrooms and fry, stirring, until they are lightly browned. Add the reserved bacon and onions and the mushrooms to the beef. Return the pan to the heat and cook for a further 30 minutes.

Boeuf en daube
This is often served with noodles, boiled, drained and dressed with some of the sauce from the pot and grated cheese. If you are cooking the daube the day before, do not add the olives until the time comes to reheat it. Alternatively, a mixture of finely chopped garlic and parsley,

sometimes with anchovies or capers added, is sprinkled on just before serving.
SERVES SIX

3 lb (1½ kg) braising beef
2 tablespoons olive oil
½ lb (225 g) salt pork, diced
4 onions, quartered
4 celery stalks, chopped into
    1-inch (2-cm) pieces

Meat and game

Pot roast with prunes

SERVES SIX TO EIGHT

4 lb (2 kg) rolled rump roast of beef
Salt and pepper
2 tablespoons oil
2 garlic cloves, chopped
Thinly pared rind of 1 lemon
½ cup (125 ml) port
1¼ cups (315 ml) beef stock
½ lb (225 g) prunes, pitted
½ lb (225 g) small white onions
Beurre manié

Rub the beef with the salt and pepper. Heat the oil in a Dutch oven and brown the beef on all sides. Add the garlic, lemon rind, port and stock. Cover the Dutch oven tightly and cook over very low heat or in a 300°F (150°C) oven for 2 hours.

Soak the prunes in water while the meat is cooking. At the end of the 2 hours, add the prunes and onions. Cover the Dutch oven and cook for another 30 minutes or until the meat is tender when pierced with a fork. Transfer the meat to a warm serving dish, surround with the prunes and onions and keep hot.

Skim as much fat as possible off the top of the cooking liquid and return the Dutch oven to the heat. Add the beurre manié a little at a time, stirring constantly until the sauce has thickened. Adjust the seasoning. Strain the sauce into a gravy boat and serve with the meat, prunes and onions.

Beef olives

Although olives are not included in this recipe, they may be added both to the stuffing and to the sauce at the end of the cooking time. Serve beef olives with mashed potatoes.

SERVES FOUR

8 slices lean beef, pounded out thinly, approximately 3 × 4 inches (8 × 10 cm)
1 tablespoon butter
2 bacon slices, chopped
1 onion, finely chopped
1 carrot, finely diced
1 celery stalk, finely chopped
1¼ cups (315 ml) beef stock
1 tablespoon tomato paste
Salt and pepper
Bouquet garni
2 tablespoons beurre manié

STUFFING
1 tablespoon butter
1 bacon slice, chopped
1 small onion, finely chopped
¼ cup (25 g) fresh white bread crumbs
½ lb (225 g) ground veal
1 tablespoon chopped mixed herbs
Salt and pepper
2 tablespoons beef stock

First make the stuffing. Melt the butter in a small frying pan. Add the bacon and onion and fry, stirring, until softened. Combine the remaining ingredients in a bowl. Mix in the bacon and onion.

Lay the meat slices on a board. Spread the stuffing on the meat and roll up, tying the rolls with thread.

Heat the butter in a frying pan. Add the meat rolls and brown them. Lift out the meat and set aside. Add the bacon and vegetables to the pan and fry, stirring, until they are lightly browned. Put the meat rolls on top of the vegetables. Mix the stock with the tomato paste and pour it over the meat. Season to taste, add the bouquet garni and bring to a boil. Cover the pan, reduce the heat to low and simmer the beef olives for 1½ hours or until tender.

Lift out the beef olives, remove the thread, put them in a warm serving dish and keep hot. Strain the sauce and return it to the pan. If the sauce is too thin, add the beurre manié a little at a time, stirring over low heat until it has thickened. Pour the sauce over the beef olives and serve.

Oxtail stew

This is a good stew to make the day before you are going to serve it. Simmer the stew for about 3 hours, then chill it until the next day. Remove all the fat from the top and simmer for another hour.

SERVES FOUR TO SIX

1 oxtail, cut into pieces and soaked for 4 hours in cold water
2 tablespoons seasoned flour
¼ cup (50 g) lard or drippings
2 onions, thinly sliced
2 carrots, thinly sliced

2 celery stalks, thinly sliced
Beef stock or water
Bouquet garni
Salt and pepper
Chopped parsley

Put the oxtail into a large pan of cold water, bring to a boil gradually and then simmer for about 10 minutes, skimming off the scum as it rises. Drain the oxtail pieces, dry well and roll in the seasoned flour.

Melt the lard or drippings in a heavy-bottomed pan and brown the oxtail on all sides. Remove the oxtail, put in the onions, carrots and celery and cook gently, stirring, for a few minutes, then put the oxtail back on top of them. Pour in enough stock or water to come halfway up the meat, add the bouquet garni and season well. Cover the pan tightly, reduce the heat to low and simmer very gently for 3½ to 4 hours or until the meat is very tender. Sprinkle the parsley on top and serve.

Osso buco (braised shank of veal)

Traditionally a mixture of finely chopped garlic, parsley and grated lemon rind called a gremolata is sprinkled on top, and the dish is served with saffron-flavored risotto milanese.

SERVES FOUR

¼ cup (50 g) butter
4 pieces veal shank, about 2 inches (5 cm) thick
¾ cup (175 ml) white wine or veal stock
1 lb (450 g) ripe tomatoes, peeled and coarsely chopped
1 garlic clove, crushed
Salt and pepper

GREMOLATA
1 garlic clove, finely chopped
2 tablespoons finely chopped parsley
Finely grated rind of ½ lemon

Melt the butter in a large frying pan. Add the veal and fry, turning occasionally, until browned. Pour in the wine or stock and simmer for 15 minutes. Add the tomatoes and garlic, season well and continue cooking, with the

pan uncovered, until the cooking liquid is reduced a little.

Cover the pan and cook for 1 hour over low heat. Uncover and cook for one more hour. More liquid may be added if necessary.

About 10 minutes before serving, mix together the gremolata ingredients, sprinkle over the meat and serve.

Blanquette de veau

Serve the blanquette with new potatoes, baby carrots and peas.

SERVES FOUR TO SIX

2-lb (900-g) shoulder or breast of veal, boned and cut into square pieces
3 cups (750 ml) veal stock
1 carrot
1 onion, stuck with 2 cloves
1 celery stick
Bouquet garni
Salt and pepper
6 tablespoons butter
12 small white onions
½ lb (225 g) mushrooms
2 tablespoons flour
2 egg yolks
½ cup (125 ml) cream
Grated nutmeg
Lemon juice

Put the veal into a large Dutch oven. Pour in enough stock to cover the meat. Add the carrot, onion, celery and bouquet garni. Season well and bring to a boil. Reduce the heat to low, cover the pot and simmer gently for 1½ hours.

Meanwhile, melt two tablespoons of the butter in a small frying pan. Add the onions and fry them gently, stirring, for 5 minutes. Add the mushrooms and fry, stirring, for 2 minutes. Using a slotted spoon, transfer the onions and mushrooms to the Dutch oven 15 minutes before the end of the cooking time.

After 1½ hours lift out the meat, the onions and the mushrooms. Strain and reserve the cooking liquid, discarding the carrot, onion, celery and bouquet garni. Return the meat, onions and mushrooms to the Dutch oven and keep warm and covered.

Melt the remaining butter in a saucepan. Stir in the flour to make a roux. Gradually pour in 1¾ cups of the cooking liquid, stirring constantly to prevent lumps from forming. Bring the sauce to a boil and cook until it thickens slightly, stirring occasionally. Remove the pan from the heat.

Combine the egg yolks with the cream in a small bowl. Stir in 2 to 3 spoonfuls of the hot sauce. Pour the egg mixture into the sauce, stirring. Add a pinch of nutmeg and a squeeze of lemon juice and adjust the seasoning. Pour the sauce over the meat and vegetables. Return the Dutch oven to low heat. When the blanquette is heated through, serve immediately.

Kidneys braised in red wine

SERVES FOUR

2 tablespoons butter
1 tablespoon olive oil
4 veal kidneys
1 tablespoon flour
2 bacon slices
2 carrots, diced
1 onion, diced
1 small turnip, peeled and diced
Salt and pepper
1¼ cups (315 ml) red wine
Bouquet garni
½ lb (225 g) mushrooms
2 tomatoes, peeled, seeded and coarsely chopped
1 tablespoon chopped fresh parsley

Preheat the oven to 325°F (170°C).

Heat the butter and the oil in a frying pan. Add the kidneys and sauté them, turning them over to cook on both sides. Add the flour and let it brown.

Put the bacon into an earthenware casserole, cover with the mixed vegetables and season well. Remove the kidneys from the pan and put them on top of the vegetables. Add the wine to the pan and bring it to a boil, stirring in any residue in the pan. Pour it over the kidneys, add the bouquet garni and bake for 30 minutes. Stir in the mushrooms and tomatoes. Cook for another 10 minutes.

Using a slotted spoon, lift out the kidneys and mushrooms. Purée the sauce, pushing the vegetables through a sieve into a saucepan, or purée it in a blender for a few minutes. Adjust the seasoning, return the kidneys and mushrooms to the sauce, reheat for 5 minutes and serve sprinkled with parsley.

Red-cooked pork

This Chinese dish from the Shanghai area uses soy sauce to darken the food and give it its characteristic color. Serve the pork with plain, boiled rice.

SERVES TWELVE

6-lb (3-kg) pork hock, boned, rolled and tied
1 onion, sliced
8 tablespoons soy sauce
8 tablespoons red wine
1 tablespoon chopped ginger root
3 tablespoons sugar
2 tablespoons oil
2 teaspoons cornstarch mixed with 2 tablespoons cold water

Preheat the oven to 350°F (180°C).

Put the pork in a large Dutch oven, pour in boiling water to cover the meat and bring back to a boil. Reduce the heat, cover the pot and simmer gently for about 20 minutes.

Remove the pot from the heat, lift out the meat and set aside. Pour away all but 2 cups of the cooking liquid and skim off all the fat and scum. Return the meat to the pot with all the remaining ingredients except the cornstarch. Cover the pot and put it in the oven for 3 to 4 hours, turning the meat every 30 minutes.

To serve, lift the pork out and cut it into serving pieces. Put it on a heated serving dish and keep warm. Stir the cornstarch mixture into the sauce and simmer for 1 minute. Strain the sauce over the meat and serve at once.

Cassoulet

This excellent winter dish improves on reheating. There are many versions of it, depending on what is at hand; in the recipe given here, quantities and indeed ingredients (apart from the beans) are not critical. Preserved goose (*confit d'oie*) is sold, canned, in many delicatessens.

SERVES EIGHT

2 lb (900 g) dried white beans, soaked overnight and drained
2 onions, sliced
½ lb (225 g) salt pork, cubed
4 garlic cloves, crushed
Salt and pepper

Bouquet garni
4 cups (1 liter) veal stock or water
4 to 6 tablespoons drippings
Wing and leg of preserved goose (*confit d'oie*) or 1½-lb (700-g) boned shoulder of lamb, cubed
1-lb (450-g) boned shoulder of pork, cubed
1 lb (450 g) garlic sausage, thickly sliced
Toasted bread crumbs

Place the beans in a large saucepan with the onions, salt pork, garlic, seasoning and bouquet garni. Pour in the stock or water, adding more if necessary to cover the ingredients, and bring to a boil. Cover the pan, reduce the heat and simmer gently for 1 hour. Remove the pan from the heat and drain. Discard the bouquet garni and reserve the liquid.

Preheat the oven to 300°F (150°C).

Meanwhile, melt the drippings in a large pan and brown the goose or lamb and the pork. Put a layer of the beans into an earthenware casserole, then the goose or lamb, the pork and the garlic sausage. Cover with the rest of the beans. Pour in 1 cup of the reserved liquid, spread a layer of bread crumbs on top and put the casserole into the oven for at least 1½ hours.

More liquid can be added as necessary during the baking time, and the crust that forms on top is usually pushed down and stirred into the mixture and more toasted bread crumbs spread on top, a process which can be repeated several times. In the finished dish most of the liquid should have been absorbed, leaving the meat and beans succulent but not swimming in liquid.

Lancashire hot pot

Irish stew is similar to this and uses the same ingredients, but Lancashire hot pot is more succulent, with very little stewing liquid. Traditionally a deep, straight-sided pot is used. Mutton is the meat which should be used for this dish, but if it is not available use lamb.

SERVES SIX

3 lb (1½ kg) mutton rib chops, cut into cubes
Salt and pepper
2 to 3 lb (900 g to 1½ kg) potatoes, cut into very thin slices
1 lb (450 g) onions, sliced
1 cup (250 ml) beef stock

Preheat the oven to 325°F 170°C).

Fill an earthenware dish with well-seasoned layers of meat,

Meat and game

onion and potato in that order, finishing with a layer of potatoes neatly arranged in overlapping slices. Pour in the stock. Cover the dish and cook for 2½ to 3 hours.

Navarin printanier

This is a spring stew, made with fresh young vegetables. If you use mutton instead of lamb, double the cooking time of the meat.

SERVES SIX

6 tablespoons drippings
3-lb (1½-kg) shoulder or breast of lamb, cut into 1½-inch (3-cm) cubes
2 tablespoons flour
1 garlic clove, crushed
2 cups (500 ml) veal stock or water
1 teaspoon tomato paste, mixed with 1 tablespoon water
Salt and pepper
Bouquet garni
20 small onions
1 lb (450 g) young carrots, sliced
3 small turnips, cubed
Pinch of sugar
1 lb (450 g) new potatoes
2 lb (900 g) young green beans, sliced
1 lb (450 g) early peas, shelled
Chopped parsley

Melt 4 tablespoons of the drippings in a large frying pan. When the fat is very hot, add the meat and brown it, turning the pieces, over high heat. Pour off most of the fat, reduce the heat, sprinkle the flour over the meat and let it brown, stirring constantly. Stir in the garlic, stock or water, tomato paste, seasoning and bouquet garni. Cover the pan and simmer for 45 to 60 minutes.

Meanwhile, melt the remaining drippings in another pan. Add the onions, carrots, turnips and sugar and fry, turning the vegetables frequently, until they are well browned.

Add the potatoes to the meat and cook for 10 minutes. Add the onions, carrots and turnips and simmer for 5 minutes. Add the beans and peas and simmer for a final 10 minutes or until all the vegetables are cooked and the meat very tender.

If necessary skim the fat off the top of the stew. Sprinkle the parsley on top and serve.

Jugged hare

In this traditional English dish blood is used to thicken the sauce. If you prefer not to use the blood, a little extra beurre manié can be used instead. The stew takes a long time to make, but is well worth the effort. It improves with keeping and can be reheated the next day. Make the stuffing on the day the stew is to be eaten.

SERVES SIX

1 hare, cut into serving pieces, the blood reserved
4 tablespoons seasoned flour
4 tablespoons drippings
2 large onions, chopped
2 carrots, sliced
2 celery stalks, sliced
Sprig rosemary
2 to 3 sprigs thyme
1 teaspoon allspice
Strip of lemon rind
Salt and freshly ground black pepper
2 to 4 tablespoons beurre manié
1 tablespoon red currant jelly
6 tablespoons port or red wine

MARINADE
1 cup (250 ml) red wine
1 tablespoon oil
1 onion, coarsely chopped
1 bay leaf
1 sprig thyme
6 juniper berries, crushed
Salt and pepper

STUFFING
6 tablespoons finely diced bacon
1 onion, finely chopped
¾ cup (75 g) fresh white bread crumbs
2 tablespoons chopped suet
1 tablespoon chopped parsley
1 tablespoon fresh marjoram or 2 teaspoons dried marjoram
Salt and pepper
1 egg plus 1 egg yolk, beaten
Oil for frying

Mix together the marinade ingredients. Put the pieces of hare into a large, shallow dish, pour over the marinade and leave for at least 6 hours, turning from time to time.

Three warming meat stews : from left to right, Lancashire hot pot, cassoulet and goulash.

Preheat the oven to 325°F (170°C).

Remove the hare from the marinade. Strain and reserve the marinade. Dry the hare with a cloth and roll in the seasoned flour.

Melt the drippings in a Dutch oven and brown the pieces of hare on all sides. Add the onions, carrots and celery, cook for 1 to 2 minutes, then pour over the marinade and just enough water to cover the meat. Add the herbs, allspice and lemon rind, and season well with salt and pepper. Cover the Dutch oven tightly and bake for 3½ to 4 hours.

Remove the Dutch oven from the oven. Lift out the pieces of hare. Strain the cooking liquid into a saucepan and return the hare to the Dutch oven.

Remove and discard the herbs and rub the vegetables through a sieve into the saucepan. Add the beurre manié a little at a time, stirring constantly, and bring to a boil. Remove from the heat and gradually add some of this hot gravy to the reserved blood, mixing well, then pour it back into the pan, still mixing. Stir in the red currant jelly and port or red wine. Strain the sauce onto the hare and reheat gently.

While the hare is reheating, make the stuffing. Cook the bacon and the onion together in a saucepan until soft. Combine the bread crumbs, suet, herbs and seasoning in a bowl. Add the bacon and onion and mix well. Add enough of the beaten egg to bind the ingredients together. Shape into balls the size of a walnut. Fry until golden. Serve with the hare.

Rabbit stew

This stew can also be made with hare; use red wine instead of white and cook gently for at least 3½ to 4 hours.

SERVES FOUR

4-lb (2-kg) rabbit, cut into pieces
2 tablespoons seasoned flour
4 tablespoons butter
1 cup (250 ml) chicken stock
½ cup (125 ml) white wine
2 teaspoons tomato paste mixed with 1 tablespoon water
1 garlic clove, crushed
Bouquet garni
Salt and pepper
2 tablespoons heavy cream mixed with 2 teaspoons cornstarch
1 tablespoon chopped parsley

Coat the rabbit pieces with the flour. Heat the butter in a Dutch oven. Add the rabbit pieces and fry until brown on all sides.

Pour in the stock, wine and tomato paste. Add the garlic, bouquet garni and seasoning and bring to a boil. Reduce the heat to low, cover the Dutch oven and cook gently (or place in a 325 F/170°C oven) for 1½ to 2 hours or until the rabbit is tender. Transfer the rabbit pieces to a warm serving dish and keep hot.

Stir the cream into the cooking liquid and simmer for a few seconds until the sauce thickens. Remove the bouquet garni. Pour the sauce over the rabbit. Sprinkle the parsley on top and serve.

Braised venison with juniper berries and sour cream

Serve with puréed celeriac, braised celery or turnips and green beans.

SERVES SIX

3 lb (1½ kg) boned shoulder of venison, cut into 2-inch (5-cm) cubes
4 tablespoons seasoned flour
6 tablespoons butter
4 onions, sliced
2 tablespoons red currant jelly
12 chestnuts, peeled and boiled until tender
2 teaspoons lemon juice
½ cup (125 ml) sour cream or light cream
Salt and pepper

MARINADE
1½ cups (375 ml) red wine
2 tablespoons olive oil
10 juniper berries, crushed
Salt and pepper
1 onion, sliced
Bouquet garni

Put the ingredients for the marinade into a saucepan, bring to a boil, simmer for 20 minutes and allow to cool.

Put the venison into a deep earthenware bowl. When the marinade is room temperature, pour it over the venison. Cover the bowl and marinate the venison in a cool place for 2 days. Turn and baste the meat at least twice a day.

Preheat the oven to 325°F (170°C).

Drain the meat, dry it and roll in seasoned flour. Strain and reserve the marinade.

Melt the butter in a Dutch oven. Add the venison and fry, stirring, until browned on all sides. Add the onions and let them brown. Stir in any remaining seasoned flour, let it brown and gradually mix in the reserved marinade, stirring constantly. Cover the Dutch oven and bake in the oven for 2 hours. Stir in the red currant jelly, chestnuts and lemon juice and cook for 15 minutes more. Stir in the sour cream and adjust the seasoning.

Vegetables

Stewing, braising and casseroling can improve and transform the flavor of many vegetables. Those that have a somewhat bland flavor when simply boiled or steamed are given additional taste and texture by combining them with other contrasting vegetables. Such dishes as ratatouille, which is a superb stew made with tomatoes, eggplants, peppers and onions, or a mushroom and herb casserole can be served by themselves as a main course.

Strictly speaking, fruit should not be stewed as their qualities are most enhanced by gentle poaching. For the general treatment of fruit in liquid, and for purées, see the section on boiling and steaming.

Braised lettuce

This is a good dish to make in late summer when there is a glut of lettuces. Serve as an accompaniment to roast or broiled meat.

SERVES FOUR TO SIX

4 heads romaine lettuce
1 tablespoon butter
4 bacon slices
1 onion, chopped
1 carrot, chopped
½ cup (125 ml) chicken or veal stock, hot
Salt and freshly ground black pepper
Bouquet garni

Preheat the oven to 350°F (180°C).

Keep the lettuces whole, wash them well and trim the base as neatly as possible without detaching any leaves.

Blanch the lettuces in boiling salted water for 5 minutes. Drain them and put into a bowl of cold water at once. Drain again, squeezing the lettuce to remove any excess moisture.

Grease a large ovenproof casserole with the butter. Line the bottom of the casserole with the bacon. Cover the bacon with the onion and carrot and lay the lettuce heads on top. Pour in the stock, season well and add the bouquet garni.

Lay a piece of buttered waxed paper on top of the lettuce heads, cover the casserole and put into the oven for 45 minutes.

Lift out the lettuce heads, arrange them in a warm serving dish and keep warm. Put the casserole over high heat and boil the cooking liquid for 5 to 10 minutes or until it is well reduced. Strain the liquid over the lettuce and serve.

Braised chestnuts with Chinese cabbage

SERVES FOUR TO SIX

5 tablespoons oil
2 tablespoons dried shrimp
½-inch (1-cm) piece fresh ginger root, peeled and finely chopped
1 lb (450 g) chestnuts, peeled, skinned and boiled for 25 minutes
4 medium-sized dried Chinese mushrooms, soaked for 30 minutes, drained, stalks removed and caps quartered
1½ lb (700 g) Chinese cabbage, washed, drained and coarsely chopped
½ cup (125 ml) chicken stock
4 tablespoons soy sauce
2 tablespoons dry sherry
1½ tablespoons sugar

Heat the oil in a large frying pan. Add the shrimp, ginger, chestnuts and mushrooms and stir over moderate heat for 2 minutes. Add the cabbage and cook, stirring, for 1 minute.

Pour in the stock, soy sauce and sherry. Add the sugar and cook over low heat for 20 to 25 minutes, stirring frequently.

Red cabbage with apples

SERVES FOUR

3 tablespoons diced salt pork
2 onions, thinly sliced
2 lb (900 g) red cabbage, finely shredded
½ cup (125 ml) hard cider or apple wine
Salt and pepper
1 tablespoon brown sugar
3 tart apples, peeled, cored and sliced

Sauté the salt pork in a large casserole until the fat runs. Add the onions and fry, stirring, until they are soft. Add the cabbage, cider, salt, pepper and sugar. Stir well, cover the pan and simmer for 1 hour. Stir in the apples and cook for another hour.

Casseroled celery

SERVES FOUR

2 heads celery, trimmed and cut into short lengths
¼ cup (50 g) butter
½ cup (125 ml) chicken or vegetable stock
Salt and pepper

Blanch the celery in boiling salted water for 5 minutes and drain.

Melt the butter in a heavy casserole, add the celery and cook, turning the pieces over, until they are lightly browned. Pour in the stock, season to taste and simmer for 1 to 1½ hours or until the celery is tender.

Buttered Belgian endive

SERVES FOUR

1½ lb (700 g) Belgian endive
Sugar
¼ cup (50 g) butter
2 tablespoons water
Juice of ½ lemon
½ teaspoon salt

Drop the endive into boiling water to which a little sugar has been added, blanch for 5 minutes and drain.

Melt the butter in a heavy pan and add the endive. Cook for 3 minutes over low heat.

Add the water, lemon juice and salt and bring to a simmer. Cook, covered, over very low heat for 1 hour or bake in a 300°F (150°C) oven for 1 hour.

Braised onions

SERVES FOU

2 lb (900 g) medium-sized onions, peeled
Salt
½ cup (125 g) butter or bacon fat
¼ cup (50 g) sugar
Pepper
Chicken or veal stock

Preheat the oven to 350°F (180°C).

Parboil the onions in boiling salted water for 15 minutes.

Melt the butter or bacon fat in a heavy casserole. Add the onions and the sugar and cook over low heat, turning the onions occasionally, for 5 to 10 minutes. Season well and put the casserole into the oven for 1 hour or until the onions are tender and a rich gold color. Baste from time to time, and if the onions get too dry pour in a little stock.

Leeks provençal

This dish may be served hot, or cold as a first course or salad.

SERVES FOUR TO SIX

4 tablespoons olive oil
8 leeks, washed and cut into short lengths
1 green pepper, cored, seeded and thinly sliced
1 lb (450 g) tomatoes, peeled and quartered
12 large black olives, halved and pitted
Juice and rind of 1 lemon
Salt and pepper

Heat the oil in a large frying pan. Add the leeks and stir well. Cover the pan, reduce the heat to low and cook gently for 10 minutes, stirring occasionally.

Add the pepper, tomatoes, olives, lemon rind and juice, salt and pepper. Cover the pan and cook for 15 minutes. Remove the lemon peel and serve.

Sauerkraut

You can make your own sauerkraut or buy it in jars or cans. If you buy it, see that it is pickled in brine and not in vinegar.

Serve with ham or corned beef.

SERVES FOUR

1 lb (450 g) sauerkraut
4 bacon slices, chopped
1 carrot, quartered
1 onion, cut in half
Bouquet garni
Salt and pepper
Chicken or veal stock

Boil the sauerkraut in salted water for 10 minutes and drain well.

Heat the bacon in a heavy pan until the fat runs. Add the sauerkraut, carrot, onion and bouquet garni and season with salt and pepper. Pour in enough stock to cover the cabbage and bring to a boil. Reduce the heat, cover the pan and simmer gently on top of the stove or in a 300°F (150°C) oven for 1 hour.

Remove the pan from the heat or oven and drain the sauerkraut. Discard the carrot, onion and bouquet garni and serve.

Mushroom and herb casserole

If fresh herbs are available, use them in preference to dried ones but double the quantities.

SERVES FOUR

2 tablespoons butter
4 bacon slices, cut into
    pieces
1 garlic clove, crushed
¼ teaspoon thyme
¼ teaspoon oregano
¼ teaspoon basil
¼ teaspoon rosemary
¾ teaspoon paprika
1½ lb (700 g) mushrooms
Salt and black pepper
¾ cup (175 ml) tomato sauce,
    hot
1 cup (125 g) grated
    Parmesan cheese

Preheat the oven to 375°F (190°C).

Melt the butter in a wide, heavy pot. Add the bacon and fry, stirring, until the fat runs. Add the garlic, herbs and paprika, reduce the heat and cook for 2 minutes. Add the mushrooms and cook for 3 minutes, stirring. Season well.

Pour the tomato sauce over the mushrooms. Sprinkle the Parmesan cheese on top and cook on the top shelf of the oven for 10 minutes or until the top is slightly browned and bubbling.

Ratatouille

Ratatouille may be eaten either hot—as an accompaniment to other dishes—or cold, in smaller quantities, as an hors d'oeuvre.

SERVES FOUR

5 tablespoons olive oil
3 onions, thinly sliced
2 garlic cloves, chopped
2 green peppers, seeded and
    sliced into thin strips
1 red pepper, seeded and
    sliced into thin strips
3 medium-sized eggplants,
    degorged
4 zucchini, sliced
4 large tomatoes (or ½ lb/
    225 g canned tomatoes),
    peeled and chopped
Salt and freshly ground
    black pepper
¼ teaspoon each fresh or
    dried rosemary, thyme
    and basil

Heat the oil over low heat in a heavy casserole. Add the onions and garlic and cook for 5 minutes or until they are soft, but not brown. Add the peppers, eggplants and zucchini, stir well and cook over very low heat for at least 30 minutes, stirring from time to time.

Add the tomatoes and season well with salt and black pepper. Add the herbs and cook for 30 minutes more on low heat.

Stuffed peppers

Serve the peppers hot or cold, as an hors d'oeuvre or main dish.

SERVES FOUR

4 large or 8 small peppers
1 lb (450 g) lean ground beef
Grated rind and juice of
    1 lemon
⅔ cup (125 g) rice, washed
    and drained
1 teaspoon dried mint
1 teaspoon turmeric
1 teaspoon salt
1 teaspoon sugar
Cayenne pepper
2 tablespoons olive oil
2 tablespoons tomato paste,
    mixed in 1 cup (250 ml)
    water

Cut the tops off the peppers and remove the seeds and pith. Reserve the tops.

Put the ground beef, lemon rind and juice, rice, mint, turmeric, salt, sugar and a pinch of cayenne into a bowl and mix well. Stuff the peppers with the mixture.

Heat the oil in a saucepan just large enough to hold the peppers. Put the peppers into the pan, spoon a little of the tomato paste mixture on top of each pepper and cover them with the reserved tops. Pour the remaining tomato paste mixture around the peppers, reduce the heat, cover the pan and cook gently for 40 to 50 minutes or until the peppers are tender and the rice cooked.

Peperonata

This Italian dish may be served hot or cold, on its own or with meat and poultry.

SERVES SIX

4 tablespoons olive oil
1 large Bermuda onion,
    thinly sliced
2 garlic cloves, crushed
1½ lb (700 g) red peppers,
    cored, seeded and cut into
    strips
2 lb (900 g) ripe tomatoes,
    peeled and chopped
Salt

Heat the oil in a frying pan. Add the onion and garlic and fry until the onion is soft and lightly colored.

Add the peppers, cover the pan and cook gently for 20 minutes, stirring occasionally.

Add the tomatoes, season to taste with salt and cook, uncovered, for 30 minutes or until the tomatoes are cooked to a pulp.

Caponata

This Sicilian dish is traditionally served piled on a platter with slices of spiny lobster or canned tuna fish arranged on top.

SERVES FOUR TO SIX

Olive oil
6 cups (900 g) diced egg-
    plants, degorged
1 head celery, stalks cut into
    small pieces
1 large onion, sliced
8 tablespoons tomato paste,
    mixed with 4 tablespoons
    water
1 tablespoon sugar
2 tablespoons capers
½ cup (125 g) black olives
    pitted and quartered
6 anchovies, soaked in
    warm water for 15
    minutes, drained and
    chopped
½ cup (125 ml) wine vinegar
Salt and pepper

Heat some oil—the amount of oil is difficult to estimate as eggplants tend to absorb it rapidly—in a large frying pan and fry the eggplants gently, turning them until they are browned all over. Using a slotted spoon, lift them out and drain.

Put the celery in boiling water and blanch for 1 minute.

Heat 4 tablespoons of oil in a large saucepan. Add the onion and fry until soft. Stir in the tomato paste and sugar and cook, stirring, for 15 minutes or until the mixture is reduced and dark.

Add the celery, eggplants, capers, olives, anchovies and vinegar. Season if necessary and simmer for 10 minutes.

Cereals

Cereals, because of their absorbent qualities and their relatively neutral flavor, are an ideal base for a stew or casserole containing several other more distinctive ingredients. The cereals most commonly used are rice, barley, cracked wheat, hominy (coarsely ground corn) and kasha (coarsely ground buckwheat, millet or barley).

There are several methods of casseroling cereals, but two in particular will serve for most purposes. Either add the cereal and the liquid after the other main ingredients and the flavorings have been cooked gently in butter or oil, or cook the cereal first in butter or oil with a little onion and garlic and a few spices before adding the rest of the ingredients and the cooking liquid.

Contrasting textures add interest to cereal-based stews and casseroles: for example, olives, nuts, chopped peppers or dried fruit.

Creole jambalaya

This is an adaptation of a jambalaya from Louisiana. The dish was probably introduced to New Orleans by early Spanish explorers.

SERVES FOUR

6 tablespoons olive oil
1 large onion, chopped
2 garlic cloves, crushed
1 large green pepper, seeded and chopped
1¼ cups (225 g) long-grain rice, washed, soaked in cold water for 30 minutes and well drained
¾ lb (350 g) cooked ham, diced
1½ lb (700 g) tomatoes, skinned and chopped
1¼ cups (300 ml) water
½ teaspoon dried thyme
2 tablespoons chopped parsley
Salt and pepper
½ to 1 teaspoon cayenne pepper
¾ lb (350 g) shelled shrimp, deveined

Heat the oil in a large sauté pan. Add the onion, garlic and green pepper and fry, stirring, until the onion is golden. Add the rice and fry, stirring constantly, for 3 minutes. Stir in the ham, tomatoes, water, thyme, parsley, salt, pepper and cayenne and bring to a boil.

Cover the pan tightly, reduce the heat to low and simmer for 30 minutes or until the rice is tender and most of the liquid has been absorbed. Stir in the shrimp 5 minutes before the end of the cooking time.

Rissotto alla Milanese

Good Italian rice such as Arborio or Vialone is the most suitable for making risotto. Risotto alla Milanese is served on its own or with Osso buco.

SERVES FOUR

¼ cup (50 g) butter
1 small onion, peeled and chopped
2 tablespoons beef marrow (optional)
2 cups (350 g) Italian rice
½ cup (125 ml) white wine
5 cups (1¼ liters) chicken stock, boiling
4 saffron threads, soaked in 2 tablespoons hot chicken stock for 10 minutes
¼ cup (25 g) grated Parmesan cheese

Melt half the butter in a large pan and cook the onion until it is golden. Stir in the bone marrow, if you are using it, and the rice and fry for 2 minutes. Add the wine, reduce the heat to low and cook until it has been absorbed. Add the hot stock, a cupful at a time, waiting until one cup has been absorbed before adding the next. After half the stock has been absorbed, check to see if the rice is cooked. If the rice is not tender, add another cupful of stock and check the rice again when it has been absorbed. It will take between 20 and 30 minutes for all the stock to be used. As the end of the cooking time is reached, stir the rice with a fork to prevent sticking. When the rice is cooked, mix in the saffron mixture, the remaining butter and the cheese and serve.

Bulghur pilaff

SERVES FOUR

½ cup (125 g) butter
1 onion, chopped
1½ cups (225 g) cracked wheat (bulghur), washed and drained
½ lb (225 g) mushrooms, cleaned and sliced
2½ cups (625 ml) chicken stock
Salt and pepper

Melt the butter in a saucepan. Add the onion and cook gently until it is soft. Stir in the cracked wheat and the mushrooms, increase the heat and cook for about 5 minutes, stirring frequently. Add the chicken stock and seasoning and bring to a boil. Cook rapidly for about 5 minutes, then lower the heat and simmer for 10 minutes or until the liquid has been absorbed. Remove from the heat. Place a clean cloth over the pan, cover with a lid; let stand for about 15 minutes before serving.

Tomato rice

SERVES SIX TO EIGHT

1 onion, chopped
1 garlic clove, chopped
1 lb (450 g) tomatoes, blanched, peeled and chopped
4 tablespoons vegetable oil
2 cups (350 g) long-grain rice, washed, soaked in cold water for 30 minutes and drained
3¾ cups (925 ml) chicken stock
Salt
Cayenne pepper

Put the onion, garlic and tomatoes into a blender and reduce to a purée.

Heat the oil in a heavy pan. Add the rice and cook, stirring, over low heat until the oil has been absorbed, taking care that the rice does not burn. Add the tomato and onion purée and the stock. Season to taste with salt and a large pinch of cayenne and bring to a boil. Cover the pan and cook, over the lowest possible heat, for about 25 minutes or until the rice is tender.

Paella Valenciana

Paella may include both meat and seafood, seafood only, or simply vegetables.

Paella can be served with a green or mixed salad.

SERVES FOUR TO SIX

4 tablespoons olive oil
3 garlic cloves, halved
1 onion, chopped
3 tomatoes, blanched, peeled and chopped
1 sweet red pepper, seeded and sliced
1 chicken, cut into serving pieces
1 teaspoon paprika
2 cups (350 g) rice
¼ teaspoon powdered saffron
3¾ cups (925 ml) chicken stock
1 lb (450 g) peas, shelled
½ lb (225 g) shelled shrimp
16 mussels, scrubbed and beards removed

Heat the oil in a large, shallow sauté pan. Add the garlic and cook gently for 2 to 3 minutes to flavor the oil. Remove and discard the garlic.

Add the onion, tomatoes, red pepper, chicken pieces and paprika. Cook for 10 minutes, stirring frequently.

Add the rice and cook for 2 to 3 minutes more, stirring constantly. Stir in the saffron, pour in the stock and bring to a boil. Add the peas and shrimp and cook, uncovered, over low heat for 15 minutes or until almost all the liquid has been absorbed.

Place the mussels on top of the rice. Cover the pan and cook for 6 to 8 minutes until the mussels open. Discard any that remain closed. Serve hot.

Biryani

Of central Asian origin, Biryani is a favorite dish in Pakistan.

Serve it with a yogurt and cucumber salad, various chutneys and relishes.

SERVES FOUR TO SIX

½ cup (125 g) plus 2 tablespoons butter
2 onions, finely chopped, plus 1 onion, finely sliced
1-inch (2-cm) piece fresh ginger root, peeled and finely chopped
4 garlic cloves, crushed
1 green chili, finely chopped
2 teaspoons cumin seeds
2 lb (900 g) boned leg or shoulder of lamb, cut into cubes
1-inch (2-cm) piece stick cinnamon
6 cloves
6 whole cardamom pods
1¼ cups (315 ml) yogurt, mixed with ½ cup (125 ml) water
Salt
2 cups (350 g) basmati rice, washed and soaked in water for 30 minutes
½ teaspoon saffron threads, soaked in 3 tablespoons boiling water for 20 minutes
4 tablespoons slivered, blanched almonds
4 tablespoons raisins
2 hard-cooked eggs, quartered

Melt ¼ cup of the butter in a large saucepan. Add the finely chopped onions, ginger, garlic, chili and cumin seeds and fry, stirring frequently, over moderately low heat until the onions are soft.

Add the lamb, increase the heat and fry, turning the cubes over, for 10 minutes or until they are well browned. Add the cinnamon, cloves, cardamom, the yogurt and water mixture and 1 teaspoon of salt and bring to a boil. Cover the pan, reduce the heat to low and simmer for 30 minutes or until the lamb is nearly cooked.

Preheat the oven to 350°F (180°C).

Meanwhile, cook the rice in plenty of boiling salted water for 2 minutes. Remove the pan from the heat and drain the rice.

Paella Valenciana and barley and vegetable casserole.

Melt ¼ cup of the remaining butter in a casserole. Spread one-third of the rice over the bottom of the casserole, sprinkle with 1 tablespoon of the saffron water and spoon half the lamb mixture over the rice. Repeat the layers ending with the rice and saffron.

Cover the casserole and put it in the oven for 40 minutes or until the rice is cooked.

Meanwhile, prepare the garnish. Heat the remaining butter in a small frying pan and fry the sliced onion, stirring frequently, until it is golden brown. Using a slotted spoon, remove the onion and drain on paper towels.

Add the almonds and raisins to the frying pan and fry, stirring, until lightly browned.

Remove the casserole from the oven and garnish with the fried onions, almonds, raisins and hard-cooked eggs.

Barley and vegetable casserole

Serve this dish with roast meat or poultry, or on its own.

SERVES FOUR

6 tablespoons butter
1 large onion, finely chopped
4 celery stalks, chopped
¾ cup (125 g) diced turnips
1½ cups (225 g) sliced carrots
⅔ cup (125 g) pearl barley
2 cups (500 ml) chicken stock, boiling
1½ teaspoons salt
Black pepper
½ teaspoon thyme
1 tablespoon chopped parsley

Preheat the oven to 350°F (180°C). Melt the butter in a large frying pan. Add the onion and fry gently, stirring occasionally, until it is soft and golden. Add the celery, turnips and carrots and cook for 10 minutes, stirring to coat with the butter.

Stir in the barley. Remove the pan from the heat and spoon the mixture into a well-buttered casserole. Pour in the stock, season well with salt and black pepper and add the thyme.

Cover the casserole and put it in the oven for 45 to 60 minutes or until the barley is tender and all the stock has been absorbed.

Serve garnished with the parsley.

Broiling

Broiling is a quick, efficient way of cooking meat, poultry, young game birds, fish, cheese and some fruit and vegetables. One of the main advantages of this method is that little fat, and usually no liquid, is used, but the disadvantages are that only good-quality, and therefore expensive, cuts of meat are required and the cooking must be done only minutes before the food is put on the table.

Barbecuing is closely related to broiling, so the food is usually prepared and cooked in exactly the same way, but with different utensils, and using a different source of heat (coals, charcoal or wood).

Preheat the broiler before you start cooking. The broiler rack or skewers on which the food is to be cooked should be brushed with fat or oil to prevent sticking, and if a rotisserie is to be used for meat, make sure that you put the spit through the center of the meat or bird to insure that it turns easily and cooks evenly.

The cuts of meat that are most suitable for broiling are steaks, ham slices, chops, cutlets or bacon slices. Shoulder or leg of lamb and leg and fillets of pork may be cut into cubes and used for kebabs, and whole legs may be spit-roasted. Sausages and such variety meats as kidney and liver often accompany broiled chops. Large kidneys should be cut in half and skewered to keep them flat.

Game is hardly ever broiled or barbecued, but young, tender game birds or poultry can be cooked this way very successfully. Small birds, for example quail, may be cooked whole if they are split down the backbone and spread out flat. Larger birds may be cut in half or in pieces.

All meat, poultry and game birds may be marinated in a mixture of oil, herbs and spices before being broiled. This not only insures that the meat will be tender but adds to the flavor.

Fish and shellfish may also be marinated before being broiled. Shellfish and small fish, such as mackerel, whiting, sole, herring or mullet may be cooked whole, but cut larger fish into steaks or cutlets. Firm-fleshed fish are the most suitable for kebabs: use cod, halibut or haddock cut into cubes.

Mushrooms, tomatoes, eggplants, onions and peppers can all be broiled, and they are often added to meat or fish kebabs.

Broiled grapefruit is a popular first course, but there are other fruit that can be broiled—pear or peach halves, slices of pineapple or bananas for example. They can be served as an accompaniment to meat, game or poultry, or by themselves as a first course or dessert. Bananas may also be cut into chunks and wrapped in slices of bacon before being broiled.

Fish and shellfish

Mussels with garlic butter 128

Broiled oysters 128

Oysters on skewers 128

Haddock kebabs 127
Boiled fennel 92,
Deep-fried parsley 153

Red mullet with dill butter 127
Asparagus 92,
Cottage fries 151

Sea bass with herbs flambé 127
Belgian endive, orange and watercress salad 213, Potato croquettes 151

Broiled halibut steaks with orange sauce 127
Petits pois à la française 91, Soufflé potatoes 150

Broiled salmon steaks 127
Sauce hollandiase 67,
Broiled mushrooms 134, Zucchini 93

Broiled lobster 127
Sauce hollandaise 67,
Lyonnaise potatoes 151,
Asparagus 92

Lobster thermidor 128
Avocado salad 213

Scallop brochettes 128
Green salad 213,
Boiled rice 97

Seafood en brochette 128
Boiled rice or noodles 97, Ratatouille 121

Herring with mustard sauce 126
Potato croquettes 151,
Steamed broccoli 92

Deviled herring 126
Spinach purée 92,
Green salad 213

Cod rarebit 127

Clams with Gruyère sauce 128
Green salad 213

Poultry and game birds

Broiled chicken livers 130

Chicken brochettes 130

Poussins with lemon butter 130
Boiled potatoes, peas 93

Spatchcock chicken 130 Mashed potatoes, Snow peas 93, Cottage Fries 151, Chestnuts with Chinese cabbage 120

Deviled turkey legs 130
Green salad 213,
Boiled rice 97

Broiled partridge à la diable 130
Spinach purée 92,
Zucchini 93,
Shoestring potatoes 150

Broiled quail with orange and sage sauce 131
Green salad 213,
Potato chips 150

Meat and game

Pork saté 133

Lebanese kebabs 132

Minute steaks 132
Shoestring potatoes 150
Petit pois à la française 91

Tournedos Rossini 132
Green salad 213

Hamburgers 132
Tomato sauce 69,
French fries 150

Broiled pork chops 133
Cottage fries 151,
Spinach purée 92

Ham steaks with apricots 133
Mashed potatoes 93,
Braised lettuce 120,
Shell beans 92

Stuffed pork chops 133
Celery, apple and walnut salad 213,
Potatoes à la dauphinoise 180

Mixed grill 132
Mashed potatoes 93

Vegetables, Fruit and dairy products

Broiled grapefruit 134

Grapefruit anisette 134

Welsh rabbit 135
Green salad 213

Broiled tomatoes 134

Broiled mushrooms 134

Peaches with wine 134
Sauce sabayon 69

Broiled pineapple with rum 134
Cream

Cheese toast 134

Cheese and walnut fingers 135

Broiled Roquefort 135

First courses

Main courses

Light lunch-supper dishes

Accompaniments

Desserts

Miscellaneous

Fish and shellfish

All fish which are to be broiled should be brushed with oil or melted butter. Make two or three diagonal cuts in such round, oily fish as herring, mackerel or trout, to allow the heat to penetrate. Put the fish on a greased rack, skin side away from the heat if the fish has been filleted, and cook under or over a moderate heat until the flesh flakes easily when tested with a knife.

Cooking times depend on the thickness of the fish: a thin fillet may need only six to eight minutes, whereas a thick steak or a large whole mackerel may take fifteen or sixteen minutes. Baste when necessary with melted butter or oil, and season just before bringing the fish to the table or serve with savory butter.

Such shellfish as lobster and spiny lobster must be killed just before broiling, and then coated with a sauce or brushed with melted butter and sprinkled with grated cheese. A 1¼- to 1½-pound (575- to 700-g) lobster will take about fifteen minutes to cook through.

Herring with mustard sauce

SERVES FOUR

- 2 tablespoons French mustard
- 1 tablespoon cream
- 1 cup (250 ml) hot béchamel sauce
- 4 herring, gutted
- 1 tablespoon oil or melted butter

First make the sauce. Stir the mustard and cream into the béchamel sauce and keep hot. Preheat the broiler to moderate. Brush the herring all over with the oil or butter and place them on the broiler rack. Broil for 3 to 4 minutes on each side and serve immediately with the mustard sauce.

Deviled herring

SERVES FOUR

- 4 herring, cleaned and gutted
- 4 tablespoons French mustard
- 4 tablespoons white bread crumbs, mixed with ½ teaspoon salt and black pepper and ¼ teaspoon cayenne pepper
- 2 tablespoons melted butter
- 1 lemon, quartered

Preheat the broiler to fairly low.

Score the skin of the herring on both sides. Coat them with mustard and then roll in the seasoned bread crumbs. Sprinkle over the melted butter. Broil for about 8 minutes, turning once. Serve with lemon wedges.

Haddock kebabs

Serve haddock kebabs with a green salad, savory rice or triangles of buttered toast.

SERVES FOUR

8 slices bacon
**2 lb (900 g) haddock steaks,
 1 inch (2 cm) thick**
2 tablespoons seasoned flour
**16 small onions or 4 medium
 onions, quartered**
**16 tiny tomatoes or 8
 medium-sized tomatoes,
 halved**
**¼ cup (50 g) melted butter,
 seasoned with salt and
 black pepper**

LEMON SAUCE
Juice of 1 lemon
**1 tablespoon chopped fresh
 parsley**

1 cup (250 ml) hot béchamel sauce made with milk in which the rind of 1 lemon has infused for 15 minutes

First make the sauce. Stir the lemon juice and parsley into the prepared béchamel. Keep hot.

Divide each bacon slice in half. Cut the fish into 16 cubes, roll them in seasoned flour and wrap a piece of bacon around each cube.

Blanch the onions for 5 minutes and drain them.

Preheat the broiler to high. Thread 4 skewers with pieces of fish, onion and tomato. Brush all over with seasoned butter and broil until cooked through, turning the skewers frequently to ensure that the kebabs are cooked on all sides.

Serve with the lemon sauce.

Red mullet with dill butter

SERVES TWO

**4 medium-sized red mullet,
 cleaned and gutted**
2 tablespoons olive oil
1 lemon, cut into wedges

DILL BUTTER
**3 tablespoons butter,
 softened**
**1 tablespoon finely chopped
 fresh dill weed**
1 teaspoon lemon juice
1 garlic clove, crushed
Salt and black pepper

Make the dill butter first. Mix the softened butter with the dill, lemon juice, garlic and seasoning. Set aside.

Preheat the broiler to moderate. Brush the fish with the oil and broil for about 5 minutes on each side. Transfer the mullet to a warm platter and spread with the dill butter. Serve with lemon wedges.

Cod rarebit

SERVES FOUR

**1½ lb (700 g) cod fillets or 4
 cod steaks**
2 tablespoons melted butter
**⅔ cup (50 g) grated Cheddar
 cheese**
2 tablespoons cream

*Sea bass with herbs flambé is a
spectacular dinner party dish.*

Salt and black pepper
4 slices hot toast

Preheat the broiler to fairly low.

Brush the fish with melted butter and broil for about 15 minutes, turning once.

Mix the grated cheese with the cream and seasoning and place spoonfuls of the mixture evenly over the fish. Continue to broil until the cheese has melted and browned.

Serve on the hot toast.

Sea bass with herbs flambé

SERVES FOUR

**3-lb (1½-kg) sea bass, cleaned
 and gutted**
2 to 3 tablespoons oil
Salt and black pepper
**2 or 3 sprigs each of thyme,
 rosemary and fennel, and
 additional sprigs for
 garnish**
3 tablespoons Pernod

Preheat the broiler to moderate.

Make two or three slits on either side of the fish. Brush the fish all over with the oil and season with salt and pepper. Put sprigs of herbs into the incisions and into the gut cavity. Broil the fish for about 20 minutes, turning once.

Place the fish on a heatproof serving dish that has been lined with sprigs of herbs. Warm the Pernod, ignite it and pour over the fish. Serve immediately.

Broiled halibut steaks with orange sauce

This method of broiling white fish keeps it moist. It is also suitable for skinned whole flounder and sole.

SERVES FOUR

Grated rind of 1 orange
**1 tablespoon chopped fresh
 chives**
**1 cup (250 ml) béchamel
 sauce, hot**
4 halibut steaks
1 tablespoon seasoned flour
¼ cup (50 g) butter
Juice of ½ orange

First prepare the sauce. Stir the grated orange rind and chives into the béchamel. Keep the sauce hot until the fish is ready.

Before heating the broiler, remove the wire rack from the

broiler pan and grease the bottom of the pan.

Coat the steaks in the seasoned flour and lay them in the broiler pan. Dot them with butter and cook under medium heat for 5 minutes on each side, basting frequently with butter to keep the fish moist.

Transfer the fish to a warm serving dish, sprinkle with the orange juice and serve the sauce separately.

Broiled salmon steaks

A hollandaise sauce may be served with the salmon instead of the maître d'hôtel butter.

SERVES FOUR

4 large salmon steaks
¼ cup (50 g) melted butter
Salt and black pepper
**¼ cup (50 g) maître d'hôtel
 butter**
Lemon wedges

Preheat the broiler to moderate.

Brush the fish with melted butter and broil for 3 to 5 minutes on each side or until the fish is cooked.

Transfer the fish to a warm serving dish and season lightly. Divide the maître d'hôtel butter between the salmon steaks and serve with lemon wedges.

Broiled lobster

SERVES TWO

½ cup (125 g) melted butter
**2 uncooked lobsters (about
 1 lb/450 g each) split in
 half and prepared, claws
 cracked**
Salt and black pepper
**4 tablespoons fresh white
 bread crumbs**
Parsley

Preheat the broiler to moderate.

Pour half the melted butter over the flesh of the lobsters and place them, shell sides down, with the claws, under a medium broiler. Cook for 15 minutes or until the lobsters are cooked and the shells bright red. Season well.

Meanwhile, heat the remaining butter in a small pan, add the bread crumbs and fry until they are golden. Sprinkle the bread crumbs on the lobsters and broil until the crumbs are lightly browned. Garnish with parsley.

Fish and shellfish

Lobster thermidor

This dish is best served with a mixed green salad.

SERVES FOUR

4 uncooked lobsters (about 1 lb/450 g each), split in half and prepared, claws cracked
Olive oil
3 tablespoons finely chopped shallots
1 tablespoon chopped fresh tarragon
1 tablespoon chopped fresh parsley
½ cup (125 ml) white wine
2 tablespoons butter
2 tablespoons flour
1 cup (250 ml) milk
1 cup (250 ml) heavy cream
Pinch cayenne pepper
Salt and black pepper
1 egg yolk, beaten
2 teaspoons French mustard
3 tablespoons grated Parmesan cheese

Preheat the broiler to fairly low.

Place the lobsters, shell sides down, with the claws, on an oiled broiler pan. Brush them with oil and broil for about 15 minutes or until the lobsters are cooked and the shells bright red.

Meanwhile, put the shallots, herbs and wine in a small saucepan and bring to a boil. Simmer until all but 2 tablespoons of the liquid has evaporated. Strain the liquid and set aside.

Melt the butter in another pan and stir in the flour. Gradually add the milk and cream, stirring constantly. Add the cayenne and seasoning to taste. Pour in the reduced wine and cook until the sauce thickens. Remove the pan from the heat and stir in the egg yolk and mustard. Keep the sauce warm in a double boiler, stirring frequently to prevent a skin forming.

When the lobsters are cooked, remove them from the broiler. Increase the broiler heat to high.

Remove the tail meat and meat from the cracked claws and cut it into small cubes. Add half the sauce to the lobster meat, mix well and fill the tail shells of the lobsters with this mixture. Pour the rest of the sauce over the lobsters, coating the meat. Sprinkle with the cheese and broil for about 5 minutes or until the tops are golden.

Scallop brochettes

Serve these brochettes on a bed of rice with a green salad or by themselves as a first course.

SERVES FOUR

16 small scallops, removed from their shells
16 small mushrooms, wiped clean
1 large orange, cut into 16 pieces
8 mint leaves, cut in half

MARINADE
¼ cup (65 ml) olive oil
¼ cup (65 ml) white wine
1 garlic clove, crushed
Salt and freshly ground black pepper
Juice of 1 lemon

Mix the marinade ingredients in a shallow dish and add the scallops, stirring to coat them well. Set aside in a cool place for 1 hour.

Preheat the broiler to moderate. Remove the rack.

Drain the scallops and reserve the marinade. Thread the scallops alternately with the remaining ingredients on four long skewers. Line the broiler pan with foil and lay the skewers in the pan. Broil for 20 minutes, basting with the marinade and turning them over frequently. Transfer the brochettes to warm plates and serve immediately.

Seafood en brochettes

SERVES FOUR

12 large mussels, steamed and removed from their shells
4 slices bacon, each stretched and cut into 3 and rolled up
12 jumbo shrimp, shelled
12 small mushrooms
1 green pepper, cored, seeded and cut into 12 pieces
1 garlic clove, crushed
4 tablespoons butter
Salt and black pepper
Parsley sprigs

Preheat the broiler to moderate.

Thread the mussels, bacon rolls, shrimp, mushrooms and green pepper alternately onto 4 long skewers.

Put the garlic, butter, salt and pepper into a saucepan and heat very gently until the butter

has melted. Brush the brochettes with the melted butter and broil for about 8 minutes, turning them over frequently until they are cooked.

Garnish with parsley sprigs.

Mussels with garlic butter

This dish makes an excellent first course served with French bread.

SERVES FOUR

24 large mussels, cooked
½ cup (125 g) butter, softened
2 garlic cloves, crushed
1½ tablespoons finely chopped fresh parsley
6 tablespoons fine white bread crumbs

Preheat the broiler to hot.

Remove the mussels from their shells and place each one in a half shell.

Mix together the butter, garlic and parsley. Spread it equally over the mussels. Sprinkle with the bread crumbs.

Place the mussels in a shallow broiler pan and broil for about 3 minutes or until the butter has melted and the crumbs are golden.

Oysters on skewers

This dish is served as a first course.

SERVES FOUR

12 oysters, removed from their shells with the liquid reserved
12 small mushrooms
4 tablespoons melted butter
1 teaspoon lemon juice
3 tablespoons dried white bread crumbs
Freshly ground black pepper
4 large lemon slices

Preheat the broiler to low.

In a shallow pan, poach the oysters for 1 minute in their own liquid. Arrange them alternately with the mushrooms on small skewers.

Mix the melted butter and lemon juice and dip the skewers in this mixture before rolling them in the bread crumbs.

Place on an oiled broiler rack and broil for about 4 minutes, sprinkling with the butter and turning them over frequently.

Season with the pepper and serve at once with lemon slices.

Clams with Gruyère sauce

SERVES FOUR

24 clams
2 tablespoons butter
1 shallot, finely chopped
2 teaspoons chopped fresh parsley
½ cup (125 ml) heavy cream
2 tablespoons grated Gruyère cheese
Salt and pepper
1 tablespoon dried bread crumbs

Open the clams, wash off any sand and return them to their half shells.

Melt the butter in a small saucepan and cook the shallot until soft. Add the parsley, cook for another minute and then add the cream. Simmer for 1 minute before adding the cheese, salt and freshly ground pepper.

Preheat the broiler to moderately high.

Place the clams in a broiler pan and pour the sauce over them. Sprinkle with the bread crumbs. Broil for about 5 minutes and serve at once.

Broiled oysters

Serve these broiled oysters as a first course.

SERVES TWO

1 bunch watercress, stalks trimmed off and leaves finely chopped
¼ cup (65 ml) cream
1 teaspoon lemon juice
Pinch cayenne pepper
Salt
2 tablespoons grated Parmesan cheese
12 oysters, cleaned and top shells removed
2 tablespoons dried white bread crumbs

Preheat the broiler to moderate.

Put the watercress, cream, lemon juice, cayenne pepper and salt in a small saucepan and cook over low heat until the watercress is cooked. Rub the mixture through a fine sieve into a small bowl and stir in the cheese.

Lay the oysters on a broiler pan. Spoon the sauce equally over each oyster and sprinkle with the bread crumbs.

Place the pan under the broiler for 5 minutes or until the top is golden and bubbling. Serve hot.

Compound butters

Compound butters can be made with almost any savory flavorings, providing the flavorings are not too liquid.

Compound butters are always chilled before being used, and can either be served in small pots or cut into fancy shapes. They are always served with hot food unless spread on toast.

Maître d'hôtel butter

¼ **cup (50 g) butter**
2 teaspoons lemon juice
2 teaspoons finely chopped fresh parsley
Salt and black pepper

Cream the butter and add the lemon juice very gradually, a few drops at a time. Mix in the parsley and seasoning.

Egg and chive butter

¼ **cup (50 g) butter, softened**
2 yolks of hard-cooked eggs
Salt and freshly ground black pepper
1 tablespoon chopped fresh chives
1 teaspoon French mustard

Put the butter and egg yolks in a small bowl and mash the yolks into the butter until the mixture is smooth and evenly combined. Beat in the remaining ingredients.

Orange butter

Lemon can be substituted for orange, in the same quantities, to make a lemon butter.
¼ **cup (50 g) butter**
Grated rind of ½ orange
2 teaspoons orange juice
Salt and black pepper

Soften the butter, mix in the orange rind and juice and season to taste.

Shallot butter

¼ **cup (50 g) butter**
2 shallots, peeled, chopped and pounded

Soften the butter and mix well with the shallots. Rub the butter mixture through a fine sieve.

Shrimp butter

½ **cup (50 g) shrimp, cooked and shelled**
¼ **cup (50 g) butter, softened**
¼ **teaspoon salt**

Pound the shrimp in a mortar to make a smooth paste. Place the butter and salt in a small mixing bowl and gradually beat in the shrimp. Rub the butter mixture through a fine sieve.

Garlic butter

2 garlic cloves, peeled and crushed
¼ **cup (50 g) butter**

Pound the garlic and beat into the butter. Rub the butter mixture through a fine sieve.

Mustard butter

¼ **cup (50 g) butter**
1 tablespoon French mustard

Soften the butter and mix in the mustard slowly, blending well.

Herb butter

Tarragon, chives, or chervil and chives may be used to make a herb butter. Use approximately 1½ tablespoons of herbs to ¼ cup (50 g) of butter. Blanch the herbs in boiling water before pounding them. Add them to the softened butter and season well. Rub the butter mixture through a fine sieve.

Tomato butter

1 tablespoon tomato paste
¼ **cup (50 g) butter**

Beat the tomato paste into the softened butter.

Anchovy butter

4 anchovy fillets
¼ **cup (50 g) butter**
1 teaspoon lemon juice
Black pepper

Pound the anchovy fillets to a paste and work them into the softened butter with the lemon juice and freshly ground black pepper. Rub the butter mixture through a fine sieve.

Delicately flavored compound butters are the perfect accompaniment to broiled fish or meat—or spread them on melba toast to accompany salads.

Poultry and game birds

To broil poultry or game birds, brush the whole, halved or cut-up birds with plenty of melted butter, oil or marinade as the meat tends to become dry. Broil under a moderate heat until the juices run clear when the meat is pierced: about twelve to fourteen minutes for small pieces, or a small bird such as quail, and twenty to thirty minutes for a spring chicken skewered flat, or large pieces.

Poussins with lemon butter

A poussin is a 4- to 6-week-old chicken weighing between ½ and 1 pound (225 and 450 g), and is only sufficient for 1 portion. A larger bird, up to 2 pounds (900 g), is called a double poussin.

SERVES FOUR

4 poussins
Salt and pepper
6 tablespoons lemon butter

Preheat the broiler to moderate.

Using a sharp knife, cut the poussins through the breastbone and, with your hands, crack the two halves until they lie flat.

Grease the rack in the broiler and lay the birds on it, bone side up. Season well with salt and pepper. Spread generously with the lemon butter.

Broil—the birds must be at least 3 inches (8 cm) below the heat—for 8 minutes, baste well with more butter and broil for 7 minutes more. Turn the birds over and broil, basting once, for another 15 minutes. Test by piercing the thighs with the point of a sharp knife—if the juices run clear the birds are done. Serve immediately.

Chicken brochettes

Serve chicken brochettes with fried rice and a variety of salads.

SERVES FOUR

4 chicken breasts, boned
32 small onions
32 cherry tomatoes, or 8 medium tomatoes, quartered
2 green peppers, cut into pieces

MARINADE
4 tablespoons olive oil
4 tablespoons lemon juice
2 garlic cloves, crushed
1 teaspoon salt
¼ teaspoon cayenne pepper

Mix the marinade ingredients in a bowl. Cut the chicken breasts into 1-inch (2-cm) cubes and add them to the marinade. Set aside for at least 2 hours, turning the chicken occasionally.

Preheat the broiler to hot.

Thread 8 skewers with the chicken and vegetables.

Broil the brochettes on one side for about 4 minutes, turn and broil 4 minutes more or until the meat is cooked. Serve at once.

Spatchcock chicken

Spatchcock means a bird killed and cooked immediately. This rarely happens today, but the name lives on to denote a simple dish of broiled spring chicken. Spring chickens, also known as broilers, are 3 months old and weigh between 2 and 2½ pounds (900 g and 1 kg). Two birds will feed 4 people.

SERVES FOUR

2 chickens (broilers)
Salt and pepper
Juice of 1 lemon
½ cup (125 g) butter, melted
1 garlic clove, crushed
2 teaspoons flour
½ cup (125 ml) white wine
Lemon wedges

Split the chickens in half down the back. Cut out the backbone. Season well, sprinkle with lemon juice and set aside for 10 minutes.

Preheat the broiler to moderate.

Brush the birds lavishly with the butter and place them bone side up on a greased rack under the broiler—they should be at least 3 inches (8 cm) from the heat. Broil for about 30 minutes on each side, basting regularly.

Pierce the thighs with a skewer or the point of a sharp knife—if the juices run clear the birds are cooked.

Put the broiled chickens on a heated serving dish, cover and keep hot in a low oven.

Pour the butter from the broiler into a saucepan, adding any left over from basting. Add the garlic and fry over gentle heat for a few seconds. Stir in the flour. Pour in the wine and cook, stirring, until the sauce comes to a boil. Adjust the seasoning and add a little lemon juice.

Serve the chicken garnished with the lemon wedges, and with the sauce served separately in a gravy boat.

Broiled chicken livers

SERVES SIX

6 slices bacon
6 (approximately ½ lb/225 g) chicken livers, cleaned and halved
12 wooden cocktail picks soaked in cold water

Preheat the broiler to high.

Flatten the bacon slices and cut them in half. Wrap each chicken liver half in a strip of the bacon and secure with a cocktail pick.

Put the rolls under the broiler and broil, turning, for 10 minutes or until the bacon is crisp on all sides—the liver should be slightly pink on the inside.

Deviled turkey legs

SERVES FOUR

4 turkey legs
Salt and black pepper
1 tablespoon French mustard
1 tablespoon lemon juice
6 tablespoons melted butter

Skin the turkey legs and make two or three deep incisions in the meat of each leg. Season well, coat with the mustard and lemon juice and rub into the meat. Set aside for 1 hour.

Preheat the broiler to moderate.

Brush the turkey legs with melted butter. Put them in the broiler pan and place 4 inches below the heat for 15 minutes or until cooked.

Transfer to a warm dish and serve at once.

Broiled partridge à la diable

SERVES FOUR

2 young partridges
½ cup (125 g) melted butter
Salt and pepper
½ cup (50 g) fresh white bread crumbs
1 lemon, thinly sliced
¼ cup (50 g) black olives, pitted
1 bunch watercress, washed

SAUCE A LA DIABLE
1½ teaspoons butter
1 shallot, finely chopped
¾ cup (175 ml) wine vinegar
1 cup (250 ml) espagnole sauce
2 tablespoons tomato paste
Worcestershire sauce
Salt and pepper
Cayenne pepper

First prepare the sauce. Heat the butter in a small saucepan, add the shallot and fry gently until soft. Pour in the vinegar and boil until it is reduced by half.

Stir in the espagnole sauce and tomato paste and cook, covered, for 5 minutes. Season to taste with Worcestershire sauce, salt, pepper and cayenne. Keep hot until the partridges are ready.

Preheat the broiler to moderate. Split the partridges down the back, open them out and flatten. Keep them flat by threading them on 2 skewers. Brush with the melted butter and season with salt and freshly ground pepper.

Broil for about 10 minutes each side, brushing frequently with the butter. Remove the partridges from under the broiler and coat with the bread crumbs. Return to the broiler and broil gently for another 5 minutes, basting frequently with the butter until the crumbs are

golden. Test the birds by piercing the thighs with the point of a sharp knife—if the juices run clear the birds are cooked. Remove from under the broiler.

Arrange the birds on a warm serving dish, garnish with slices of lemon, the olives and watercress. Serve with the sauce in a gravy boat.

Broiled quail with orange and sage

Quail can be broiled with almost any herb, providing the flavor is not too aggressive.

SERVES TWO

½ cup (125 g) butter
Juice and grated rind of
 1 orange
2 teaspoons finely chopped
 fresh sage
1 small garlic clove,
 crushed
½ teaspoon French mustard
4 quail, cleaned and split
 through the backbones
4 sprigs watercress
1 cup (250 ml) applesauce

Preheat the broiler to moderate.

Put the butter, orange juice and rind, sage, garlic and mustard in a small saucepan and place over low heat until the butter has melted.

Place the quail, skin sides up, on a baking sheet. Pour over the butter sauce and place the sheet under the broiler. Broil

for about 7 minutes on each side, basting with the butter sauce, until the quail are cooked. Test by piercing the thighs with the point of a sharp knife—if the juices run clear the birds are cooked. Serve immediately, garnished with the watercress, and with the applesauce served separately in a gravy boat.

Meat and game

Use only tender cuts of meat for broiling—beefsteaks and lamb chops are ideal. Pork chops must be marinated, covered with glaze or well basted during cooking because the meat tends to be dry. Pork is never eaten underdone so be careful to broil it until it is cooked through.

Nick the fat on the meat to prevent it curling during cooking. If you have an adjustable broiler, the meat should be about three inches (8 cm) from the heat source. Always preheat the broiler and grease the rack or skewers.

Season with salt after cooking because salt draws out the juices and tends to make the meat tougher.

Prick sausages before broiling to release the fat and to prevent them bursting during cooking.

Mixed grill

SERVES FOUR

4 lamb chops
4 lambs' kidneys, split, cores removed and secured open with wooden cocktail sticks
2 tomatoes, halved
¼ lb (125 g) mushrooms
5 tablespoons melted butter
8 sausages
4 bacon slices
1 bunch watercress, washed

Preheat the broiler to moderate. Line the broiler pan with foil. Brush the chops, kidneys, tomato halves and mushrooms with the butter.

Place the chops and sausages in the broiler pan and cook for 2 to 3 minutes. Add the lambs' kidneys and continue to cook for 5 minutes more. Turn all the meat over and add the bacon, tomatoes and mushrooms. Cook for another 3 minutes, then turn the bacon and mushrooms and cook for 2 to 3 minutes longer until they are ready.

Lower the pan away from the heat if the meat is browning too fast.

Remove the cocktail sticks from the kidneys. Transfer everything to a hot platter, pour over the pan juices and garnish with watercress.

Minute steaks

SERVES FOUR

4 minute steaks, ¼ inch (½ cm) thick
1 tablespoon olive oil
Salt and black pepper
1 cup (250 ml) béarnaise sauce

Preheat the broiler to high.

Brush the steaks with oil and cook for 1 minute on each side. Transfer them to a warm dish, pour over the pan juices, season and serve at once with the béarnaise sauce.

Tournedos Rossini

SERVES FOUR

½ cup (125 g) butter
4 slices French bread
4 slices pâté de foie gras
½ lb (225 g) mushrooms
4 tournedos, 1½ inch (3 cm) thick
¼ cup (65 ml) Madeira
1 cup (250 ml) demi-glace sauce

Broiling Times	
Sirloin steak 1 in (2 cm) thick	MODERATE HEAT
High heat for 1 min each side then	about 5 min (rare)
	about 10 min (well done)
Fillet steak 1½–2 in (3–5 cm) thick	
High heat for 1 min each side then	8–10 min (rare)
	12–16 min (well done)
Lamb chops 1½ in (3 cm) thick	16–20 min
Pork chops 1½ in (3 cm) thick	20–25 min
Smoked ham slices	20–25 min
Bacon slices	about 5 min
Liver	4–8 min
Kidneys	5–10 min
Sausages	15–20 min

Preheat the broiler to high.

Melt 4 tablespoons of the butter in a large frying pan. Add the bread and fry on both sides over moderate heat until golden and crisp. Drain the croutons on paper towels and keep warm on a serving dish.

Add 2 tablespoons more of butter to the frying pan and cook the slices of foie gras very quickly over high heat, turning once, until they are golden. Remove from the pan and keep warm in another dish.

Add the mushrooms to the pan and cook gently while the steaks are being broiled.

Melt the remaining butter and brush it over the steaks. Cook under the broiler for about 3 minutes on each side. Pour any juices from the broiler pan over the mushrooms in the frying pan.

Put one tournedos on top of each crouton on the serving dish, lay a slice of foie gras on each steak and top with a cooked mushroom. Arrange the remaining mushrooms around the tournedos. Reserve the liquid in the frying pan and keep the serving dish warm while the sauce is prepared.

Stir the Madeira and the demi-glace into the juices in the frying pan. Bring to a boil. Pour some of the sauce into the serving dish and serve the rest separately.

Lebanese kebabs

Serve Lebanese kebabs with pitta and a tomato and olive salad.

SERVES FOUR

1½ lb (700 g) boned leg or shoulder of lamb, cut into ½-inch (1-cm) cubes
1 onion, finely chopped
½ cup (125 ml) natural yogurt
2 tablespoons chopped mint
Salt and pepper
1 tablespoon olive oil
1 garlic clove, crushed

Put the meat in a large bowl. Mix all the remaining ingredients together and pour over the meat. Cover the bowl and refrigerate for 8 hours or overnight, stirring occasionally.

Preheat the broiler to high.

Drain the meat and thread onto 4 skewers. Broil for 8 to 10 minutes, basting frequently with the marinade and turning the skewers, until the meat is cooked.

Hamburgers

Additions can include fresh or dried herbs, finely chopped onion and crushed garlic. Grated carrot will make the hamburger more juicy and a slice of bread crumbled into the meat will both lighten and "stretch" it. The yolk of an egg will help to bind the mixture. Serve with potato chips, sliced raw onion and sliced tomatoes.

SERVES FOUR

1 lb (450 g) ground steak
Salt and black pepper
4 soft rolls, split and toasted

Preheat the broiler to high.

Mix the meat and seasoning together and shape the mixture into 4 hamburgers about 1 inch (2 cm) thick. Broil for 3 minutes on each side if you like your hamburgers rare, 4 to 5 minutes each side for medium and 6 minutes each side for well done.

Serve inside the rolls.

Pork saté

Serve as a starter or main course.

SERVES FOUR TO EIGHT

2 lb (900 g) pork fillet, cut into 1-inch (2-cm) cubes

MARINADE
Juice of 1 lemon
½ to 1 teaspoon cayenne pepper
3 garlic cloves, crushed
1 tablespoon oil
2 tablespoons soft brown sugar
2 tablespoons molasses
8 tablespoons soy sauce

PEANUT SAUCE
3 tablespoons oil
1 onion, finely chopped
2 garlic cloves, crushed
½ to 1 teaspoon cayenne pepper
½ teaspoon turmeric
2 teaspoons ground coriander

3 tablespoons smooth peanut butter
1 cup (50 g) shredded coconut blended with 1 cup (250 ml) scalded milk, cooled and strained
Salt

Thread the pork cubes onto skewers. Mix all the marinade ingredients together in a shallow dish. Put the skewers into the marinade and set aside for 3 to 4 hours, turning the skewers and basting the meat occasionally.

Meanwhile, prepare the sauce. Heat the oil in a saucepan. Add the onion and garlic and fry, stirring, until golden. Add the cayenne, turmeric and coriander and fry for 1 minute. Stir in the peanut butter and pour in the coconut milk. Bring to a boil, stirring. Reduce the heat to low, cover the pan and simmer for 20 minutes. Stir in 5 tablespoons of the marinade. Taste the sauce and add salt if necessary.

Preheat the broiler to moderate. Grease the broiler rack. Broil the pork, basting with the marinade, for 5 minutes on each side or until the pork is cooked.

Pour the peanut sauce into individual bowls or saucers and serve with the saté.

Broiled pork chops

SERVES FOUR

4 loin pork chops
1 orange, thinly sliced

GLAZE
2 tablespoons honey
Rind and juice of 1 orange
1 teaspoon lemon juice
1 teaspoon soy sauce
Salt and black pepper

Preheat the broiler to moderate.

Mix the ingredients for the glaze in a saucepan and bring to a boil. Simmer for 3 minutes.

Nick the fat on the chops. Grease the broiler rack. Put the chops on the rack and brush them with the glaze. Broil, basting frequently, for about 10 minutes. Turn the chops, brush with the glaze and broil, basting occasionally, for 10 minutes or until the chops are cooked.

Serve immediately, garnished with the orange slices.

Stuffed pork chops

SERVES FOUR

⅓ cup (50 g) prunes, simmered until tender in ½ cup (125 ml) sweet
cider, pitted and chopped
½ cup (50 g) fresh white bread crumbs
1 teaspoon rubbed sage
Salt and pepper
½ small onion, grated
1 tablespoon butter, melted
1 small egg yolk, beaten
4 pork chops
1 tablespoon oil

Preheat the broiler to hot.

Mix all the ingredients except the pork chops and oil.

With a sharp, pointed knife, cut the meat away from the bone of the chops. Cut an incision in the meat at the leanest part, making a pocket for the stuffing. Fill the pockets with the stuffing mixture and sew them up with trussing thread.

Brush with oil and broil for about 15 minutes on each side.

Ham steaks with apricots

Pineapple rings may be used instead of the apricots. Serve with garlic mashed potatoes and boiled peas or broccoli.

SERVES FOUR

4 slices smoked ham, 1 inch (2 cm) thick
1 lb (450 g) canned apricots, drained
2 tablespoons butter, cut into pieces
¼ cup (50 g) soft brown sugar
Sage leaves to garnish

Preheat the broiler to moderate.

Nick the fat on the ham. Broil the ham for 12 minutes on each side.

Arrange the apricots on top of the ham slices, dot with the butter and sprinkle the sugar on top. Return the ham to the heat and broil until the apricots are browned.

Serve garnished with the sage leaves.

Vegetables, fruit and dairy products

The vegetables that are most commonly broiled are mushrooms (the large, open ones) and tomatoes.

Tomatoes may be broiled whole or cut across in half. Brush with oil and cook for about ten to fifteen minutes. Broil the rounded sides of tomato halves first to prevent the soft, uncooked pulp from slipping out of the skin. Serve broiled mushrooms or tomatoes on toast or as an accompaniment to fish, meat or poultry.

Slices of degorged eggplant may also be broiled. Brush them with oil and cook until they are brown on both sides.

In the south of France a delectable first course is made with broiled green peppers. Put the whole peppers under high heat until their skins blister and can be rubbed off easily under cold running water. Core and seed the peppers, cut them into strips and marinate in a herb-flavored vinaigrette for at least thirty minutes.

With very few exceptions (for example grapefruit, peaches and pineapple), fruit is never broiled.

Dairy products and cereals, with the exceptions of cheese and bread, are never cooked under a broiler. The best cheese for broiling are hard and semi-hard cheeses, such as Cheddar, Edam, Gruyère, Parmesan and Cheshire.

Broiled tomatoes

SERVES FOUR

4 large tomatoes
6 tablespoons dry
  bread crumbs
1 garlic clove, crushed
1 tablespoon chopped fresh
  basil
1 tablespoon chopped
  parsley
1 tablespoon grated
  Parmesan cheese
Salt and pepper
Melted butter or olive oil

Preheat the broiler to moderate.

Cut the tops off the tomatoes and scoop the flesh into a bowl. Turn the tomatoes upside down on paper towels to drain.

Mix the chopped tomato pulp with the bread crumbs, garlic, herbs, cheese and seasoning. Mix in a little melted butter or oil. Fill the tomatoes with this mixture, sprinkle with butter or oil and broil for about 10 minutes or until they are heated through.

Broiled mushrooms

For plain broiled mushrooms brush the mushroom caps with melted butter, season to taste and broil them cap sides up for about 3 minutes. Turn them over and broil for 2 minutes more. Serve the mushrooms on toast.

SERVES FOUR

12 large mushrooms
3 tablespoons butter
1 garlic clove, crushed
1 small onion, chopped
6 tablespoons dry bread
  crumbs
Salt and pepper
2 teaspoons chopped parsley
1 tablespoon melted butter

Preheat the broiler to moderate.

Wipe the mushrooms. Remove the stalks and chop them finely.

Melt the butter in a small saucepan and gently fry the mushroom stalks, garlic and onion for 3 to 4 minutes. Add the bread crumbs, seasoning and parsley and cook for 2 minutes more. Fill the caps with the mixture. Put them in a broiler pan that has been lightly greased. Sprinkle the tops with the melted butter and broil for 5 minutes. Serve immediately.

Broiled grapefruit

SERVES FOUR

2 grapefruit, halved
4 tablespoons sherry
4 teaspoons brown sugar

Preheat the broiler to hot.

Sprinkle the grapefruit halves with sherry and spread with the sugar. Cook under the broiler for a few minutes until glazed.

Grapefruit anisette

SERVES FOUR

2 pink-fleshed grapefruit,
  halved
4 teaspoons Pernod
2 tablespoons sugar
8 mint leaves, washed

Preheat the broiler to hot.

Sprinkle the grapefruit with the Pernod and soak for 5 minutes. Sprinkle with the sugar and cook under the broiler, 5 to 6 inches (13 to 15 cm) from the heat, for about 8 minutes or until glazed.

Garnish with mint leaves and serve at once or let cool.

Peaches with wine

SERVES FOUR

4 large, ripe peaches, halved
  and seeded
4 tablespoons white wine or
  dry sherry
4 tablespoons soft brown
  sugar
2 tablespoons butter, cut into
  small pieces
½ cup (125 ml) whipping
  cream, whipped

Preheat the broiler to hot.

Put the peaches, cut sides up, in a broiler pan. Fill the centers with the wine or sherry, sprinkle with the sugar and dot with the butter. Place under the broiler until the sugar has melted and the wine is hot.

Serve with whipped cream.

Broiled pineapple with rum

Kirsch may be used instead of rum.

SERVES FOUR TO SIX

1 ripe pineapple
4 to 6 tablespoons Jamaican
  rum
4 tablespoons soft brown
  sugar
1 pint (500 ml) good-quality
  vanilla ice cream

Preheat the broiler to moderate.

Cut the pineapple in half lengthwise. Scoop out the flesh and cut into small cubes. Toss the flesh with the rum and return to the shells. Cover the leaves with foil.

Put the pineapple halves in the broiler pan, sprinkle with the sugar and broil until the sugar has melted.

If the pineapple is too near the heat, the rum may ignite, but the flames will soon subside if the broiler pan is lowered.

Remove the foil and serve at once with the ice cream.

Cheese toast

MAKES SIXTEEN PIECES

4 slices bread
2 tablespoons butter
1¼ cups (125 g) grated
  Cheddar cheese
¼ teaspoon baking powder
1 egg, separated
Salt and pepper

Preheat the broiler to hot.

Remove the crusts from the bread and cut each slice into 4 triangles. Toast lightly and butter on one side. Keep warm.

Mix the cheese, baking powder, egg yolk and seasoning. Beat the egg white until it is stiff and fold it in. Spread the mixture thickly on the toast and place under the broiler until brown and puffed.

Welsh rabbit

To make a buck rabbit, put a poached egg on a Welsh rabbit.

SERVES FOUR

$2\frac{1}{2}$ cups (225 g) grated
  Cheddar cheese
2 tablespoons butter
1 teaspoon prepared
  mustard
3 tablespoons beer
Salt and pepper
Cayenne pepper
4 slices bread, toasted and
  kept warm

Preheat the broiler to hot.

Mix the cheese, butter, mustard, beer and seasoning in a small saucepan over low heat. Stir until completely blended.

Pour over the toast and broil until brown.

Cheese and walnut fingers

MAKES TWENTY-FOUR FINGERS

8 slices brown bread,
  toasted and kept warm
$\frac{3}{4}$ cup (175 g) cream cheese
$\frac{1}{3}$ cup (50 g) chopped walnuts
Salt and pepper

Preheat the broiler to hot.

Mix the cheese, nuts and seasoning and spread onto the toast. Cut each slice into three. Broil until lightly browned.

Dishes to broil : cheese toast, grapefruit and tomatoes.

Broiled Roquefort

SERVES TWO TO FOUR

4 slices bread
2 tablespoons butter
4 slices chicken or ham
$\frac{1}{4}$ lb (125 g) Roquefort
  cheese, creamed

Preheat the broiler to hot.

Toast the bread slightly and butter it. Place a slice of meat on each piece of toast, spread with the cheese and broil.

Frying and sautéing

Pan frying, sautéing, deep-fat frying and stir-frying are all ways of cooking food in hot fat.

For pan frying use a good-quality heavy frying pan and only a small amount of drippings, lard, polyunsaturated margarine, butter or oil, or a mixture of butter and oil.

Sautéing is closely related to pan frying, but only butter or oil or a mixture of both is used. Heat the pan well and add just enough fat to grease the pan. When it is hot, add the food. Cook briskly, shaking the pan frequently to keep the food moving so that it browns on all sides evenly and does not stick.

Often after a preliminary sautéing a little liquid is added, the pan covered and the food cooked over gentle heat until done. A straight-sided sauté pan with a lid is useful, particularly for poultry and meat.

For deep-fat frying you need a deep, heavy saucepan fitted with a frying basket. The saucepan must never be more than two-thirds full of fat because if it bubbles over onto the stove the fat might catch fire. On the other hand, there must be enough fat to cover the food.

A deep-frying thermometer is the most accurate way of judging the temperature of the fat. Keep it in hot water and wipe it dry before putting it in the hot oil. If a thermometer is not available, use a one-inch (2-cm) cube of day-old bread to estimate the temperature. When the fat is hot, drop in the cube and check the time it takes to brown with a kitchen timer. If it takes thirty-five seconds to brown the temperature will be approximately 400°F (204°C); if it takes forty seconds it will be approximately 375°F (190°C); if it takes fifty seconds it will be approximately 360°F (182°C) and if it takes fifty-five seconds it will be approximately 350°F (176°C).

Most foods require a temperature of about 375°F (190°C), but some, such as potato chips, whitebait, croutons and precooked foods, require a second frying at a temperature of about 400°F (204°C).

Stir-frying is a method of frying practiced by the Chinese, who use a large pan with a rounded base called a wok. (As an alternative use a large, heavy frying pan.) Cut the food into small pieces and fry it quickly in a little hot oil, stirring constantly. It may take only fifteen seconds to cook and rarely takes more than five minutes.

Fish and shellfish

Fried whitebait 138
Sauce tartar 68,
Brown bread 198

Sautéed soft roes 138

Clam fritters 140

New England fried scallops 140
Deep-fried parsley 153

Fried fish 138
Sauce tartar 68,
French fries 150

Fish cakes 138
Tomato sauce 69,
Mashed potatoes 93,
Green beans 92

Fritto misto di mare 138
Sauce tartar 68

Bass à la provençale 138
Garlic bread 189,
Boiled fennel 92

Filets de sole meunière 140
Lemon butter 129,
Boiled potatoes 93,
Casseroled celery 120

Herring in oatmeal 140
Tomato sauce 69,
Leeks 93

Trout with almonds 140
Cottage fries 151

Fillets of sole à la panetière 140
Green salad 213

Fried eels 140
Sauce hollandaise 67,
Spinach purée 92

Kedgeree 140
Green salad 213

Stir-fried giant shrimp 140
Stir-fried bean sprouts 153

Sautéed frogs' legs à la niçoise 141
Potato croquettes 151,
Green beans 92

Fried scampi 141
Sauce tartar 68,
Brown bread 198

Squirrel fish 141
Stir-fried bean sprouts 153

Bean sprouts and shrimp Chinese style 141

Poultry and game birds

Chicken Maryland 142
Potato croquettes 151,
Corn fritters 153,
Sautéed bananas 154

Chicken sauté à la bordelaise 142

Chicken sauté à l'italienne 142
Cottage fries 151,
Spinach 92

Chicken Kiev 144
Steamed broccoli 92,
Mashed potatoes 93,
Zucchini 93

Deep-fried chicken 144
Sauce tartar 68,
French fries 150

Chicken lemon sauté 144
Soufflé potatoes 150,
Snow peas 93

Poulet sauté chasseur 144
Large croutons 158,
Green beans 92

Chicken sauté paprika 145
Rösti 151, Spinach 92

Guinea hen with juniper berries 145
Green bean salad 212,
Garlic mashed potatoes 180

Sautéed partridge jubilee 145
Green salad 213,
Cottage fries 151

Meat and game

Wild duck à la seville 145
Belgian endive, orange and watercress salad 213, Potato chips 150

Chicken kromeski 144
Green salad 213, Broccoli, Spinach 92

Chicken with almonds 145
Stir-fried bean sprouts 153

Stir-fried chicken and mushrooms 145

Chicken liver sauté 145
Large croutons 158

Steak au poivre 146
Broiled tomatoes 134, Potato croquettes 151

Steak Diane 146
Braised onions 120, Broccoli 92, Cottage fries 151

Beef stroganoff 146
Green salad 213, Steamed rice 97

Entrecôte à la viennoise 146
Sauce béarnaise 67, Fried mushrooms 152

Veal Zurich style 147
Rösti 151, Petit pois à la française 91

Veal cutlets Milanese style 147
Green salad 213, Cottage-fries 151

Fondue bourguignonne 148

Veal marsala 148
Zucchini 93, Fried mushrooms 152

Noisettes of lamb with stuffed tomatoes 148
Leeks provençal 120, Cottage fries 151

Saltimbocca 148
Spinach 92

Sautéed venison steaks 148
Brussels sprouts with chestnuts 91, Celeriac 93

Veal chops en papillote 148
New potatoes 93, Green beans 92

Sautéed sweetbreads Saint Médard 149
Celery, apple and walnut salad 213, Braised onions 120

Meatballs with sweet and sour sauce 149
Fried rice 158

Entrecôte au poivre vert 149
Green beans 92, Carrot and parsnip purée 91

Tournedos au vin rouge 149
New potatoes, Peas 93

Wiener schnitzel 149
Broccoli 92, Cottage fries 151

Sautéed liver and bacon 149
Fried mushrooms 152, Mashed potatoes 93

Fruit and Vegetables

Bubble and squeak 152
Broiled bacon 132

Pipérade 153
Large croutons 158

Fried apples and bacon 155

Pakoras with mint chutney 152

Potatoes
chips 150, French fries 150, Shoestring 150, soufflé 150, Cottage fries 151, Lyonnaise 151, Parisienne 151, croquettes 151, Rösti 151, scones 152

Onions 152

Mushrooms 152
Duxelles 152

Fritters
eggplant 153, corn 153, cauliflower cheese 152, banana and bacon 154, apple 154, special apple 154, apricot 154, winter 154

Sautéed eggplants 152
Stir-fried bean sprouts 153
Deep-fried parsley 153

Sautéed bananas 154

Apples with Calvados 155

Caramelized pineapple 155

Salted almonds 155

Cereals

Fried bread 158

Croutons 158

Fried rice 158

Crusty noodles 158

Crêpes Suzette 157

Beignets soufflés 158

Pancakes 156

Drop scones 157

Blini 157

English crumpets 157

English muffins 157

Waffles 157

English doughnuts 157

American doughnuts 158

French toast 158

Fritter batter 156

Eggs and dairy products

Fried mozzarella cheese 162

Mozzarella in carrozza 162

Fried eggs 160
Beurre noir 68

Scrambled eggs 160

Scrambled eggs with mushrooms 160

Scrambled eggs with cheese 160

Scotch woodcock 160

French omelet 160
Green salad 213

Omelet fines herbes 160
Green salad 213

Mushroom omelet 160
Green salad 213

Cheese omelet 160
Green salad 213

Omelet Arnold Bennett 160
Green salad 213

Spanish omelet 161
Green salad 213

Egg fu-yung 161

Scotch eggs 161
Salads: Potato 93, Tomato 213

Scrambled eggs with chicken 162

Scrambled eggs with chicken livers 162
Scrambled eggs with smoked salmon 162
Green salad 213

Bean sprouts with omelet shreds 162

Huevos rancheros 162

Kuku sabsi 161

Ajja 162

Omelet au Grand Marnier 161

Omelet flambé 161

First courses
Main courses
Light lunch-supper dishes
Accompaniments
Desserts
Miscellaneous

Fish and shellfish

The nicest way to pan fry fish is in butter, which is then poured over the fish when it is served. A milk and flour or egg and bread crumb coating may be used for all types of fish, but the Scottish way of frying herring in coarse oatmeal adds an even more interesting flavor and crunchy texture.

For deep frying, fish is usually coated with batter. Heat the oil to a temperature of 375°F (190°C) and fry the fish until it is golden brown. Fillets and small whole fish will take from five to eight minutes.

Scallops, jumbo shrimp and precooked mussels may also be coated with batter and deep fried and take about three to four minutes.

Fried fish

SERVES FOUR

2 lb (900 g) white fish fillets, skinned
Oil
1¾ cups (425 ml) fritter batter

Dry the fish well on absorbent paper towels. Heat the oil to 375°F (190°C).

Coat the fish with the batter and lower into the hot fat. Fry for 5 minutes or until the fish is crisp and golden.

Fish cakes

SERVES FOUR

1 lb (450 g) fish, steamed or boiled
½ lb (225 g) potatoes, boiled
3 tablespoons cream
2 tablespoons butter
¼ lemon
2 tablespoons chopped parsley
Salt and pepper
1 egg, beaten
Toasted bread crumbs
Oil
1 lemon, cut into wedges

Flake the fish and remove any skin or bones. Mash the potatoes with the cream and butter until smooth. Add a squeeze of lemon juice and blend with the fish, parsley and seasoning. With floured hands, shape the mixture into eight round, flat patties. Chill for at least 1 hour to make the patties firm.

Dip the patties in the beaten egg, then in the bread crumbs, and either deep fry at 375°F (190°C) for about 6 minutes or pan fry for 10 to 12 minutes. Drain on paper towels. Garnish with lemon wedges and serve.

Fried whitebait

SERVES FOUR

1 lb (450 g) whitebait
2 tablespoons seasoned flour
Oil
Cayenne pepper
2 lemons, cut into quarters

Put the whitebait and the flour in a plastic or paper bag and shake gently until the whitebait are well coated.

Heat the oil to 375°F (190°C). Using a frying basket, lower a few whitebait at a time into the oil and fry for about 2 minutes. Drain well on paper towels. When all the whitebait are fried and drained, put them all together in the frying basket. Reheat the oil until it reaches 400°F (204°C) and plunge the basket in the oil for 1 minute to crisp the whitebait. Drain well, sprinkle with cayenne pepper and serve immediately with the lemon quarters.

Fritto misto di mare

SERVES FOUR TO SIX

1 lb (450 g) calamary (squid or inkfish), ink sac and cuttlebone removed
Salt
4 to 8 red mullet (smaller ones are best), cleaned
2 lb (900 g) large and small shrimp, unshelled
1 cup (125 g) seasoned flour
Oil

Cut the body and tentacles of the calamary into ¼-inch (½-cm) rings. Bring some salted water to a boil in a saucepan. Add the calamary and boil for about 25 minutes or until tender. (Large calamary will take longer to cook.) Drain the calamary.

Roll all the fish in the flour until lightly coated. Heat the oil to 375°F (190°C). Add the fish a few at a time. Fry the larger fish for 10 to 15 minutes and the smaller pieces for 5 to 8 minutes or until they are golden. Serve immediately.

Sautéed soft roes

SERVES TWO

¼ cup (50 g) butter
1 small onion, finely chopped
½ lb (225 g) soft herring roes, cut into pieces
2 tablespoons seasoned flour
2 tablespoons sherry
4 toast triangles
1 tablespoon chopped fresh parsley

Melt the butter in a frying pan and fry the onion gently until soft. Coat the roes lightly with the seasoned flour and add them to the pan. Fry gently for 2 to 3 minutes, stirring to prevent them sticking. Add the sherry; cook for 1 to 2 minutes. Serve on hot toast, sprinkled with parsley.

Bass à la provençale

SERVES FOUR

2 sea bass, about 1½ lb (700 g)
Oil
2 tablespoons seasoned flour
2 cups (500 ml) tomato sauce
2 garlic cloves, finely chopped
3 tablespoons bread crumbs

Preheat the broiler to moderate.

Scale the bass and make shallow diagonal cuts in the skin. Heat plenty of oil—enough to come halfway up the fish—in the frying pan. Roll the fish in the flour and fry on both sides until cooked through. Transfer the fish to an ovenproof dish and cover with the sauce.

Heat 1 tablespoon of oil in a small frying pan and fry the garlic gently for a few seconds. Sprinkle the garlic and the bread crumbs over the sauce and put the dish under the broiler. Cook until the crumbs are browned.

Delicious fritto misto di mare is made from a selection of deep fried fish and shellfish.

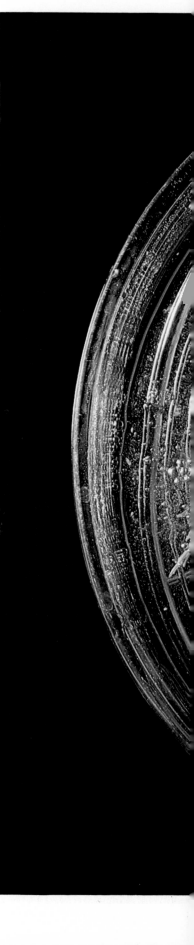

Fish and shellfish

Filets de sole meunière
SERVES FOUR

2 sole, about 1½ lb (700 g) each, filleted
2 tablespoons seasoned flour
¼ cup (50 g) butter
2 teaspoons lemon juice
1 lemon, quartered
1 tablespoon chopped fresh parsley

Skin the sole fillets carefully and pat them dry with paper towels. Roll the fillets in the seasoned flour.

Melt half the butter in a frying pan. Add the fillets and fry for 2 to 3 minutes over moderate heat, shaking the pan to keep the fish from sticking. When brown, turn the fillets over and fry for 2 to 3 minutes more on the other side or until the fish are cooked. Transfer the fish to a warm dish and keep hot.

Wipe the pan with paper towels and return to the heat. Add the remaining butter and when it has turned golden, stir in the lemon juice. Pour the butter over the fish, garnish with the lemon wedges, sprinkle with parsley and serve immediately.

Herring in oatmeal
SERVES FOUR

4 herring, cleaned
1 tablespoon lemon juice
Salt and pepper
4 tablespoons oatmeal
¼ cup (50 g) butter or drippings

Split the fish down the back and remove the backbones. Score the skin. Brush with the lemon juice and season well. Roll the herring in the oatmeal until they are completely coated.

Heat the butter or drippings in a frying pan and add the herring, skin side up. Fry for about 5 minutes on each side or until browned and cooked. Drain on paper towels and serve at once.

Trout with almonds
SERVES FOUR

4 trout, washed and cleaned
2 tablespoons seasoned flour
6 tablespoons butter
2 lemons
4 tablespoons slivered almonds

Roll the trout in the seasoned flour. Melt 4 tablespoons of the butter in a large sauté or frying pan. Fry the trout for about 5 minutes on each side or until well browned and cooked. Transfer the fish to a warm serving dish and keep hot.

Add the remaining butter and when it has melted, add the juice of ½ lemon. Add the almonds and fry, shaking the pan occasionally, until golden. Pour the almonds and butter over the trout. Garnish with the remaining lemons cut into quarters.

Fillets of sole à la panetière
A la panetière originally meant that the dish was presented in a hollowed-out loaf, or in croustades. A pastry case is lighter and more suited to modern tastes. A variation would be to serve each portion in an individual puff-pastry shell.
SERVES FOUR

2 sole, filleted
2 tablespoons seasoned flour
½ cup (125 g) butter
1 lb (450 g) mushrooms, chopped
½ cup (125 ml) cream
Salt and pepper
Grated nutmeg
10-inch (25-cm) puff-pastry shell, baked and kept warm.

Trim the sole fillets, flatten, fold over once and dip into the seasoned flour.

Melt half the butter in a frying pan. Add the mushrooms and fry until soft. Remove the pan from the heat and stir in the cream. Return to very low heat and cook for a few minutes longer, but do not allow the cream to boil or it will curdle. Season with salt, pepper and a pinch of grated nutmeg and keep hot.

Heat the remaining butter in a frying pan. Sauté the fillets for about 5 minutes on each side or until cooked through. Arrange the fish around the inside of the puff-pastry shell and fill the center with the mushrooms.

Fried eels
SERVES FOUR

2 lb (900 g) small eels, skinned
½ cup (125 ml) milk
4 tablespoons seasoned flour
Oil for deep frying
1 lemon, quartered
Parsley sprigs

Score the eels. Twist them into figure-eight shapes and secure them with skewers. Put the milk into a bowl. Put the eels in the milk and leave for a few minutes and then roll them in the flour.

Heat the oil to 375°F (190°C). Add the eels and fry until crisp, golden and cooked. Drain on paper towels and serve on a folded napkin. Garnish with lemon quarters and parsley.

Kedgeree
In the nineteenth century, the British in India developed kedgeree from a local dish of rice cooked with lentils called kicheri. Bearing little resemblance to the original dish, kedgeree is most often made from leftover fish and rice. Although it is traditionally served at breakfast, try it as a supper dish accompanied by a crisp green salad.
SERVES FOUR

6 tablespoons butter
1 lb (450 g) finnan haddie, cooked, skin and bones removed, and flaked
½ lb (225 g) long-grain rice, boiled
2 hard-cooked eggs, chopped
Salt and pepper
Milk
Chopped parsley

Melt the butter in a large saucepan. Add the flaked fish and rice, and stir over moderate heat until heated through. Stir in the eggs and seasoning. If the mixture looks too dry, add 1 to 2 tablespoons of milk. Garnish with parsley and serve.

Clam fritters
Serve clam fritters as an hors d'oeuvre.
SERVES FOUR

24 small clams
1 cup (250 ml) fritter batter
Oil for deep frying
Lemon wedges
Parsley sprigs
1 cup (250 ml) tartar sauce

Put the clams in a saucepan with a little water and set over moderate heat for about 7 minutes. Remove the clams from the shells and pat them dry, discarding any that have not opened.

Heat the oil to 375°F (190°C). Dip the clams into the batter and deep fry for about 4 minutes or until golden. Arrange the clams in a basket lined with a napkin and garnish with lemon and parsley. Serve with tartar sauce.

New England fried scallops
Scallops can be deep fried, but their flavor is better enhanced by sautéing them in butter.
SERVES FOUR

12 scallops
White wine
2 tablespoons oil
1 tablespoon lemon juice
Salt and pepper
1 teaspoon chopped parsley
1 egg, beaten
Browned bread crumbs
¼ cup (50 g) butter
¼ cup (50 g) tarragon butter
1 lemon, cut into quarters

Prepare the scallops and put them into a saucepan with enough white wine to cover. Simmer for 3 to 4 minutes. Set them aside to cool, then cut them in half across.

Mix together the oil, lemon juice, seasoning and parsley in a bowl. Toss the scallops in this mixture and marinate for 30 minutes. Drain well and dip them in the beaten egg and coat with bread crumbs.

Melt the butter in a frying pan. Add the scallops and fry until browned on all sides. Serve with the tarragon butter and the lemon quarters.

Stir-fried giant shrimp
For this adaptation of a Chinese dish use any large shrimp about 5 inches (13 cm) in length. Serve the shrimp as a first course or as part of a Chinese meal.
SERVES FOUR

8 jumbo shrimp, shelled, uncooked
Salt
2½ tablespoons soy sauce
2½ tablespoons dry sherry
1 tablespoon tomato paste
1 tablespoon vinegar
1 teaspoon Chinese chili sauce
3 tablespoons oil

1 small onion, finely
   chopped
½-inch (1-cm) piece fresh
   ginger root, peeled and
   sliced
1 garlic clove, crushed
1 teaspoon sugar

Rub the shrimp all over with salt. Mix the soy sauce, sherry, tomato paste, vinegar and chili sauce in a small bowl. Set aside.

Heat the oil in a large frying pan. Add the onion, ginger and garlic and stir-fry for 30 seconds. Add the shrimp and stir-fry for 1 minute. Sprinkle the sugar over the shrimp and pour in the soy and sherry mixture. Cook, stirring constantly, for 5 minutes. Serve immediately.

Bean sprouts and shrimp Chinese style

SERVES FOUR

4 tablespoons oil
1 piece candied ginger,
   cut into fine strips
½ lb (225 g) snow peas
3 celery stalks, cut into fine
   strips
¼ lb (125 g) dried Chinese
   mushrooms, soaked in
   water for 20 minutes,
   drained and chopped
1 lb (450 g) bean sprouts
1 teaspoon salt
1 garlic clove, finely
   chopped
1-inch (2-cm) piece fresh
   ginger root, finely
   chopped
½ lb (225 g) shelled shrimp
Pepper
1 tablespoon soy sauce
2 teaspoons cornstarch
   mixed with 2 tablespoons
   cold water
1 tablespoon dry sherry

Heat half the oil in a wok or large frying pan and fry the ginger, snow peas and celery for 3 minutes. Add the mushrooms and bean sprouts and fry, stirring constantly, for about 3 minutes. Stir in the salt. Using a slotted spoon, lift out the vegetables and set aside.

Add more oil to the pan, if necessary, and fry the garlic and the ginger root until golden. Add the shrimp and cook, stirring, for 1 minute. Season with pepper. Return the vegetables to the pan. Mix the soy sauce

with the cornstarch mixture and sherry, add it to the pan and continue to stir-fry over gentle heat for about 4 minutes. Serve immediately.

Sautéed frogs' legs à la niçoise

SERVES FOUR

12 pairs frogs' legs
1 cup (250 ml) milk
½ cup (125 g) seasoned flour
2½ tablespoons oil
6 tomatoes, peeled and
   coarsely chopped
1 onion, finely chopped
1 garlic clove, crushed
Salt and pepper
4 tablespoons clarified butter
1 tablespoon chopped parsley

Dip the frogs' legs in the milk and coat with the seasoned flour. Heat ½ tablespoon of the oil in a saucepan. Add the tomatoes, onion and garlic, season well and cook over medium heat. Heat the remaining oil with the clarified butter in a frying pan and sauté the frogs' legs for about 10 minutes, turning once, or until browned on both sides.

Coating and frying fish

To fry fish in bread crumbs, dip them first in egg and milk.

Coat the fish all over in fresh or dried bread crumbs.

To deep fry fish in batter, dip them in a bowl of batter.

Drop the coated fish into hot oil and fry until golden.

Arrange the frogs' legs on a serving dish. Put a spoonful of tomato mixture on top of each pair of legs and sprinkle with parsley before serving.

Fried scampi
A single coating of egg and bread crumbs can be used, but the double coating gives the fish a much crisper exterior. This recipe will serve two people as a main course and four as a first course.

SERVES TWO TO FOUR

2 egg yolks, mixed with
   3 tablespoons milk
1 cup dried white
   bread crumbs
1 lb (450 g) jumbo shrimp,
   shelled
Vegetable oil for deep frying
1 cup (250 ml) tartar sauce

Put the egg yolk mixture on one plate and the bread crumbs on another. Dip each shrimp first in the egg yolk mixture and then in the bread crumbs, coating them all over. Repeat the process to give them a double coating.

Heat the oil to 375°F (190°C).

Put all the coated shrimp into a deep-frying basket and lower it into the oil. Fry the shrimp for about 3 minutes or until they are cooked through and a deep golden color on the outside.

Line a warm serving dish with a cloth or paper napkin. Place the shrimp in the dish and serve immediately, with the tartar sauce in a separate bowl.

Squirrel fish

SERVES FOUR

2-lb (900-g) sea bass, cleaned
   and head removed
4 tablespoons flour
Oil for deep frying
2 tablespoons oil
1 onion, thinly sliced
4 dried Chinese mushrooms,
   soaked for 20 minutes in
   cold water, drained and
   caps chopped
2 tomatoes, skinned and
   chopped
4 tablespoons thinly sliced
   bamboo shoots
3 tablespoons chicken stock
3 tablespoons wine vinegar
2 tablespoons sugar
1 tablespoon soy sauce
1 tablespoon tomato paste
1 tablespoon cornstarch,
   mixed with 4 tablespoons
   water

Split the fish but leave the tail intact. Cut out the backbone. Open out the fish and score the flesh with crisscross cuts to within ¼ inch of the skin. Dredge with flour.

Heat the oil to 350°F (176°C). Fry the fish for 5 minutes. Lift out the fish and drain.

Heat the 2 tablespoons of oil in a frying pan. Add the onion and stir-fry for 1 minute. Add the mushrooms, tomatoes and bamboo shoots and stir-fry for 2 minutes.

Combine the stock, vinegar, sugar, soy sauce, tomato paste and cornstarch. Pour the mixture into the pan and cook, stirring constantly, until the sauce is thick. Remove from the heat. Reheat the oil in the deep-frying pan to 375°F (190°C) and fry the fish again for 2 minutes or until it curls.

Drain the fish and put it on a serving dish. Pour the sauce over the top and serve.

Poultry and game birds

In the West the poultry that is most commonly cut into quarters or small pieces and fried is chicken and turkey, but in the Middle East many very small birds are fried in butter, sprinkled with lemon juice and served between pieces of hot pitta.

For pan frying, coat chicken or turkey pieces with seasoned flour or egg and bread crumbs. After the initial browning reduce the heat and cook for fifteen to twenty minutes or until tender. Test by piercing the meat with the point of a sharp knife—if the juices run clear the meat is cooked.

The length of time it takes to sauté chicken or turkey depends on the size of the pieces and whether or not liquid is to be added after the initial browning. The leg or thigh takes longer to cook than the breast or a wing, but should not take longer than about twenty-five to thirty minutes.

Game birds and small chickens may be cut in half and cooked slowly and gently in plenty of butter—a little wine, water or stock may be added after browning.

Chicken Maryland

This traditional American dish may be served with corn fritters and crisp bacon rolls.

SERVES FOUR

4-lb (2-kg) chicken, cut into serving pieces
¾ cup (75 g) seasoned flour
Bacon fat or oil for frying
1½ tablespoons flour
1 cup (250 ml) cream
1 cup (250 ml) milk
Salt and pepper

Coat the chicken pieces thoroughly in the seasoned flour.

In a large sauté pan heat 1 to 1½ inches (2 to 3 cm) of bacon fat or oil. When the oil or fat is very hot, add the chicken pieces and fry, turning occasionally, until browned on all sides. Reduce the heat to low, cover the pan and cook for 25 minutes or until the chicken is cooked. Alternatively, after the initial browning, transfer the chicken pieces to a covered ovenproof dish and cook in a 375°F (190°C) oven for 30 minutes.

Test by piercing the meat with the point of a sharp knife— if the juices run clear the chicken is cooked. Transfer the chicken pieces to a warm serving dish and keep hot.

Pour away all but 4 tablespoons of the fat or oil in the pan. Stir in the flour and cook, stirring, for 2 minutes. Add the milk and cream gradually, stirring constantly to prevent lumps from forming. Bring the sauce to a simmer and cook slowly until it is thick and smooth. Season to taste.

Pour the sauce into a gravy boat and serve with the chicken.

Chicken sauté à la bordelaise

SERVES FOUR

¼ cup (50 g) butter
2 tablespoons olive oil
4-lb (2-kg) chicken, cut into pieces
1 garlic clove, crushed
½ cup (125 ml) chicken stock
5 tablespoons white wine
1 teaspoon meat glaze
1 tablespoon tomato paste
Salt and black pepper
3 artichoke hearts, cooked, cut in quarters and fried in butter
1 lb (450 g) potatoes, sautéed
Deep-fried onion rings
Deep-fried parsley sprigs

Heat the butter with the oil in a frying pan and sauté the chicken pieces until they are brown on all sides. Reduce the heat, cover and cook for about 30 minutes or until the chicken is tender. Test by inserting the point of a sharp knife into the meat—if the juices run clear the chicken is cooked. Transfer the chicken to the center of a large, warm serving dish and keep hot.

Add the garlic to the frying pan and fry for 1 minute. Stir in the stock, wine, meat glaze, paste and seasoning. Bring to a boil and cook, stirring constantly, until the sauce is reduced and slightly thickened. Strain the sauce over the chicken. Surround the chicken with the remaining ingredients and serve.

Chicken sauté à l'italienne

SERVES FOUR

4-lb (2-kg) chicken, quartered
Salt and pepper
3 tablespoons butter
1 tablespoon olive oil

ITALIAN SAUCE

½ cup (125 ml) white wine
3 tablespoons duxelles
1 cup (250 ml) demi-glace sauce
2 tablespoons tomato paste
Salt and pepper
1 tablespoon chopped ham
1 teaspoon chopped tarragon
1 teaspoon chopped chervil
1 tablespoon chopped parsley

Rub the chicken pieces with salt and pepper.

Heat the butter and oil in a frying pan and cook the chicken pieces gently, turning them occasionally, for 30 to 40 minutes or until they are cooked. Test by inserting the point of a sharp knife into the meat—if the juices run clear, the chicken is cooked.

While the chicken is cooking, prepare the sauce. Mix the wine and the duxelles in a saucepan and bring to a boil. Boil rapidly until the wine is reduced by half. Stir in the demi-glace sauce and the tomato paste. Taste the sauce and add seasoning if necessary. Stir in the ham, tarragon, chervil and 1 teaspoon of the parsley.

Transfer the chicken to a warm serving dish. Keep hot.

Pour the Italian sauce into the frying pan. Bring to a boil, stirring and scraping the pan to dislodge the sediments.

Pour the sauce over the chicken, garnish with the remaining parsley and serve.

From left to right : chicken Kiev, chicken sauté à la bordelaise, and chicken Maryland.

Poultry and game birds

Chicken Kiev

Flatten the chicken breasts between sheets of waxed paper.

Make the butter filling, shape it into a rectangle and chill.

Enclose one-quarter of the butter in each chicken breast.

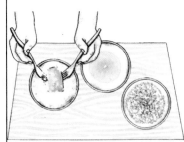

Fasten with toothpicks and coat in flour, egg and bread crumbs.

Fry the chicken rolls in hot oil until crisp and golden brown.

Chicken Kiev

SERVES FOUR

4 chicken breasts, skinned and boned
¼ cup (50 g) butter
1 tablespoon chopped fresh parsley
1 teaspoon chopped fresh tarragon
2 garlic cloves, crushed
Grated rind and juice of ½ lemon
Salt and pepper
Seasoned flour
1 egg, beaten
¾ cup (125 g) dry bread crumbs
Oil for deep frying
1 lemon, quartered
1 bunch watercress, washed

Place the chicken breasts between 2 pieces of waxed paper and flatten with a mallet or rolling pin.

Cream the butter in a mixing bowl. Beat in the herbs, garlic, lemon rind and seasoning and moisten with a teaspoon of the lemon juice. Shape the butter into a rectangle and chill in the refrigerator until firm.

Cut the chilled butter in 4 equal pieces and put 1 piece into the center of each flattened chicken breast. Roll up tightly, folding in the edges so that the butter is completely encased, and secure each roll with a toothpick. Coat the chicken rolls first with flour, then with egg and then with the bread crumbs. Put them on a plate and chill in the refrigerator for at least 1 hour.

Heat the oil to 375°F (190°C). Fry the chicken rolls for about 7 minutes or until they are golden. Drain well, transfer to a warm platter. Garnish with the lemon wedges and watercress.

Deep-fried chicken

SERVES TWO

2 tablespoons soy sauce
4 tablespoons lemon juice
½-inch (1-cm) piece fresh ginger root, peeled and grated
1 lb (450 g) cooked chicken, cut into 1½-inch (3-cm) cubes
Oil for deep frying
1 cup (250 ml) fritter batter
1 lemon, quartered

Mix the soy sauce, lemon juice and ginger in a large bowl for the marinade. Marinate the chicken, turning occasionally, for at least 1 hour and preferably longer.

Remove the chicken from the marinade and dry well on paper towels.

Heat the oil to 375°F (190°C). Coat the chicken cubes in the batter. Lower them into the oil in small batches and fry until golden. Using a slotted spoon, remove the chicken pieces and drain on paper towels. When all the chicken pieces have been fried increase the heat of the oil and return the whole batch in a frying basket to the hot oil for a few seconds to crisp.

Drain and transfer the chicken pieces to a warm serving dish and serve with lemon quarters.

Chicken lemon sauté

SERVES FOUR

4-lb (2-kg) chicken, cut into pieces
Salt and pepper
1 tablespoon oil
¼ cup (50 g) butter
1 tablespoon flour
Rind and juice of 1 lemon
½ cup (125 ml) chicken stock
2 tablespoons dry vermouth
2 teaspoons chopped fresh tarragon
4 tarragon sprigs

Season the chicken pieces.

Heat the oil and butter in a large frying pan and sauté the chicken pieces for 8 to 12 minutes, until they are evenly browned.

Transfer the chicken to a warm dish and keep hot.

Pour off all but 1 tablespoon of the fat. Stir in the flour and cook for 2 minutes. Add the lemon juice and rind, stock, vermouth and chopped tarragon. Stir over moderate heat until the sauce has thickened.

Return the chicken pieces to the pan. Cover the pan and simmer the chicken pieces very gently for 25 to 30 minutes or until they are cooked. Test by piercing the meat with the point of a sharp knife—if the juices run clear the chicken is cooked. Transfer the chicken pieces to a warm serving dish, strain the sauce over the chicken and garnish with the tarragon sprigs.

Poulet sauté chasseur

SERVES FOUR

3 tablespoons butter
1 tablespoon oil
4-lb (2-kg) chicken, cut into serving pieces
½ lb (225 g) mushrooms, sliced
1 shallot, chopped
½ cup (125 ml) white wine
1 cup (250 ml) chicken stock
1 tablespoon tomato paste
1 tablespoon brandy
Salt and pepper
1 teaspoon finely chopped fresh tarragon
1 teaspoon finely chopped fresh chervil
1 tablespoon finely chopped fresh parsley
2 tablespoons beurre manié

Heat the butter and oil in a large frying pan and sauté the chicken pieces for 15 minutes or until they are well browned.

Reduce the heat and continue frying for 15 minutes. Add the mushrooms and shallot and fry, stirring, for 3 to 4 minutes or until the chicken is cooked. Test by inserting the point of a sharp knife into the meat—if the juices run clear the chicken is cooked. Transfer the chicken to a warm serving dish and keep hot.

Pour the wine into the pan and bring to a boil for 1 minute. Stir in the stock, tomato paste, brandy, seasoning, tarragon, chervil and 1 teaspoon of the parsley. If the sauce is too thin, stir in a little beurre manié, until slightly thickened.

Pour the sauce over the chicken, sprinkle the remaining parsley on top and serve.

Chicken kromeski

SERVES FOUR

1½ cups (350 g) ground cooked chicken
1 teaspoon dried dill weed
1 cup (50 g) chopped mushrooms, cooked
Salt and pepper
1 egg yolk
6 tablespoons very thick béchamel sauce, made with 1 tablespoon each butter and flour to 6 tablespoons milk
8 bacon slices
Oil for deep frying
1¼ cups (315 ml) fritter batter
1 cup (250 ml) tomato sauce

Mix the chicken, dill weed, mushrooms, seasoning, egg yolk and béchamel together. With well-floured hands, shape the mixture into 8 croquettes.

Lay the bacon flat on a board, put 1 croquette on each slice and roll up. Chill for 1 hour.

Heat the oil to 375°F (190°C). Dip the rolls in the batter and fry for 3 to 4 minutes or until golden brown. Drain on paper towels and serve hot with the tomato sauce.

Chicken with almonds
SERVES TWO TO FOUR

4 cups (450 g) diced chicken breasts
1 tablespoon cornstarch
2 tablespoon soy sauce
2 tablespoons dry sherry
1 teaspoon sugar
2 tablespoons oil
½-inch (1-cm) piece fresh ginger root, peeled and finely chopped
6 scallions, sliced
2 garlic cloves, crushed
⅔ cup (125 g) almonds, blanched and split
Pepper

Rub the chicken cubes all over with the cornstarch. Set aside.

Combine the soy sauce, sherry and sugar in a bowl.

Heat the oil in a large frying pan. Add the ginger, scallions and garlic and stir-fry for 30 seconds. Add the chicken and stir-fry for 2 minutes. Add the almonds and fry for 1 minute. Pour in the soy sauce mixture and some pepper and cook for 1½ minutes. Serve immediately.

Chicken sauté paprika
SERVES FOUR

4 lb (2 kg) chicken pieces
Salt and pepper
¼ cup (50 g) butter
2 tablespoons paprika
1 cup (250 ml) cream

Rub the chicken pieces all over with salt and pepper.

Melt the butter in a large frying pan and fry the chicken pieces gently on all sides without browning. Stir in the paprika. Cover the pan and cook gently for about 30 to 35 minutes or until the chicken is tender. Test by piercing the meat with the point of a sharp knife—if the juices run clear the chicken is cooked.

Transfer the chicken pieces to a warm serving dish and keep hot.

Pour the cream into the frying pan. Stir and scrape the pan to mix and bring to a boil. Boil until the cream is reduced by half.

Adjust the seasoning to taste, if necessary. Pour the sauce over the chicken and serve.

Stir-fried chicken and mushrooms
SERVES FOUR

1 lb (450 g) boned chicken breasts, cut into ½-inch (1-cm) cubes
Salt
1 tablespoon cornstarch
2 tablespoons sherry
2 tablespoons soy sauce
4 tablespoons oil
1 garlic clove, crushed
½-inch (1-cm) piece fresh ginger root, peeled and grated
1½ heaping cups (50 g) dried mushrooms, soaked in water for 20 minutes and chopped
½ cup (50 g) water chestnuts, cut into small cubes

Rub the chicken all over with salt and cornstarch. Set aside.

Mix the sherry and soy sauce in a small bowl. Set aside.

Heat 3 tablespoons of the oil in a wok or a large frying pan over high heat. Stir in the garlic, ginger and mushrooms and stir-fry for 15 seconds. Add the chicken pieces. Stir-fry for 4 minutes. Pour in the sherry and soy sauce, reduce the heat and cook for 30 seconds. Add the water chestnuts and cook for 30 seconds more.

Guinea hen with juniper berries
Guinea hen has dry flesh, so cook it very gently.
SERVES FOUR

6 tablespoons butter
2 guinea hens, cut in half
Juice and thinly pared rind of 1 orange
6 juniper berries, bruised
Salt and pepper
½ cup (125 ml) Dubonnet

Melt the butter in a large frying pan over low heat. Add the guinea hens and cook them gently, turning occasionally, for 15 minutes. Add the orange rind, juniper berries and seasoning and continue frying gently for another 15 minutes until the birds are browned.

Pour in the orange juice, scrape and stir to mix and bring to a simmer. Cover the pan and simmer very gently for 20 to 30 minutes or until the birds are cooked. Test by piercing the thighs with the point of a knife. If the juices run clear, the birds are cooked.

Lift out the birds and set aside on a plate. Remove the orange peel and juniper berries if desired. Pour the Dubonnet into the pan. Increase the heat and stir, scraping the bottom of the pan. Simmer the sauce for 30 seconds. Return the birds to the pan, baste with the sauce and simmer for 30 seconds or until hot. Serve immediately.

Wild duck à la Seville
Sweet oranges may be substituted for the Sevilles, but the flavor is less interesting.
SERVES FOUR

¼ cup (50 g) butter
1 tablespoon oil
2 small wild ducks or 1 large mallard, cut into pieces
½ cup (125 ml) stock
2 Seville oranges
4 sugar cubes
2 tablespoons wine vinegar
Juice of ½ lemon
Salt and black pepper

Heat the butter and oil in a large frying pan and sauté the duck pieces until they are well browned on all sides. Pour in the stock, cover the pan and cook for about 20 minutes or until the duck is cooked. Test by inserting the point of a sharp knife into the meat—if the juices run clear the duck is cooked. Remove the duck pieces to a warm serving dish and keep hot.

Meanwhile, pare the rind from 1 orange, cut it into julienne strips and blanch. Remove the zest from the other orange by rubbing the skin with the sugar cubes.

Crush the cubes and stir into the pan with the vinegar, juice of 1 orange, lemon juice and seasoning. Bring to a boil and cook until syrupy. Taste and add more sugar or seasoning if necessary.

Strain the sauce over the duck, and garnish with the orange rind.

Sautéed partridge jubilee
SERVES FOUR

¼ cup (50 g) butter
2 tablespoons olive oil
2 young partridges, halved
4 slices brown bread, cut in half diagonally
3 tablespoons bacon fat
¼ lb (100 g) pâté de foie
½ lb (225 g) ripe black cherries, pitted
1 teaspoon sugar
1 teaspoon lemon juice
Salt and pepper
8 tablespoons Madeira
1 bunch watercress, washed

Heat the butter with the oil and sauté the partridges until browned on all sides. Continue cooking for about 25 minutes, until the birds are tender.

Meanwhile, fry the bread in the bacon fat, drain and spread with the pâté. Put the fried bread on a warm serving dish and put the partridges on top.

Return the frying pan to the heat and stir in the cherries, sugar, lemon juice, seasoning and Madeira. Bring to a boil. Pour the sauce over the partridges and serve at once, garnished with watercress.

Chicken liver sauté
SERVES FOUR

1½ lb (700 g) chicken livers
¼ cup (50 g) butter
1 Bermuda onion, finely chopped
½ cup (125 ml) red wine
½ teaspoon dried thyme
¼ bay leaf
Salt and pepper

Remove any skin or membrane from the chicken livers and cut each liver into quarters.

Melt the butter and fry the onion until it begins to color. Add the chicken livers and fry quickly for 2 minutes.

Stir in the wine, herbs and seasoning. Cover and simmer for 3 to 4 minutes. Remove the bay leaf and serve at once.

Meat and game

The most suitable cuts of meat for pan frying are beef fillet, club sirloin steak, lamb or pork chops, veal chops and cutlets and liver and kidneys. Sausages, hamburgers and bacon may also be cooked in this way.

To fry steak, nick the fat around the outside to prevent the meat from curling up during cooking. Put the pan over high heat. Add just enough fat to grease the bottom of the pan. Fry the steak quickly on both sides to seal in the juices. Reduce the heat to moderate and cook, turning the meat occasionally, until the steak is done—a one-inch (2-cm) fillet steak will cook rare in four minutes. A one-and-a-half-inch (3-cm) steak will take about ten minutes. Season only when cooking is completed. Serve the steak with the deglazed pan juices poured over it.

Cook chops and cutlets in the same way but after the initial browning turn the heat down to fairly low and cook for a longer period—about sixteen to twenty minutes. Well-flattened veal scallops, fried either plain or coated with flour or egg and bread crumbs are ready as soon as they are browned on both sides. Coat thinly sliced liver with seasoned flour and fry for about six to eight minutes. Slit kidneys, skin and fry, flat side first, for about three to four minutes on each side over gentle heat. Prick sausages before frying to prevent them from bursting and fry for fifteen to twenty minutes or until they are well browned all over and cooked through. To fry bacon slices, snip the rinds, if necessary, and cook for about five minutes.

Steak au poivre

The best steaks for this dish are fillets. If club steaks are used, score any fat to prevent the steaks from curling up.

SERVES FOUR

1 to 3 tablespoons peppercorns, depending on taste
4 steaks, about 1 inch (2 cm) thick, weighing at least ½ lb (225 g) each
2 tablespoons butter
1 tablespoon olive oil
Salt
2 tablespoons brandy
¼ cup (65 ml) demi-glace sauce

Crush the peppercorns with a pestle or rolling pin. Wipe the steaks dry and press the crushed peppercorns into both sides of the meat using your palm.

Heat the butter and oil together in a heavy frying pan until very hot. Put in the steaks and fry for 3 to 4 minutes on each side for medium rare, less for rare. Transfer the steaks to a hot dish and sprinkle with salt. Pour the brandy and demi-glace into the hot pan and boil rapidly for 30 seconds, scraping in all the sediment sticking to the pan. Pour the sauce over the steaks and serve at once.

Steak Diane

SERVES FOUR

4 fillet steaks, ¾ inch (2 cm) thick
2 tablespoons butter
1 tablespoon olive oil
1 tablespoon lemon juice
1 tablespoon Worcestershire sauce
1 teaspoon French mustard
1 shallot, finely chopped
2 tablespoons chopped parsley

Flatten the steaks between waxed paper to about ¼ inch (½ cm) thick with a mallet.

Heat the butter and oil together in a heavy frying pan until they are very hot. Put in the steaks and fry for 1 minute on each side if you like them medium rare, longer if you like them well done. Transfer the steaks to a warm serving dish and keep hot.

Add the lemon juice, Worcestershire sauce, mustard and shallot to the pan. Cook for one minute over medium heat, stirring all the time. Stir in the parsley. Pour the sauce over the steaks and serve.

Beef stroganoff

The success of this dish lies in the quick frying of the meat in very hot butter until brown all over.

SERVES FOUR

1½ to 2 lb (700 to 900 g) fillet steak
4 tablespoons clarified butter
2 medium-sized onions, thinly sliced
½ lb (225 g) small mushrooms, sliced
Salt and pepper
½ cup (125 ml) sour cream

Cut the steak into thin strips, slightly on the diagonal, about ½ inch (1 cm) wide and 2 inches (5 cm) long.

Melt the butter in a large sauté pan and fry the onions until soft. Add the mushrooms and cook gently for 2 to 3 minutes.

Using a slotted spoon, transfer the onions and mushrooms to a plate and keep hot. Increase the heat, adding more butter to the pan if necessary. When the butter is very hot, put in the beef and fry quickly for 4 to 5 minutes. Return the onions and mushrooms to the pan and season well. Cook for another minute or two. Pour in the sour cream, let it come to just under boiling point and serve immediately.

Entrecôte à la viennoise

SERVES FOUR

4 sirloin steaks, ¾ inch (2 cm) thick
Salt
1 teaspoon paprika
2 tablespoons plain plus 2 tablespoons seasoned flour
4 tablespoons butter or lard
2 onions, sliced into rings

Put the steaks between 2 sheets of waxed paper and beat with a rolling pin or mallet to flatten them. Season with salt and paprika and coat the steaks with the plain flour. Melt the butter or

Three easy-to-make meat dishes: from top to bottom, sweet and sour meatballs, Wiener schnitzel and entrecôte au poivre vert.

lard in a frying pan over high heat and fry the steaks on both sides for 4 minutes until brown. Transfer to a warmed serving dish and keep hot.

Dip the onion rings in the seasoned flour and fry in the hot fat. Drain well on paper towels and arrange on top of the steaks. Serve at once.

Veal Zurich style

SERVES FOUR

1½ lb (700 g) boned leg of
   veal
3 tablespoons seasoned flour
4 tablespoons butter
1 tablespoon finely chopped
   shallots
½ teaspoon paprika (optional)
½ cup (125 ml) dry white
   wine
½ cup (125 ml) cream
Salt and pepper

Slice the veal as thinly as possible across the grain and cut these slices into thin strips. Toss in seasoned flour.

Heat the butter in a sauté pan. Add the chopped shallots and fry for 1 to 2 minutes. Add the veal and sauté over high heat for 2 minutes or until well browned. Sprinkle with paprika, if you are using it. Reduce the heat, pour in the wine and bring to simmering point. Stir in the cream and reheat, but do not boil. Adjust the seasoning and serve at once.

Veal cutlets Milanese style

SERVES FOUR

4 veal cutlets
Salt and pepper
1 egg, beaten
⅓ cup (50 g) dried fine bread
   crumbs
4 tablespoons butter
1 tablespoon olive oil

Flatten the cutlets. Season well, then dip in beaten egg and coat with the bread crumbs.

Heat the butter and oil together and when hot, fry the cutlets for 3 to 4 minutes on each side or until cooked through.

Meat and game

Fondue bourguignonne

The cooking is done by each guest at the table, where the oil is kept hot over an alcohol burner. Long skewers or fondue forks are a necessity.

SERVES FOUR TO SIX

2 lb (900 g) fillet or sirloin steak
1 cup (250 ml) corn oil
4 bowls of sauces such as béarnaise, horseradish, mayonnaise, aioli, tartar and chili

Cut the steak into ½-inch (1-cm) cubes, trimming off any fat or gristle. Heat the oil in the fondue pan until it is bubbling and very hot. Divide the meat between the guests and let each one in turn skewer a piece of meat and fry it in the hot oil. The meat is then dipped into one of the sauces before being eaten.

Veal Marsala

SERVES FOUR

8 small, thin veal scallops
Salt and pepper
2 tablespoons flour
¼ cup (50 g) butter
1 teaspoon lemon juice
3 tablespoons Marsala wine
2 tablespoons finely chopped parsley

Flatten the pieces of veal. Season with salt and pepper and roll in the flour. Melt the butter in a heavy frying pan and sauté the veal for 3 to 4 minutes on each side or until golden.

Add the lemon juice and Marsala, stir well to mix with all the pan juices and simmer for 1 to 2 minutes. Serve sprinkled with parsley.

Noisettes of lamb with stuffed tomatoes

SERVES FOUR

8 lamb noisettes (3 oz/75 g each, cut from rib)
Salt and pepper
6 tablespoons butter
1 small onion, finely chopped
¼ lb (125 g) mushrooms, chopped
2 slices ham, chopped
2 teaspoons chopped mint
1 garlic clove, crushed
3 tablespoons yogurt
8 small tomatoes
8 round croutons, hot

½ cup (150 ml) veal stock
2 teaspoons tomato paste
Fresh mint sprigs
1 lemon, sliced

Season the noisettes and set aside.

Preheat the oven to 350°F (180°C). Melt half the butter in a saucepan and fry the onion until transparent. Add the mushrooms, ham, mint and garlic. Stir over moderate heat until the mushrooms are tender. Remove the pan from the heat and stir in the yogurt.

Cut the tops off the tomatoes and scoop out the centers. Fill the tomatoes with the mushroom and ham mixture and put them into a baking dish. Bake for 20 minutes.

Meanwhile, melt the rest of the butter in a frying pan and fry the noisettes for 5 to 8 minutes on each side or until cooked and brown. Arrange the croutons on a serving dish, put a noisette on each crouton and keep hot. Deglaze the pan with the stock. Boil until reduced by about half and stir in the tomato paste. Spoon the sauce over the noisettes, arrange the tomatoes in the center of the dish and garnish with the mint sprigs and lemon slices.

Saltimbocca

SERVES FOUR

8 thin veal scallops, about 3 inches (8 cm) across
Salt and pepper
8 slices prosciutto or mild-cured ham
8 sage leaves
¼ cup (50 g) butter
4 tablespoons white wine

Flatten the veal well. Season lightly with salt and pepper. Put a sage leaf and then a slice of ham on top of each piece of veal. Roll and secure with a toothpick.

Heat the butter in a large frying pan. When the butter is foamy, add the rolls and fry briskly on all sides for 6 to 8 minutes or until they are cooked through and golden.

Transfer the scallops to a warm dish and keep hot while you make the sauce.

Stir the wine into the juices in the pan and bring to a boil,

scraping and stirring. Pour over the scallops and serve.

Sautéed venison steaks

SERVES FOUR

4 venison steaks, ¾ inch (2 cm) thick
Salt and black pepper
1 onion, sliced
Rind and juice of ½ lemon
8 juniper berries, crushed
½ teaspoon dried thyme
½ cup (125 ml) vermouth
2 tablespoons olive oil
¼ cup (50 g) butter
2 tablespoons red currant jelly
1 lemon, sliced
Watercress

Season the steaks well on both sides and put them into a dish.

Mix together the onion, the lemon rind and juice, the juniper berries, thyme, vermouth and oil. Rub this into the steaks, cover the dish and refrigerate for at least 1 day.

Drain the meat and dry on paper towels. Reserve the marinade. Heat the butter in a heavy frying pan. Fry the venison over low heat for about 10 to 12 minutes on each side. Cover the pan and cook for 20 minutes more, turning once. Transfer the steaks to a warm serving dish and keep hot.

Strain the marinade into the pan, add the red currant jelly and bring to a boil, stirring. Adjust the seasoning and pour the sauce over the steaks. Garnish with the lemon and watercress.

Veal chops en papillotes

The chops are brought to the table in their paper wrappings.

SERVES FOUR

2 tablespoons butter
4 veal chops
Waxed paper or parchment paper
Oil
8 slices ham, the same size as the veal chops
8 tablespoons duxelles
Salt and pepper

Melt the butter in a frying pan and fry the chops for 10 minutes on each side or until they are cooked through.

Preheat the oven to 400°F (200°C).

Cut the waxed paper into 4 heart-shaped pieces. Lightly oil the paper. Lay 1 slice of ham on one half of each heart. Spread 1 tablespoon of duxelles on each slice and cover with the veal chops. Spread another tablespoon of duxelles on each chop and cover with another slice of ham. Season to taste.

Fold the other half of the paper hearts over and fold the edges like a hem. Put the papillotes in a baking dish and bake for 15 minutes or until the paper is puffed up and beginning to turn brown.

Remove the papillotes from the oven and serve immediately.

Making papillotes

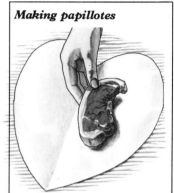

Put the ham and veal chop on a heart-shaped piece of paper.

Cover with duxelles and another slice of ham.

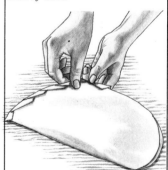

Fold the paper heart in half and pleat the edges to seal it.

Sautéed sweetbreads Saint Médard

Calves' sweetbreads are considered to be the most delicately flavored of all variety meats. If you are using lambs' sweetbreads, you will need ¼ pound (125 g) per person.

SERVES TWO

1 pair calf's sweetbreads, soaked, blanched and trimmed
2 tablespoons seasoned flour
4 tablespoons butter
1 tablespoon oil
1 tablespoon brandy
Salt and freshly ground black pepper
Nutmeg
¼ lb (125 g) mushrooms, sliced
⅓ cup (50 g) black olives, pitted and sliced
4 tablespoons Madeira wine
Juice of ½ lemon
½ cup (125 ml) sour cream
8 fried bread triangles

If you have time, press the sweetbreads between two pieces of waxed paper with a weight on top for at least 2 hours or overnight. This improves the texture and gives the sweetbreads an even thickness.

Slice the sweetbreads in half horizontally and coat them in the flour. Heat the butter and oil in a frying pan and sauté the sweetbreads until golden on both sides. Heat the brandy in a ladle or small saucepan, ignite it, pour it over the sweetbreads and shake the pan gently until the flames die down. Season with salt, pepper and a little grated nutmeg.

Add the sliced mushrooms and olives and cook for 1 to 2 minutes more. Stir in the Madeira and simmer for 5 minutes. Add the lemon juice and the sour cream. Reheat but do not boil. Garnish with the fried bread.

Serve at once.

Sautéed liver and bacon

SERVES FOUR

8 bacon slices
2 onions, cut into rings
1 lb (450 g) lambs' liver, thinly sliced
1 tablespoon well-seasoned flour
¾ cup (175 ml) stock
1 tablespoon chopped fresh tarragon (optional)
1 tablespoon butter
4 tomatoes, cut in half crosswise and broiled

Fry the bacon and onions in a heavy frying pan. Transfer the bacon and onions to a warm serving dish and keep hot. Toss the liver in the seasoned flour and cook for about 2 minutes on each side. Transfer to the serving dish and keep hot.

Deglaze the frying pan with the stock, add the chopped tarragon, if you are using it, and the butter.

Pour the sauce over the liver and serve at once, garnished with the broiled tomatoes.

Meatballs with sweet and sour sauce

These meatballs may be served with other sauces or with yogurt or sour cream. If you prefer a more spicy flavor, add finely chopped ginger root, green chili and garlic to the meat mixture and leave out the mushrooms.

SERVES FOUR

1½ lb (700 g) ground meat, pork and beef mixed
1 small onion, finely chopped
1 cup (50 g) finely chopped mushrooms
1 teaspoon salt
1 teaspoon sugar
¼ teaspoon cayenne pepper
2 tablespoons fresh white bread crumbs
1 egg yolk
3 tablespoons soy sauce
Flour
4 to 6 tablespoons oil

SAUCE

2 tablespoons oil
2 tablespoons brown sugar
1 teaspoon soy sauce
1½ cups (450 g) canned pineapple chunks, drained and the liquid reserved
2 tablespoons wine vinegar
3 carrots, thinly sliced on the diagonal
2 green peppers, thinly sliced
1 tablespoon cornstarch
3 tomatoes, quartered

Combine all the ingredients for the meatballs except the oil. With floured hands, form the mixture into walnut-sized balls.

Heat the oil in a large frying pan and fry the meatballs for about 5 minutes or until they are cooked and well browned.

Using a slotted spoon, transfer the meatballs to a plate and set aside.

To make the sauce, rinse out the pan and return it to the heat. Pour in the oil, stir in the sugar, soy sauce, all but 3 tablespoons of the reserved pineapple liquid and the vinegar. Bring to a boil. Add the carrots and green pepper, reduce the heat and simmer for 2 minutes.

Mix the cornstarch with the reserved 3 tablespoons of pineapple liquid and stir it into the pan. Cook for 1 minute and add the pineapple chunks, meatballs and tomatoes. Simmer for a few minutes until the meatballs are heated through. Serve immediately.

Entrecôte au poivre vert

SERVES FOUR

2 tablespoons butter
4 club steaks
Salt
2 tablespoons brandy
½ cup (125 ml) cream
2 tablespoons canned green peppercorns

Melt the butter in a large, heavy frying pan over moderate heat. Add the steaks and fry them for 1 minute on each side. Reduce the heat to moderate and cook for a further 1 to 2 minutes on each side. Remove the steaks, season with salt and keep them hot on a warm serving dish.

Add the brandy to the pan and stir, scraping the bottom of the pan to dislodge the sediment. Stir in the cream and peppercorns and, when the sauce is hot but not boiling, remove the pan from the heat and pour it over the steaks. Serve immediately.

Tournedos au vin rouge

Tournedos are cut from the heart of the tenderloin and should be at least 1 to 1½ inches (2 to 3 cm) thick. Serve the tournedos with new potatoes and young peas.

SERVES FOUR

¼ cup (50 g) butter
1 tablespoon olive oil
4 tournedos
½ cup (125 ml) red wine
4 round croutons, hot
2 tablespoons meat glaze
Salt and pepper
2 teaspoons chopped fresh tarragon

Melt 1 tablespoon of the butter with the oil in a heavy frying pan. When the fat is very hot, add the tournedos and fry for 1 minute on each side to brown.

Pour in the wine, cook for a few seconds, then reduce the heat to low and cook gently for about 3 to 4 minutes.

Arrange the croutons on a warm serving dish. Put the steaks on top of the croutons and keep hot.

Increase the heat, stir the meat glaze into the wine and boil until reduced and syrupy. Remove the pan from the heat. Cut the remaining butter into small pieces and stir into the sauce one piece at a time. Season to taste and stir in the tarragon. Pour the sauce over the steaks and serve.

Wiener Schnitzel

The scallops for this dish should be large, round and paper thin. They are best served crisp, dry and straight from the frying pan. Serve with a mixed salad.

SERVES FOUR

4 large veal scallops
2 tablespoons seasoned flour
1 egg, beaten
Dried white bread crumbs
4 to 6 tablespoons butter
1 to 2 tablespoons olive oil
1 lemon, peeled and sliced
2 hard-cooked eggs, the whites and yolks separated and finely chopped
4 to 8 green olives, pitted and halved
8 anchovies (optional)
1 to 2 tablespoons chopped capers (optional)

Flatten the scallops well. Dip them into the seasoned flour, then in the egg and coat with bread crumbs.

Heat the butter and oil in a heavy pan and sauté the scallops for 3 to 4 minutes on each side until golden brown. Drain well on paper towels and serve garnished with the lemon slices and eggs, olives, anchovies and capers if desired.

Serve immediately.

Vegetables

A very wide variety of vegetables may be fried or sautéed.

For pan frying very little fat is required—about one tablespoon of oil or butter for one pound (450 g) of vegetables. Cut or slice the vegetables evenly. Heat the fat in a frying or sauté pan and when it is very hot, add the vegetables. Reduce the heat to low, cover the pan and cook, stirring occasionally, until the vegetables are tender.

To stir-fry, cut root vegetables into small, even-sized pieces, shred cabbage finely or cut into pieces and leave such vegetables as snow peas whole. Cooked uncovered throughout, the vegetables are stirred constantly over high or moderately high heat and rarely take longer than five minutes to cook. About two tablespoons of oil will be required for one pound (450 g) of vegetables.

Many vegetables are suitable for deep frying, but with few exceptions—potatoes, sweet potatoes and parsley, for example—they must be dipped into batter first. Heat the oil for deep frying vegetables (except potatoes) to 350° to 375°F (176° to 190°C). French fries and soufflé potatoes are fried twice; French fries at 330°F (165°C) and then again at 375° to 400°F (190° to 204°C) and soufflé potatoes at 250°F (121°C) and 400°F (204°C). Soak potatoes in ice-cold water for thirty minutes before frying to remove excess starch.

Deliciously crisp vegetable fritters made with eggplants, mushrooms and zucchini.

French fries

SERVES FOUR

4 large potatoes
Oil for deep frying
Salt

Peel the potatoes and cut them into ½-inch (1-cm) thick sticks, using either a special cutter or a sharp knife.

As the potatoes are cut, put them into enough cold water to cover. Put all the potatoes into a colander and rinse them under cold running water. Alternatively, soak in ice water for 30 minutes. Drain and dry them with a clean towel.

Heat the oil to 330°F (165°C).

Put small batches of potatoes at a time in the frying basket and fry, shaking the basket gently, for about 2 to 3 minutes. Remove the potatoes and drain on paper towels.

When all the potatoes have been fried once, heat the oil to 375°F (190°C) and fry them again for 3 to 4 minutes more or until they are crisp and golden brown. Remove and drain well on paper towels. Keep warm in an uncovered serving dish in the oven. Sprinkle the potatoes with plenty of salt and serve immediately.

Shoestring potatoes

Shoestring potatoes are prepared like French fries except that they are cut into matchstick shapes and fried for a shorter time.

Potato chips

Potato chips are made from wafer-thin slices of potato (a vegetable slicer gives the best results) and fried for 2 to 4 minutes at 375°F (190°C).

Soufflé potatoes

Soufflé potatoes are difficult to make. They do not always puff up. Use old starchy potatoes cut very thinly lengthwise (cut the slices in half if they are too big). Soak in ice water for 30 minutes, drain and dry well.

Heat the oil to 250°F (121°C) and fry the potatoes for 4 minutes. Lift out and drain. Increase the temperature of the oil to 400°F (204°C) and fry the potatoes again until they puff up.

Sprinkle with salt before serving.

Cottage fries

In Europe these are known as sauté potatoes. The Provençal version has chopped garlic and parsley added just before the potatoes are ready.

SERVES FOUR TO SIX

2 lb (900 g) old potatoes, peeled
6 tablespoons butter, or 2 tablespoons oil and 2 tablespoons butter
Salt and pepper

Boil the potatoes until they are just tender. Drain and let cool. Cut into ¼-inch (½-cm) thick slices.

Melt the butter or butter and oil in a large frying pan and when it is hot, add the potato slices and seasoning.

Sauté for about 5 minutes, shaking the pan occasionally, or until the undersides are well browned. Turn the whole batch of potatoes over and continue cooking, as before, until the potatoes are lightly browned.

Arrange in a warm dish, season and serve at once.

Lyonnaise potatoes

Prepare as above, adding 4 thinly sliced onions with the potatoes.

Parisienne potatoes

Using a metal scoop, cut potatoes into balls and boil until nearly tender. Drain and sauté in butter in a frying pan until cooked through and golden brown.

Potato croquettes

The croquettes may be varied by mixing the mashed potatoes with chopped herbs, grated onion, cheese or a little chutney.

Croquettes may also be pan fried in 3 tablespoons butter and 4 tablespoons oil.

SERVES FOUR

2 lb (900 g) old potatoes, peeled, boiled and mashed
4 egg yolks
2 tablespoons butter
1½ teaspoons salt
½ teaspoon black pepper
About ½ cup (125 ml) hot milk
1 egg, beaten
1⅓ cups (125 g) dry white bread crumbs

Mix the potatoes, egg yolks, butter and seasoning in a large bowl. Add enough hot milk to make a firm paste and beat well until it is quite smooth.

With floured hands, divide the mixture into even-sized pieces made from about 2 tablespoons of potato. Set aside in the refrigerator on a lightly floured tray, in a single layer, and chill for 30 minutes or until firm.

Roll the pieces into cork shapes and dip them first into the beaten egg, then in the bread crumbs, coating them all over.

Heat the oil to 375°F (190°C). Put a few of the croquettes in a single layer into a frying basket and lower into the hot oil. Fry for 3 to 5 minutes or until they are golden brown on all sides. Drain well on paper towels and keep hot while you fry the remaining croquettes.

Rösti

A Swiss specialty, rösti is often served as a breakfast dish. Chopped onion, ham or grated cheese can be added to the potatoes before frying.

SERVES FOUR

2 lb (900 g) potatoes
Salt and pepper
6 tablespoons butter

Cook the potatoes in their skins in boiling water for 10 minutes. Drain and let them cool. When they are room temperature, peel them and grate the flesh coarsely into a bowl. Mix with salt and pepper to taste.

Melt half the butter in a large, heavy frying pan and when it is sizzling, add the potatoes, smoothing the top down lightly. Fry over moderate heat, loosening the base occasionally with a spatula to prevent sticking.

After about 10 minutes, press the potatoes down with the spatula to form a cake. Invert a plate over the frying pan and turn the rösti out onto it. Melt the remaining butter in the pan. Slide the rösti back into the frying pan and cook the other side, shaking the pan occasionally for 10 to 15 minutes more or until the underside is golden and crisp.

Turn the rösti out onto a warm plate.

Serve at once.

Vegetables

Bubble and squeak

The quantities of potato and greens can be varied according to what is available, but the traditional proportions are half and half.

The mixture may be cooked as one large pancake or formed into individual cakes. Serve with broiled sausages or bacon.

SERVES FOUR

½ lb (225 g) mashed potatoes
½ lb (225 g) cooked green or white cabbage, greens or Brussels sprouts, coarsely chopped
Salt and freshly ground black pepper
¼ cup (50 g) bacon fat, drippings or butter

Mix the potatoes, cabbage and seasoning in a bowl.

Melt the fat in a large frying pan. Put the potato mixture into the pan and press it down well. Fry for about 4 minutes on each side until it is lightly browned and heated through. Slide onto a warm serving plate and serve.

Potato scones

This Irish/Scottish dish is not really a scone at all—it is more like a thick pancake.

Potato scones may be eaten hot with plenty of butter and syrup or honey, or served with bacon or sausages.

MAKES ABOUT TWELVE

1 lb (450 g) freshly boiled potatoes, mashed
6 tablespoons butter, melted
1 teaspoon salt
1 cup (125 g) flour

Mix the potatoes, butter and salt in a bowl. Add the flour gradually (the quantity required will depend upon the flouriness of the potatoes) until a soft dough forms. The dough must not be too dry.

On a lightly floured board, roll out the dough to about ¼ inch (½ cm) thick. Cut into large circles, about 6 to 8 inches (15 to 20 cm) in diameter, and then carefully cut each circle into quarters.

Cook either on an ungreased hot griddle or in a lightly greased heavy frying pan for about 4 minutes on each side or until the scones are lightly browned. Serve immediately.

Fried onions

Fried onions are cooked gently to produce a soft, almost creamy texture. The addition of cream and egg yolks makes this an excellent filling for a quiche.

SERVES FOUR

3 tablespoons butter
1 lb (450 g) onions, thinly sliced
Salt and pepper

Melt the butter in a heavy frying pan and stir in the onions, coating well with butter. Season to taste. Cover and fry very gently over very low heat, stirring frequently, for 15 minutes. Uncover the pan and fry for 20 minutes more or until the onions are golden and tender.

Deep-fried onions

SERVES FOUR

1 lb (450 g) large onions, cut into ¼-inch (½-cm) slices
1 cup (250 ml) fritter batter 1
Oil for deep frying

Heat the oil to 375°F (190°C). Separate the onion slices into rings. Dip the rings into the batter and fry them for 2 to 4 minutes or until golden brown. Remove with a slotted spoon and drain well on several layers of paper towels. Serve hot.

Fried mushrooms

SERVES FOUR

¼ cup (50 g) butter
1 lb (450 g) mushrooms, wiped clean and sliced, halved or left whole, depending on size
Salt and pepper

Melt the butter in a large, heavy frying pan. Add the mushrooms, season well and fry, stirring, for about 5 minutes.

Serve the pan juices with the mushrooms.

Deep-fried mushrooms

Serve hot as a first course with tartar sauce.

SERVES FOUR TO SIX

1 egg, well beaten
1 cup (100 g) fresh white bread crumbs
1 lb (450 g) mushrooms, wiped clean
Oil for deep frying

Put the egg on one plate and the bread crumbs on another and coat the mushrooms first with the egg and then the bread crumbs.

Heat the oil to 375°F (190°C). Drop in the mushrooms and fry for about 3 minutes or until they are lightly browned. Drain well and serve hot.

Duxelles

A useful flavoring for soups, sauces, stuffings and stews.

MAKES EIGHT TABLESPOONFULS

1 lb (450 g) mushrooms, wiped clean
½ cup (125 g) butter
2 shallots, chopped
Salt and black pepper
Nutmeg

Chop the mushrooms finely, including the stalks. Put them on a clean cloth or on a paper towel, twist the towel and squeeze out any moisture.

Melt the butter in a frying pan and fry the shallots gently for about 5 minutes.

Stir in the mushrooms and seasoning and cook over moderate heat, stirring constantly, for 40 to 50 minutes or until almost all the moisture has evaporated and the mixture is thick and rich.

Remove the pan from the heat and use immediately or store in the refrigerator.

Cauliflower cheese fritters

Broccoli may be prepared in the same way, but the cheese should be omitted from the batter.

SERVES FOUR TO SIX

1 cauliflower, washed
Oil for deep frying
2 tablespoons grated Parmesan cheese
1¼ cups (315 ml) fritter batter

Separate the cauliflower into florets and cook in boiling salted water for 5 minutes. Drain well and dry on paper towels. Set aside.

Heat the oil to 375°F (190°C).

Mix the cheese into the batter. Dip each floret in the batter and drop it into the oil. Fry for 4 to 5 minutes or until the fritters are golden brown.

Remove the fritters from the oil with a slotted spoon, drain well on several paper towels and serve hot.

Pakoras with mint chutney

Pakoras are Indian fritters. They are spicy and salty and usually served with a chutney. Use any vegetable: whole spinach leaves, partially cooked cauliflower florets or thinly sliced potatoes. Gram (chick-pea) flour, or besan as it is called, is available at Indian or Pakistani food stores.

SERVES FOUR

1 cup (125 g) gram flour
1 to 2 teaspoons chili powder
1 teaspoon salt
½ teaspoon baking powder
Oil for deep frying
4 onions

MINT CHUTNEY

1 handful mint leaves, stalks removed
½ cup (125 ml) yogurt
Juice of 1 lemon
2 green chilies, cores and seeds removed
4 tablespoons shredded coconut
1 teaspoon salt
½ teaspoon sugar

First make the chutney. Put all the ingredients into a blender and blend until smooth. Taste and adjust the seasoning. Put in a bowl and refrigerate for 3 hours.

To make the fritters, sift the flour, chili powder, salt and baking powder into a bowl. Beat in enough water to make a light batter.

Heat the oil to 375°F (190°C).

Slice the onions and push into rings. Dip the rings into the batter and fry them singly. Alternatively, slice the onions thinly, mix with the batter and fry several spoonfuls at a time.

Fry the onions until brown and crisp. Drain on paper towels and serve immediately with the chutney.

Sautéed eggplants

Other vegetables may be sautéed in the same way, but parsnips, Jerusalem artichokes, celeriac, salsify and sweet potatoes should be boiled until just tender, sliced and then sautéed.

SERVES FOUR

¼ cup (50 g) butter
2 medium-sized eggplants, cut in ¼-inch (½-cm) slices, degorged, rinsed and patted dry

½ cup (125 ml) tomato sauce, kept hot
Chopped fresh parsley

Melt the butter in a large, heavy frying pan and sauté the eggplants, turning occasionally, until golden brown on both sides. Lift from the pan with a slotted spoon, allowing any excess butter to drip back into the pan.

Transfer to a warm dish, pour over the tomato sauce and garnish with parsley.

Serve at once.

Eggplant fritters
Zucchini and squash may be prepared in the same way.

SERVES FOUR

2 medium-sized eggplants, cut into ¼-inch (½-cm) slices or sticks, degorged, rinsed and thoroughly dried
1 cup (250 ml) fritter batter
Oil for deep frying

Heat the oil to 375°F (190°C).

Coat the eggplants in batter and fry for 3 to 4 minutes or until golden brown.

Remove the eggplants from the oil with a slotted spoon, drain well on paper towels and serve at once.

Corn fritters
Serve as an accompaniment to Chicken Maryland.

SERVES FOUR

1 cup (125 g) self-rising flour
1 large egg, beaten
½ cup (125 ml) milk
Salt and freshly ground black pepper

2 cups (300 g) canned corn, drained, or 5 to 6 cobs of corn, cooked and stripped of kernels
¼ cup (50 g) butter

Sift the flour into a bowl. Make a well in the center and pour in the egg and milk. Add seasoning to taste and stir to draw the flour gradually into the liquid. When all the flour is incorporated, beat well until the batter is smooth. Stir in the corn.

Melt the butter in a large frying pan and when it is hot, drop in large spoonfuls of batter and fry for 2 to 3 minutes on each side or until the fritters are crisp.

Pipérade
Pipérade can be served as a first course by itself, or as a light main dish on croutons or slices of fried ham.

SERVES TWO

2 tablespoons olive oil
2 shallots, finely sliced
1 garlic clove, crushed
4 green peppers, cored, seeded and cut into strips
1 red pepper, cored, seeded and cut into strips
1½ lb (700 g) ripe tomatoes, peeled and chopped
1 tablespoon chopped fresh herbs

4 eggs, lightly beaten with plenty of salt and freshly ground pepper

Heat the oil in a large frying pan over moderate heat. When the oil is hot, add the shallots and fry them until they are golden. Add the garlic and peppers and fry until the peppers are nearly tender. Stir in the tomatoes and herbs and cook until the tomatoes have formed a pulp.

Pour in the eggs and cook, stirring once or twice, until the mixture sets lightly. Serve immediately on warm plates.

Deep-fried parsley
Fried parsley is used as a garnish for a variety of dishes, particularly broiled or fried fish.

SERVES FOUR

1 large handful fresh parsley, washed if necessary and thoroughly dried
Oil for deep frying

Cut off the parsley stalks, leaving only the leaves.

Heat the oil to 375°F (190°C) and lower the parsley into the oil in a frying basket. The oil will hiss and bubble vigorously for 1 to 2 minutes. As soon as the hissing stops, remove the basket. The parsley should be very crisp and green. Drain well and serve at once.

Stir-fried bean sprouts
Almost any vegetable may be used—whole snow peas, shredded Chinese cabbage, sliced green beans or diced bamboo shoots. Small pieces of raw or cooked meat, fish or shellfish may be added.

SERVES FOUR

2 tablespoons vegetable oil
1 onion, thinly sliced
2 teaspoons finely shredded ginger root
1 lb (450 g) bean sprouts, washed
Salt

Heat the oil in a large frying pan or wok and fry the onion and ginger, stirring constantly, for 2 minutes.

Add the bean sprouts and salt to taste and stir-fry for 2 minutes more. Serve immediately.

Fruit

Fruit for pan frying or sautéing should be quite ripe but not mushy. Those most successfully cooked in this way are apples, pineapples, bananas, peaches and apricots. Serve them as an accompaniment to meat, game and poultry dishes—apples, for example, go well with bacon, and peaches complement pork or goose.

Pan-fried fruit may also be served for dessert, and they taste especially good if they are marinated in wine or liqueur for an hour or so before cooking. Add a little sugar and such spices as cinnamon, nutmeg, allspice or ginger and a few drops of lemon juice halfway through the cooking time when the fruit have been turned.

All the fruit suitable for pan frying may also be dipped into fritter batter and deep fried.

Special apple fritters
SERVES FOUR

4 tart, crisp apples, peeled and cored
1 tablespoon lemon juice
Grated rind of 1 lemon
1 tablespoon apricot brandy
4 tablespoons confectioners' sugar, sifted
6 tablespoons apricot jam
4 tablespoons water
¼ lb (125 g) macaroons, finely crushed
1 cup (250 ml) fritter batter
Oil for deep frying
½ cup (125 ml) whipping cream, lightly whipped

Cut the apples into thick rings. Put them on a plate and sprinkle with the lemon juice, lemon rind, apricot brandy and 3 tablespoons of the sugar. Turn the apple rings in the mixture to coat them.

Put the jam and water into a saucepan. Bring to a boil, then simmer for 5 minutes. Strain the glaze, and if it is not thick enough to coat the spoon, return it to the pan and cook a little longer.

Coat each apple ring with the glaze. Put the macaroon crumbs on a plate. Dip the apple rings into the crumbs to coat well on both sides. Put the apple rings on a plate and set aside for 15 minutes.

Heat the oil to 375 °F (190°C). Have the batter ready in a bowl. Using a skewer or fork, dip the apple rings into the batter and then drop them into the oil. Fry, turning once or twice, until they are crisp and golden brown. Drain on paper towels. Dust with the remaining confectioners' sugar and serve hot with the cream.

Apple fritters

The prepared fruit may be marinated in liqueur and then drained before being dipped into batter.

Other fruit that may be used are bananas or pear halves, pineapple or orange slices and pitted cherries. Prunes should be marinated in tea or port and pitted. Stuff each one with a blanched almond.

SERVES FOUR

4 large apples, peeled, cored and cut into ¼-inch (½-cm) thick rings
½ cup (125 g) vanilla sugar
1½ cups (375 ml) fritter batter
Oil for deep frying
Confectioners' sugar

Dip the apples rings into the vanilla sugar and then coat them in the batter. Heat the fat to 375°F (190°C) and fry the apple rings for about 4 minutes or until they are golden. Drain well, sprinkle over the sugar and serve.

Apricot fritters

Peach halves or whole strawberries may also be used. Marinate the apricots in the juice of freshly squeezed oranges. Drain before coating in batter.

Winter fritters

Soak mixed dried fruit in sherry for several hours. Drain, mix into the batter and fry several spoonfuls at a time. Drain and dredge with confectioners' sugar.

Sautéed bananas, caramelized pineapple and apple fritters.

Banana and bacon fritters
SERVES FOUR

2 large bananas, cut in half lengthwise
8 bacon slices, cut across in half
1 cup (250 ml) fritter batter
Oil for deep frying

Cut the banana halves into 4 pieces, making 16 in all. Wrap each piece in bacon and secure with a large wooden toothpick.

Heat the oil to 375°F (190°C). Dip the bacon rolls into the batter and drop into the oil. Fry until golden brown and crisp.

Sautéed bananas
SERVES FOUR

¼ cup (50 g) butter
4 bananas, peeled and sliced lengthwise

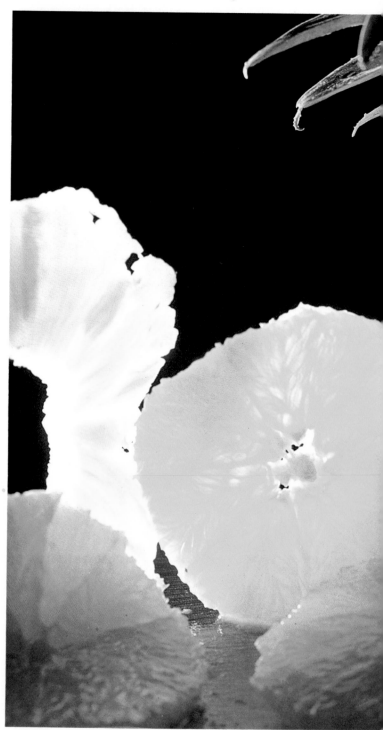

1 tablespoon soft brown
  sugar
**Juice and grated rind of 1
  orange**
1 tablespoon slivered
  almonds, toasted

Melt the butter in a large frying
pan and, when it is hot, add the
bananas. Cook for 3 minutes,
then turn the bananas carefully.
Sprinkle over the sugar, orange

juice and rind and cook for 3
minutes more. Transfer the
bananas to a warm serving platter, pour over the juices and
scatter the almonds on top. Serve
at once.

Fried apples and bacon
SERVES THREE TO FOUR

2 tablespoons butter
8 bacon slices

2 tablespoons brown sugar
1 lb (450 g) tart apples,
  peeled, cored and sliced

Melt the butter in a frying pan,
add the bacon and fry until crisp.
Remove the bacon from the pan,
put it into a warm serving dish
and keep hot.

Add the sugar to the pan and
stir well. Add the apple slices
and cook for about 5 minutes or

until they are very soft and well
caramelized.

Transfer the apples to the
serving dish and serve at once.

Apples with Calvados
SERVES FOUR

$\frac{1}{4}$ **cup (50 g) butter**
**2 lb (900 g) eating apples,
  peeled, cored and sliced**
$\frac{1}{4}$ **cup (50 g) sugar**
Grated rind of $\frac{1}{2}$ lemon
2 tablespoons Calvados

Melt the butter in a large frying
pan. Add the apples, sugar and
lemon rind and cook for about
4 minutes, shaking the pan once
or twice, until the apples begin
to change color. Pour over the
Calvados, cook for 2 minutes
more and serve at once.

Caramelized pineapple
SERVES FOUR

$\frac{1}{4}$ **cup (50 g) butter**
2 tablespoons honey
**1 pineapple, peeled, cut in
  $\frac{1}{2}$-inch (1-cm) slices and
  cored**
1 tablespoon brown sugar
Juice of $\frac{1}{2}$ lemon
4 tablespoons toasted almonds

Melt the butter in a large frying
pan. Stir in the honey and, when
the mixture bubbles, add the
pineapple rings. Sprinkle with
the sugar and cook quickly for 1
minute. Turn, baste with the
syrup and sprinkle with the
lemon juice.

Overlap the pineapple rings
on a warm serving platter,
sprinkle the almonds on top and
serve at once.

Salted almonds

For deviled almonds add $\frac{1}{4}$ to $\frac{1}{2}$
teaspoon cayenne pepper while
frying.

SERVES FOUR

1 tablespoon oil
**$1\frac{1}{3}$ cups (225 g) almonds,
  blanched**
Salt

Heat the oil in a large frying pan.
Add the almonds and fry, turning them frequently, until
golden brown. Remove and
spread on paper towels. Toss
the almonds in salt while they are
still warm.

Cereals

Pancakes, fritters, waffles, crumpets—so many of the foods made with batter are easy to cook, inexpensive and delicious.

For pancakes, use a special straight-sided pancake pan or a heavy frying pan about six inches (15 cm) in diameter. Ideally it should be made of cast-iron and seasoned when newly bought (see page 8). Any pan kept exclusively for pancakes should never be washed, just lightly oiled and wiped clean.

Waffles can only be cooked in a special waffle iron, which should be seasoned in a similar way to a pancake or omelet pan. It should not need further greasing as waffle batter is fairly buttery.

Crumpets and muffins are best cooked on a lightly greased griddle or on a heavy baking sheet.

The other cereals that can be fried are rice, noodles and bread, which can be served as accompaniments to a wide variety of dishes.

Fritter batter 1

For a sweet batter add 2 teaspoons of fine granulated sugar to the flour.

MAKES ABOUT ONE CUP (250 ML)
- **1 cup (125 g) all-purpose flour**
- **¼ teaspoon salt**
- **1 tablespoon cooking oil**
- **1 egg, separated**
- **½ cup (125 ml) tepid beer, milk or water, or a combination of these**

Sift the flour and salt into a mixing bowl. Make a well in the center and pour in the oil and egg yolk. Using a wire whisk, mix the oil and egg yolk together, gradually drawing in the flour and adding the liquid a little at a time. Beat the batter until smooth and creamy.

If beer is used, cover the bowl and set the batter aside for at least 2 hours.

Beat the egg white until stiff and fold into the batter. Use immediately.

Fritter batter 2

MAKES ABOUT ONE CUP (250 ML)
- **½ cake compressed yeast**
- **½ cup (125 ml) warm water**
- **1 cup (125 g) all-purpose flour**
- **¼ teaspoon salt**
- **1 tablespoon cooking oil or melted butter**
- **1 egg white, stiffly beaten (optional)**

Dissolve the yeast in half the water. Set aside in a warm place for 10 minutes or until puffed up and frothy.

Sift the flour and salt into a mixing bowl. Make a well in the center and pour in the yeast. Using a wire whisk, gradually draw in the flour, adding the remaining water and the oil or butter a little at a time. Beat the batter until smooth and creamy. Leave, covered, in a warm place for about 1 hour.

If a crisper fritter is required, fold in the stiffly beaten egg white just before the batter is used.

Pancakes (crêpes)

If the first pancakes are to be kept warm while the remainder are being cooked, overlap them on a lightly buttered baking dish and keep covered in a moderate oven. Alternatively, a large plate can be placed over a saucepan of hot water, the pancakes stacked on the plate and covered with a second plate.

Pancakes can be cooked in advance, cooled and stored for later use. They may be stacked, with a piece of waxed paper between each one, and stored in an airtight container in the refrigerator for 2 to 3 days or in the freezer for 3 months.

Serve pancakes in the traditional Shrove Tuesday fashion with a squeeze of lemon juice and fine granulated sugar. Or fill with jam or ice cream, roll and dust with confectioners' sugar.

MAKES ABOUT TWELVE
- **1 cup (125 g) all-purpose flour**
- **Pinch salt**
- **1 whole egg plus 1 egg yolk, beaten**
- **2 tablespoons butter, melted**
- **1 cup (250 ml) milk, or half milk and half water**
- **Butter for frying**

Sift the flour and salt into a mixing bowl. Make a well in the center and put in the eggs and melted butter. Using a wire whisk, beat the eggs and melted butter together, incorporating the flour gradually and adding the milk a little at a time. Beat until smooth.

Heat a frying pan and melt ½ tablespoon of butter, rolling it around the base and sides of the pan. When it is very hot (if a few drops of water flicked into the pan spit and jump, the pan is hot enough), pour in a tablespoon of batter and tip the pan so that it runs all over the base. If the first pancake is too thick, add a little more liquid to the batter.

After about 30 seconds the underside of the pancake will be golden and cooked. Either toss the pancake by flicking the pan sharply upward with a firm movement of the wrists or turn carefully with a pancake turner.

If the pan should become very dry, melt another small pat of butter before cooking the remaining batter.

Pancakes (Crêpes)

Melt some butter in a pancake pan and when it is very hot, pour in the pancake batter.

Swirl the batter around the pan and cook one side. Flip the pancake over carefully.

Crêpes Suzette

To make the filling, rub sugar cubes over the orange skins to extract the zest.

Using a metal spatula, spread a little of the orange butter evenly over each crêpe.

Fold the crêpes into quarters and lay them, overlapping, in a baking dish.

Warm the brandy and Cointreau slightly, ignite and pour over the crêpes. Serve hot.

Crêpes Suzette

SERVES SIX

6 sugar cubes
2 oranges
½ cup (125 g) sweet butter
1 tablespoon orange juice
5 tablespoons Cointreau
12 paper-thin crêpes
4 tablespoons brandy

Preheat the oven to 425°F (220°C).

Rub the sugar cubes all over the rind of the oranges until they completely absorb all the oil. Put the sugar in a bowl and crush the cubes.

Cream the butter. Add the crushed sugar and beat until smooth. Beat in the orange juice and 1 tablespoon of the Cointreau.

Spread the crêpes with the orange butter. Fold the crêpes into quarters like a handkerchief and lay them, overlapping, in a baking dish. Cover and put in the oven for 5 minutes.

Put the remaining Cointreau and brandy in a small saucepan, warm slightly, set alight and pour flaming onto the crêpes. Serve immediately.

Drop scones

These small, thick pancakes may be eaten hot with butter, jam, honey or syrup or can be cooled and stored for several days in an airtight container. They can then be eaten cold or toasted.

MAKES ABOUT TWELVE

2 cups (225 g) self-rising flour
Pinch salt
1 tablespoon sugar
2 eggs, beaten
1 tablespoon corn syrup
1 cup (250 ml) milk
Oil or butter

Sift the flour and salt into a mixing bowl and add the sugar.

Make a well in the center and pour in the eggs and syrup. Using a wooden spoon, beat the eggs and syrup, gradually drawing in the flour and adding the milk by degrees. When the batter has the consistency of thick cream, stop adding the milk.

Lightly grease a griddle or heavy frying pan with oil or butter and put it over moderate heat. Drop spoonfuls of the batter onto the griddle. After 2 to 3 minutes bubbles will appear on the surface and the underside will be golden. Turn the scones, using a pancake turner. Cook the second side for 2 to 3 minutes or until golden.

Blini

These light yeast pancakes are a Russian specialty traditionally served with caviar and sour cream. They may also be served with smoked roe, chopped hard-cooked egg and melted butter.

Blini should be no larger than 2 to 3 inches (5 to 8 cm) in diameter.

MAKES ABOUT FORTY

½ cake compressed yeast
¼ teaspoon sugar
½ cup (125 ml) warm water
1½ cups (175 g) buckwheat flour
1½ cups (375 ml) warm milk
1½ cups (175 g) all-purpose flour
3 eggs, separated
½ teaspoon salt
2 tablespoons melted butter
½ cup (125 g) butter

Mash the yeast with the sugar in a small bowl. Mix in the water and set aside in a warm place for about 10 to 15 minutes or until the yeast is puffed up.

Put the buckwheat flour in a large mixing bowl, beat in the yeast mixture and enough of the milk to make a smooth batter the consistency of thick cream. Cover the bowl with a cloth and leave in a warm place for 2 hours or until the batter has risen and doubled in bulk.

Meanwhile, make a second batter. Put the all-purpose flour into another bowl and beat in the egg yolks, salt, melted butter and the remaining milk. Combine the two batters, cover the bowl and leave in a warm place for 30 minutes.

Beat the egg whites until stiff, fold into the batter, cover again and leave in a warm place for 20 minutes more.

Heat a large, heavy frying pan or griddle. Add 1 tablespoon of the butter and when it is sizzling, pour in 4 separate tablespoons of the batter to make 4 blini. Cook for about 1 minute or until golden. Turn the pancakes and if necessary add more butter. Cook for 1 minute. Keep warm while you cook the remainder.

English crumpets

Crumpet or muffin rings and a griddle or a heavy baking sheet are needed for making crumpets.

MAKES TEN

½ cake compressed yeast
¼ teaspoon sugar
1 cup (250 ml) milk, lukewarm
2 cups (225 g) all-purpose flour
¼ teaspoon salt

Mash the yeast with the sugar in a small bowl. Beat in 2 tablespoons of the milk and set aside in a warm place for 15 minutes or until puffed up and frothy.

Put the flour and salt in a large, warm mixing bowl, make a well in the center and pour in the yeast and the rest of the milk. Mix thoroughly, gradually drawing in the flour, until the batter has the consistency of thin cream. Add more warm milk if necessary. Cover the bowl with a cloth and put in a warm place for 45 minutes or until the batter has doubled in bulk.

Lightly grease a griddle or heavy baking sheet. Use as many rings as the griddle or baking sheet will take and heat.

Pour about 2 tablespoons of the batter into each ring; the batter must fill the ring to a depth of about ¼ inch (½ cm). Cook for about 5 minutes or until bubbles appear and the batter is slightly set and golden brown underneath. Remove the rings, turn the crumpets and cook on the second side until golden. Toast before eating.

English muffins

Serve muffins toasted and buttered, on their own or with scrambled or poached eggs.

MAKES EIGHT

2 cups (225 g) all-purpose flour
½ teaspoon salt
2 teaspoons baking powder
2 tablespoons sugar
1 egg
¼ cup (50 g) butter, melted
⅔ cup (150 ml) buttermilk

Sift the flour, salt and baking powder into a large bowl and mix in the sugar.

Beat the egg lightly in another bowl. Mix in the butter and the buttermilk.

Mix the buttermilk mixture into the dry ingredients quickly and lightly to make a soft dough. Ignore any lumps and do not overmix the dough.

Using floured hands, divide the dough into 8 pieces. Roll each piece into a ball, then flatten it with your hand or with a rolling pin until it is about ½ inch (1 cm) thick. Use muffin rings if you want to make quite sure that the muffins keep their shape. Cook on both sides on a greased griddle until they are lightly browned.

Waffles

Waffles can be eaten plain, with maple syrup, jam or honey or the batter can be prepared with pieces of finely chopped bacon, fruit or grated cheese.

MAKES ABOUT TWENTY

1½ cups (175 g) all-purpose flour
¼ teaspoon salt
2 teaspoons baking powder
1 tablespoon sugar
2 large eggs, separated
1 cup (250 ml) milk
4 tablespoons melted butter

Sift the flour, salt, baking powder and sugar into a large mixing bowl. Make a well in the center and pour in the egg yolks. Add the milk and butter and mix quickly and lightly—it does not matter if the batter is lumpy and not smooth.

Beat the egg whites until stiff and fold into the batter.

Have the waffle iron heated, pour in enough batter to cover the base of the iron, close the lid and cook until no more steam escapes from the iron—about 2 to 4 minutes. Serve at once, very hot.

English doughnuts

These doughnuts may be slit with the point of a sharp knife and stuffed with 1 teaspoon of jam or jelly.

MAKES TWELVE

1 cake compressed yeast
6 tablespoons sugar
½ cup (125 ml) milk, warmed
2 cups (225 g) all-purpose flour
¼ teaspoon salt
¼ cup (50 g) butter
1 egg, beaten
Oil for deep frying

Mix the yeast with the ¼ teaspoon of sugar in a small bowl. Add 2 tablespoons of the warm milk and mix until smooth. Set aside in a warm place for 15 minutes or until it is puffed up and frothy.

Sift the flour and salt into a warm bowl. Rub the butter into the flour. Stir in 2 tablespoons of the sugar.

Make a well in the flour mixture and pour in the yeast, the remaining milk and egg. Mix well to make a dough and knead until smooth. Cover the bowl with a cloth and let stand in a warm place for 45 minutes or until the dough has risen and doubled in bulk.

Turn out the dough and knead for 5 minutes. Roll the dough out on a floured board to about ¼ inch (½ cm) thick. Using a well-floured, plain 2-inch (5-cm) cutter, cut the dough into circles.

Put the doughnuts on a lightly floured baking sheet in a warm place for 30 minutes or until they have doubled in size.

Heat the oil to 375°F (190°C) in a deep frying pan. Fry 4 to 5 doughnuts at a time for about 3 to 5 minutes until they are golden brown, turning them once.

Using a slotted spoon, lift them out and drain well on paper towels. Let cool a little and sprinkle with the remaining sugar. Eat hot.

American doughnuts

MAKES TWELVE

1 egg
¼ cup (65 ml) milk
¼ cup (50 g) butter, melted
2 cups (225 g) flour
2 teaspoons baking powder
Salt
Grated nutmeg
Ground cinnamon
3 tablespoons fine granulated sugar
Oil for deep frying

Beat the egg in a small bowl. Beat in the milk and butter.

Sift the flour, baking powder and a pinch each of salt, nutmeg and cinnamon into a large bowl. Stir in 2 tablespoons of the sugar. Make a well in the center and pour in the egg and milk mixture. Mix it in well to make a dough. Add more milk if the dough is too firm.

Cover the dough and put it in the refrigerator for 30 minutes.

Roll out the dough on a lightly floured board until it is ½ inch (1 cm) thick. Using a 2½-inch (6-cm) biscuit cutter, cut out circles. Use a 1½-inch (3-cm) cutter to cut out the centers. Let the doughnuts sit for 10 minutes.

Heat the oil to 375°F (190°C) in a deep frying pan. Add the doughnuts and fry for 5 minutes or until they are golden brown. Using a slotted spoon, lift out the doughnuts and drain well.

Dust the doughnuts with the remaining sugar.

Beignets soufflés

These French fritters may be served just sprinkled with fine granulated sugar or with a sauce.

SERVES SIX

Oil for deep frying
1 recipe choux pastry
Fine granulated sugar

LEMON SAUCE

3 tablespoons sugar
1 level teaspoon cornstarch
1¼ cups (315 ml) water
2 tablespoons butter
Rind and juice of 1 lemon

First make the sauce. Mix the sugar and cornstarch together in a saucepan. Pour in the water gradually and stir to mix until the sauce begins to bubble. Simmer for 1 minute, then remove from the heat. Stir in the butter and the lemon rind and juice.

Heat the oil to 370°F (180°C). Drop teaspoonfuls of the choux pastry into the hot oil and fry until golden brown. Drain, dust with sugar and serve with the sauce.

French toast

French toast may be served with jam or a fruit purée.

SERVES FOUR

¼ cup (65 ml) milk
1 egg, beaten
Pinch salt
1 tablespoon vanilla sugar
4 slices day-old white bread, crusts removed
¼ cup (50 g) butter

Beat the milk, egg, salt and sugar and put it in a dish.

Put the bread in the egg and milk mixture and set aside for 5 minutes, turning once.

Heat the butter in a frying pan and when it is sizzling, put in the bread and fry for 2 to 3 minutes on each side or until golden.

Using a pancake turner, lift out the French toast, hold over the pan for a few seconds to drain and serve immediately.

Fried bread

Serve with fried egg and bacon or as an accompaniment to meat or poultry dishes.

SERVES TWO

3 tablespoons bacon fat or drippings
2 slices day-old bread, halved

Heat the fat in a frying pan and when it is very hot, put in the bread and fry quickly on both sides until lightly browned.

Lift with a pancake turner, hold over the pan for a few seconds to drain and serve at once.

Croutons

Croutons can be made in all sizes and shapes. Large croutons are used as a base on which to put steaks and noisettes. Small croutons are used as garnishes for soups.

They may be sautéed in butter or deep fried in oil and are prepared from thick slices of day-old white bread cut into squares, circles or heart shapes.

If the croutons are sautéed, the butter should not be too hot. Turn them after 2 to 3 minutes or when golden brown. To deep fry, heat the oil to 375°F (190°C). Use a frying basket and drain well on paper towels. Sprinkle croutons over soup at the last minute.

Fried rice

This dish must be planned ahead of time, because the rice must be boiled the day before you intend to serve it. Let the rice cool then refrigerate for 24 hours.

SERVES FOUR TO SIX

1¼ cups (225 g) rice, cooked and drained
3 tablespoons oil
2 garlic cloves, peeled and finely chopped
½ lb (225 g) lean pork or chicken, cut into thin strips
3 tablespoons soy sauce
Freshly ground black pepper
2 eggs
6 scallions, sliced (including the green part)

Heat the oil in a heavy frying pan until it is very hot. Add the garlic and pork or chicken and fry for 5 minutes, stirring occasionally. Add the cooked rice, soy sauce and pepper to taste. Fry, stirring constantly, until the rice is heated through and the meat is cooked. This should take no more than 5 minutes. Taste and add more soy sauce if necessary.

Beat the eggs and stir them quickly into the meat and rice. Cook for 1 to 2 minutes or until the eggs just begin to set.

Remove the pan from the heat, mix in the scallions and serve.

Crusty noodles

These noodles make a good accompaniment to roast beef.

SERVES FOUR

1 lb (450 g) fine noodles
1 teaspoon salt
¼ cup (50 g) butter
Pepper

Thirty minutes before you want to fry the noodles, cook them in plenty of boiling salted water for about 2 minutes—timed after the water has returned to a boil. Empty the noodles into a strainer and wash thoroughly in hot water to remove the starch. Drain and let cool.

Heat a 7-inch (18-cm) heavy frying pan. Add the butter and when it sizzles, put in the noodles and stir them around. Sprinkle with pepper and more salt, if necessary. Reduce the heat to low and let the noodles cook very slowly for 10 to 15 minutes or until there is a light brown crust on the bottom. Using a spatula, lift up the edge of the noodles—if the bottom is not set in a brown crust, continue frying for a few more minutes.

Clockwise: English muffins and waffles for tea and crêpes Suzette for a dinner party dessert.

Eggs and dairy products

Frying brings out the best in eggs. Methods include scrambling, making omelets, and of course frying them whole as in eggs and bacon.

Scrambling is one of the most delicate ways of cooking eggs. The heat should be gentle and the moment the eggs begin to set well the pan should be drawn off the heat—the heat of the pan is sufficient to finish cooking the eggs. Use a heavy pan, preferably with a nonstick coating—unlined pans are difficult to clean after scrambling eggs.

A little milk or cream—one tablespoon for two eggs—may be stirred in at the end of the cooking time. In that case, reduce the amount of butter used.

There are three types of omelet: the French omelet, which is slightly liquid in the middle, the fluffy soufflé omelet, which is more often served as a dessert, and the Spanish omelet, a more solid dish, which is made in a way also used to make Egyptian, Persian and Chinese omelets.

Ideally an omelet pan should be made of iron, and seasoned before it is used (see page 8). If possible it should only be used for making omelets and it should never be washed—just oil it lightly and wipe it with a clean cloth.

The size of the pan is important. If the base of the pan is five inches (13 cm) in diameter it will make a two- to three-egg omelet; if it is seven inches (18 cm) it will make a four-egg omelet, and if it is nine inches (23 cm) it will make a six-egg omelet.

Fillings for omelets are spread off center just before the omelet is folded and turned out.

Fried eggs

These are the traditional eggs of bacon and eggs. If bacon has been cooked in the frying pan before the eggs, use the bacon fat to fry them.

Fried eggs are also delicious served with beurre noir.

SERVES TWO TO FOUR

2 tablespoons bacon fat, drippings or butter
4 eggs
Salt and pepper

Heat the fat in a frying pan over low heat and break in the eggs. Tip the pan slightly so that the eggs can be basted with the fat. (Some people prefer the eggs cooked without basting—in this case, cover immediately with a lid.)

Cook the eggs for about 3 minutes, basting several times until the whites set. Season with salt and pepper. Using a pancake turner, lift the eggs out of the fat, hold over the pan until any excess fat has run off and transfer to hot plates. Serve at once.

If desired, the eggs may be turned over carefully during the frying, but do not attempt this until the eggs have begun to set.

Scrambled eggs

Scrambled eggs are very versatile and can be combined successfully with many vegetables, cheeses, smoked meats and fish. They may be served hot or cold by themselves, or in small vol-au-vent or tomato cases.

SERVES TWO

4 eggs
Salt and freshly ground black pepper
3 tablespoons butter
2 slices buttered toast, kept hot

Break the eggs into a bowl and season well. Using a fork, lightly beat the eggs until the whites and yolks are blended.

Melt half the butter over low heat and pour in the eggs. Using a wooden spoon, and keeping the heat low, stir the eggs, pulling large curds from the base of the pan. At the same time add the remaining butter a little at a time.

When almost all the egg has formed moist curds, remove the pan from the heat. Stir until cooked and creamy. Spoon onto the hot toast. Serve immediately.

Scrambled eggs with mushrooms

Allow 1 cup (50 g) of sliced mushrooms for each person. Sauté the mushrooms in butter in a separate pan.

Put the eggs on hot buttered toast and pour over the mushrooms and juices.

Scrambled eggs with cheese

Allow ¼ cup (25 g) of grated hard cheese or creamed soft cheese for each person. Just before the eggs are removed from the heat, stir in the cheese. Serve at once with broiled tomatoes.

Scotch woodcock

Have ready one slice of hot toast spread with anchovy paste for each person. Season the eggs with salt and cayenne and scramble as usual. Just before the eggs are ready, stir in 1 tablespoon of cream per portion. Spoon the eggs onto the toast and serve at once.

French omelet

SERVES ONE TO TWO

2 to 3 eggs
Salt and freshly ground black pepper
1 tablespoon butter

Break the eggs into a bowl, season well and beat lightly with a fork.

Heat the omelet pan until it is very hot over moderate heat. Add the butter and swirl it around the pan. It will melt instantly. When it foams, pour in the eggs and shake the pan gently backward and forward. The eggs will begin to set at once, so stir with a fork, drawing in large flakes of cooked eggs from the sides of the pan. In 1 to 2 minutes the omelet will be nearly cooked. Tilt the pan away from you and, using a spatula, lift up the edge of the omelet so that some of the un-cooked egg will run from the middle of the omelet onto the base of the pan. Leave on the heat for a few seconds more so that the bottom can take on a golden color.

Tilt the pan and flip half the omelet over. Turn onto a warm plate and serve at once.

Omelet fines herbes

For each serving add 1 tablespoon of mixed chopped fresh herbs to the eggs while they are being beaten.

Mushroom omelet

Allow 2 tablespoons of mushrooms for each serving. Chop the mushrooms and sauté them in a little butter. Fill the omelet, fold over and serve.

Cheese omelet

Allow ½ cup (50 g) of grated Parmesan, Cheddar and Parmesan or Gruyère and Parmesan per person. Beat the cheese with the eggs or sprinkle it on the omelet just before folding and serving.

Omelet Arnold Bennett

SERVES TWO

4 tablespoons butter
½ lb (225 g) finnan haddie, cooked, skinned, boned and flaked
4 eggs, separated
½ cup (125 ml) cream
Salt
2 tablespoons grated Parmesan cheese

Melt half the butter in a small saucepan, stir in the finnan haddie and heat through.

Preheat the broiler to high.

Beat the egg yolks with half the cream and season to taste. Stir in the fish.

Beat the egg whites until they form soft peaks and fold into the egg yolk and fish mixture.

Melt the remaining butter in a large omelet pan. Pour in the egg mixture, shake the pan once or twice and cook until just set.

Slide the unfolded omelet onto an ovenproof serving dish, pour over the remaining cream, sprinkle the cheese on top and put under the broiler for a few seconds to brown. Serve immediately.

Spanish omelet

Eaten hot or cold, a Spanish omelet may include such ingredients as sweet peppers, spinach, peas, mushrooms, parsley, ham, anchovies or slices of chorizo sausage.

SERVES FOUR

3 tablespoons olive oil
1 garlic clove, crushed
2 large onions, sliced
2 large potatoes, peeled and cut into ¼-inch (½-cm) cubes
Salt
6 eggs

Heat the oil in a frying pan. Add the garlic, onions, potatoes and salt to taste. Cover the pan and cook gently, stirring occasionally, for 15 to 20 minutes or until the potatoes are cooked through. Using a slotted spoon, lift out the vegetables.

Break the eggs into a bowl and beat lightly with a fork to mix the whites and yolks. Stir in the cooked vegetables. Reheat the oil in the pan and when it is very hot, pour in the egg and vegetable mixture, spreading it to fill the pan evenly. Cook for 5 minutes, shaking the pan occasionally. When the bottom has set, put a plate over the pan and invert the omelet onto the plate, then slide it back into the pan and brown the other side. Alternatively, brown the top of the omelet under a hot broiler.

Cut into wedges and serve.

Omelet au Grand Marnier

SERVES TWO

3 eggs
Grated rind and segments of 1 orange
1 tablespoon sugar
2 tablespoons Grand Marnier
1 tablespoon butter

Beat the eggs with the orange rind, half the sugar and the Grand Marnier.

Preheat the broiler to high.

Melt the butter in an omelet pan, and when it is hot, pour in the egg mixture and cook as for a French omelet. When it is almost ready, put the orange segments on one half of the omelet, leave for 30 seconds, fold in half and turn onto a warm serving dish.

Sprinkle the omelet with the remaining sugar and glaze under the broiler for 30 seconds. Serve at once.

Omelet flambé

Make sure you have one end of the skewer wrapped in a cloth when you are heating it.

SERVES TWO

4 eggs
Salt
1 tablespoon sugar
1 tablespoon butter
4 tablespoons Jamaican rum, cognac, whisky or Calvados

Beat the eggs, a pinch of salt and half the sugar together with a fork. Melt the butter in an omelet pan. Pour in the egg mixture and cook as for a French omelet. Fold and slide onto an ovenproof dish. Sprinkle the rest of the sugar on top of the omelet. Heat a skewer until it is red-hot and mark the top of the omelet with a crisscross pattern. Warm the rum, pour over the omelet and ignite. Serve immediately.

Egg fu-yung

A traditional Chinese omelet, egg fu-yung may include a variety of ingredients such as mushrooms, shrimp, chicken and ham.

SERVES TWO

2 tablespoons cooking oil
2 scallions, chopped
1½ cups (125 g) bean sprouts, washed
4 eggs
1 teaspoon soy sauce
Salt and pepper
½ cup (50 g) cooked crabmeat, flaked

Heat 1 tablespoon of oil in a frying pan and stir-fry the scallions and the bean sprouts for 2 minutes. Using a slotted spoon, lift out the scallions and bean sprouts and set aside on a plate.

Lightly beat the eggs with the soy sauce and seasoning. Heat the remaining oil in the frying pan. Pour in the egg mixture. Quickly stir in the crabmeat, scallions and bean sprouts. When the bottom sets, turn the omelet over using a pancake turner. Cook for 1 minute and serve.

Scotch eggs

Scotch eggs may be served hot or cold and will keep for several days in a refrigerator.

SERVES FOUR

¾ lb (350 g) sausage meat
Salt and pepper
Pinch mace
4 hard-cooked eggs, shelled
1 egg, beaten
⅓ cup (50 g) dry bread crumbs
Oil for deep frying

In a large bowl mix the sausage meat, seasoning and mace. Divide the mixture into four pieces. Flatten each piece between the palms of your hands. Put an egg in the center of each piece and bring the sides up to enclose the egg completely.

Dip the coated eggs in beaten egg and then in bread crumbs; press the crumbs on firmly.

Heat the oil to 375°F (190°C). Fry the scotch eggs until the coating is well browned. Drain well.

Kuku sabsi

This omelet from Iran can be made from any green leaf vegetable.

SERVES FOUR

3 tablespoons butter
1 onion, sliced
½ lb (225 g) spinach, washed, drained and finely chopped
2 tablespoons chopped fresh herbs
1 tablespoon chopped walnuts
Salt and pepper
6 eggs, lightly beaten

Melt the butter in a frying pan and fry the onion until soft. Add the spinach, herbs and walnuts and fry, stirring, for 2 to 3 minutes. Season well and pour in the eggs. Stir with a fork for a few seconds. Reduce the heat and cook until the eggs have almost set.

Preheat the broiler to hot. Put the pan under the broiler until the omelet is lightly browned. Cut into wedges and serve.

Making an omelet

As the eggs begin to set, stir the bottom with a fork.

Tilt the pan and, with a spatula, lift up the edge of the omelet.

When the omelet is cooked, fold one half over the other.

Slide the folded omelet onto a heated plate and serve at once.

Eggs and dairy products

Huevos rancheros

SERVES TWO

2 tablespoons olive oil
1 garlic clove, crushed
1 onion, finely chopped
1 green pepper, cored,
  seeded and finely chopped
1 lb (450 g) tomatoes, peeled
  and chopped
½ teaspoon cayenne pepper
Salt and pepper
4 slices ham, cut into
  strips
4 eggs, fried and kept hot

Heat the oil in a frying pan. Add the garlic, onion and pepper and fry for 5 minutes. Add the tomatoes, cayenne pepper and salt and pepper to taste. Simmer the mixture uncovered, stirring occasionally, until it is thick.

Stir in the ham. Spoon the mixture onto a heated serving plate. Arrange the fried eggs on top and serve.

Scrambled eggs with chicken livers

SERVES FOUR

2 tablespoons butter
2 bacon slices, diced
8 chicken livers, cut into
  quarters
Salt and pepper
6 eggs, lightly beaten
4 slices hot buttered toast
1 tablespoon chopped
  parsley

Melt the butter in a frying pan and fry the bacon for 1 minute. Add the chicken livers and fry, stirring, for 1 to 2 minutes or until lightly cooked. Season well and pour in the eggs. Reduce the heat and cook gently, stirring, until the eggs are just set.

Pile the eggs onto the toast, sprinkle with parsley and serve.

Scrambled eggs with smoked salmon

SERVES FOUR

¼ cup (50 g) butter
4 slices smoked salmon,
  chopped
8 eggs, lightly beaten
2 teaspoons chopped chives
Salt and pepper
4 slices hot buttered toast

Melt the butter in a saucepan, add the salmon and heat very gently. Pour in the eggs and cook, stirring, until lightly set. Stir in the chives. Taste the mixture and season if necessary. Spoon the mixture onto the toast and serve immediately.

Bean sprouts with omelet shreds

SERVES TWO

4 eggs
2 teaspoons soy sauce
3 tablespoons oil
½-inch (1-cm) piece fresh
  ginger root, peeled and
  finely chopped
3 scallions, finely sliced
½ lb (225 g) bean sprouts

Lightly beat the eggs with the soy sauce. Heat half the oil in a frying pan and pour in the eggs. Let the eggs set in a thin omelet. When the omelet is browned underneath, lift it out and cut it into large shreds.

Add the remaining oil to the pan and stir-fry the ginger and scallions for 1 minute. Add the bean sprouts and stir-fry for 2 minutes. Add the omelet shreds and fry for 1 minute more. Serve immediately.

Ajja

Omit or halve the amount of green chilies in this spicy Tunisian dish if you are not used to the taste of hot food.

SERVES FOUR

2 tablespoons olive oil
1 lb (450 g) Spanish chorizo
  sausage, cut into ½-inch
  (1-cm) slices
2 onions, sliced
2 garlic cloves, crushed
1 to 2 green chilies, chopped
1 lb (450 g) tomatoes, peeled
  and chopped
3 green peppers, sliced
Salt and freshly ground
  black pepper
6 eggs, lightly beaten

Heat the oil in a large sauté pan. Add the sausage and fry, stirring, until browned. Add the onions, garlic and green chilies and fry for 2 to 3 minutes. Add the tomatoes and peppers and cook, stirring, for 10 minutes. Add salt and pepper to taste.

Pour in the eggs, reduce the heat to low and cook, stirring, until the eggs have just set. Serve immediately.

Scrambled eggs with chicken

SERVES FOUR

2 tablespoons butter
2 cups (225 g) cooked
  chicken, cut into strips
4 scallions, chopped
Pinch cayenne pepper
Salt and black pepper
6 eggs
2 tablespoons sour cream

Melt the butter in a saucepan over moderate heat.

Mix all the ingredients together in a bowl. Pour into the saucepan and cook, stirring, until lightly set. Serve hot.

Mozzarella in carrozza

Fried cheese sandwiches are a popular dish in southern Italy. The name literally means mozzarella in a carriage.

SERVES FOUR

16 thin slices of bread from
  a small sandwich loaf
1 lb (450 g) mozzarella
  cheese, cut into thin slices
2 eggs
2 tablespoons milk
Salt
Oil for deep frying

Trim the crusts off the bread slices. Sandwich a layer of mozzarella between two slices of bread.

Beat the eggs, milk and a little salt together on a plate. Dip the sandwiches in the egg mixture, turning to coat them well. Set aside for 30 minutes.

Heat the oil to 375°F (190°C). Fry the sandwiches until they are golden brown on both sides. Drain on paper towels. Serve immediately.

Fried mozzarella cheese

SERVES FOUR

1 lb (450 g) mozzarella
  cheese, thinly sliced
Flour
2 eggs, lightly beaten
Dry bread crumbs
Oil for deep frying

Dust the cheese slices with flour. Dip them in the egg and then in the bread crumbs to coat them well.

Heat the oil to 375°F (190°C) and fry the cheese until golden brown on both sides. Drain on paper towels. Serve immediately.

Roasting and baking

True roasting—one of the most primitive methods of cooking known to man—has, along with the spit, jack and the servant to turn it, long since disappeared from Western kitchens. It still survives, however, almost unchanged in parts of Greece, Spain, Italy and in many countries of the Middle East where suckling pigs, lamb or kid are roasted whole, flavored with garlic and sprigs of rosemary, marjoram or fennel.

What we now call roasting is really baking and this too is a time-honored method of cooking. The nomads of Central Asia still use their age-old clay ovens and in the remoter parts of some European countries the old "robber-style" cooking in underground ovens continues to this day.

Only good-quality meat and poultry should be used for roasting. The poorer cuts and older birds may be baked in pies or turned into meat loaves and pâtés. Almost any kind of fish and some shellfish are suitable for baking. Many vegetables, plain or stuffed, fruit, dairy products and cereals are transformed by baking into delicious desserts, pies, turnovers, soufflés, cakes and breads.

Fish and shellfish

Crab au gratin 168
Melba toast 81

Crab soufflé 168
Green salad 213

Baked scallops 169

Finnan haddie flan 169
Green salad 213

Salmon baked in foil 166
Sauces: Hollandaise, Mousseline 67
New potatoes 93,
Broccoli 92

Baked mackerel 166
Cottage fries 151,
Belgian endive, orange and watercress salad 213

Baked fish with olives 166
Fennel 92,
Boiled potatoes 93

Roast stuffed bass 167
Cottage fries 151

Truites en papillotes 167
Green salad 213

Sole Ormondville 167
Green salad 213

Indonesian baked fish 168

Halibut with lemon sauce 168
Cottage fries 151

Roast carp with julienne vegetables 168

Kulibyaka 169
Green salad 213

Fish pie 169
Tomato salad 213

Eel pie 169
Broccoli 92

Poultry and game birds

English roast chicken 170
Bread sauce 69,
Peas 93,
Roast potatoes 180

French roast chicken 170
Green salad 213,
Glazed carrots 91,
Garlic mashed potatoes 180

Roast duck with apricots 170
Casseroled celery 120,
Potato croquettes 151,
Peas 93

Roast turkey 172
Bread sauce 69,
Brussels sprouts 92,
Potato croquettes 151

Guinea hen with apples 172
Large croutons 158,
Green beans 92

Goose with sauerkraut 172
Broccoli 92,
Boiled potatoes,
Zucchini 93

Pheasant with celery 172
Potato chips 150

Roast partridge with vine leaves 173
Large croutons 158,
Spinach purée 92

Country chicken pie 173
Peas 93

Game pie 173
Belgian endive, orange and watercress salad 213

Meat and game

Roast ribs of beef with Yorkshire pudding 174
Horseradish sauce 89
Glazed carrots 91
Broccoli 92

Stuffed loin of pork 177
Brussels sprouts 92,
New potatoes 93

Beef Wellington 174
Green salad 213,
Zucchini 93

Haunch of venison 178
Casseroled celery 120,
Garlic mashed potatoes 180

Roast breast of veal with sour cream and tarragon 174
Spinach purée 92,
Braised onions 120,
Roast potatoes 180

Pork pie 178
Salads:
Carrot and apple 213,
Potato 93

Roast shoulder of lamb with herb stuffing 176
Mint sauce 69,
Lima beans 92,
Roast potatoes 180

Cornish pasty 179
Green salad 213

Crown roast 176
Mint sauce 69,
Green beans 92,
Garlic mashed potatoes 180

Steak and kidney pie 179
Glazed carrots 91,
New potatoes 93

Baked ham 178
Cumberland sauce 69
Belgian endive, orange and watercress salad 213 New potatoes 93

Honey-glazed ham 178
Celery, apple and walnut salad 213,
Sweet potato soufflé 180

Roast suckling pig 178
Applesauce 69,
Peas 93,
Roast potatoes 180

Roast pork 176
Baked apples 184,
Green beans 92,
Mashed potatoes 93

Pork spareribs 177
Green salad 213

Vegetables

Stuffed grape leaves 182

Baked spiced avocados 183

Mushroom vol-au-vents 181

Eggplant à la nîmoise 180

Ham-stuffed potatoes 180
Tomato salad 213

Finnan haddie potatoes 180
Steamed fennel 92

Stuffed baked squash 181
Garlic mashed potatoes 180

Moussaka 181
Green salad 213

Boston baked beans 180
Boston steamed bread 99

Baked tomatoes 182

Baked stuffed onions 183

Belgian endive au gratin 181

Baked potatoes 180

Garlic mashed potatoes 180

Potatoes à la dauphinoise 180

Sweet potato soufflé 180

Fruit

Mince pies 184
Brandy butter 69

English apple pie 184
Whipped cream

Apple dumplings 184
Custard sauce 69

French apple flan 184
Whipped cream

Apple strudel 184
Whipped cream

Rhubarb crumble 185

Cherry flan 185

Lemon meringue pie 185

Pear tart 186

Date bars 186

Clafoutis 186

Pineapple upside-down cake 186
Whipped cream

Cereals

Macaroni cheese 188
Green salad 213

Baked pasta with seafood 188

Cannelloni di spinace 188
Green salad 213

Lasagne 189
Green salad 213

Pizza Napoletana 188
Pizza con cozze 188
Pizza alla francescana 188
Green salad 213

Baked chicken pancakes 189

Garlic bread 189

Rice pudding 189
Fruit sauce 69

Oatmeal and apple pudding 189
Whipped cream

Bread and butter pudding 189

Cakes, pastries and cookies 190-7

Breads 198-201

Eggs and dairy products

Quiche Lorraine 203
Green salad 213

Tarte au Gruyère 203
Green salad 213

Oeufs sur le plat 203
Brown bread 198

Cheese soufflé 203

Chocolate soufflé 204

Baked custard 204

Caramel custard 204

Petit pots de crème au chocolat 204

Meringue hazelnut gâteau 205

Meringues 204
Meringue baskets 205

Pavlova 205

Baked Alaska 205

Queen of puddings 205

Raspberry tart 205

First courses

Main courses

Light lunch-supper dishes

Accompaniments

Desserts

Miscellaneous

Fish and shellfish

Whole fish, steaks or fillets may be baked in the oven with a little butter and seasoning. Preheat the oven to about 375°F (190°C) and cook until the flesh is opaque and comes away from the bone easily.

Whole fish can be stuffed with all sorts of different mixtures. Sometimes the stuffing mixture is spread over fish fillets, which are then rolled up before being baked. Alternatively, the stuffing mixture may be used as a bed on which whole fish, steaks or fillets are cooked. A very little liquid may also be added—use fish stock, white wine, cider or lemon juice.

A topping of grated cheese and bread crumbs gives baked fish a pleasantly crisp crust. Alternatively, bake the fish in a cheese, béchamel or velouté sauce with bread crumbs and a few small pieces of butter sprinkled on top.

When shellfish are cooked in the oven they are usually coated in a sauce or made into soufflés or gratins.

Salmon baked in foil

This is an excellent way of dealing with large fish when you have no poaching kettle to steam them in; the foil keeps all the flavor and juices in. An hour will be enough to cook a fish, or piece of fish, weighing up to 6 pounds (3 kg); allow 10 minutes per pound for fish larger than this.

Smaller fish can be cooked in the same way. Trout, for instance, will cook in 20 to 30 minutes. Salmon steaks can be sprinkled with lemon juice, seasoning, butter and herbs and individually wrapped in foil; they will cook in about 20 minutes—test with a fork.

Serve hot salmon with hollandaise or mousseline sauce, boiled new potatoes and a lettuce and cucumber salad. Cold salmon is traditionally served with mayonnaise or a sauce verte, boiled potatoes and a cucumber salad.

SERVES SIX TO EIGHT

Butter or oil
4-lb (2-kg) salmon (or salmon trout, turbot or other firm fish), cleaned
Lemon juice
Parsley, rosemary, thyme or dill sprigs
Salt and pepper
1¼ cups (315 ml) sauce mousseline

Preheat the oven to 325°F (170°C).

Tear off a piece of foil large enough to enclose and seal in the fish. If the fish is to be served hot, grease the foil with butter; if it is to be served cold, grease the foil with oil. Sprinkle the inside of the fish with lemon juice, seasoning, a little butter and some sprigs of fresh herbs.

Wrap the foil around securely and seal the edges well so that no juices or steam can escape. Bake for 1 hour.

If the salmon is to be served hot, remove the foil and skin the fish. Leave it to rest for 10 to 15 minutes before serving (5 minutes in the case of salmon steaks or smaller fish). Serve the fish and sauce separately.

Baked mackerel

SERVES FOUR

4 small mackerel, filleted
Salt and pepper
2 tablespoons oil
2 large onions, chopped
1 garlic clove, chopped
2 tomatoes, peeled and chopped
1 green and 1 red pepper, seeded and sliced
2 teaspoons lemon juice
½ cup (125 ml) tomato juice
2 tablespoons butter

Preheat the oven to 350°F (180°C).

Season the mackerel fillets. Heat the oil in a large frying pan. Fry the onions and garlic until soft. Add the tomatoes, peppers and seasoning and cook for 1 minute. Put the vegetables in a baking dish. Arrange the mackerel fillets on top of the vegetables, sprinkle the fish with lemon juice and pour the tomato juice over the top. Dot with the butter, cover the dish and bake for 30 minutes.

Baked fish with olives

Freshly caught fish are usually best when cooked quite simply. This recipe from southern Italy can be used for bass, red mullet or other firm fish.

SERVES FOUR

2-lb (900-g) fresh bream or large red mullet, scaled and cleaned
Salt
Olive oil
Vinegar
½ cup (125 g) pitted green olives

Preheat the oven to 350°F (180°C).

Dry the fish with paper towels. Lightly salt the insides. Put a little olive oil into a baking dish and lay the fish on top. Sprinkle lightly with vinegar and a little more salt, cover with the olives and bake for 20 to 30 minutes. Serve immediately.

Fish baked in foil retains its natural flavor and juices.

Roast stuffed bass

SERVES FOUR

3- to 4-lb (1½- to 2-kg) bass or
  4 small bass, cleaned
4 tomatoes, peeled and diced
2 onions, diced
¼ cup (65 ml) white wine

STUFFING
1 cup (125 g) soft bread
  crumbs
Milk
3 tablespoons olive oil
1 large onion, diced
1 shallot, diced
¼ lb (125 g) mushrooms,
  chopped
1 tablespoon chopped chives
1 tablespoon chopped
  parsley
1 tablespoon chopped
  chervil
Salt and pepper
1 egg, beaten

First make the stuffing: soak the bread crumbs in a little milk and squeeze them dry.

Heat the oil in a frying pan. Add the onion and shallot and fry for about 5 minutes. Add the mushrooms and herbs and continue cooking for another 3 to 4 minutes. Remove the pan from the heat. Stir in the bread crumbs, season well and bind with the beaten egg. Stuff the fish and sew up or secure with wooden cocktail picks.

Preheat the oven to 325°F (170°C).

Put the tomatoes and onions in a baking dish, add the wine and lay the fish on top. Cover with foil and bake for 1 hour (or 30 minutes if using small bass). Remove the string or cocktail picks and serve.

Truites en papillotes

SERVES FOUR

2 tablespoons butter
4 trout, filleted
1 tablespoon heavy cream
1 teaspoon Pernod
8 tablespoons duxelles
Oil
Salt and freshly ground
  black pepper
1 tablespoon finely chopped
  parsley

Preheat the oven to 350°F (180°C). Melt the butter in a frying pan. Fry the trout fillets gently for 2 to 3 minutes or until they are half cooked.

Stir the cream and Pernod into the duxelles.

Cut 4 hearts out of foil or waxed paper large enough to enclose 2 fillets with space to spare around the edge. Brush with oil. Spread a little of the duxelles on one half of each heart and put 2 fillets on it. Season to taste. Cover with more of the duxelles and sprinkle a little parsley on top. Fold over the other half of the heart and secure by folding the edges like a hem. Cook on a baking sheet for 20 minutes or until the hearts are puffed up. Serve in the hearts.

Sole Ormondville

SERVES FOUR

4 sole, filleted
Salt and pepper
3 tablespoons butter
1 teaspoon lemon juice
⅔ cup (150 ml) dry white
  wine or cider
1 pint (1 lb/450 g) mussels,
  scrubbed
4 tablespoons court bouillon
¼ lb (125 g) shelled cooked
  shrimp
½ lb (225 g) small
  mushrooms
1 teaspoon flour
Cayenne pepper
⅔ cup (150 ml) cream
1 egg yolk, beaten
8 small triangles fried bread

Preheat the oven to 350°F (180°C).

Season the fillets and fold them over. Butter a baking dish with 1 tablespoon of the butter and arrange the fillets in it. Sprinkle the fish with the lemon juice and pour over the wine or cider. Cover the dish with foil and bake for 10 to 15 minutes or until cooked.

Meanwhile, put the mussels in a saucepan with the court bouillon and bring to a boil. Cover the pan, reduce the heat and simmer for 5 minutes. Remove the mussels from their shells, discarding any that have not opened.

Melt the remaining butter in a frying pan and sauté the shrimp and mushrooms for 2 minutes.

Arrange the fish on a serving dish, surrounded by the mussels, shrimp and mushrooms. Strain the liquid from the baking dish into a saucepan. Heat until boiling. Remove the pan from the heat. Mix the flour and a pinch of cayenne with the cream and stir it into the pan. Return the pan to low heat and cook at just below simmering point until thickened. Pour the sauce onto the egg yolk, beating well. Season to taste, pour the sauce over the fish and serve garnished with triangles of fried bread.

Fish and shellfish

Indonesian baked fish

This recipe is suitable for such fish as herring or mackerel, haddock, shad or whiting.

SERVES FOUR

2 lb (900 g) fish fillets
1 garlic clove, finely chopped
Salt and pepper
¼ cup (50 g) butter
2 tablespoons soy sauce
2 tablespoons lemon juice
Chili powder

Preheat the oven to 375°F (190°C).

Sprinkle the fish with the chopped garlic, salt and pepper. Put into a buttered baking dish and bake for 15 minutes.

Melt the butter in a small pan and stir in the soy sauce, lemon juice and a pinch of chili powder. Pour this over the fish and cook for another 15 to 20 minutes.

Halibut with lemon sauce

SERVES FOUR

¼ cup (50 g) butter
4 halibut steaks
Salt and pepper
1 onion, finely chopped
2 celery stalks, finely chopped
¼ lb (125 g) mushrooms, finely chopped
2 tomatoes, peeled and chopped
1 tablespoon mixed chopped herbs (parsley, dill, thyme or rosemary)
1 lemon, sliced

SAUCE
Juice of 1 lemon
2 teaspoons cornstarch
½ cup (125 ml) fish stock
1 egg, beaten
Salt and pepper

Preheat the oven to 375°F (190°C).

Grease a baking dish with a little of the butter. Remove the bone from the center of each halibut steak. Sprinkle the fish steaks with salt and pepper and arrange them in the baking dish. Melt the remaining butter in a frying pan and fry the onion and celery until soft. Add the mushrooms and fry, stirring, until soft. Add the tomatoes, seasoning and herbs.

Spoon the mixture into the center of each steak. Cover with greased waxed paper, then with foil. Bake for 20 to 25 minutes or until the fish is cooked.

Meanwhile, make the sauce. In a small bowl mix the lemon juice with the cornstarch. Heat the stock in a pan, add a little to the cornstarch mixture, mix thoroughly and return to the pan and cook, stirring, for 1 minute. Remove the pan from the heat, allow the sauce to cool for 1 minute and pour over the egg, beating constantly. Season to taste.

Remove the fish from the oven and take off the foil and paper. Pour the sauce over the fish and garnish with the lemon slices. Serve immediately.

Roast carp with julienne vegetables

SERVES SIX

3-lb (1½-kg) carp, cleaned
Salt and pepper
Vinegar
Rosemary, thyme and parsley sprigs
2 tablespoons soy sauce
¼ cup (50 g) butter, cut into pieces
1 garlic clove, finely sliced
½-inch (1-cm) piece fresh ginger root, finely sliced
2 carrots
½ cucumber
4 scallions
2 tablespoons chicken stock

Soak the carp in cold salted water for 30 minutes.

Preheat the oven to 375°F (190°C).

Rinse the fish in vinegar and water and dry on thick paper towels.

Rub the fish with plenty of salt and pepper. Arrange a bed of herbs in a roasting pan and lay the carp on the herbs. Sprinkle the soy sauce over the fish and cover with the butter, garlic and ginger. Place a piece of greased waxed paper over the fish to prevent it from burning. Roast for 30 to 40 minutes.

Meanwhile cut the carrots, cucumber and scallions into small julienne strips. Put the vegetables into a saucepan, cover with salted water and simmer for 5 minutes. Drain and set aside. Arrange the fish on a serving dish and garnish with the vegetables. Pour the stock into the roasting pan and bring to a boil. Strain the sauce over the fish and serve immediately.

Crab au gratin

SERVES FOUR

1 teaspoon anchovy paste
1 cup (250 ml) mornay sauce
1 large crab (about 2 lb/ 900 g), cooked, the meat removed and the small claws reserved
Juice of 1 lemon
½ cup (50 g) grated Parmesan cheese
¼ cup (25 g) fresh white bread crumbs
2 tablespoons butter
1 lemon, cut into wedges

Preheat the oven to 350°F (180°C).

Mix the anchovy paste into the mornay sauce. Scrub the shell of the crab and dry thoroughly. Mix the dark crabmeat with 4 tablespoons of the sauce and 1 tablespoon of the lemon juice. Spread this mixture in the bottom of the shell. Mash the rest of the crabmeat with the remaining lemon juice and pile it into the shell. Mask with the remaining sauce.

Toss the cheese and bread crumbs together, sprinkle them over the crabmeat, dot with butter and bake for 20 minutes or until the top is golden brown. Serve garnished with the small claws and the lemon wedges.

Crab soufflé

Serve with a green salad.

SERVES TWO TO THREE

2 tablespoons plus 1 teaspoon butter
3 tablespoons grated Parmesan cheese
½ lb (225 g) cooked crabmeat
1 cup (250 ml) milk
¼ cup (25 g) flour
1 teaspoon tomato paste
Tabasco sauce
1 teaspoon dry mustard
Salt and pepper
3 eggs yolks
4 egg whites

Preheat the oven to 350°F (180°C).

Grease an 8-inch (20-cm) soufflé dish with a teaspoon of the butter and sprinkle 1 tablespoon of the grated cheese over the bottom and sides. Put a waxed paper collar around the soufflé dish. Flake the crabmeat and set it aside in a small bowl.

Heat the milk to just under boiling point and set aside. Melt the remaining butter in a saucepan. Stir in the flour and cook for 1 to 2 minutes. Gradually add the hot milk, stirring constantly until smooth. Blend in the tomato paste, Tabasco to taste, the mustard and seasoning.

Beat the egg yolks in a bowl. Stir in a little of the hot sauce then add the mixture to the pan with the crabmeat. Cool the sauce. Beat the whites until stiff and fold them into the sauce. Pour the mixture into the soufflé dish. Sprinkle with the remaining cheese and bake for 35 minutes or until the soufflé has risen and is firm to the touch but creamy inside. Remove the waxed paper collar and serve immediately.

Baked scallops

SERVES FOUR

8 large scallops, cleaned
¾ cup (175 ml) white wine
½ cup (125 ml) water
½ lemon
3½ tablespoons butter
½ lb (225 g) mushrooms, sliced
1½ tablespoons flour
½ cup (125 ml) cream
Salt and pepper
Cayenne pepper
⅔ cup (50 g) Gruyere cheese, grated

Preheat the oven to 375°F (190°C).

Put the scallops in a saucepan with the wine, water and a squeeze of lemon juice and simmer for 5 minutes. Drain the scallops; strain and reserve the cooking liquid. Cut each scallop into quarters.

Melt 2 tablespoons of the butter in a frying pan and fry the mushrooms for 2 to 3 minutes.

Melt the remaining butter in a saucepan. Stir in the flour to make a roux. Remove the pan from the heat and gradually pour in the cooking liquid, stirring constantly. Bring to a boil and cook for 5 minutes. Stir in the cream and boil until the sauce is thick and syrupy. Season to taste with salt, pepper and cayenne.

Mix the scallops and mush-rooms into the sauce. Divide the mixture between 4 scallop shells. Sprinkle the cheese on top. Put the shells on a baking sheet and bake on the top shelf of the oven for 10 to 15 minutes or until golden brown and bubbling.

Kulibyaka

This Russian fish pie can be made with any fine-flavored fish. There are many versions, including one using meat and vegetables, but the classic one is with salmon and rice. Brioche dough may be used instead of pastry.

SERVES FOUR

Puff pastry made with 2 cups (225 g) flour
¾ lb (350 g) salmon
Salt and pepper
Lemon juice
¾ cup (75 g) cooked rice
2 tablespoons chopped parsley
1 tablespoon chopped dill
7 tablespoons butter
1 cup (50 g) chopped mushrooms
1 onion, finely chopped
2 hard-cooked eggs, chopped
Nutmeg

Preheat the oven to 450°F (230°C).

Roll out the pastry to a rectangle 16 by 8 inches (40 by 20 cm), lift it onto a greased baking sheet and set aside to rest.

Put the fish into a saucepan with a little salt, lemon juice and water to cover. Bring to a simmer and cook for 10 minutes. Remove the salmon from the pan and leave to cool. Flake the fish in a bowl and mix in the rice, herbs and seasoning.

Melt 3 tablespoons of the butter in a frying pan and fry the vegetables until soft. Put half the fish and rice mixture on one half of the pastry. Spread with chopped egg and the mushroom and onion. Season, add a pinch of nutmeg, and cover with the rest of the fish. Dampen the edges of the pastry, fold over and seal. Make diagonal cuts across the top of the pastry and bake for 40 minutes.

Remove the pie from the oven. Melt the remaining butter and brush the pastry, pouring the excess into the pie through the cuts. Serve hot.

Fish pie

SERVES FOUR

1½ lb (700 g) cooked white fish
1¾ cups (425 ml) béchamel sauce
Salt and pepper
Cayenne pepper
1 tablespoon anchovy paste (optional)
2 hard-cooked eggs, sliced
1½ lb (700 g) mashed potatoes
1 egg, beaten
2 tablespoons cream
Nutmeg
2 tablespoons butter, melted

Preheat the oven to 375°F (190°C).

Flake the fish and mix it with the béchamel sauce. Season well, adding a pinch of cayenne pepper and the anchovy paste if you are using it. Turn the mixture into a deep pie dish and cover with the sliced eggs.

Beat the potatoes with the egg, cream and a little grated nutmeg. Pile it over the fish mixture or squeeze it over using a large-nozzled pastry tube. Sprinkle with melted butter and bake for 20 to 25 minutes until golden brown on top.

Eel pie

SERVES FOUR

Puff pastry for 1-crust 9-inch (23-cm) pie
2 lb (900 g) eel fillets, cut into 2-inch (5-cm) pieces
2 tablespoons butter
½ cup (125 g) stuffed olives, chopped
4 hard-cooked eggs, sliced
Salt and pepper
Nutmeg
2 tablespoons chopped parsley
½ cup (125 ml) white wine
Milk or beaten egg to glaze
2 tablespoons demi-glace sauce

Preheat the oven to 350°F (180°C).

Roll out the pastry to fit the top of a deep pie dish and leave to rest. Blanch the eel pieces in boiling salted water for 2 minutes, drain and cool.

Grease the pie dish with a little of the butter. Layer the eel pieces with the olives and hard-cooked egg slices, sprinkling

each
grate
Po
top
cut
of
the
br
beaten egg, decor
leaves and make a cut in the middle to allow the steam to escape. Bake for 1 hour, or until the pastry is golden brown. When ready to serve pour the demi-glace through the cut in the pastry. Serve hot or cold.

Finnan haddie flan

SERVES SIX

3 tablespoons butter
2 onions, chopped
¼ lb (125 g) mushrooms, sliced
2 tomatoes, peeled and diced
1 lb (450 g) finnan haddie
½ cup (125 ml) milk
Pepper
Mace
Bay leaf
½ cup (125 ml) cream
3 eggs
Grated rind of 1 lemon
Salt
10-inch (25-cm) baked plain pastry pie shell

Preheat the oven to 350°F (180°C).

Melt the butter in a frying pan and fry the onions until soft. Add the mushrooms and cook for 2 to 3 minutes until the juices run. Add the tomatoes and cook for 1 minute. Remove the pan from the heat. Allow to cool.

Put the haddock into a saucepan with the milk, pepper, mace and bay leaf to taste, and simmer very gently for 10 minutes. Remove the fish, discard the skin and bones and flake the flesh. Reserve the cooking liquid.

Beat the cream and eggs together, add the lemon rind, and strain in the reserved cooking liquid. Season if necessary taking into account the saltiness of the smoked haddock.

Put the vegetable mixture into the piecrust, spreading it over the bottom. Put the fish on top and pour over the egg and cream mixture. Bake for 30 to 40 minutes or until the top is puffed up and golden brown.

...ng is the traditional method of cooking young ...try and game birds. A lean bird should be larded with ...ty bacon slices or salt pork and well basted during ...ooking. You can also put a little butter inside the bird or stuff it with a variety of fruit or vegetables—sautéed mushrooms and onions, for example—or just a few herbs and a little garlic.

A very fatty bird like a goose or a duck should be roasted on a rack placed over a baking pan. The pan may need to be emptied of fat during the cooking time.

Most birds are roasted until they are cooked through. Test by inserting the tip of a knife into the bird's thigh, which is the part that takes longest to cook: if the juices run clear, the bird is cooked.

English roast chicken

The traditional accompaniments are crisply broiled bacon rolls and bread sauce.

Sausages are often baked separately in the oven—they take 45 to 60 minutes to brown and cook through—and are then served with the chicken.

SERVES FOUR

4-lb (2-kg) chicken, giblets reserved
2 tablespoons drippings or bacon fat
Salt and pepper
1 onion sliced
1 carrot, sliced
Thyme or marjoram
1 cup (250 ml) bread sauce, kept hot

Preheat the oven to 375°F (190°C).

Rub the chicken with the drippings or bacon fat and put it in a roasting pan. Roast for 25 minutes on each side, basting every 15 minutes. Season the bird well and turn it onto its back for the last 30 minutes or until done. Insert the tip of a sharp knife into one thigh—if the juices run clear the chicken is cooked.

While the chicken is roasting put the giblets, onion, carrot and a pinch of thyme or marjoram in a saucepan with 2 cups (500 ml) of water and bring to a boil. Reduce the heat and simmer. When the chicken is cooked, transfer it to a serving dish and keep hot. Pour off most of the fat from the roasting pan and strain in the giblet stock. Set the pan over moderate heat and boil, stirring in all the sediment, until the gravy is reduced and well flavored. Strain the gravy into a heated gravy boat. If you prefer a thickened gravy, mix 1 teaspoon of arrowroot (or cornstarch) with a little cold water and mix it into the roasting pan. Cook, stirring constantly, until the gravy has thickened.

Serve the chicken with the gravy and bread sauce.

French roast chicken

SERVES FOUR

4-lb (2-kg) chicken, with giblets
1 onion, sliced
1 carrot, sliced
Thyme or marjoram
¼ cup (50 g) butter
Salt and pepper
4 slices bacon
Fresh tarragon or parsley sprigs
1 lemon slice

First make the stock. Put the giblets, onion, carrot and a pinch of thyme or marjoram in a saucepan with 2 cups (500 ml) of water and bring to a boil. Reduce the heat and simmer for 1½ hours. Remove the pan from the heat and strain the stock into a bowl. Set aside.

Preheat the oven to 375°F (190°C). Spread the chicken with 2 tablespoons of the butter. Season well and cover the breast with the bacon slices. Put a few sprigs of tarragon or parsley inside the chicken with the remaining butter, salt, pepper and the lemon slice.

Roast the bird as for English roast chicken, but use the stock for basting. Remove the bacon for the last 15 minutes to allow the breast to brown.

Make the gravy as for English roast chicken, but without the arrowroot or cornstarch, and reduce the quantity of gravy by boiling it down to no more than 1¼ cups.

Roast duck with apricots

Serve with potato croquettes.

SERVES THREE TO FOUR

5-lb (2½-kg) duck, trussed
Salt and pepper
Rind and juice of 1 orange
1 lb (450 g) apricots, blanched, peeled and halved
½ cup (125 ml) Madeira
¼ cup (50 ml) veal stock
1 teaspoon sugar
1 teaspoon cornstarch

Preheat the oven to 425°F (220°C).

Rub the duck with salt and pepper. Put the orange rind inside the cavity. Prick the duck all over with a fork. Put the duck on its back on a rack in a roasting pan and bake for 20 minutes.

Reduce the oven temperature to 350°F (180°C). Put the orange juice in a small pan and bring to just under boiling point. Turn the duck on its side, baste with some of the orange juice and cook for 20 minutes. Turn it on its other side, baste with the remaining orange juice and cook for 20 minutes more.

Remove the duck from the oven and put it in an earthenware baking dish. Arrange the apricot halves around the duck. Pour off all the fat from the roasting pan. Put the pan over moderate heat and pour in the Madeira and stock. Stir and scrape the bottom of the pan to amalgamate the sediments with the wine. Season to taste and stir in the sugar. Mix the cornstarch with a tablespoon of water and mix it into the sauce. Bring the sauce to a boil and boil for 1 minute. Pour the sauce over the duck.

Return the baking dish to the oven and bake for 30 minutes or until the duck is cooked.

Two traditional English dishes : a raised game pie and roast chicken garnished with broiled bacon rolls and sausages.

Poultry and game birds

Roast turkey

There are several ways of roasting turkeys. Very large birds can be wrapped in foil and cooked at 250°F (130°C) overnight, the heat being increased only in the last 30 minutes when the foil is removed, to brown the bird. Or roast the turkey at 300°F (150°C) allowing 15 minutes per pound plus 1 hour.

SERVES TEN

10-lb (4½-kg) turkey
½ cup (125 g) butter
Salt and pepper
Drippings
2 tablespoons flour
2 cups (500 ml) giblet stock

CHESTNUT STUFFING

1 lb (450 g) chestnuts, peeled
2 cups (500 ml) chicken stock
1 lb (450 g) sausage meat
2 tablespoons chopped parsley
2 tablespoons butter
1 onion, finely chopped
Salt and freshly ground black pepper

Preheat the oven to 375°F (190°C).

First make the stuffing. Put the chestnuts into a saucepan with the stock and bring to a boil. Reduce the heat, cover the pan and simmer for 40 minutes or until the chestnuts are tender.

Purée the chestnuts in a food mill or blender. Mix the purée with the sausage meat and parsley in a bowl.

Heat the butter in a frying pan and fry the onion until soft. Add the onion to the other ingredients, season to taste and mix well. Put the stuffing into the cavity and crop of the bird. Secure with a skewer or sew up with strong thread.

Mash the butter with the salt and pepper and smear all over the turkey. Heat plenty of drippings—at least 1 inch (2 cm) in depth—in the roasting pan. Put the bird in on its side, cover with foil and roast for 1¼ hours. Turn the bird on its other side and roast for 1¼ hours. Turn the bird on its back and roast for 70 minutes more. Baste regularly every 20 minutes. Take the foil off for the last 30 minutes for the breast to brown. Test by piercing the thigh with a sharp knife—if the juices run clear the turkey is cooked.

When the turkey is cooked, lift it out of the pan onto a carving board or large dish. Pour most of the fat out of the roasting pan. Stir in the flour. Scrape in all the bits from the sides and cook, stirring, over heat until the flour is golden. Add the giblet stock. Boil for 1 to 2 minutes and strain into a gravy boat and serve with the turkey.

Guinea hen with apples

SERVES TWO

1 guinea hen
Salt and pepper
Bacon
6 tablespoons butter
3 firm sweet apples, thinly sliced
¾ cup (175 ml) whipping cream
6 tablespoons Calvados (optional)

Preheat the oven to 375°F (190°C).

Season the bird well and cover with the bacon. Heat 4 tablespoons of the butter in a frying pan and gently fry the apples for 2 to 3 minutes. Melt the remaining butter in a baking dish and put in the guinea hen. Arrange the apple slices around it and pour over half of the cream. Roast, basting from time to time, for about 45 minutes or until the bird is done. Test by inserting a sharp knife into the thigh— if the juices run clear the bird is cooked.

Remove the bird to a serving dish and keep warm. Stir the rest of the cream into the apples, reheat gently, add the Calvados if liked, adjust the seasoning and serve with the guinea hen.

Goose with sauerkraut

SERVES EIGHT

10-lb (4½-kg) goose
Salt and pepper
2 lb (900 g) sauerkraut, braised and kept hot
8 frankfurters, hot
1 cup (250 ml) white wine
1 cup (250 ml) giblet stock

STUFFING

2 tablespoons butter
2 Bermuda onions, sliced
2 lb (900 g) sausage meat
1½ cups (175 g) soft bread crumbs
1 teaspoon caraway seeds
Salt and pepper

Preheat the oven to 425°F (220°C).

First make the stuffing. Melt the butter in a frying pan and fry the onions until soft. Put them in a bowl and mix in the sausage meat, bread crumbs, caraway seeds and seasoning. Put the stuffing into the goose and sew it up with strong thread.

Prick the goose all over with a fork and rub with salt and pepper. Put the bird on its side on a rack in the roasting pan and roast for 20 minutes.

Lift out the bird and pour off the fat from the roasting pan. Reduce the oven temperature to 325°F (170°C) and roast, turning the bird, for 3 hours more or until the goose is tender and the juices run clear when the thigh is pierced with the point of a sharp knife.

Put the goose on a large serving dish. Surround it with the sauerkraut and frankfurters and keep hot.

Pour away all the fat from the roasting pan. Pour in the wine and stock and bring to a boil, stirring. Boil rapidly until the gravy is reduced by half. Pour the gravy into a gravy boat and serve with the goose.

Pheasant with celery

SERVES TWO TO THREE

1 pheasant, trussed
Salt and pepper
½ cup (125 g) butter
1 carrot, quartered
1 onion, quartered
2 slices bacon
4 celery hearts
Juice of ½ lemon
½ tablespoon flour
½ cup (125 ml) stock or white wine
½ cup (125 ml) whipping cream

Preheat the oven to 375°F (190°C).

Season the pheasant well. Melt 2 tablespoons of the butter in a heavy ovenproof casserole. Put in the pheasant and brown the bird on all sides over moderate heat. Put in the carrot and onion. Lay the bacon over the bird's breast and roast for about 50 minutes. Baste frequently.

Meanwhile, quarter the celery hearts. Put them into a saucepan with a little salted water and the lemon juice and bring to a boil. Reduce the heat to low, cover the pan and cook for 20 minutes.

When the pheasant is cooked, lift it out and keep it warm. Discard the bacon, onion and carrot. Sprinkle the flour into the casserole and cook on top of the stove, stirring, until smooth. Gradually blend in the stock or

---

Roasting poultry and game birds

Chicken		
20 min per lb	375°F (190°C)	
(2 lb dressed weight minimum cooking time 50 to 60 minutes)		
Duck		
20 min per lb	425°F (220°C) for first 20 min then 350°F (180°C)	
Goose (stuffed)		
20 min per lb	425°F (220°C) for the first 20 min then 325°F (170°C)	
Turkey (stuffed)		
20 min per lb plus 20 min	375°F (190°C)	
(unstuffed)		
15 min per lb plus 15 min		
Guinea-hen		
45 to 60 min	375°F (190°C)	
Pheasant		
50 or 60 min	425°F (220°C) or 375°F (190°C)	
Pigeon		
25 to 30 min	425°F (220°C)	
Wild duck (rare)		
30 min	425°F (220°C)	
Grouse and partridge		
30 to 40 min	425°F (220°C)	
Woodcock, snipe and quail (rare)		
15 to 20 min	425°F (220°C)	

wine. Bring to a boil, stirring. Stir in the cream. Season to taste.

Drain the celery and put in the dish with the sauce. Put the pheasant on top. Reheat in the oven for about 8 minutes and serve.

Roast partridge (or quail) with vine leaves

It is traditional in many countries to enclose small game birds in vine leaves. All the juices and flavor are retained, just as in modern cooking with foil. Serve the birds on croutons of bread fried in butter, if liked. One partridge is usually enough for 2 people, but allow one quail per person.

SERVES FOUR

2 partridge (or 4 quail)
Salt and pepper
6 tablespoons butter
Bacon
Vine leaves

Preheat the oven to 425°F (220°C). Season the insides of the birds with salt and pepper and put a little butter inside each one. Cover the breasts with bacon and enclose the birds in vine leaves. Put them into a well-buttered baking dish in which they will fit nicely and roast for 30 minutes or until the juices run clear when the thighs are pierced with a knife.

Country chicken pie

SERVES FOUR

1 lb (450 g) cooked chicken, diced
4 thick slices ham, cut into ½-inch (1-cm) cubes
2 cups (500 ml) béchamel sauce
1 tablespoon butter
2 cups (125 g) sliced mushrooms
Salt and pepper
Pastry for a single crust pie
Beaten egg to glaze

Preheat the oven to 425°F (220°C).

Mix the chicken and ham with the béchamel sauce.

Melt the butter in a small frying pan. Add the mushrooms and fry for 2 to 3 minutes. Mix the mushrooms into the chicken mixture. Season and spoon the mixture into a pie dish.

Roll out the dough. Dampen the rim of the pie dish with water. Lift the dough and lay it on the pie dish and flute the edges. Brush the dough with beaten egg and prick with a fork. Bake for 25 minutes or until the pastry is golden brown.

Game pie

SERVES EIGHT

2 lb (900 g) mixed game
Hot-water pastry for a double crust pie
¼ lb (125 g) bacon slices
1 lb (450 g) sausage meat
¼ lb (125 g) mushrooms, sliced
Salt and pepper
2 tablespoons chopped fresh thyme, sage and marjoram
Beaten egg to glaze
½ cup (125 ml) well-flavored aspic

Preheat the oven to 400°F (200°C).

Remove the meat from the game and cut into strips. Line a greased pie pan with the hot-water crust dough, saving a third of the dough for the lid. Put the bacon in a layer at the bottom of the pie shell. Cover with a layer of sausage meat then layer the game, the rest of the sausage meat and the mushrooms. Season well between each layer and sprinkle with the herbs.

Roll out the remaining dough to make the lid. Dampen the edges of the dough and cover the pie. Press to seal, trim and decorate. Brush with the beaten egg. Make a hole in the center of the lid for the steam to escape. Bake for 30 minutes. Reduce the temperature of the oven to 300°F (150°C) and bake for another 1½ hours. Remove the pie from the oven and allow to cool.

Heat the aspic just enough to melt it and pour it into the pie through a funnel placed in the steam vent. Chill the pie for at least 6 hours before serving.

Carving a turkey

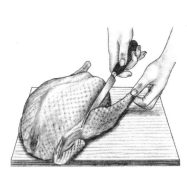

Holding the drumstick, cut off the leg including the thigh. Then cut off the wing.

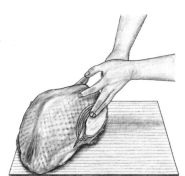

Hold the knife parallel to the body. Carve downward, cutting the white meat in thin slices.

Separate the drumstick from the thigh by cutting through the joint. Slice the thigh thinly.

Hold the drumstick upright and carve the meat in thin slices or serve the drumstick whole.

Carving a chicken

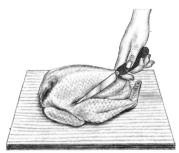

Cut off the legs. Separate the thighs from the drumsticks. Cut off the wings.

Cutting downward, carve the breast in neat slices from either side of the breastbone.

Carving a duck

Using a knife or poultry shears, cut the wings and legs from either side of the body.

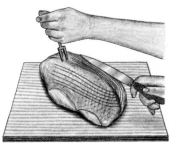

Make a downward cut on each side of the breastbone. Cut thick parallel slices from both sides.

Meat and game

Large pieces of meat or game are the best for roasting because small pieces tend to dry up during cooking. Very lean meat should be larded or barded and basted frequently during cooking.

Put beef into a very hot oven for the first fifteen minutes to brown the outsides and seal in the juices, then lower the heat a little for the rest of the cooking time. With the exception of beef, most meat and game is usually well cooked, but in France lamb is often served slightly rare.

Raised meat pies should be made a day in advance to allow time for the inside of the pastry to absorb some of the meat juices.

Roast ribs of beef with Yorkshire pudding
Serve the beef with horseradish sauce or mustard.

SERVES SIX

Drippings
Standing rib roast of beef chined and trimmed at the end (about 6 to 7 lb/3 kg)
1 teaspoon Dijon mustard
Salt and pepper
2 lb (900 g) peeled potatoes, cut into even-sized pieces
1¼ cups (315 ml) stock or water

YORKSHIRE PUDDING
1 cup (125 g) flour
Salt
1 egg
1 cup (250 ml) milk

Preheat the oven to 450°F (230°C).

Heat 4 tablespoons of drippings in a roasting pan. Rub the beef fat with the mustard, salt and pepper and stand, fat-side up, in the roasting pan. Roast for 1¾ to 2 hours, reducing the oven temperature after 15 minutes to 375°F (190°C). The higher temperature will seal the meat.

After 15 minutes add the potatoes and turn them in the fat. Turn the potatoes once or twice during the rest of the cooking time to brown on all sides.

Meanwhile, make the batter for the Yorkshire pudding. Sift the flour and a pinch of salt into a bowl. Make a well in the center and break in the egg. Add half the milk and mix with the egg. Stirring slowly, mix in the flour to make a batter. Gradually add the remaining milk. Thirty minutes before the beef is cooked pour a teaspoon of the hot drippings into 6 individual Yorkshire pudding pans or muffin tins and put them on the top rack of the oven to heat. After 5 minutes pour the batter into the pans and let cook for about 20 minutes. If one large pan is used, the cooking time will be about 30 minutes.

Transfer the meat to a carving board and the potatoes and Yorkshire puddings to a heated dish. Keep hot. Carefully pour off the fat from the roasting pan, leaving the meat juices behind. Add the stock or water. Bring to a boil and stir, scraping the sides of the pan. Strain the gravy into a heated gravy boat.

Beef Wellington
If you prefer, wrap the beef in a rich pie crust instead of using puff pastry.

Serve beef Wellington with green beans, zucchini or ratatouille.

SERVES SIX TO EIGHT

1 beef fillet about 3 lb (1½ kg)
1 tablespoon oil
Salt and pepper
Duxelles made from 1 lb (450 g) mushrooms, cooled
¼ lb (100 g) pâté de foie gras
2 recipes puff pastry
Beaten egg to glaze
1 cup (250 ml) Madeira sauce

Preheat the oven to 425°F (230°C).

Rub the beef all over with the oil and salt and pepper. Put the meat on a rack and roast for 40 minutes.

Take the meat out of the oven and set aside to cool completely.

Meanwhile, mix the duxelles with the foie gras. When the meat has cooled, spread the top and sides with the duxelles mixture.

Roll out the pastry dough into a rectangle ¼ inch (½ cm) thick and large enough to enclose the fillet. Put the fillet, top side down, onto the pastry dough. Enclose the meat in the dough to make a neat package. Dampen and seal the ends. Reserve the trimmings.

Put the meat on a baking sheet with the seam side down.

Roll out the trimmings and cut out pastry leaves. Brush the top of the pastry with the beaten egg and arrange the pastry leaves on top in a decorative pattern. Brush with more egg. Pierce the pastry in 3 places.

Bake for 40 minutes or until the pastry is puffed up and golden brown. Serve with the Madeira sauce.

Roast breast of veal with sour cream and tarragon
Instead of tarragon use a few sprigs of rosemary or marjoram. Serve the veal with mashed potatoes, purple or green sprouting broccoli and glazed carrots or sautéed zucchini.

SERVES SIX

1 boned breast of veal, weighing about 3 lb (1½ kg) when boned
Salt and pepper
6 tablespoons butter
2 medium-sized onions, chopped
1 cup (125 g) soft brown bread crumbs
1 tablespoon chopped tarragon
Grated rind of 1 lemon
1 tablespoon lemon juice
Salt and freshly ground black pepper
2 eggs, beaten
1 cup (250 ml) veal stock (made from the bones)
⅔ cup (150 ml) sour cream
Few tarragon sprigs

Preheat the oven to 375°F (190°C).

Lay the veal flat on a board, skin side down. Season with salt and pepper.

Melt 3 tablespoons of the butter in a frying pan and fry the onions until soft. Remove the pan from the heat and mix in the bread crumbs, tarragon, lemon rind and juice. Season to taste and bind with the egg. Spread the stuffing over the veal and roll up like a jelly roll. Secure with string. Melt the remaining butter in a roasting pan. Put in the meat and roast for about 1¾ hours, basting frequently with the juices.

Transfer the meat to a heated serving dish. Pour the stock into the pan and bring to a boil on top of the stove, scraping in the bits. Boil until reduced by half. Remove the pan from the heat, allow to cool a little and stir in the sour cream and the tarragon sprigs. Reheat but do not boil. Adjust the seasoning.

Remove the string and carve the meat into slices. Pour over a little of the sauce, serving the rest in a gravy boat.

A classic dish : a rib roast of beef with Yorkshire pudding.

Roasting meat and game

Beef (on the bone) 15 min per lb plus 15 min	450°F (230°C) for first 15 min then 375°F (190°C)
Beef (boned) 20 min per lb plus 10 min	
Mutton (on the bone) 25 min per lb plus 25 min	400°F (200°C) for first 15 min then 375°F (190°C)
Lamb (on the bone) 20 min per lb plus 20 min	375°F (190°C)
Lamb (boned) 30 min per lb plus 20 min	
Pork (on the bone) 35 min per lb	425°F (220°C) for first 20 min then 325°F (170°C)
Pork (boned) 45 min per lb	
Veal 25 min per lb plus 25 min	375°F (190°C)
Venison 25 min per lb plus 30 min	375°F (180°C) then 475°F (240°C) for last 30 min

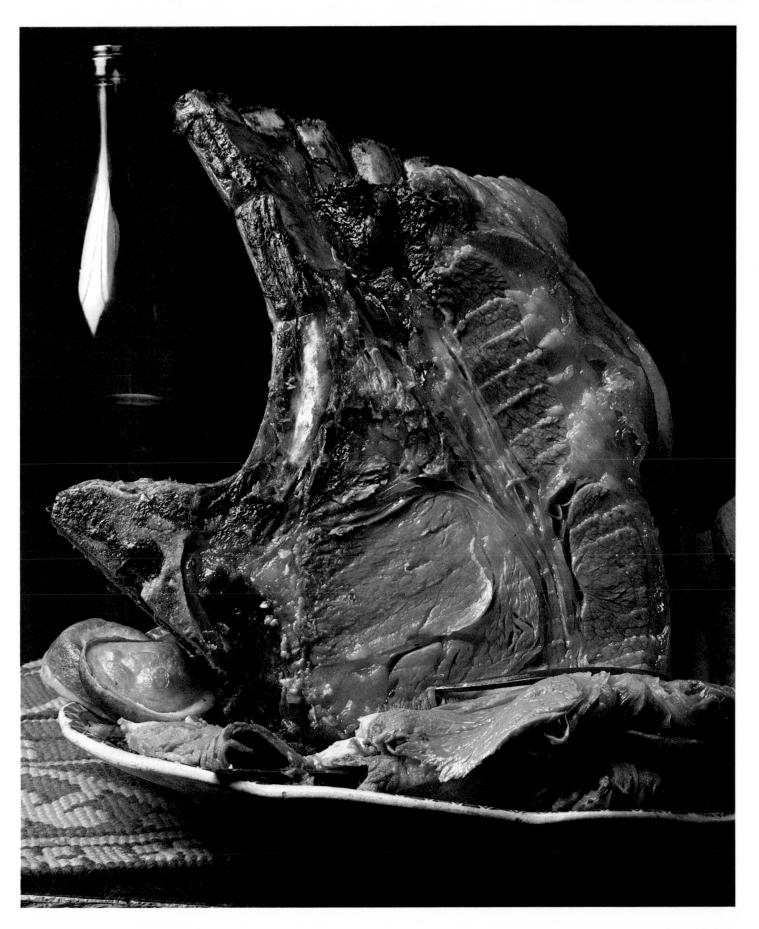

Meat and game

Roast shoulder of lamb with herb stuffing

Use other herbs such as rosemary, chervil, basil, marjoram or mint in the stuffing. Serve the lamb with roasted potatoes and shell or lima beans.

SERVES SIX

1 boned shoulder of lamb weighing 3½ lb (1½ kg)
3 tablespoons drippings
Salt and pepper
1 cup (250 ml) stock made from the lamb bones

STUFFING
3 tablespoons butter
1 onion, chopped
1 garlic clove, chopped
1 cup (125 g) fresh bread crumbs
6 tablespoons chopped parsley
1 teaspoon chopped thyme
Salt and pepper
2 eggs, beaten

Preheat the oven to 375°F (190°C).

To make the stuffing, melt the butter in a frying pan and fry the onion and garlic until soft. Remove the pan from the heat and stir in the rest of the stuffing ingredients. Open up the meat and put the mixture in the center. Roll and tie securely. Put the drippings and meat in a roasting pan, sprinkle with salt and pepper and roast for about 2 hours, basting frequently. Lift out the meat and keep warm.

Pour off most of the fat from the pan. Put the roasting pan over heat and pour in the stock. Bring to a boil, stirring and scraping the bottom of the pan. Boil for 12 to 13 minutes. Adjust the seasoning. Pour the gravy into a gravy boat and serve with the meat.

Crown roast

The stuffing for a crown roast is a matter of taste—use the herb stuffing from the roast shoulder of lamb or combine 2 cups (225 g) of cooked rice, 1 lightly fried chopped onion and 2 chopped garlic cloves, 2 tablespoons each of golden raisins, chopped almonds and walnuts, seasoning to taste, and the juice of ½ lemon.

SERVES SIX

1 crown roast (approximately 12 chops)
Approximately 4 to 6 cups (450 to 700 g) stuffing
Drippings
1¼ cups (315 ml) strong stock
Salt and pepper

Preheat the oven to 375°F (190°C).

Fill the crown roast with the stuffing. If you are using the rice stuffing, dot the top with a little butter.

Heat the drippings in a roasting pan. Put the crown roast in the pan. Cover each bone with a piece of foil to prevent it from burning. Roast for 1¼ to 1½ hours, basting occasionally.

Transfer the meat to a serving dish and keep warm. Remove the pieces of foil and replace them with chop frills if you like.

Pour off most of the fat from the pan. Add the stock and bring to a boil on top of the stove, scraping and stirring. Season to taste and strain into a heated gravy boat.

Serve immediately.

Roast pork

The choicest cut for roasting is the loin, but other common roasting cuts are the shoulder or leg. There is a basic difference between the French and English methods of roasting: the French remove the skin first, whereas the English leave it on to become crisp, delicious crackling. If roasting pork in the French style, rub the meat with crushed thyme (or marjoram) and bay leaf about an hour before cooking.

To roast pork in the English style, score the skin and rub it with fat and salt. Roast according to the chart—the crackling should be crisp at the end of the cooking time. Serve with applesauce or baked apples and gravy.

SERVES FOUR TO SIX

3 lb (1½ kg) boned loin of pork, skinned and rolled
2 garlic cloves, slivered
Sage
1 teaspoon black peppercorns, coarsely crushed
Rind and juice of 1 lemon
½ teaspoon salt
1 tablespoon olive oil
1 cup (250 ml) white wine

Carving a shoulder of lamb

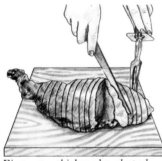

First cut a thick wedge-shaped slice. Then carve to your left.

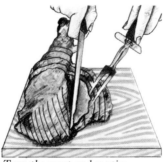

Turn the meat and continue slicing down to the bone.

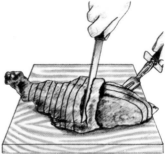

Now carve from the first cut down to the shank bone.

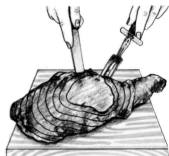

Turn the meat over, cut away the fat and slice across.

Carving a leg of lamb

First cut a thick wedge-shaped slice then carve on either side.

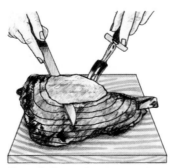

Turn the leg over, cut away the fat and carve across.

Carving ribs of beef

Remove the chine bone, loosen the meat from the ribs and slice.

Make downward cuts, slanting the knife to get larger slices.

Preheat the oven to 375°F (190°C).

Trim the pork of any excess fat. Using a sharp knife, make a number of incisions in the meat and insert the garlic slivers and a little sage. Mix the peppercorns, lemon rind and juice, salt and olive oil together and rub over the pork.

Put the pork on a rack in a roasting pan and roast for 2 to 2¼ hours or until the meat is thoroughly cooked. Test the meat by piercing it in the center with a sharp knife—if the juices run clear it is done.

Lift out the meat and put it on a carving board and keep warm. Pour away the fat in the roasting pan and put in the wine. Put the pan over heat and bring the wine to a boil, stirring and scraping. Boil rapidly to reduce the gravy. Adjust the seasoning and serve.

Stuffed loin of pork

SERVES SIX TO EIGHT

½ lb (225 g) prunes, soaked for 3 hours in cold water and drained

2 medium-sized tart apples, peeled, cored and finely chopped
2 teaspoons brown sugar
Finely grated rind of 1 lemon
5 lb (2½ kg) boned loin of pork
¼ cup (50 g) butter
2 tablespoons white wine
1 cup (250 ml) sour cream

Put the prunes into a saucepan with enough cold water to cover. Bring to a boil over moderate heat and simmer for 15 minutes or until the prunes are tender.

Drain the prunes, and when they are cold enough to handle, remove the pits and chop the flesh. Mix with the apples, sugar and lemon rind.

Lay the pork, fat side down, on the work surface. Cover the meat, to within 1 inch (2 cm) of the short ends, with the prune stuffing and roll it up tightly. Tie the roll at ½-inch (1-cm) intervals with trussing string.

Preheat the oven to 350°F (180°C).

Melt the butter in a roasting pan over moderate heat. Add the pork roll and brown it well on all sides.

Roast the meat for about 3½ hours or until it is cooked and the juices run clear when it is pierced with the point of a sharp knife.

Remove the meat from the oven and carve it into thick slices. Put the slices on a warmed serving dish and keep hot.

Pour off all the fat from the roasting pan. Put the pan over moderate heat and add the wine. Scrape the bottom of the pan to dislodge any sediment. Add the cream and cook gently until the sauce is hot and smooth. Pour the sauce over the pork and serve immediately.

Pork spareribs

SERVES FOUR

3½ to 4 lb (1½ to 2 kg) pork spareribs, trimmed and cut into 2-rib pieces

MARINADE

4 tablespoons clear honey
Juice of 1 lemon
1 tablespoon French mustard
2 tablespoons tomato paste
3 tablespoons soy sauce
¼ teaspoon cayenne pepper
Salt
1 teaspoon grated ginger root
2 garlic cloves, crushed

Combine the marinade ingredients in a saucepan, and simmer for 2 minutes. Set aside to cool.

Put the spareribs into a large dish. Pour over the marinade and set aside for at least 12 hours, turning once.

Preheat the oven to 350°F (180°C).

Drain the spareribs and put them into a roasting pan. Reserve the marinade.

Roast the spareribs for 1 hour. Lift out the ribs and pour away the fat. Increase the oven temperature to 425°F (220°C) and put the ribs back into the roasting pan, brush with the marinade and return to the oven for 15 minutes or until crisp. Brush once again with the marinade during the last five minutes.

Raised pork pie

Press the dough over an upturned, lightly greased jar.

Turn right side up, remove the jar, put in the filling and cover.

Put a double thickness of paper around the pie and tie to secure.

After baking, pour the stock through a funnel into the pie.

Beef Wellington

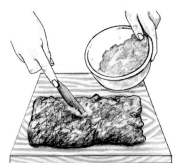

Spread the top and sides of the fillet with pâté and duxelles.

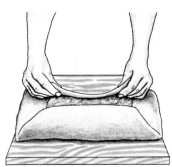

Roll out the pastry and put the fillet in the center.

Enclose the meat in the pastry, dampen well and seal the ends.

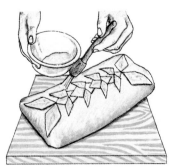

Decorate the top with pastry leaves and brush with beaten egg.

Meat and game

Roast suckling pig

SERVES ABOUT FIFTEEN

**1 suckling pig weighing
about 12 lb (6 kg)**
4 tablespoons seasoned flour
¼ cup (50 g) butter
**1 lb (450 g) mushrooms,
chopped**
½ lb (225 g) pig's liver, chopped
4 lb (2 kg) ground veal
2 teaspoons salt
½ teaspoon pepper
1 teaspoon allspice
**2 tablespoons each parsley
and thyme**
1 teaspoon sage
½ cup (125 ml) sherry
2 eggs, beaten
1 lb (450 g) chestnuts, peeled
2 cups (500 ml) chicken stock
1 stuffed green olive
16 small red apples, baked
**1¾ cups (425 ml) cranberry
sauce**

Preheat the oven to 450°F
(220°C).

Rub the suckling pig with the
seasoned flour. Cover the feet,
ears and tail with foil.

Melt the butter in a frying pan
and fry the mushrooms until
soft. Tip the mushrooms into a
large mixing bowl. Add the liver,
veal, salt, pepper, allspice, herbs,
sherry and eggs and mix well.

Stuff the pig with the mixture
and sew up. Put a block of wood
in its mouth and arrange it,
kneeling, on a rack in the oven
with a roasting pan underneath.
Roast for 15 minutes, then reduce
the oven temperature to 325°F
(170°C) and continue roasting
for about 9 hours or for 35
minutes per pound (weighed
with stuffing), until thoroughly
cooked. Baste frequently with
the pan drippings.

Meanwhile, put the chestnuts
in a saucepan, cover with the
stock and simmer for 40 minutes
or until they are tender. Drain
the chestnuts. Empty the roasting pan of almost all the drippings, put in the chestnuts and
roast for the last 30 minutes.

Cover the pig with foil if it
is browning too much. When
cooked transfer the pig to a
wooden board, put a slice of olive
in each eye socket and replace
the block in its mouth with a red
apple.

Garnish with the chestnuts
and the baked apples, filled with
the cranberry sauce.

To carve, first separate the
shoulders and legs from the carcass. Then cut the ribs into
chops.

Baked ham

This method of cooking is ideal
for whole hams that may be too
large to fit into a saucepan.

SERVES TEN

**1 ham, about 15 lb (7 kg),
soaked in cold water
overnight**
8 cups (900 g) flour
2½ cups (625 ml) water

Preheat the oven to 300°F
(160°C).

Rinse and dry the ham. Remove the skin. Put the flour in a
large bowl and mix in the water
to make a dough. Roll out the
dough large enough to enclose
the ham completely. There must
be no gaps or holes in the dough.
Dampen the edges and seal. Put
in a large roasting pan and bake
for 6 hours or for 25 minutes per
pound plus 30 minutes.

Take the ham out of the oven
and remove and discard the
pastry covering. The ham is now
ready to be served, glazed in the
oven or covered in browned
bread crumbs.

Honey-glazed ham

SERVES TEN

**1 baked or boiled ham,
about 15 lb (7 kg)**

GLAZE

½ cup (125 g) honey
**Grated rind and juice of 1
orange**
**1 tablespoon prepared
mustard**
About 24 whole cloves

Preheat the oven to 425°F
(210°C).

Score the ham fat diagonally at
1-inch (2-cm) intervals, first in
one direction, then in the other,
to make a diamond pattern.

Mix the honey with the orange
rind, mustard and enough orange
juice to make a spreadable mixture. Spread the ham with the
glaze. Stud the corners of each
diamond with the cloves. Put the
ham in a roasting pan and bake
for 30 minutes.

Remove from the oven. Cool
completely before serving.

Haunch of venison

Serve with braised celery and
garlic mashed potatoes.

SERVES EIGHT TO TEN

**5 lb (2½ kg) haunch of
venison**
**½ lb (225 g) salt pork, cut into
strips**
Salt
2 tablespoons whisky
**½ cup (125 ml) whipping
cream**
**16 to 20 prunes, soaked and
simmered for 10 minutes**
**12 chestnuts, peeled and
simmered in stock for 40
minutes**
2 lemons, cut into wedges
**1½ cups (375 ml) cranberry
sauce**

MARINADE

2 cups (500 ml) red wine
4 tablespoons wine vinegar
8 tablespoons olive oil
Bouquet garni
12 peppercorns, bruised
6 juniper berries, bruised
3 cloves
2 carrots, sliced
2 celery stalks, sliced
2 onions, sliced

Lard the venison with the salt
pork. Combine all the marinade
ingredients in a large bowl. Put
the venison into the marinade
and leave for 2 days, turning
occasionally.

Preheat the oven to 350°F
(180°C).

Lift out and dry the venison.
Strain and reserve the marinade.
Put the herbs, celery, carrots and
onions from the marinade into a
roasting pan. Rub the venison
with a little salt and put it on top
of the herbs and vegetables.
Roast for 2 hours basting occasionally with the reserved
marinade.

Increase the oven temperature
to 400°F (200°C) and cook for
30 minutes. Lift out the venison
and put it on a heated serving
dish. Warm the whisky in a ladle,
ignite it and pour it over the meat.
Keep the venison warm while
you make the gravy.

Pour off the fat from the roasting pan. Pour in the remaining
marinade and bring to a boil
on top of the stove, stirring and
scraping the bottom of the pan.
Boil until the liquid is reduced
by one-third. Remove the roasting pan from the heat and stir in

the cream, adjust the seasoning
and strain the gravy.

Arrange the prunes and chestnuts around the venison together
with the lemon wedges. Serve
with the cranberry sauce and
gravy.

Pork pie

SERVES FOUR

**Hot water pastry for a
2-crust 9-inch (23-cm) pie**
**¾ lb (350 g) lean pork, cut
into ¾-inch (2-cm) cubes**
**½ lb (225 g) breakfast bacon,
thinly sliced and cut into
pieces**
1 teaspoon sage
½ teaspoon allspice
¼ teaspoon salt
Pepper
Beaten egg
**1¼ cups (315 ml) degreased
jellied stock, made from
pig's feet**

Preheat the oven to 350°F
(180°C).

Lightly grease the outer base
and sides of a 2-pound (900 g)
jam jar, and grease a baking
sheet.

Set aside one-quarter of the
pastry dough for the lid and keep
warm. Spread the remaining
dough into a circle and put it over
the base of the upturned jam jar.
Press the dough down evenly
over the jar with your hands until
it reaches the shoulder of the jar
and is about ½ inch (1 cm) thick
all around. Set aside to cool.

Cut a double thickness of
brown or waxed paper the same
depth as the dough case and
long enough to go around its
circumference. Wrap the paper
around the dough and secure it
in place with paper clips or
string.

Turn the jam jar right side up
onto the baking sheet and gently
lift out the jar leaving the dough
case.

Mix the pork, bacon, sage,
allspice and salt and pepper in a
bowl. Carefully fill the dough
case with the meat and trim the
top level with the meat.

Press the remaining dough
into a circle to make the lid. Put
it on top of the pie, dampen the
edges and pinch to seal.

Use any trimming to make
leaves or flowers. Dampen them
and arrange on top of the pie.

Brush with the beaten egg. Pierce a hole in the center of the pie to allow the steam to escape. Bake the pie for $2\frac{1}{4}$ hours, removing the paper collar halfway through the cooking time.

Remove the pie from the oven and let cool.

Heat the jellied stock until it has melted. Using a funnel placed in the steam vent, pour in the cooled stock until it comes to just below the pie lid.

Chill the pie in the refrigerator for at least 4 hours.

Steak and kidney pie

SERVES FOUR

$1\frac{1}{2}$ **lb (700 g) round steak, trimmed of all fat and cut into 1-inch (2-cm) cubes**
$\frac{1}{2}$ **lb (225 g) kidney, cut into 1-inch (2-cm) cubes**
1 tablespoon seasoned flour
3 tablespoons drippings
2 medium-sized onions, chopped
$\frac{1}{2}$ **lb (225 g) mushrooms, quartered**
Bouquet garni
1 cup (250 ml) beef stock
Salt and pepper
1 recipe English flaky pastry
1 egg, beaten

Roll the meat in the seasoned flour, coating it well.

Melt the drippings in a sauté pan. Add the meat, a few pieces at a time and fry quickly until browned all over. Transfer the meat as it browns to a saucepan.

Add the onions to the sauté pan, fry until lightly browned and add to the meat. Fry the mushrooms for 2 to 3 minutes and put them in the saucepan. Put in the bouquet garni. Pour the stock into the sauté pan and bring to a boil, stirring and scraping the bottom of the pan. Season to taste and pour the stock over the meat and vegetables. Cover the pan and simmer over very low heat for $1\frac{1}{2}$ hours or until the meat is tender. Discard the bouquet garni.

Preheat the oven to 375°F (190°C).

Using a slotted spoon, transfer the meat and vegetables to a deep pie pan. If the cooking liquid is too thin, thicken it by boiling it down or by adding a little beurre manié, or a spoonful of flour mixed in cold water. Pour the

boiling liquid into the pie pan.

Roll out the pastry dough to make a lid. Dampen the edges of the pie pan and put the dough on top. Trim and press down to seal. Flute the edges. Use the trimmings to make flowers and leaves and decorate the top of the pie. Make a hole in the center for the steam to escape and brush all over with the egg.

Bake for 40 minutes or until the top is puffed up and golden.

Cornish pasty

SERVES TWO TO FOUR

Pie pastry made from 2 cups (225 g) flour, and lard
1 egg, lightly beaten

FILLING
$\frac{1}{2}$ **lb (225 g) rump steak or tenderloin of beef, finely chopped**
2 tablespoons finely chopped onion
$\frac{1}{4}$ **lb (125 g) potatoes, thinly sliced**
2 tablespoons chopped turnip
Salt and pepper
Thyme

Preheat the oven to 350°F (180°C). Lightly grease two baking sheets.

First make the filling. Mix the meat with the vegetables. Season well with the salt, pepper and a large pinch of thyme.

Divide the dough in half and

Three ways of baking meat in pastry: beef Wellington, top left; Cornish pasty, top right and pork pie.

roll each half into a circle about 8 inches (20 cm) in diameter.

Divide the filling between the two circles, laying it down the middle. Brush around the edges of the dough with the beaten egg. Lift the dough on either side of the filling to meet on top and pinch to seal all along the edge.

Pierce the pasties with a sharp knife to make 2 vents for the steam to escape.

Put the pasties on the baking sheets, brush all over with the egg and bake for 1 hour.

Vegetables

Most root vegetables and vegetable fruit can be cooked in the oven. Small new potatoes can be baked in foil with a little butter, salt and pepper and a sprinkling of mint or parsley. Larger potatoes may be baked in their jackets, or peeled and quartered, parboiled for five minutes and roasted around a large piece of meat—they will take about forty minutes. Alternatively, potatoes can be cooked au gratin with cheese and cream.

For a main course there is a wide range of recipes for stuffed vegetable fruit. Eggplants, tomatoes, zucchinis and peppers make excellent cases for such ingredients as rice and ground meat, flaked fish and shellfish, grated cheese, dried fruit, herbs and nuts.

Baked potatoes

Baked potatoes are delicious with just a pat of butter, but they can also be scooped out, mixed with other ingredients and baked again for 10 minutes.

SERVES FOUR

4 fairly large potatoes, scrubbed clean and dried
2 tablespoon butter

Preheat the oven to 375°F (190°C).

Prick the potatoes all over with a fork and then rub them with the butter. Place them on the oven rack or on a baking sheet and bake for 1 to 1½ hours or until the skin is very crisp and the potatoes are tender in the center—test them with a fork. Serve hot.

Ham-stuffed potatoes

SERVES FOUR

4 hot baked potatoes
2 tablespoons butter
1 cup (125 g) diced smoked ham
2 teaspoons chopped fresh chives
2 tablespoons heavy cream
Salt and freshly ground black pepper

Preheat the oven to 375°F (190°C).

Cut a thin slice off the top of each potato and set it aside. Using a teaspoon, scoop the flesh out into a bowl, taking care to keep the skins intact. Add the remaining ingredients and mash them together with a fork. Spoon the mixture into the skins and place them upright in a baking dish small enough to prevent the potatoes from falling over. Replace the lids if you like or replace them just before serving if you want the top to brown. Bake for 10 to 15 minutes or until very hot. Serve immediately.

Finnan haddie potatoes

SERVES FOUR

Scoop out the flesh of 4 baked potatoes and mix it with ½ pound (225 g) flaked cooked finnan haddie and 2 tablespoons sour cream.

Garlic mashed potatoes

SERVES FOUR

2 lb (900 g) potatoes, mashed
¼ cup (50 ml) cream
¼ cup (50 g) butter
2 large egg yolks
4 garlic cloves, crushed
Salt and pepper
Small pinch nutmeg

Preheat the oven to 375°F (190°C).

Put all the ingredients into a mixing bowl and beat well with a wooden spoon to mix the ingredients together thoroughly. Spoon the mixture into a pastry tube with a large star nozzle and either squeeze out the mixture into a baking dish, or squeeze out individual circles on a greased baking sheet.

Place the dish or baking sheet in the oven and bake for 20 minutes or until lightly browned.

Potatoes à la dauphinoise

SERVES FOUR

¼ cup (50 g) butter
1 garlic clove, crushed
2 lb (900 g) potatoes, peeled, thinly sliced and washed
1¼ cups (125 g) grated Gruyère cheese
Salt and pepper
Grated nutmeg
1¼ cups (315 ml) scalded milk or cream
1 egg, beaten

Preheat the oven to 350°F (180°C).

Mash half the butter with the garlic clove and use it to grease a shallow baking dish. Place a layer of potatoes in the bottom of the dish and sprinkle with a little of the cheese, salt, pepper and nutmeg. Repeat the layers until you have used all the potatoes and nearly all the cheese. Beat the milk or cream and egg together and strain the mixture over the potatoes. Sprinkle over the remaining cheese. Cut the remaining butter into small pieces and dot it over the top. Bake for about 1¼ hours or until the potatoes are tender and the top is golden. Serve at once.

Sweet potato soufflé

SERVES FOUR

1 teaspoon olive oil
1 lb (450 g) sweet potatoes, boiled and mashed
4 tablespoons cream
1 tablespoon sugar
Salt
2 tablespoons butter
1 orange
3 egg yolks
½ teaspoon ground cinnamon
Pinch grated nutmeg
4 egg whites, stiffly beaten

Preheat the oven to 375°F (190°C).

Using the teaspoon of oil, grease a medium-sized soufflé dish and set it aside.

Put the potato in a bowl and add the cream, sugar, salt and butter. Beat the mixture with a wooden spoon until smooth.

Grate the orange rind and add it to the purée, with the chopped orange flesh. Beat in the egg yolks, with the cinnamon and nutmeg. Fold in the stiffly beaten egg whites. Pour the mixture into the soufflé dish and bake for 45 minutes or until the soufflé is well risen and golden brown on the top. Serve immediately.

Boston baked beans

This is traditionally served with Boston steamed bread.

SERVES SIX

2 lb (900 g) dried beans, soaked overnight in cold water and drained
¼ cup (50 g) dark brown sugar
4 tablespoons molasses
Salt and pepper
1 tablespoon dry mustard
1 lb (450 g) salt pork, cut into 2-inch (5-cm) cubes, blanched for 5 minutes in boiling water and drained
1 onion, peeled

Put the beans into a large saucepan and add enough cold salted water to cover. Bring to a boil over high heat, skimming off the scum as it rises. Reduce the heat to low, cover the pan and simmer for 1 hour, adding more boiling water if necessary. Drain the beans in a colander.

Preheat the oven to 250°F (130°C).

Mix the sugar, molasses, salt, pepper and mustard together. Layer the beans, molasses mixture and salt pork in a deep ovenproof casserole and bury the onion in the middle. Add enough boiling water to cover and put the lid on the casserole. Bake for 6 to 8 hours or until the beans are tender. As the water evaporates, add more because the beans must be kept moist. Remove the lid for the last hour of baking to let the top brown. Serve hot.

Eggplant a la nîmoise

SERVES TWO

3 tablespoons olive oil
1 large eggplant, cut in half, degorged, rinsed and dried
1 cup (125 g) cooked rice
3 tomatoes, peeled, seeded and chopped
1 tablespoon tomato paste
1 garlic clove, crushed
1 tablespoon chopped fresh basil
1 teaspoon chopped fresh chives
Salt and pepper

Preheat the oven to 350°F (180°C).

Heat the oil in a frying pan and add the eggplant, skin side up. Reduce the heat to low, cover the pan and cook for about 10 minutes. Remove the eggplant halves from the pan and drain them well. Scoop out the pulp with a teaspoon, leaving the skin intact. Chop the pulp and mix with the rice, tomatoes, tomato paste, garlic, basil and chives. Season to taste. Fill the skins with the stuffing and place them in a baking dish. Sprinkle with a little oil from the frying pan and bake for about 35 minutes. Serve at once.

Moussaka

SERVES FOUR

Olive oil
1½ lb (700 g) eggplants, thinly sliced, degorged, rinsed and patted dry
2 tablespoons butter
1 onion, finely chopped
3 large garlic cloves, crushed
1½ lb (700 g) ground lamb
1½ lb (700 g) tomatoes, chopped
2 tablespoons tomato paste
1 teaspoon dried thyme
1 teaspoon dried rosemary
Salt and freshly ground black pepper
1½ cups (375 ml) mornay sauce
2 large egg yolks
2 tablespoons grated Parmesan cheese

Pour a little olive oil into a large frying pan—it should be just enough to make a thin film over the bottom. Heat the frying pan over fairly high heat and, when hot, add enough eggplant slices to cover the base in a single layer. Press the slices down so they are coated with some of the oil and turn them over quickly. Fry for 1½ minutes on each side or until they are lightly browned.

Set the fried slices aside on a plate and continue frying the remaining slices in the same way, adding more oil to the pan.

When all the eggplants have been fried, set them aside and make the meat sauce. Melt the butter in a saucepan and add the onion. Fry, stirring, for 5 minutes then add the garlic and lamb and fry for about 8 minutes or until the lamb is browned. Stir in the tomatoes, tomato paste, thyme, rosemary and plenty of salt and pepper. Reduce the heat to low, cover the pan and simmer, stirring occasionally, for 15 minutes. Remove the pan from the heat and set aside.

Preheat the oven to 375°F (190°C).

Mix the mornay sauce with the egg yolks and set aside.

Layer the eggplant slices and meat sauce in a large, round baking dish, beginning and ending with the eggplant. Spoon the mornay sauce over the last layer of eggplant slices to cover them completely, and sprinkle over the Parmesan cheese. Bake in the oven for about 1 hour or until the top is well browned.

Mushroom vol-au-vents

SERVES FOUR

2 tablespoons butter
½ lb (225 g) small mushrooms, sliced
1 cup (125 g) cubed cooked ham
1¼ cups (315 ml) velouté sauce
3 tablespoons cream
⅔ cup (50 g) grated Gruyère cheese
Salt and pepper
4 vol-au-vent cases

Preheat the oven to 375°F (190°C).

Melt the butter in a saucepan.

Add the mushrooms and fry, stirring, for 3 to 4 minutes.

Stir in the ham, velouté sauce, cream, Gruyère cheese and salt and pepper to taste.

Spoon the mixture into the vol-au-vent cases and bake for 10 to 15 minutes or until bubbling on top and heated through.

Belgian endive au gratin

This dish can also be made with broccoli, celery and fennel.

SERVES FOUR

1 teaspoon butter
1 tablespoon sugar
1 teaspoon lemon juice
4 large heads Belgian endive, washed and trimmed
4 large slices lean ham
1¼ cups (315 ml) mornay sauce
2 tablespoons cream
1 tablespoon grated Parmesan cheese

Preheat the oven to 375°F (190°C). Using the teaspoon of butter, grease a medium-sized baking dish and set it aside.

Fill a medium-sized saucepan with salted water and add the sugar and lemon juice. Bring to a boil over moderate heat and add the Belgian endive. When the water has come back to a boil, reduce the heat to low and simmer for 10 minutes. Drain and reserve 2 tablespoons of the cooking liquid.

Wrap one Belgian endive in each ham slice and place the rolls in a baking dish. Mix the mornay sauce with the reserved cooking liquid and the cream and pour over the rolls to cover them completely. Sprinkle with the Parmesan cheese and bake for 30 minutes. Serve hot.

Stuffed baked squash

This needs no vegetable accompaniment other than garlic mashed potatoes or croquette potatoes.

SERVES FOUR

3 lb (1½ kg) squash
1 tablespoon oil
2 onions, chopped
¾ lb (350 g) sausage meat
2 tomatoes, skinned and chopped
2 tablespoons tomato paste
½ cup (50 g) cooked rice
Salt and pepper
½ teaspoon dried sage
1 tablespoon butter
1 cup (250 ml) tomato sauce, hot

Preheat the oven to 375°F (190°C).

Cut the stalk end off the squash and set it aside. Scoop the seeds out of the squash with a metal spoon and discard them. Bring a large saucepan of salted water to a boil. Add the squash and blanch it for 5 minutes. Drain well and set aside.

Heat the oil in a small frying pan and fry the onions, stirring, for 6 minutes or until soft. Stir in the sausage meat and cook, stirring, for 15 minutes. Stir in the tomatoes, tomato paste, rice, seasoning and sage. Remove the pan from the heat and stuff the mixture into the squash. Replace the stalk end, securing it with skewers or toothpicks.

Using the butter, grease a piece of foil large enough to enclose the squash. Wrap the squash in the foil and place it in a baking pan. Put in the oven and bake for 1 hour or until tender. Remove the squash from the oven and unwrap it. Cut it into thick slices and serve with the tomato sauce.

Vol-au-vent cases

To make a large vol-au-vent, cut out a circle of puff pastry.

Lightly score a smaller circle and a pattern on the dough.

Small cases are made with two sizes of biscuit cutters.

Once baked, the insides are scooped out. Retain the lids.

Vegetables

Stuffed grape leaves

Pickled grape leaves can be bought from Greek grocers. Blanch fresh leaves in boiling water for 2 minutes.

SERVES FOUR

½ lb (225 g) ground lamb
½ cup (125 g) uncooked rice, washed, soaked in cold water for 30 minutes, blanched for 2 minutes and drained
3 tablespoons tomato paste
2 tablespoons chopped mint
Salt and pepper
2 garlic cloves, crushed, plus 1 garlic clove, sliced
2 tablespoons lemon juice
16 grape leaves
1 cup (250 ml) hot chicken stock

Preheat the oven to 325°F (170°C).

Put the lamb, rice, 1 tablespoon of the tomato paste, half the mint, salt, pepper, crushed garlic and lemon juice in a bowl and mix together well.

Lay a leaf out flat on your work surface. Put a little filling on the stem end of the leaf and fold the stem end over. Fold the sides inward and roll up the leaf, from the stem end, to make a tight, cigar-shaped package.

Lay the grape leaves in a greased, shallow baking dish in a single layer, packing them in tightly so they do not open out during cooking. Pack the garlic slices and remaining mint between the packages.

Mix the chicken stock with the remaining tomato paste and pour the mixture over the rolls. Place the dish in the oven and bake for 1 hour or until the rice inside the leaves is tender.

Baked tomatoes

SERVES FOUR

8 large tomatoes, washed
Salt and pepper
Dried basil
1 tablespoon butter
1 shallot, finely chopped
¾ lb (350 g) mushrooms, sliced
4 cups (450 g) cooked diced chicken
2 tablespoons cream
4 tablespoons bread crumbs

4 tablespoons grated Gruyère cheese
2 tablespoons grated Parmesan cheese
Nutmeg
4 tablespoons melted butter

Preheat the oven to 375°F (190°C).

Cut the tops off the tomatoes and scoop out the flesh. Sprinkle the insides with a little salt, pepper and basil. Put the tomatoes in a greased baking dish.

Melt the butter in a saucepan. Add the shallot and fry gently, stirring, until it is soft. Add the mushrooms and fry for 2 minutes. Stir in the chicken and cream and season to taste. Stuff the tomatoes with this mixture.

From left to right : stuffed grape leaves, baked tomatoes, baked stuffed onions and baked spiced avocados.

Mix the bread crumbs, Gruyère and Parmesan together and season lightly. Spoon this over the chicken mixture. Grate a little nutmeg over the filling and sprinkle liberally with the melted butter.

Bake for 15 minutes or until the tomatoes are heated through and brown and bubbling on top.

Baked stuffed onions
SERVES FOUR

3 large onions, boiled until tender and drained
2 tablespoons butter
2 tablespoons fresh white bread crumbs
½ lb (225 g) lean ground beef
1 tablespoon chopped parsley

Salt and pepper
2 tablespoons heavy cream
2 tablespoons melted butter

Preheat the oven to 375°F (190°C).

When the onions are cool enough to handle, slit each one on one side down to the center and carefully slip off about 8 of the largest layers. Chop up one of the remaining onions and discard the other two.

Melt the butter in a frying pan and add the chopped onion. Fry, stirring, until it is golden.

Put the fried onion in a mixing bowl and add the bread crumbs, beef, parsley, salt and pepper and cream. Beat well with a wooden spoon to mix. Put 2

teaspoons of the filling on each layer and roll up the layers.

Place rolls upright in a greased baking dish, sprinkle over the melted butter and bake for 30 minutes or until browned.

Baked spiced avocados
SERVES FOUR

2 large ripe avocados
2 garlic cloves, crushed
1 teaspoon salt
Few drops Tabasco sauce
1 tablespoon ground coriander
1 teaspoon cumin seeds
¼ teaspoon ground ginger
2 teaspoons mixed spice
½ lb (225 g) cooked shrimp
2 tablespoons sour cream

1 teaspoon lemon juice
4 lemon wedges

Preheat the oven to 350°F (180°C).

Cut the avocados in half and remove the seeds. Using a teaspoon, scoop all the flesh out into a bowl, being careful not to damage the skins.

Mash the avocado flesh with a fork until it is smooth. Stir in the remaining ingredients, except the lemon wedges. Pile the mixture into the reserved skins and carefully transfer them to a baking dish. Place the dish in the oven and bake for 20 minutes. Transfer the avocados to individual plates and serve with the lemon wedges.

Fruit

Simple but delicious desserts can be made by baking such fruit as apples, pears or bananas: for example, core and stuff the apples or pears with a mixture of raisins, honey, cloves and cinnamon, score the skin, brush with melted butter and bake in a fairly hot oven until tender. Bananas are much improved if they are baked with a little butter, rum, brown sugar and lemon juice and even the hardest pears are delicious cooked in red wine.

Fruit pies are usually covered with plain pie pastry, pâte sucrée or flaky pastry. A nine-inch (23-cm) pie pan will take about two pounds (900 g) of fruit. Although the traditional fillings such as apple and cherries are always popular, try mixing such fruit as strawberries and rhubarb, prunes and apricots or peaches and oranges.

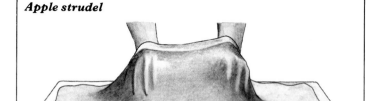

Apple strudel

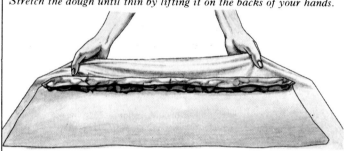

Stretch the dough until thin by lifting it on the backs of your hands.

Lay the filling in a strip then lift the cloth to roll the dough over.

Mince pies

MAKES ONE 8-INCH (20-CM) PIE
OR TWELVE INDIVIDUAL PIES

Pastry for a double-crust pie
3 cups (700 g) mincemeat
Sugar

Preheat the oven to 425°F (220°C).

Roll out two-thirds of the pastry dough and line an 8-inch (20-cm) pie pan. Spoon in the mincemeat. Roll out the remaining dough and cover the pie.

Bake for 40 to 50 minutes. Individual pies will take 20 to 25 minutes.

Mincemeat

Mincemeat will keep for up to 1 year in a cool place.

MAKES ABOUT NINE POUNDS
(4 KG)

1 lb (450 g) currants, coarsely chopped
1 lb (450 g) seedless raisins, coarsely chopped
1 lb (450 g) golden raisins, coarsely chopped
½ lb (225 g) candied peel, chopped
3 large apples, grated
1 lb (450 g) suet, shredded
¼ lb (100 g) almonds, chopped
2¼ cups (450 g) soft brown sugar
Rind and juice of 2 lemons
1 teaspoon mixed spice
1 teaspoon ground nutmeg
⅔ cup (150 ml) brandy

Wash and dry the fruit. Mix all the ingredients together, moistening with the brandy. Spoon the mixture into jars. Cover tightly and keep for at least 1 month before using.

English apple pie

SERVES FOUR TO SIX

2 lb (900 g) tart apples, peeled, cored and thinly sliced
1 quince, peeled, cored and thinly sliced
Granulated sugar
Pastry for a single-crust pie

Preheat the oven to 400°F (200°C).

Layer the apple and quince in a pie pan. Sprinkle each layer with sugar. Shape the top layer of apples in a dome to come above the top of the pan. Pour in ¼ cup of water.

Roll out the pastry dough ¼ inch (½ cm) thick. Cut a strip of dough to go around the top of the pie pan. Dampen the strip and press it down on the rim of the pan. Lay the rest of the dough on top to form a lid. Trim the dough and flute the edges. Brush the top with water and dredge with sugar.

Bake for 15 minutes. Reduce the oven temperature to 375°F (190°C) and continue baking for 25 minutes.

Apple dumplings

SERVES SIX

2 recipes shortcrust pastry
6 tart apples, peeled and cored
½ cup (125 g) brown sugar
1 teaspoon ground cinnamon
12 cloves
Milk
Sugar
2 cups (500 ml) custard sauce

Preheat the oven to 400°F (200°C). Lightly grease a large

baking sheet with butter.

Divide the pastry dough into 6 equal pieces, reserving a little for decoration. Pat each piece into a circle. Put an apple on each circle and work the dough up the sides of the apple, leaving the top open. Mix the sugar and cinnamon together. Spoon the mixture into the centers of the apples, putting 2 cloves in each cavity. Seal the pastry over the tops of the apples.

Put the apples upside down on the baking sheet. Roll out the reserved pastry dough and cut out leaves. Decorate the apple dumplings, brush with milk and dust with sugar. Bake for 30 minutes.

Serve hot with the custard.

French apple flan

SERVES FOUR TO SIX

1 recipe pâte sucrée
1½ lb (700 g) tart apples, peeled, cored and sliced
2 tablespoons sugar
Grated rind of 1 lemon
4 green dessert apples, cored and thinly sliced
3 tablespoons melted butter
4 tablespoons strained marmalade, warm

Preheat the oven to 425°F (220°C).

Roll out the pastry dough and line a 9-inch (23-cm) pie pan with it. Build up a fluted rim and bake blind. Reset the oven to 400°F (200°C).

Meanwhile, simmer the cooking apples with a tablespoon of water until soft. Mash with a wooden spoon to make a purée. Stir in the sugar and lemon rind. Set aside to cool slightly.

Fill the pastry shell with the apple purée. Arrange the sliced apples in overlapping circles on top of the purée. Brush with the butter. Bake for 25 minutes or until the apples are lightly browned. Remove from the oven and brush the top with the marmalade.

Serve hot or cold.

Apple strudel

Serve apple strudel warm or cold with whipped cream.

SERVES TEN TO TWELVE

1 recipe strudel pastry
1 cup (225 g) butter, melted
Sifted confectioners' sugar

STRUDEL FILLING

4 tablespoons toasted bread crumbs
⅔ cup (100 g) raisins
3 lb (1½ kg) tart apples, peeled, cored and finely sliced
Grated rind of 1 lemon

1 tablespoon lemon juice
¼ cup (50 g) ground almonds
2 cups (125 g) blanched,
    toasted, chopped almonds
½ cup (125 g) sugar
2 teaspoons ground
    cinnamon

First prepare the filling. Lightly mix all the ingredients together in a bowl.

To shape the strudel, cover a large table with a cloth or sheet. Dust the cloth lightly with flour. Put the dough in the center of the cloth and roll it out as thinly as possible.

Put your hands, palms downward, under the dough. Gradually stretch the dough by lifting it on the backs of your hands until it is paper thin. Work your way around the table stretching the dough to a uniform thickness.

If a few small holes appear in the dough do not worry. When the dough is as thin as paper, straighten the edges with a pair of scissors. Preheat the oven to 425°F (220°C). Grease 2 or 3 baking sheets.

Brush the dough with two-thirds of the butter. Starting at one of the shorter ends, lay the filling in a long strip on the dough. Leave a clear 2-inch (5-cm) margin on each side and in front of you. Fold the margins of the two longer sides over the filling and brush the folds with butter.

Now lift up the cloth in front of you and roll the dough over the filling. Continue rolling until the filling is completely rolled up in the dough.

Using a sharp knife, cut the strudel into lengths to fit on the baking sheets. Put the strudel on

the baking sheets with the seams underneath. Brush generously with butter and put in the oven. Reduce the oven temperature to 350°F (180°C) and bake for 45 minutes or until the strudel is golden brown on top.

Serve the strudel warm or cold, dusted with confectioners' sugar.

Rhubarb crumble
Use other fruit—apples, apples and black currants, red currants or gooseberries—to make crumble. Serve with cream or with a custard sauce.

SERVES FOUR

2 lb (900 g) rhubarb, cut into chunks
Grated rind of 1 large orange
½ cup (125 g) sugar

CRUMBLE TOPPING
1 cup (125 g) flour
1 teaspoon ground cinnamon
6 tablespoons butter
2 tablespoons sugar

Preheat the oven to 375°F (190°C). Butter a medium-sized soufflé or deep baking dish.

Put the rhubarb, orange rind and sugar into the baking dish and mix well.

To make the crumble, mix the flour and cinnamon in a bowl. Work in the butter and mix in the sugar. Pile the crumble mixture on top of the fruit. Do not worry if the topping is higher than the top of the dish, it will sink when the fruit cooks and softens.

Bake the crumble for 45 to 60 minutes or until the top is browned and well settled.

Serve hot or cold.

Cherry flan
When dark Bing cherries are in season use 1½ pounds (700 g) of fresh cherries, remove the pits and poach in a syrup made of 1 cup (250 ml) of water and 5 tablespoons of sugar for 5 minutes. Drain the cherries, return the syrup to the pan and boil it until it thickens. Serve the flan with whipped cream.

SERVES SIX

Almond pastry for a single-crust 9-inch (23-cm) pie
1 lb (450 g) canned, pitted sour cherries
1 tablespoon arrowroot
Grated rind of 1 large lemon
2 tablespoons sugar
1 egg
¼ cup (50 ml) whipping cream

Preheat the oven to 425°F (220°C).

Roll out the pastry dough and with it line a 9-inch (23-cm) pie pan. Bake blind. Remove the pastry shell from the oven and reduce the temperature to 375°F (190°C).

Drain the cherries. Measure out ⅔ cup of the syrup into a saucepan and mix in the arrowroot. Bring the mixture to a boil, stirring, and cook for 1 minute or until thick and smooth.

Arrange the cherries in the pastry shell and spoon the thickened syrup over the top.

Mix the lemon rind with the sugar in a bowl. Add the egg. Put the bowl over barely simmering water and beat until the mixture is thick and pale and leaves a trail when the beater is lifted.

Remove the bowl from the heat and gently fold in the cream. Pour the mixture over the cher-

ries. Bake for 30 minutes or until the top is lightly browned. Serve cool.

Lemon meringue pie
SERVES FOUR TO FIVE
Rich pastry for a single-crust pie
3 tablespoons cornstarch
1 cup (250 ml) water
2 tablespoons sugar
Pinch salt
3 egg yolks
Rind and juice of 2 lemons
2 egg whites
¼ teaspoon cream of tartar
½ cup (125 g) sugar

Preheat the oven to 425°F (220°C).

Roll out the pastry dough, line an 8-inch (20-cm) fluted pie pan and bake blind. Reset the oven to 325°F (170°C).

Mix the cornstarch with the water, sugar and salt in a saucepan. Stir over low heat until the mixture is thick and bubbling. Remove the pan from the heat. Lightly beat the egg yolks in a bowl. Stir in a little of the hot cornstarch mixture then pour into the saucepan, beating all the time. Stir in the lemon rind and juice. Cool the mixture for 15 minutes, stirring occasionally, then pour it into the pastry shell. Set aside to cool.

Meanwhile, beat the egg whites with the cream of tartar until stiff. Gradually beat in the sugar, saving a spoonful to sprinkle on the top. Pile the meringue onto the pie to cover the filling completely. Sprinkle the sugar over the top. Bake for 20 to 25 minutes or until the meringue is crisp and golden. Serve cool.

Baking blind
Baking blind is a method of baking pastry shells without a filling. To prevent the dough in the bottom of the shell from rising, the bottom and sides are lined with foil or waxed paper and weighed down with dried beans or rice. The pastry is baked at 425°F (220°C).
The foil and beans or rice are removed after 15 minutes and the shell is baked for 5 minutes more to brown. Store the beans or rice and use again for baking.

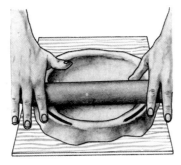
Line the pan with pastry dough.

Trim and flute the edges.

Line with foil and beans or rice.

Fruit

Pear tart

SERVES FOUR TO SIX

**Rich pie pastry for 1-crust
9-inch (23-cm) pie**
1½ tablespoons sugar
1 cup (250 ml) water
**1½ lb (700 g) pears, peeled,
quartered and cored**
1¼ cups (315 ml) cream
1 vanilla bean
2 egg yolks
2 teaspoons cornstarch
**2 tablespoons preserved
ginger, chopped**
**1 tablespoon split blanched
almonds, toasted**

Preheat the oven to 425°F
(220°C).

Roll out the pastry dough, line
a 9-inch (23-cm) pie pan with it
and bake unfilled.

Reset the oven to 325°F
(170°C).

Dissolve 1 tablespoon of the
sugar in the water in a saucepan.
Add the pears and poach them
gently for 12 minutes or until
just tender. Remove the pan
from the heat and let the pears
cool in the syrup.

Scald the cream and the
vanilla bean and set aside for 10
minutes. Remove the vanilla
bean. Beat the egg yolks with the
cornstarch and the remaining
sugar. Stir in the hot cream.

Drain the pears and arrange
them in the pie shell. Sprinkle
the chopped ginger over them.
Strain the custard over the pears.
Bake the tart for 45 minutes or
until the custard is lightly set.

Sprinkle the almonds over the
top and serve warm.

Date bars

MAKES 12

½ lb (225 g) pitted dates
½ cup (125 ml) water
1⅓ cups (125 g) rolled oats
**1 cup (125 g) whole wheat
flour**
2 tablespoons brown sugar
½ teaspoon ground allspice
½ cup (125 g) butter, softened

Preheat the oven to 350°F
(180°C).

Put the dates and water in a
small saucepan and simmer for
15 minutes or until the dates are
soft. Mash the dates into a pulp.
Set aside to cool.

Mix the oats, flour, sugar and
allspice together. Rub in the

butter and mix well together.

Lightly butter a 1½ inch (3-cm)
deep, 8-inch (20cm) square pan.
Spread half the flour and butter
mixture over the bottom of the
pan, pressing it down evenly.
Spread the date pulp over the
top and the remaining flour and
butter mixture over the dates
with your finger-tips.

Bake for 30 minutes. Remove
the pan from the oven. Cut the
mixture into bars in the pan.
Let cool completely before removing from the pan.

Clafoutis

Although the traditional fruit
used in a clafoutis is cherries,
other fruit may also be used.

SERVES FOUR TO SIX

3 eggs
3 tablespoons sugar
**1 cup (125 g) all-purpose
flour**
Pinch salt
2 tablespoons melted butter
1¼ cups (315 ml) milk
**1 lb (450 g) pitted black
cherries**
**2 tablespoons butter, cut into
pieces**
**1 tablespoon confectioners'
sugar**
**1¼ cups (315 ml) custard
sauce**

Preheat the oven to 400°F
(200°C). Butter a 9-inch (23-cm)
pie pan.

Beat the eggs and sugar in a
large bowl until foamy and pale.
Gradually beat in the flour,
salt, the melted butter and milk.
Put the cherries in the pie pan.
Pour over the batter, dot with
the butter and bake for 30
minutes or until the top is firm
to the touch. If the top begins to
brown too much, cover with foil.
Sprinkle with confectioners'
sugar and serve warm with the
custard.

Pineapple upside-down cake

Serve this cake as a dessert with
whipped cream.

SERVES FOUR TO SIX

**½ cup (125 g) soft dark brown
sugar**
**¼ cup (50 g) plus ½ cup (125 g)
butter**
**1 lb (450 g) canned pineapple
slices, drained**
5 to 6 candied cherries

½ cup (125 g) sugar
2 eggs
1 cup (125 g) self-rising flour
¼ teaspoon vanilla extract

Preheat the oven to 350°F
(180°C).

Put the brown sugar and ¼ cup
of the butter in a 10-inch (25-
cm) oval dish about 2 inches
(5 cm) deep. Put the dish in the
oven for a few minutes until the
sugar and butter have melted.

Remove the dish from the oven

and spread the sugar and butter mixture evenly. Arrange the pineapple slices on top. Put the candied cherries in the centers of the pineapple slices. Set aside.

Cream the sugar with the remaining ½ cup of butter in a bowl until the mixture is pale and fluffy.

Beat in the eggs one by one with a tablespoon of flour. Mix in the vanilla extract and fold in the remaining flour. Pour the cake mixture over the pineapple slices and bake for 30 to 40 minutes or until a knife inserted into the sponge comes out clean.

Remove the cake from the oven and cool for 20 minutes. Turn out onto a serving dish. Serve cool.

Three delightful fruit desserts to serve hot or cold : lemon meringue pie, apple dumplings and rhubarb crumble.

Cereals

Macaroni cheese
SERVES FOUR

¼ cup (50 g) plus 1 teaspoon
  butter
½ lb (225 g) macaroni,
  cooked and drained
Salt and pepper
2½ cups (575 ml) mornay
  sauce
2 large ham slices, diced
⅔ cup (50 g) grated Cheddar
  cheese
½ cup (50 g) soft white bread
  crumbs

Preheat the oven to 425°F
(220°C). Grease a medium-sized
baking dish with the teaspoon of
butter.

Put the macaroni in a mixing
bowl with half the butter, the
salt, pepper, mornay sauce and
ham. Mix gently then pour into
the baking dish. Sprinkle with
the cheese and bread crumbs and
dot with the remaining butter.
Bake for 10 to 15 minutes or
until the top is lightly browned.

Baked pasta with seafood
SERVES FOUR

1 teaspoon vegetable oil
½ lb (225 g) pasta shells,
  cooked and drained
½ lb (225 g) cooked shelled
  mussels
1 cup (125 g) cooked shelled
  shrimp
2½ cups (575 ml) béchamel
  sauce
1 teaspoon anchovy paste
½ cup (50 g) grated Parmesan
  cheese
2 tablespoons butter

Preheat the oven to 425°F
(220°C).

Grease a large baking dish
with the teaspoon of oil.

Mix all the ingredients except
the cheese and butter together
and spoon into the baking dish.
Sprinkle with the cheese and dot
with the butter. Bake for 10 to
15 minutes or until the top is
well browned and bubbling.
Serve immediately.

Pizza dough
MAKES TWO PIZZAS

½ cake compressed yeast
¼ teaspoon sugar
½ cup (125 ml) lukewarm
  water
2 cups (225 g) all-purpose
  or bread flour
½ teaspoon salt
1 tablespoon plus 2
  teaspoons olive oil

Put the yeast, sugar and 2 tablespoons of the water into a small
bowl and mash the mixture with
a fork to make a smooth paste.
Set the bowl aside in a warm,
draft-free place for about 15
minutes or until the mixture is
puffed up and frothy.

Sift the flour and salt into a
bowl and make a well in the
center. Pour in the yeast mixture,
the remaining water and the
tablespoon of oil. Mix the liquids
together, gradually incorporating the flour. Mix the dough with
your hands until it begins to
leave the sides of the bowl. Turn

the dough out onto a lightly
floured surface and knead it for
about 10 minutes or until it is
smooth and elastic.

Rinse, dry and lightly grease
the mixing bowl. Shape the
dough into a ball and place it in
the bowl. Cover the bowl with a
damp cloth and set aside in a
warm, draft-free place for about
1 hour or until the dough has
doubled in bulk.

Turn the dough out onto the
work surface again and knead it
for 3 minutes. Divide the dough
in half and shape each half into a
ball. Flatten each ball by pressing down with your palm until
it forms a circle about ¼ inch
(½ cm) thick. Brush the top of
the dough with the remaining
olive oil.

The pizza base is now ready
to be covered with whichever
mixture you are using and baked
in the oven.

Pizza Napoletana
This is the classic Neapolitan
pizza—simple but delicious.

MAKES TWO PIZZAS

1 recipe pizza dough,
  shaped into 2 circles
8 medium-sized tomatoes,
  blanched, skinned and
  chopped
Salt and freshly ground
  black pepper
8 thin slices of mozzarella
  cheese
8 anchovy fillets
6 black olives, halved and
  pitted
1 teaspoon chopped fresh
  oregano
1 teaspoon chopped fresh
  basil
2 teaspoons olive oil

Preheat the oven to 450°F
(230°C).

Lightly grease a large baking
sheet. Put the two pizza dough
circles on the sheet.

Put half the tomatoes on each
pizza and sprinkle with a little
salt and lots of black pepper.
Put 4 slices of mozzarella cheese
on each pizza and garnish with
the anchovies and olives.
Sprinkle over the herbs and
moisten with the olive oil.

Bake the pizzas for about 20
minutes or until the cheese has
melted and is bubbling. Serve
hot or cold.

Pizza con cozze
Make in exactly the same way as
pizza Napoletana, but substitute
16 cooked and shelled mussels
for the anchovies, adding them
in the last 5 minutes of baking
time. Sprinkle the top liberally
with coarsely ground black
pepper.

Pizza alla Francescana
MAKES TWO PIZZAS

1 recipe pizza dough,
  shaped into 2 circles
1 tablespoon olive oil
2 cups (125 g) thinly sliced
  mushrooms
4 medium-sized tomatoes,
  skinned and chopped
6 slices prosciutto ham,
  cut into thin strips
1 teaspoon chopped fresh
  basil
Salt and pepper
8 thin slices mozzarella
  cheese

Preheat the oven to 450°F
(230°C).

Lightly grease a baking sheet.
Put the two pizza circles on the
baking sheet.

Heat the oil in a small saucepan and add the mushrooms. Fry
for 2 minutes, stirring constantly. Add the tomatoes and
cook for 5 minutes, stirring
occasionally.

Remove the pan from the heat
and spread half the mixture
over each pizza. Cover the mixture with the ham strips and
sprinkle over the basil and plenty
of salt and pepper. Lay the
cheese slices over the top.

Place the baking sheet in the
oven and bake for about 15 to 20
minutes or until the cheese has
melted and is bubbling.

Cannelloni di spinace
If you are using fresh pasta, cut
two large sheets of thinly rolled-
out pasta into oblongs about 3 ×
4 inches (8 × 10 cm). Cook the
pasta as usual, drain it and cool.
Put about 1 tablespoon of filling
along one edge of each oblong
and roll them up, placing them
seam sides down in the baking
dish.

SERVES FOUR

2 tablespoons butter
1 onion, finely chopped
2 garlic cloves, crushed

½ lb (225 g) ground veal
1 small package (150 g) frozen chopped spinach, thawed and drained
2 teaspoons chopped fresh basil
Salt and black pepper
1 egg yolk beaten with 2 tablespoons heavy cream
½ lb (225 g) cannelloni squares or tubes, cooked and drained
1¼ cups (315 ml) béchamel sauce, made with 2 tablespoons butter and flour, 1¼ cups (315 ml) milk and 3 tablespoons heavy cream
1¼ cups (315 ml) tomato sauce
2 tablespoons grated Parmesan cheese

Melt the butter in a saucepan and add the onion. Fry for 6 minutes, stirring. Add the garlic, veal, spinach, basil, salt and pepper and cook, stirring, for 5 minutes. Remove the pan from the heat and stir in the egg yolk and cream mixture. Set the mixture aside to cool.

Preheat the oven to 375°F (190°C). Lightly grease an oblong baking dish and set it aside.

Stuff the mixture into the cannelloni tubes and put them in the baking dish. Pour over the béchamel sauce and then the tomato sauce. Sprinkle over the Parmesan cheese and bake in the oven for about 30 to 40 minutes or until the top is well browned and bubbling. Serve immediately.

Lasagne

SERVES SIX

¼ cup (50 g) butter
2 onions, finely chopped
2 garlic cloves, crushed
1½ lb (700 g) lean ground beef
1 teaspoon dried rosemary
1 tablespoon chopped fresh basil
1 teaspoon dried oregano
1 lb (450 g) tomatoes, skinned and chopped
2 tablespoons tomato paste
Salt and freshly ground black pepper
4 tablespoons beef stock
2½ cups (575 ml) béchamel sauce
4 tablespoons heavy cream
1 egg yolk

4 tablespoons grated Parmesan cheese
1 lb (450 g) lasagne noodles (plain or verde), cooked and drained

Melt the butter in a saucepan and add the onions. Fry, stirring, for 6 to 8 minutes or until they are golden brown. Add the garlic and beef and fry for 8 minutes more. Stir in the rosemary, basil, oregano, tomatoes, tomato paste, salt, pepper and stock and reduce the heat to fairly low. Cover the pan and cook, stirring occasionally, for 20 minutes.

Preheat the oven to 400°F (200°C).

Mix the béchamel sauce with the cream, egg yolk and half the cheese. Layer the lasagne, meat sauce and béchamel in a large ovenproof dish in that order, ending with a layer of béchamel. Sprinkle over the remaining cheese and bake in the oven for 40 minutes or until the top is well browned.

Baked chicken pancakes

SERVES FOUR

2 tablespoons butter
1 green pepper, cored, seeded and diced
1 onion, finely chopped
1 garlic clove, crushed
½ lb (225 g) mushrooms, thinly sliced
3 tablespoons heavy cream mixed with 1 teaspoon cornstarch
Salt and pepper
1 teaspoon paprika
4 cups (450 g) diced cooked chicken
1 cup (125 g) shelled cooked shrimp
6 large pancakes
1¼ cups (315 ml) mornay sauce
2 tablespoons grated Parmesan cheese

Preheat the oven to 375°F (190°C).

Melt the butter in a saucepan and add the pepper and onion. Fry, stirring constantly, for 6 to 8 minutes or until the onion is golden. Add the garlic and mushrooms and fry for 4 minutes, stirring. Stir in the cream mixture, the salt and pepper, paprika, chicken and shrimp. Cook, stirring constantly, until the mixture

has thickened. Remove the pan from the heat.

Put one pancake into a round baking dish and spread over one-fifth of the mixture. Top with another pancake and continue making layers, ending with a pancake. Pour the mornay sauce over the top and sprinkle with the Parmesan cheese. Bake in the oven for 30 minutes or until the top is well browned. Serve immediately.

Garlic bread

SERVES FOUR TO SIX

1 medium-sized loaf French bread
¾ cup (175 g) butter, softened
2 to 3 large garlic cloves, crushed

Preheat the oven to 425°F (220°C).

Cut the bread into slices approximately 1½ inches (3 cm) thick. Put the butter and garlic into a small bowl and mash them together with a fork. Spread the butter on one side of the bread slices and put the loaf back together again. Wrap it completely in foil and bake in the oven for 20 minutes.

Line a bread basket with a paper napkin. Remove the bread from the oven and discard the foil. Arrange the bread slices in the basket and serve immediately.

Rice pudding

SERVES FOUR

⅓ cup (50 g) Carolina rice, washed and drained
2 tablespoons sugar
¼ teaspoon vanilla extract
1 cup (250 ml) milk
1 cup (250 ml) cream
2 tablespoons butter, cut into small pieces
¼ teaspoon grated nutmeg

Preheat the oven to 300°F (150°C).

Put the rice into a greased baking dish with the sugar, vanilla extract, milk, cream and the butter. Put into the oven for 25 minutes. Stir well, sprinkle with nutmeg and cook for 2 hours more, or until well browned on the outside and creamy inside.

Serve hot or cold.

Oatmeal and apple pudding

SERVES FOUR

1 teaspoon butter
4 tablespoons soft brown sugar
8 tablespoons medium oatmeal
Pinch of salt
4 tart apples, peeled, cored and thinly sliced
4 tablespoons melted butter

Preheat the oven to 375°F (190°C). Lightly grease a medium-sized baking dish with the teaspoon of butter.

Mix the sugar, oatmeal and salt together. Put some of the apple slices in the base of the dish and sprinkle over some of the oatmeal mixture, then some of the melted butter. Repeat the layers until all the ingredients have been used up, ending with some butter.

Put the dish in the oven and bake for about 40 minutes or until the apples are tender and the top of the dish is golden brown. Serve immediately.

Bread and butter pudding

SERVES FOUR

¼ cup (50 g) butter
6 slices fresh white bread, cut into triangles, crusts removed
2 tablespoons chopped peel
2 tablespoons golden raisins
2 tablespoons dark raisins or currants
2 tablespoons sugar
½ teaspoon mixed spice
3 eggs
¼ teaspoon vanilla extract
1¾ cups (425 ml) milk
1¼ cups (315 ml) cream

Lightly grease a 1-quart (1-liter) baking dish with a teaspoon of the butter. Spread the bread triangles with the remaining butter and layer them in the dish with the chopped peel, the raisins and currants, sugar and mixed spice.

Beat the eggs with the vanilla extract, milk and cream and pour the mixture over the bread. Set aside to soak for 30 minutes.

Meanwhile, preheat the oven to 350°F (180°C).

Put the pudding in the oven and bake for about 1 hour or until the custard has set and the top is lightly browned. Serve hot.

Cereals/cookies and small cakes

To prepare a cake pan, grease the inside surface with a thin layer of butter, lard or oil, then sprinkle in a little flour and tap the pan lightly until the flour is evenly distributed all over the greased area. Add a little granulated sugar to the flour if you are making a sponge cake.

For cakes that take a long time to cook, grease the pan and line it with two layers of greased waxed paper.

All ingredients for cake making should be at room temperature. Fruit and nuts should be prepared in advance, and candied cherries should be rinsed and patted dry with absorbent paper towels.

Preheat the oven to the temperature stated in the recipe. To test that the cake is baked, insert a toothpick or sharp-pointed knife into the center. If it comes out quite clean the cake is ready.

Let the cake cool in the pan for a few minutes, then run a knife around the edge and turn it out onto a wire rack.

Brownies

MAKES TWENTY-FOUR

9 squares (250 g) semisweet chocolate, broken into pieces
¾ cup (175 g) sugar
3 tablespoons water
½ cup (125 g) butter
½ teaspoon vanilla extract
3 eggs
1½ cups (175 g) all-purpose flour
1 teaspoon baking powder
⅔ cup (125 g) walnuts, chopped

Preheat the oven to 350°F (180°C).

Lightly grease a 1 × 7 × 11-inch (2 × 18 × 28-cm) baking pan.

Put the chocolate, sugar, water, butter and vanilla extract in a saucepan and stir to melt. Remove the pan from the heat and cool slightly.

Beat in the eggs. Sift the flour and baking powder over the mixture and mix in. Fold in the walnuts. Pour the mixture into the baking pan and bake for 30 minutes or until a knife inserted into the center comes out clean. Cool before cutting.

Scones

MAKES ABOUT TEN

2 cups (225 g) all-purpose flour
½ level teaspoon baking soda
Salt
2 tablespoons butter
½ cup (125 ml) buttermilk
Milk

Preheat the oven to 400°F (200°C).

Sift the flour, baking soda and a pinch of salt into a bowl. Rub in the butter, and mix to a soft dough with the buttermilk, adding more if necessary.

Turn the dough out onto a lightly floured board and knead lightly. Pat the dough out until it is 1 inch (2 cm) thick, cut into 1½-inch (3-cm) circles and brush with a little milk.

Bake for 10 to 12 minutes or until the scones are lightly browned. Serve hot.

Shortbread

MAKES TWO 6-INCH (15-CM) CIRCLES

1½ cups (175 g) all-purpose flour
¾ cup (75 g) rice flour
½ cup (125 g) plus 1 tablespoon sugar
¾ cup (175 g) butter

Preheat the oven to 350°F (180°C). Lightly grease a baking sheet.

Put the flours and ½ cup sugar in a bowl. Add the butter and cut it into small pieces, then blend it into the flour and sugar with your fingertips. Keep blending until the mixture is soft enough to form a smooth dough. Divide the dough in half. Pat into circles about 6 inches (15 cm) in diameter. Put on the baking sheet. Pinch the edges of the dough to make a pattern, and prick the surface with a fork. Mark each circle into sixths.

Bake for 10 minutes then turn down the heat to 300°F (150°C), and continue baking for about 35 to 40 minutes or until the shortbread is crisp and pale gold on the outside.

Remove the shortbread from the oven and sprinkle over the remaining sugar. When the shortbread is cool, break it into pieces and serve.

Almond cookies

MAKES ABOUT TWENTY

1½ cups (175 g) all-purpose flour
1 teaspoon baking powder
6 tablespoons butter, cut into small pieces
½ cup (50 g) ground almonds
1 cup (225 g) sugar
1 egg, beaten
1 teaspoon almond extract
Sliced blanched almonds

Preheat the oven to 350°F (180°C). Lightly grease a baking sheet and dust with flour.

Sift the flour and baking powder into a bowl. Rub in the butter then stir in the ground almonds and sugar. Make into a stiff dough with the egg and almond extract. Break off walnut-sized pieces of the dough and roll them into balls. Flatten the balls between the palms of your hands and place them on the baking sheet. Brush with cold water and place a sliced almond on each cookie. Bake for 10 to 15 minutes or until the cookies are firm. Cool on a wire rack.

Brandy snaps

MAKES ABOUT EIGHTEEN

4 tablespoons butter
4 tablespoons molasses
¼ cup (50 g) sugar
1 teaspoon lemon juice
4 tablespoons flour
1 teaspoon ground ginger
1 teaspoon brandy (optional)
½ cup (125 ml) cream

Preheat the oven to 375°F (180°C). Grease two baking sheets.

Heat the butter, molasses and sugar in a saucepan over moderate heat, stirring occasionally until the sugar has melted. Add the lemon juice and remove from the heat.

Stir in the flour and ginger and mix to a smooth dough. Add the brandy, if used.

Put teaspoonfuls of the mixture on the sheets several inches apart. Bake until the cookies are rich brown and lacy. Cool them for a moment then, while they

are still warm, wrap each one around a wooden spoon handle. Allow to become firm before removing from the handle.

If not required immediately, cool and store in a tin. When ready to serve whip the cream and, using a pastry tube, squeeze it into the brandy snaps.

Florentines

MAKES ABOUT TEN

4 tablespoons butter
¼ cup (50 g) sugar
1 tablespoon honey
1 tablespoon blanched slivered almonds
1 tablespoon chopped hazelnuts
2 tablespoons chopped candied cherries
2 tablespoons chopped candied peel
1 tablespoon chopped angelica
4 tablespoons flour
4 squares (125 g) semisweet chocolate

Preheat the oven to 350°F (180°C).

Line a large baking sheet with greased waxed paper and set it aside.

Melt the butter, sugar and honey in a medium-sized saucepan over moderate heat, stirring until the sugar has dissolved. Bring to a boil and remove the pan from the heat. Stir in the remaining ingredients except the chocolate.

Drop heaped teaspoonfuls of the mixture, spaced well apart, onto the baking sheet. Bake for 10 minutes or until the florentines have spread out and are golden brown.

Remove the baking sheet from the oven and let the florentines cool slightly before lifting them off the baking sheet with a spatula and cooling them on a wire rack.

While the florentines are cool-ing, melt the chocolate in a bowl over a pan of simmering water.

Using the spatula, spread the chocolate thickly over the back of each florentine, and run a fork over the chocolate to make an attractive pattern. Place the florentines, chocolate side up, on the wire rack and set aside until the chocolate has hardened.

Chocolate chip cookies

MAKES ABOUT TWENTY

4 tablespoons butter
½ cup (125 g) brown sugar
1 egg yolk
1 tablespoon milk
2 drops vanilla extract
1 cup (125 g) self-rising flour
½ cup (75 g) chocolate chips

Preheat the oven to 375°F (190°C).

Lightly grease a baking sheet and set it aside.

Cream the butter and sugar in a bowl. Beat in the egg yolk, milk and vanilla extract. Sift and fold in the flour. Add the chocolate chips.

Drop teaspoonfuls of the bat-ter, spaced well apart, on the baking sheet and bake for about 12 minutes or until the biscuits are golden brown.

Butter cookies

Serve plain or sandwiched to-gether with a butter cream fill-ing flavored with chocolate or orange. The cookies can be formed into finger-shaped strips, and both ends can be dipped in melted chocolate after they have cooked.

MAKES THIRTY

1 cup (225 g) salted butter
¼ cup (50 g) sugar
½ teaspoon vanilla extract
2 cups (225 g) all-purpose flour

Preheat the oven to 375°F (190°C). Lightly grease a baking sheet.

Put the butter in a mixing bowl and cream it with the sugar. Add the vanilla extract. Sift and add the flour and mix lightly to form a smooth dough. Put the dough into a pastry tube and squeeze it onto the baking sheet in various shapes.

Bake for 10 to 15 minutes or until the cookies are golden but not browned.

Cereals/pastries and cakes

Macaroons

The baking sheet may be lined with edible rice paper if you like. The paper is trimmed to the shape of the cookies after baking.

The flavor can be varied by using other nuts—for example walnuts or hazelnuts.

MAKES ABOUT TWELVE

1 egg white, beaten until stiff
⅓ cup (50 g) ground almonds
3 tablespoons sugar
1 tablespoon ground rice
2 drops almond extract
1 teaspoon water
Split blanched almonds

Preheat the oven to 325°F (170°C).

Using a metal spoon, gently blend all the ingredients except the split almonds together in a mixing bowl.

Line a baking sheet with parchment paper or rice paper and drop teaspoonfuls of the mixture, spaced well apart, on the sheet. Put 1 split almond on top of each spoonful.

Place in the oven and bake for about 20 minutes or until the macaroons are pale gold and firm on top. Cool on a wire rack before serving.

Coffee éclairs

These can also be made with a chocolate icing and filling, or just filled with sweetened whipped cream flavored with vanilla.

MAKES EIGHTEEN

1 teaspoon butter
1 recipe choux pastry dough
1¼ cups (315 ml) crème pâtissière
2 tablespoons black coffee

1¾ cups (225 g) confectioners' sugar
2 tablespoons warm water

Preheat the oven to 425°F (220°C). Using the teaspoon of butter, grease a large baking sheet and set it aside.

Put the dough into a pastry tube with a plain nozzle. Squeeze out 2- to 3-inch (5- to 8-cm) lengths of the dough, well spaced out, onto the baking sheet and bake for 15 to 20 minutes or until they are cooked and golden.

Remove the éclairs from the oven and put them on a wire rack. Slit them down one side to let the steam escape and cool.

When the éclairs are completely cold, mix the crème pâtissière with 1 tablespoon of the coffee and squeeze or spoon the mixture into the éclairs.

Sift the confectioners' sugar into a small bowl and add the remaining tablespoon of coffee and 1 tablespoon of the warm water. Beat the icing, adding more water if necessary, until it is smooth and glossy. Spread the icing over the tops of the éclairs with a spatula and set them aside for 1 hour before serving.

Danish pastries

MAKES EIGHT

½ cake compressed yeast
¼ teaspoon plus 1 tablespoon sugar
5 tablespoons warm water
2 cups (225 g) all-purpose flour
Salt
1 egg, beaten
¾ cup (175 g) butter
4 candied cherries, halved

ALMOND FILLING

2 teaspoons butter
1 tablespoon sugar
4 tablespoons ground almonds
2 drops almond extract
1 egg yolk, lightly beaten

GLAZE

1 small egg
2 tablespoons hot water
2 teaspoons sugar

Mash the yeast with ¼ teaspoon of the sugar in a small bowl. Mix in 2 tablespoons warm water. Set aside in a warm place for 15 minutes or until the mixture is puffed up and frothy.

Sift the flour, a pinch of salt and the remaining sugar into a bowl. Make a well in the center and pour in the yeast mixture, the remaining water and the egg. Mix to a soft dough, adding more water if necessary.

Cover the dough and put in the refrigerator for 10 minutes.

Allow the butter to soften slightly and spread it on waxed paper into a 3 × 9-inch (8 × 23-cm) rectangle ½ inch (1 cm) thick. Put in the refrigerator to chill.

Roll the dough into a 10-inch (25-cm) square. Put the butter in the middle and fold over the two sides to overlap in the middle. Seal the open ends.

Roll the dough into a 6 × 18-inch (15 × 45-cm) rectangle. Fold in three. Wrap in waxed paper or put in a plastic bag and refrigerate for 10 minutes.

Roll out the dough, with the narrow end facing you, to the same size. Fold in three, wrap and refrigerate.

Repeat the rolling and folding once more and put in the refrigerator for at least 2 hours before using.

Meanwhile make the filling. Cream the butter with the sugar. Beat in the ground almonds, almond extract and the egg yolk. Mix to a firm paste.

Roll out the dough into an 8 × 16-inch (20 × 40-cm) rectangle. Cut it into eight 4-inch (10-cm) squares. Place a ¾-inch (2-cm) circle of almond filling in the center. Using a sharp knife, cut from each corner to the almond filling. Fold one corner of each triangle thus formed to the center and press the points firmly into the almond paste. Put

half a candied cherry in the center.

Make the glaze by beating the egg with the water and the sugar. Brush the glaze over the pastries.

Preheat the oven to 425°F (210°C). Lightly grease a baking sheet and put the pastries on it. Slip the baking sheet into a greased plastic bag and set aside in a warm, draft-free place for 20 to 25 minutes or until the pastries are puffed up and doubled in size.

Bake the pastries for 15 minutes or until golden brown. Transfer the pastries to a wire rack to cool.

CUSTARD FILLING

1 tablespoon flour
1 tablespoon sugar
¾ cup (175 ml) cream or milk, boiling
2 egg yolks
Salt
Vanilla extract
1 teaspoon gelatin dissolved in 1 tablespoon hot water

Blend the flour and sugar in a saucepan. Gradually pour in the boiling cream or milk, stirring constantly. Bring back to a boil, stirring, and cook until thick. Remove the pan from the heat.

Beat the egg yolks with a pinch of salt and 2 to 3 drops of vanilla extract. Beat in 2 tablespoons of the hot cream mixture then beat it all in. Return the mixture to the pan and cook over very low heat for 1 minute. Stir in the gelatin and set aside to cool.

APPLE FILLING

1 large tart apple, peeled, cored and sliced
1 tablespoon brown sugar
¼ teaspoon ground cinnamon

Put the apple, brown sugar and 2 teaspoons of water into a saucepan and simmer until the apple is soft. Add the cinnamon and beat until smooth.

RAISIN FILLING

4 tablespoons butter
4 tablespoons sugar
2 tablespoons raisins
2 teaspoons ground cinnamon

Cream the butter and sugar. Mix in the raisins and cinnamon.

Danish pastries

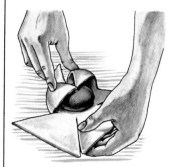

Cut the dough from the corners to the filling. Fold one corner of each triangle into the center.

Put the filling along the center line of the dough square and fold over the other two sides.

PINWHEELS

Roll out the dough to a 6 × 16-inch (15 × 40-cm) rectangle. Fill with the raisin or apple filling and roll from the short end. Cut in 1-inch (2-cm) slices.

COCKSCOMBS

Roll out the dough to an 8 × 16-inch (20 × 40-cm) rectangle. Cut the rectangle into 4-inch (10-cm) squares. Spread 2 teaspoons of apple filling across the center of each square. Fold in half and with a sharp knife make 7 slits on the folded side. Bend the pastry slightly to fan out the "teeth." Brush the pastries with the glaze and sprinkle with chopped blanched almonds.

TRIANGLES

Roll out the dough and cut as for cockscombs. Put 2 teaspoons of filling in the centers and fold over diagonally to make triangles. Brush the pastries with the glaze and sprinkle with chopped nuts.

Victoria layer cake

This is a basic recipe for cakes made by the creaming method. Whatever the size of the cake the proportion of the other ingredients to the eggs never changes—it is the weight of the eggs (in this case large, 50 g, each) in flour, sugar and fat.

MAKES ONE 7-INCH (18-CM) CAKE

**1 cup (125 g) self-rising flour
Salt
½ cup (125 g) sweet butter
4 tablespoons sugar
2 eggs
½ teaspoon vanilla extract
3 tablespoons raspberry jam
Confectioners' sugar**

Preheat the oven to 350°F (180°C). Grease and dust with flour two 7-inch (18-cm) layer cake pans.

Sift the flour and a pinch of salt into a bowl. Cut the butter into pieces and put into a warm mixing bowl. Cream the butter until softened, add the sugar and continue to beat until light and fluffy.

Add the eggs one at a time with a tablespoon of the flour, beating well after each addition. Mix in the vanilla extract.

Fold in half the remaining flour, using a large metal spoon to cut it into the batter. When mixed fold in the other half. Spread the mixture into the cake pans. Bake for about 20 minutes or until the cakes are done. Test by inserting a knife into the center of one cake—if it comes out clean the cake is ready. Cool the cakes in the pans for a few minutes before turning them onto a wire rack to cool.

When the cakes are cold spread one layer with the jam and put the other on top. Dust the top of the cake with a little confectioners' sugar.

Orange Victoria cake

Add the grated rind of 1 orange to the butter mixture. Use the juice for making a glacé icing.

Coffee and walnut cake

Mix 2 teaspoons instant coffee with the flour. Fold 2 tablespoons of chopped walnuts into the batter.

Sandwich with butter cream to which 1 teaspoon of very finely powdered coffee is added. Ice with glacé icing made with black coffee. Decorate with walnuts or dark-roast coffee beans.

Spice cake

Add 2 teaspoons of mixed spice to the flour before mixing. Decorate with vanilla glacé icing.

Seed cake

Add 2 teaspoons caraway seeds to the mixture. Bake in a 6-inch (15-cm) cake pan for 50 minutes.

Chocolate cake

Substitute 2 tablespoons of cocoa powder for 2 tablespoons of flour and sift with the flour. Ice with chocolate frosting.

Basic sponge cake

For one 9-inch (23-cm) cake increase the eggs to 4, the flour by 2 tablespoons and the sugar by 1 tablespoon.

The sponge can be made with separated eggs, the whites being beaten until stiff and then folded in after the flour has been added. This makes the sponge drier but lighter.

MAKES ONE 7-INCH (18-CM) CAKE

**3 eggs
3 tablespoons sugar
1 tablespoon water
½ teaspoon vanilla extract
6 tablespoons self-rising flour
½ cup (125 ml) whipping cream, whipped**

Preheat the oven to 350°F (180°C).

Lightly grease the bottoms and sides of two 7-inch (18-cm) layer cake pans. Line the bottom of each pan with a waxed-paper circle and grease lightly. Dust with flour, knocking out any excess. Put the eggs and sugar in a bowl and place in a pan of hot water. Beat for 10 minutes or until the mixture is very thick and creamy. Beat in the water and vanilla extract. Sift and fold in half the flour, then sift and fold in the remaining flour. Turn the mixture into the pans and bake for 10 to 12 minutes or until a knife inserted into the center comes out clean. Leave in the pans for a few minutes before turning out onto a wire rack to cool. When cold sandwich the two layers together with whipped cream.

Jelly roll

MAKES ONE JELLY ROLL

**Flour
Sugar
Basic sponge cake mixture
Confectioners' sugar
Warm jam or whipped cream**

Preheat the oven to 350°F (180°C).

Brush an 8 × 12-inch (20 × 30-cm) jelly roll pan with oil. Line the base with waxed paper, brush lightly with oil and dust with flour and sugar. Pour the sponge mixture into the pan and bake for 12 minutes.

Sprinkle a large sheet of waxed paper with confectioners' sugar and turn the pan and cake upside down onto this. Lift off the pan and peel off the paper quickly. Trim the edges, spread with warmed jam and roll up the sponge. If the roll is to be filled with cream roll up the sponge with the waxed paper and let cool completely before unrolling. Remove the paper and fill.

Génoise sponge

This is the classic French sponge cake. It may be cut into small squares or oblongs and iced or served as a large cake with whipped cream or crème pâtissière as a filling.

MAKES ONE 8-INCH (20-CM) CAKE

**¾ cup (175 g) sweet butter
6 eggs
1 cup (225 g) extra-fine granulated sugar
½ teaspoon vanilla extract
1½ cups (175 g) cake flour**

Preheat the oven to 375°F (190°C). Lightly grease and dust with flour two 8-inch (20-cm) layer cake pans.

Gently melt the butter over a pan of hot water. Let cool. Put the eggs, sugar and vanilla extract in a bowl. Place the bowl over a pan of hot water over low heat. Using a wire whisk or beater, beat the mixture for about 20 minutes or until it is pale and thick and will leave a ribbon trail when the beater is lifted. Remove from the heat.

Sift the flour into the egg mixture and fold it in carefully with a large metal spoon. Pour in the butter and quickly and lightly mix it in.

Pour the batter into the cake pans and bake for 20 to 30 minutes or until the sponge has shrunk slightly and a knife inserted into the center comes out clean.

Leave the cakes in the pans for 5 minutes before turning them out onto wire racks to cool.

Date and walnut loaf

MAKES ONE LOAF

**2 cups (225 g) all-purpose flour
1 teaspoon baking powder
½ cup (125 g) butter, cut into small pieces
½ cup (125 g) sugar
¾ lb (350 g) pitted dates, chopped
⅓ cup (59 g) chopped walnuts
1 teaspoon baking soda, mixed with 7 tablespoons slightly warmed milk
1 large egg, beaten**

Preheat the oven to 350°F (180°C).

Grease a medium-sized loaf pan and set it aside.

Sift the flour and the baking

Cereals/cakes

powder into a mixing bowl. Add the butter and work it in with your fingertips until the mixture resembles coarse bread crumbs. Stir in the sugar, dates and walnuts. Make a well in the center and pour in the baking-soda mixture and the egg. Stir the liquids together with a wooden spoon, gradually drawing in the flour mixture. Continue stirring until the mixture is smooth and fairly moist, adding a little more milk if necessary.

Spoon the mixture into the loaf pan, smoothing the top down with the back of the spoon. Put the pan in the oven and bake for about 1 hour or until the loaf has risen and is golden brown on top. Insert a toothpick into the center to check that it is cooked all the way through—the toothpick should come out dry.

Turn the loaf out onto a wire rack and cool completely before serving.

Crostata di ricotta

If ricotta cheese is not available for this Italian cheesecake, use smooth cottage cheese instead.

SERVES SIX

2 cups (225 g) all-purpose
** flour**
Salt
½ cup (125 g) butter
Grated rind of 1 lemon
1 tablespoon sugar
2 egg yolks
1 tablespoon ice water

FILLING
4 cups (900 g) ricotta cheese
4 tablespoons cream
½ cup (125 g) sugar
Grated rind and juice of 2
** lemons**
4 egg yolks
4 tablespoons raisins
2 tablespoons pine nuts
Milk

Sift the flour and a pinch of salt into a bowl. Add the butter and cut it into the flour. Work the butter into the flour until the mixture resembles coarse bread crumbs. Mix in the lemon rind, sugar, egg yolks and water. Knead lightly to make a smooth dough. Cover the dough and refrigerate for at least 1 hour.

Lightly butter a 9-inch (23-cm) pie pan. Remove a quarter of the dough, cover it and return it to the refrigerator. Roll out the remaining dough on a lightly floured board and line the pie pan with it. Prick the bottom of the dough and put it in the refrigerator for 30 minutes.

Preheat the oven to 425°F (220°C). Put the pie pan in the oven and bake blind.

Meanwhile, make the filling. Strain the ricotta cheese into a bowl. Beat in the cream, sugar, lemon rind and juice and egg yolks. Mix in the raisins.

Remove the pastry shell from the oven and reset the temperature to 350°F (180°C).

Roll out the remaining dough into a square a little larger than the diameter of the pie pan and cut it into thin strips with a sharp knife.

Spoon the ricotta filling into the pastry shell and smooth it down. Sprinkle the nuts on top. Arrange the pastry strips in a lattice pattern over the filling. Brush the strips with a little milk. Bake for 50 to 55 minutes or until the filling is firm and golden brown. Cool before serving.

Black Forest cherry cake

If fresh cherries are not available, use two 1-pound (450-g) cans of cherries—to make the syrup, use the juice from only one can and add 3 tablespoons of sugar.

MAKES ONE 10-INCH (25-CM) CAKE

1 cup (125 g) all-purpose
** flour**
¼ cup (50 g) butter
3 tablespoons sugar
1 tablespoon ground
** almonds**
Grated rind of ½ lemon
1 egg yolk

From left to right : marzipan roll, rum baba, white Christmas cake, plum cake or bride's cake, cassata alla Siciliana, and Black Forest cherry cake.

CAKE

8 eggs
1 cup (225 g) sugar
1 teaspoon vanilla extract
1½ cups (175 g) all-purpose flour
2 teaspoons baking powder
¾ cup (75 g) cocoa powder
½ cup (125 g) butter, melted

FILLING

1½ lb (700 g) black cherries, pitted
1 cup (225 g) sugar
4 cups (1 liter) whipping cream
5 tablespoons Kirsch

DECORATION

8 squares (250 g) semisweet chocolate
24 cherries, with stalks

To make the pastry base, sift the flour into a mixing bowl. Work in the butter until the mixture resembles fine bread crumbs. Stir in the sugar, ground almonds and lemon rind. Add the egg yolk and mix to a firm dough. Cover the dough and put it in the re-frigerator for 30 minutes.

Preheat the oven to 350°F (180°C). Lightly butter a 10-inch (25-cm) springform cake pan.

Roll the dough out thinly and line the bottom of the cake pan. Bake for 20 minutes. Leave the pastry in the pan for a few minutes. Transfer the pastry to a wire rack to cool.

Wipe out or wash the cake pan and grease it again with butter.

To make the cake, put the eggs, sugar and vanilla extract into a bowl and beat with a wire whisk or electric beater until the mixture is pale and thick and leaves a ribbon trail when the beater is lifted.

Sift the flour, baking powder and cocoa onto the egg mixture and fold it in gently with a large metal spoon. Gently stir in the melted butter, a spoonful at a time.

Pour the mixture into the cake pan and bake for 40 minutes or until the cake is well risen and has shrunk slightly from the sides. Test by inserting a toothpick into the center of the cake. If it comes out clean, the cake is done.

Leave the cake in the pan for a few minutes before turning it out onto a wire rack to cool.

To make the filling, put the cherries and ½ cup of the sugar in a saucepan and cook, stirring, until the sugar has dissolved. Bring to a boil slowly then remove the pan from the heat. Drain the cherries, return the juice to the pan and boil vigorously until it has reduced to a thick syrup. Pour the syrup over the cherries and set aside to cool.

Put the cream, the remaining sugar and the Kirsch in a bowl and beat until stiff.

To make the decoration, put the chocolate on waxed paper and, using a vegetable peeler, shave off curls. Put the chocolate curls in the refrigerator until they are required.

To assemble the cake, cut the cake in half horizontally. Put the pastry base on a serving dish. Spread it with a ½-inch (1-cm) layer of cream. Spoon half the cherries and syrup over the top. Cover with a layer of cake. Spread with a ½-inch (1-cm) layer of cream followed by the remaining cherries and syrup. Put the second layer of cake on top. Spread the top and sides with the remaining cream, reserving a little for decoration. Cover the sides with the chocolate curls. Arrange the cherries and the remaining chocolate curls in circles on top and swirl the remaining cream decoratively around them.

Cereals/cakes

Cassata alla Siciliana

MAKES ONE 8-INCH (20-CM) CAKE

**1 génoise sponge made with
   3 eggs**
8 tablespoons Maraschino

FILLING

**2¼ cups (350 g) mixed
   candied fruit**
3 cups (700 g) ricotta cheese
3 tablespoons sugar
**4 squares (125 g) semisweet
   chocolate coarsely grated**
**⅔ cup (125 g) chopped
   pistachio nuts**

To make the filling, reserve a few candied fruit for decoration and chop the remainder coarsely. Beat the ricotta cheese and the sugar until smooth. Mix in the chocolate, fruit and nuts.

Cut the cake into three layers horizontally. Put one layer onto the base of a springform cake pan. Sprinkle the sponge with 2 tablespoons Maraschino and spread with ½ inch (1 cm) of the filling. Put the second layer on top, sprinkle with 2 tablespoons of the liqueur and spread with ½ inch (1 cm) of filling. Put the third layer on top and sprinkle with the remaining liqueur. Clip the sides of the cake pan into place. Cover and refrigerate for 3 hours.

Remove the cake from the pan and put it on a plate. Spread the remaining ricotta mixture over the top and sides. Decorate with the reserved candied fruit.

Rum babas

MAKES SIXTEEN

1 cake compressed yeast
6 tablespoons warm milk
**2 cups (225 g) all-purpose
   flour**
½ teaspoon salt
1 tablespoon sugar
4 eggs, lightly beaten
½ cup (125 g) butter, softened
4 tablespoons clear honey
4 tablespoons water
2 tablespoons rum
1 lb (450 g) strawberries
1 cup (250 ml) cream

Grease 16 small ring molds.

Mash the yeast with the milk in a large bowl. Mix in 4 tablespoons of the flour and set aside in a warm, draft-free place for 20 minutes or until the mixture is puffed up and frothy.

Preheat the oven to 400°F (200°C).

Beat the remaining flour, the salt, sugar, eggs and butter into the yeast mixture. Beat well for 3 to 4 minutes.

Half fill the ring molds with the batter. Cover with a cloth and set aside in a warm place until the batter has risen and the molds are two-thirds full.

Bake in the top part of the oven for 12 to 15 minutes or until the babas are well risen and golden brown. Take the babas out of the oven and leave them in the molds for a few minutes, then turn them out onto a wire rack.

To make the syrup, put the honey, water and rum in a saucepan and warm over low heat.

Put the babas on a serving dish while still hot and spoon the syrup over them. When the babas are cool and you are ready to serve them, put strawberries in the middle of each baba and pour a little cream over the top.

Marzipan roll

MAKES ONE 12-INCH (30-CM) ROLL

4 tablespoons brandy
**¾ cup (125 g) candied
   cherries, halved**
**2 tablespoons chopped
   candied angelica**
**1 strip each candied lemon
   and orange peel, chopped**
**⅓ cup (50 g) chopped
   walnuts**
**⅓ cup (50 g) chopped
   hazelnuts**
2 cups (450 g) sugar
**2 cups (350 g) ground
   almonds**
¼ teaspoon almond extract
2 eggs, well beaten
2 recipes puff pastry
**1 egg yolk mixed with 2
   tablespoons milk**

Put the brandy, cherries, angelica, lemon and orange peel, walnuts and hazelnuts in a bowl and marinate for 2 hours, stirring from time to time.

Meanwhile, make the marzipan. Put the sugar and ground almonds in a bowl and mix well. Make a well in the center and pour in the almond extract and eggs. Gradually incorporate the dry ingredients, finally mixing with your hands until the mixture is smooth and quite sticky. Mix in the fruit and brandy.

Preheat the oven to 425°F (220°C). Lightly grease a baking sheet.

Roll the pastry dough out on a lightly floured board into an oblong approximately 4 × 12 inches (10 × 30 cm). Put the marzipan mixture on the dough and shape it to an oblong almost, but not quite, as wide or as long as the dough. Moisten the edges of the dough with a little water and bring the long edges up and over to seal the filling. Tuck both ends under. Make leaves out of the dough trimmings and moisten the undersides with a little water. Arrange them along the seam to cover. Paint the dough with the egg and milk mixture and very carefully transfer the roll to the baking sheet.

Bake for about 35 minutes or until the pastry is puffed up and golden brown. Remove the roll from the oven and let it cool completely on the baking sheet before cutting into slices.

Plum cake or bride's cake

To make a white Christmas cake, replace the brown sugar by white, the currants by candied pineapple, and the raisins by chopped angelica and chopped blanched almonds. Increase the candied cherries by ¾ cup (125 g). If you want to add more brandy, pierce holes in the bottom of the warm cake and pour in 3 to 4 tablespoonfuls.

MAKES ONE 10-INCH (25-CM) CAKE

**4 cups (450 g) all-purpose
   flour**
1 teaspoon baking powder
1½ cups (350 g) butter
**2¼ cups (450 g) soft brown
   sugar**
2⅔ cups (450 g) currants
2⅔ cups (450 g) dark raisins
**1½ cups (225 g) chopped
   candied peel**
**1½ cups (225 g) chopped
   citron peel**
**¾ cup (125 g) candied
   cherries**
1 teaspoon ground mace
6 eggs, beaten
½ cup (125 ml) brandy
2 tablespoons apricot jam
2 tablespoons water
1 recipe marzipan
1 recipe royal icing

Preheat the oven to 300°F (150°C).

Grease a 10-inch (25-cm) cake pan. Line it with a double thickness of greased waxed paper.

Sift the flour and baking powder together into a large bowl. Work in the butter with your fingertips. Stir in the sugar, dried fruit, peel, cherries and mace. Mix the eggs and brandy together. Using a wooden spoon or your hand, mix the eggs and brandy into the flour and fruit. When thoroughly mixed, turn into the cake pan. Spread the cake mixture evenly, hollowing out the center slightly with the back of a tablespoon dipped in cold water.

Bake for 2 hours then reduce the heat to 275°F (140°C) and bake for 1½ to 2 hours more or until the cake is dark and firm to the touch. Switch off the oven and leave the cake for 30 minutes more before turning it out onto a wire rack to cool. When the cake is cold, wrap it in foil and put it in an airtight tin for at least 30 days.

Before covering the cake with marzipan, make the jam glaze. Put the jam and water into a small saucepan and simmer for 3 to 4 minutes. Strain the mixture and keep warm.

Trim the top of the cake to straighten it and turn it upside down. The bottom of the cake will now be on the top. Brush the top of the cake with the warm glaze. Dust the work surface with a little confectioners' sugar. Take a little less than half the almond paste and roll it out into a circle the same size as the cake. Invert the cake onto the almond paste. Trim the edges and press down firmly. Turn cake right side up.

Roll the remaining paste into an oblong twice as wide as the side of the cake and half the circumference. Cut the oblong in half lengthwise and brush with the jam glaze. Roll the cake, like a wheel, along the strips of almond paste and press and smooth over the seams. Let the almond paste dry for 48 hours before covering with icing.

To ice the cake, spread two-thirds of the icing thickly over the top and sides using a spatula dipped in hot water to smooth it down. Leave the icing on the cake to harden before decorating the top and sides with the remaining icing.

Crème pâtissière or custard cream filling

This custard is used as a filling for many pastries and pies.

MAKES ABOUT 2 CUPS (500 ML)

3 egg yolks
3 tablespoons sugar
2 tablespoons cornstarch
1¾ cups (425 ml) milk
Vanilla extract
1 egg white

Cream the egg yolks with the sugar in a bowl. Beat in the cornstarch, ½ cup of the milk and a few drops of vanilla extract.

Bring the remaining milk to just under boiling point in a saucepan. Pour it gradually onto the egg mixture, stirring constantly.

Pour the mixture back into the pan and bring back to just under boiling point, stirring constantly. Remove the pan from the heat and beat until smooth. Let cool slightly.

Beat the egg white until stiff. Put one-third of the egg and milk mixture in a bowl and fold in the egg white. Fold this mixture into the rest of the egg and milk mixture and return to low heat. Cook for 2 to 3 minutes, stirring. Cool completely.

Butter cream 1

This amount will fill an 8- or 9-inch (20- or 23-cm) cake.

⅔ cup (150 ml) milk
2 egg yolks
½ cup (100 g) sugar
1 cup (225 g) sweet butter

Put the milk in a saucepan and bring to just under boiling point.

Mix the egg yolks with the sugar in a bowl. Mix in the hot milk.

Put the bowl over a pan of barely simmering water and cook, stirring, until the custard is thick enough to coat the back of the spoon. Strain and cool the custard.

Beat the butter in another bowl until soft. Beat in the custard a little at a time. Add the flavoring and use.

Butter cream 2

This quantity will fill an 8- or 9-inch (20- or 23-cm) cake.

2 tablespoons sugar
4 tablespoons water

2 egg yolks
½ cup (100 g) sweet butter

Dissolve the sugar in the water in a saucepan. Bring to a boil and boil rapidly until the syrup reaches a temperature of 215° to 220°F (101° to 104°C). Remove the pan from the heat.

Meanwhile, lightly beat the egg yolks in a bowl. Pour in the syrup, beating constantly, until the mixture is thick and fluffy.

Beat the butter until soft in another bowl. Gradually beat in the egg mixture. Add the flavoring and use.

Marzipan

MAKES 2½ POUNDS (1 KG)

2 cups (225 g) confectioners' sugar
2⅔ cups (450 g) ground almonds
1 cup (225 g) granulated sugar
2 eggs, beaten
1 tablespoon lemon juice
1 teaspoon almond extract

Sift the confectioners' sugar into a bowl with the ground almonds and granulated sugar. Stir in the eggs, lemon juice and almond extract. Using your hands, form the mixture into a ball. Dust the working surface with confectioners' sugar and turn the paste out onto it. Knead for a few minutes until smooth.

Royal icing

This amount of icing will cover a 10-inch (25-cm) cake.

3 egg whites
6 cups (700 g) confectioners' sugar, sifted
1 teaspoon lemon juice
1 teaspoon glycerin

Lightly beat the egg whites. Stir in the sugar, mixing it in with a wooden spoon a little at a time. Stir in the lemon juice and glycerin. Using a wire whisk or electric beater, beat the icing until it is smooth. Use immediately, or cover the bowl and leave up to 2 hours.

Glacé icing

This amount of icing will cover an 8- or 9-inch (20- or 23-cm) cake.

¼ cup (65 ml) water
3 cups (350 g) confectioners' sugar
5 drops tasteless cooking oil
Flavoring

Put the water in the top of a double boiler and gradually beat in the sugar, the oil and the desired flavoring. Stir over barely simmering water until the icing is warm. It should be smooth, glossy, thick and of a pouring consistency.

To use, put the cake on a wire rack, pour the icing over the top and use a spatula dipped in hot water to spread the icing evenly.

Chocolate frosting

This amount will cover one 7-inch (18-cm) cake.

1 cup (100 g) confectioners' sugar
2 tablespoons cocoa powder
¼ cup (50 g) butter
2 tablespoons black coffee
¼ cup (50 g) soft brown sugar

Sift the confectioners' sugar and cocoa together. Put the butter, coffee and the brown sugar into the top of a double boiler over

simmering water. Stir to dissolve. Add the sugar and cocoa mixture, and beat until smooth. Remove the pan from the heat and continue beating until cool and thick enough to spread.

Boiled frosting

This amount of frosting will fill and cover an 8-inch (20-cm) cake.

1½ cups (350 g) sugar
½ cup (125 ml) water
Cream of tartar
2 egg whites
Flavoring

Dissolve the sugar in the water over low heat. Stir in a pinch of cream of tartar and bring to a boil. Boil rapidly until the syrup reaches 240°F (115°C) on a candy thermometer.

Meanwhile, beat the egg whites in a bowl until stiff. Beating constantly, pour the syrup onto the egg whites. Continue beating until the icing is thick enough to spread. Beat in the flavoring.

To use, spread on the cake with a spatula dipped in hot water. Swirl icing to imitate a snowdrift or spread smoothly.

Covering and icing a cake

Brush the cake with jam glaze and cover the top with marzipan.

Roll the cake along the strip of marzipan to cover the sides.

Using a spatula, smooth the icing on the top and sides.

Decorate the cake with more icing, using a pastry tube.

Cereals/bread

Bread dough may be baked in a well-greased loaf pan, a cake pan, a ring mold or a new clay pot. Alternatively, make the dough into one of the traditional shapes—round, oval, long and thin or braided—and bake it on a greased baking sheet. Sprinkle a little flour over the top of the loaf before putting it in the oven, or glaze it with beaten egg and milk for a glossy finish, or salted water for a really crisp crust. Toppings of poppy seeds, sesame seeds or crushed wheat add taste and texture.

Experiment with additions to the dough—add prunes, dried apricots, nuts, grated cheese, olives or herbs, or mix different flours together to vary the flavor.

Sweet white bread

This sweet white bread recipe can be made into a fruit loaf by adding currants, golden or dark raisins and any other chopped candied fruit. It can be braided or shaped into rolls.

MAKES ONE BRAIDED LOAF

1 cake compressed yeast
½ cup (125 g) plus ¼ teaspoon sugar
2 tablespoons lukewarm water
6 cups (700 g) all-purpose flour
½ cup (125 g) butter
1 cup (250 ml) lukewarm milk
1 teaspoon salt
2 eggs, lightly beaten

GLAZE

1 egg yolk, lightly beaten with 1 teaspoon sugar and 1 tablespoon warm milk

Put the yeast into a small bowl and mash it with ¼ teaspoon of the sugar. Add the water and cream the mixture until it is smooth. Set aside in a warm, draft-free place for 15 minutes or until the yeast mixture is puffed up and frothy.

Sift the flour into a large mixing bowl. Add the butter and cut it into small pieces with a knife. Lightly work the butter into the flour.

Stir the remaining sugar into the milk with the salt. Continue stirring until the sugar has dissolved. Beat in the eggs.

Make a well in the center of the flour mixture and pour in the yeast mixture and the egg and milk mixture. Stir the liquids together, gradually incorporating the flour. When the dough is well mixed and coming away from the sides of the bowl, turn it out onto a lightly floured working surface and knead it for at least 10 minutes or until it is smooth and glossy.

Rinse out and dry the mixing bowl and grease it lightly. Shape the dough into a ball and place it in the bowl. Cover the bowl with a clean, damp cloth and set aside in a warm, draft-free place for about 1 hour or until the dough has doubled in bulk.

Turn the dough out onto the work surface and knead it vigorously for 5 minutes.

Divide the dough into 3 equal pieces and shape each piece into a long, thin roll. The pieces must be of equal length. Press the 3 pieces together at one end and tuck them under. Braid the pieces together and press the ends together, tucking them under as before.

Carefully transfer the braid to a greased baking sheet and brush it with the glaze. Set aside in a warm, draft-free place for 40 minutes or until the braid has doubled in bulk.

Meanwhile, preheat the oven to 475°F (240°C).

Place the bread in the oven and bake for 15 minutes. Reduce the heat to 425°F (220°C) and bake for 25 to 30 minutes more or until the bread is done and sounds hollow when the underside is rapped with your knuckles. Cool the bread on the baking sheet or, preferably, transfer it to a wire rack.

Granary bread

This bread can be baked in a loaf pan or shaped into a ball with a deep cross cut in the top before rising for the second time. It can also be baked as two small loaves.

MAKES ONE LARGE LOAF

1 cake compressed yeast
¼ teaspoon sugar
1¾ cups (425 ml) half milk, half water, lukewarm
2 tablespoons malt
1 tablespoon melted butter
8 cups (800 g) whole wheat flour
¾ cup (125 g) cracked wheat
2 teaspoons salt

Crumble the yeast into a small bowl and mash in the sugar. Add 2 tablespoons of the lukewarm liquid and blend them together until smooth. Set aside in a warm, draft-free place for 15 minutes or until the yeast is puffed up and frothy.

Mix the remaining liquid with the malt and butter, and set aside.

Put the flour into a large mixing bowl and mix in the cracked wheat and salt. Make a well in the center of the mixture and pour in the yeast mixture and the malt mixture. Stir the liquids together, gradually incorporating the flour. When the dough begins to come away from the sides of the bowl, turn it out onto a lightly floured surface and knead vigorously for at least 10 minutes or until it is smooth.

Rinse out and dry the mixing bowl and grease it lightly. Shape the dough into a ball and place it in the bowl. Cover with a clean, damp cloth and set aside in a warm, draft-free place for at least 1 hour or until it has doubled in bulk.

Turn the dough out onto the work surface and punch it once or twice to knock out the air. Knead it thoroughly and then either shape it or place it in a greased loaf pan. Put it back in a warm place and leave it to rise for 30 to 40 minutes, until it has doubled in bulk or risen to the top of the pan.

Preheat the oven to 425°F (220°C).

When the dough has risen, brush the top lightly with a little milk and place it in the oven. Bake for 10 minutes, then reduce the temperature to 375°F (190°C) and bake for 20 to 25 minutes more or until the bread is done. Test it by rapping the underside with your knuckles—it should have a hollow sound. Turn the bread out and cool on a wire rack.

Whole wheat bread

This bread is often baked in 2 medium-sized, tall new clay pots. For added texture knead in a handful of rolled oats.

MAKES ONE LARGE LOAF

1 cake compressed yeast
¼ teaspoon sugar
1½ cups (375 ml) warm water
1 tablespoon soft brown sugar or honey
2 teaspoons salt
6¾ cups (700 g) whole wheat flour

198

Put the yeast and sugar into a small bowl and mash them until smooth with 2 tablespoons of water. Set aside in a warm, draft-free place for 15 minutes or until the mixture is puffed up and frothy.

Meanwhile, mix the brown sugar or honey, salt and the remaining water together.

Put the flour into a large mixing bowl and make a well in the center. Pour in the yeast and water mixtures and mix them together, gradually incorporating the flour. When the dough is well mixed and coming away from the sides of the bowl, turn it out onto a lightly floured work surface and knead for at least 10 minutes or until the dough is smooth.

Rinse out and dry the mixing bowl and grease it lightly. Shape the dough into a ball and place it in the bowl. Cover the bowl with a clean, damp cloth and set aside in a warm, draft-free place for about 1 hour or until the dough has risen and doubled in bulk.

Turn the dough out onto the work surface and punch it once or twice to knock out the air. Knead it for about 5 minutes, then shape it or put it into a greased loaf pan.

Set aside in a warm, draft-free place for about 30 minutes or until it has doubled in bulk or risen to the top of the pan.

Meanwhile, preheat the oven to 475°F (240°C).

Place the loaf in the oven and bake for 15 minutes. Reduce the heat to 425°F (220°C) and bake for 20 to 30 minutes more or until the loaf sounds hollow when the underside is rapped with your knuckles.

Lardy cake, white bread, Chelsea buns and crisp white rolls are just a few of the good things you can make from a yeast dough.

Cereals/bread

Malt loaf

MAKES TWO SMALL LOAVES

1 cake compressed yeast
$\frac{1}{4}$ teaspoon sugar
$\frac{1}{2}$ cup (125 ml) plus 3
   tablespoons lukewarm
   water
2 tablespoons butter
2 heaping tablespoons malt
2 tablespoons molasses
1 teaspoon salt
4 cups (450 g) all-purpose
   flour
$1\frac{1}{3}$ cups (225 g) golden raisins

Crumble the yeast into a small bowl and mash in the sugar. Stir in the 3 tablespoons of water to make a smooth mixture. Set the bowl aside in a warm, draft-free place for 15 minutes or until the mixture is puffed up.

Melt the butter in the remaining water and mix in the malt, molasses and salt.

Sift the flour into a large mixing bowl. Make a well in the center and pour in the yeast mixture and the malt mixture. Mix the liquids together, gradually incorporating the flour. When the dough is well mixed and beginning to come away from the sides of the bowl, turn it out onto a lightly floured surface and knead it vigorously for 10 minutes or until it is smooth and elastic. If the dough is sticky, knead in a little more flour.

Rinse and dry the mixing bowl and grease it lightly. Shape the dough into a ball and place it in the mixing bowl. Cover the bowl with a clean, damp cloth and set it aside for $1\frac{1}{2}$ hours or until the dough has risen and doubled in bulk. Turn the dough out onto the working surface and punch it

a few times to knock out the air. Spread out the dough and work in the raisins. Shape the dough into two loaves and put it into two small, greased loaf pans. Set aside in a warm, draft-free place for about 40 minutes or until the dough has risen to the top of the pans.

Meanwhile, preheat the oven to 425°F (220°C). Bake the loaves for 10 minutes, reduce the oven temperature to 375°F (190°C) and continue baking for 20 to 30 minutes more or until the loaves have shrunk slightly from the sides of the pans and sound hollow when the undersides are rapped with your knuckles.

Cool before serving.

Lardy cake

MAKES ONE LARGE CAKE

1 cake compressed yeast
3 tablespoons sugar
1 cup (250 ml) plus 2
   tablespoons lukewarm
   water
1 tablespoon honey
1 tablespoon melted butter
1 teaspoon salt
4 cups (450 g) all-purpose
   flour
$\frac{1}{4}$ teaspoon grated nutmeg
$\frac{1}{4}$ teaspoon ground allspice
1 teaspoon ground cinnamon
$\frac{1}{2}$ cup (125 g) lard, cut into
   small pieces
$1\frac{1}{3}$ cups (225 g) currants
$\frac{1}{3}$ cup (50 g) golden raisins
$\frac{1}{3}$ cup (50 g) raisins

GLAZE

1 tablespoon honey and 1
   tablespoon sugar mixed
   with 2 tablespoons water

Crumble the yeast into a small mixing bowl and mash in $\frac{1}{4}$ teaspoon of sugar. Add the 2 tablespoons of water and mix until smooth.

Set the bowl aside in a warm, draft-free place for 15 minutes or until the yeast is puffed up and frothy.

Meanwhile, mix the honey, butter, salt and the remaining water together.

Sift the flour into a large mixing bowl and make a well in the center. Pour in the yeast mixture and the honey and water mixture. Mix the liquids together, gradually drawing in the flour. Add a little more water if the dough is too dry.

When the dough is well mixed and beginning to come away from the sides of the bowl, turn it out onto a lightly floured working surface and knead it for about 10 minutes or until it is smooth and elastic.

Rinse out and dry the mixing bowl and grease it lightly. Shape the dough into a ball and put it in the bowl. Cover the bowl with a clean, damp cloth and set it aside in a warm, draft-free place for about 1 hour or until it has risen and doubled in bulk.

Meanwhile, put the rest of the sugar, the nutmeg, allspice, cinnamon, lard and dried fruit into a mixing bowl and stir well to mix. Set aside.

Turn the dough out of the bowl and punch it once or twice to knock out the air. Knead it for 5 minutes. Roll the dough out into a large oblong. Sprinkle half the dried fruit mixture over two-thirds of the dough. Fold the remaining one-third of dough over the fruit and fold again to make a parcel. Press down on the edges to seal them. Roll the dough out and repeat the process all over again using the remaining dried fruit mixture.

Preheat the oven to 400°F (200°C).

Shape the dough into an oblong to fit a large, greased, oblong loaf pan and put it into the pan. Set the dough aside in a warm, draft-free place for 40 minutes or until it has risen to the top of the pan.

Place the cake in the oven and bake for 30 minutes. Brush the top of the cake liberally with the glaze and bake for 10 to 15

minutes more or until it is well risen and golden brown.

Cool on a rack.

Chelsea buns

The Chelsea bun mixture may also be baked as one large round.

MAKES NINE BUNS

$\frac{1}{2}$ cake compressed yeast
$\frac{1}{4}$ cup (50 g) plus $\frac{1}{4}$ teaspoon
   sugar
2 tablespoons lukewarm
   water
$\frac{1}{4}$ cup (65 ml) lukewarm
   milk
6 tablespoons melted butter
1 teaspoon salt
1 egg, lightly beaten
2 cups (225 g) all-purpose
   flour
1 teaspoon mixed spice
$\frac{1}{3}$ cup (50 g) currants
2 tablespoons candied
   cherries, chopped
2 tablespoons mixed peel

Crumble the yeast into a small bowl and mash in the $\frac{1}{4}$ teaspoon of sugar. Add the water and stir to make a smooth mixture. Set the bowl aside in a warm, draft-free place for about 15 minutes or until the yeast is puffed up and frothy.

Mix the milk, 4 tablespoons of the melted butter, the salt, the remaining sugar and egg together.

Sift the flour into a large mixing bowl and make a well in the center. Pour in the yeast mixture and the milk mixture. Mix the liquids together, gradually drawing in the flour. When the dough is well combined and beginning to come away from the sides of the bowl, turn it out onto a lightly floured surface and knead for 10 minutes or until it is smooth and elastic.

Rinse out and dry the mixing bowl and grease it lightly. Shape the dough into a ball and put it into the bowl. Cover the bowl with a clean, damp cloth and set it aside in a warm, draft-free place for about 1 hour or until the dough has risen and doubled in size.

Turn the dough out of the bowl and knead it for 5 minutes. Roll the dough into a large oblong and brush it liberally with some of the melted butter. Sprinkle over the spice and fruit and roll up the dough from the long end fairly tightly. Slice the roll quite

Crown loaf

To make a crown loaf, arrange even-sized balls of white dough in a round cake pan.

Brioche

To shape a brioche, insert a small ball of dough into the larger ball in the brioche pan.

thickly and lay each slice, cut side down, in a greased baking pan. Brush the tops with the remaining melted butter and set aside in a warm, draft-free place for about 30 minutes or until the buns have risen and almost doubled in bulk.

Meanwhile, preheat the oven to 375°F (190°C). Put the buns into the oven and bake for about 25 to 30 minutes or until they are cooked and golden brown.

Cool the buns on a wire rack.

Croissants

MAKES ABOUT TWELVE

$\frac{1}{2}$ **cup (125 ml) milk**
$\frac{1}{2}$ **cup (125 g) plus**
  2 tablespoons butter
1 cake compressed yeast
1$\frac{1}{2}$ tablespoons sugar
2 tablespoons warm water
3 cups (350 g) all-purpose
  flour
1 teaspoon salt
1 egg yolk, lightly beaten
  with 1 tablespoon milk

Put the milk into a saucepan and bring it to just under boiling point. Remove the pan from the heat and add 2 tablespoons of the butter. Let the butter melt and the mixture cool to lukewarm.

Mash the yeast with $\frac{1}{4}$ teaspoon of the sugar and the water to a smooth cream. Set aside in a warm place for 15 minutes or until the mixture is puffed up.

Sift the flour, salt and remaining sugar into a large, warm bowl. Make a well in the center and pour in the yeast mixture and the milk and butter mixture. Using your hand, mix the ingredients to a dough. Turn the dough out onto a lightly floured board. Knead for 10 minutes or until the dough is smooth and elastic.

Rinse out and dry the bowl and grease it lightly. Shape the dough into a ball and put it into the bowl. Cover with a damp cloth and set aside in a warm place for 1$\frac{1}{2}$ to 2 hours or until the dough has doubled in bulk.

Punch the dough to knock out the air and reform it into a ball. Cover it and put it in the refrigerator for 30 minutes.

Put the remaining butter between two pieces of waxed paper. Using a rolling pin, roll it out to a 6-inch (15-cm) square.

Roll out the dough on a lightly floured board to about an 8 × 12-inch (20 × 30-cm) rectangle. Put the butter in the middle. Fold the dough over the butter to enclose it completely. Roll the dough out again to a strip three times as long as it is wide. Fold the bottom third of the dough upward and the top third downward. Wrap the dough in plastic wrap or waxed paper and refrigerate for 30 minutes. Repeat the rolling out and folding twice more with the same interval of 30 minutes in the refrigerator.

After the final rolling and folding, cover with a damp cloth and leave the dough in the refrigerator for at least 1 hour or overnight.

Preheat the oven to 425°F (220°C). Lightly grease two baking sheets.

Roll out the dough $\frac{1}{4}$ inch ($\frac{1}{2}$ cm) thick on a lightly floured board. Cut the dough into 7-inch (18-cm) squares. Cut the squares in half diagonally to make triangles. Roll each triangle from the base to the apex. The pointed ends will be in the center. Shape into crescents and put on the baking sheets with the pointed end underneath. Brush with the egg mixture and bake for 15 minutes or until golden.

Brioche

MAKES ONE BRIOCHE

$\frac{1}{2}$ **cake compressed yeast**
2 tablespoons warm water
2 cups (225 g) all-purpose
  flour
1 teaspoon salt
2 tablespoons sugar
2 eggs, lightly beaten
Warm milk
$\frac{3}{4}$ cup (175 g) butter, melted

Mash the yeast in a bowl with the water. Add one-quarter of the flour and mix to a soft dough. Shape the dough into a ball and cut a cross on the top. Put the dough into a bowl of warm water for about 5 minutes or until the dough rises to the top and doubles in bulk. Lift out the dough, drain it, cover and set aside.

Meanwhile, sift the remaining flour, salt and sugar into another bowl. Make a well in the center and pour in the eggs—reserving a little for the glaze—and a little warm milk. Using your fingers, mix the egg and milk and then draw in the flour to make a sticky dough. Add more milk if necessary. Beat with your fingers by lifting the dough, throwing it down and gathering it up again. Beat for 10 minutes.

Gradually work in the butter a little at a time, beating between additions. The dough should now be smooth and less sticky. Blend the yeast ball into the dough until it is well mixed.

Lightly flour a large bowl. Put the dough into the bowl, cover with a damp cloth and leave in a warm place for 3 hours or until doubled in bulk. Punch down the dough, cover and refrigerate for at least 4 hours or overnight.

Take the dough out of the refrigerator, let it return to room temperature then knead it very gently for 2 to 3 minutes. Remove a quarter of the dough and roll the rest into a ball and put it into a lightly greased brioche mold. Make a hole in the middle with your fingers. Shape the remaining dough into a ball, then taper one end and fit it into the hole in the brioche. Cover and set aside to prove in a warm place for 30 minutes or until well risen.

Preheat the oven to 450°F (230°C).

Brush the top of the brioche with the reserved beaten egg and bake for 20 minutes. Reduce the oven temperature to 350°F (180°C) and continue baking for 30 minutes or until the top is golden brown and a toothpick inserted into the brioche comes out clean.

Remove from the oven and leave the brioche in the mold for 30 minutes before transferring it to a wire rack to cool.

Soda bread

MAKES ONE ROUND LOAF

4 cups (450 g) all-purpose
  flour
1 teaspoon salt
1 teaspoon baking soda
2 tablespoons butter
1$\frac{1}{4}$ cups (300 ml) buttermilk

Preheat the oven to 400°F (200°C).

Lightly grease a baking sheet. Sift the flour, salt and baking soda into a bowl. Work in the butter with your fingertips. Make a well in the center and pour in the buttermilk. Mix to form a spongy dough.

Turn the dough out onto a floured board and shape it into a round loaf about 2 inches (5 cm) thick. Put the loaf on the baking sheet and score the top into quarters with a sharp knife. Bake for 30 to 35 minutes or until the top is golden brown. Transfer the bread to a rack to cool completely before serving.

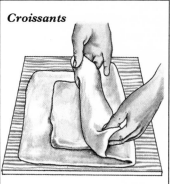

Croissants

Roll the dough into an oblong. Put the butter on the dough and fold over the edges.

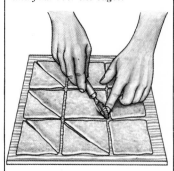

Roll the dough out thinly and cut it into squares. Cut the squares into triangles.

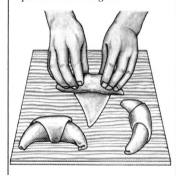

Roll each triangle from the base to the apex, then shape the rolls into crescents.

Eggs and dairy products

Baked eggs, custards and soufflés should never be over-cooked or they will be spoiled, so it is important to remember that, because the heat is retained in the dish in which they are cooked and served, they will continue to cook after they have come out of the oven.

Baked eggs are cooked in ovenproof ramekins at a temperature of 350°F (180°C) for about ten minutes or until the whites have just set.

Baked custards are cooked in a slightly cooler oven, about 325°F (170°C), for between thirty minutes and one hour, depending on whether the custard is in a large baking dish or in individual ramekin dishes. Bake in a bain-marie until a knife inserted in the center of the custard comes out clean. Leave to cool before serving.

Soufflés should always be cooked in a special straight-sided soufflé dish. Pour the soufflé mixture into the buttered dish, set it on a baking sheet in the oven and bake until the soufflé is a golden brown on the top and is well risen.

Tarte au Gruyère

SERVES FOUR

**Rich pie pastry for a 1-crust
    9-inch (23-cm) pie
2 tablespoons butter
2 tablespoons flour
½ cup (125 ml) milk
Salt and pepper
Cayenne pepper
1¼ cups (75 g) grated
    Gruyère cheese
2 eggs, separated
1 tablespoon grated
    Parmesan cheese**

Preheat the oven to 425°F (220°C).

Roll out the pastry dough and line a buttered 9-inch (23-cm) pie pan. Bake blind for 15 minutes. Remove from the oven and set aside. Reset the oven to 375°F (190°C).

Melt the butter in a saucepan. Stir in the flour to make a roux. Take the pan off the heat and gradually add the milk, stirring constantly. Return the pan to the heat and bring the sauce to a boil, stirring until very thick. Season with salt, pepper and a pinch of cayenne. Stir in the Gruyère and remove the pan from the heat.

Beat in the egg yolks and set aside until cool.

Three light and delicious baked dishes, all made with eggs : quiche Lorraine, cheese soufflé and, for dessert, caramel custard.

Beat the egg whites until stiff and fold them into the cheese mixture. Pour the mixture into the pastry shell, sprinkle the Parmesan on top and bake for 20 minutes or until the top is puffed up and golden brown.

Serve hot.

Quiche Lorraine

Serve this classic regional dish warm or cold, either by itself as a first course or with a green salad for a light lunch or supper.

SERVES FOUR AS A MAIN COURSE

**Rich pie pastry for a 1-crust
    9-inch (23-cm) pie
¼ lb (125 g) bacon, diced
1¼ cups (315 ml) heavy
    cream
1 egg plus 3 egg yolks
Salt and pepper
Nutmeg**

Preheat the oven to 425°F (220°C).

Line a 9-inch (23-cm) pie pan with the pastry dough. Bake blind for 15 minutes then set aside. Reset the oven to 375°F (190°C).

Fry the bacon gently for about 5 minutes until the fat begins to run. Using a slotted spoon, transfer the bacon to the pastry shell.

Beat the cream with the egg, egg yolks and seasoning. Pour the custard into the pastry shell, sprinkle a little nutmeg on top and bake for 30 to 40 minutes or until the top is golden brown.

Oeufs sur le plat

Bacon and eggs are extremely good cooked in this way. The bacon is first lightly fried and the fat reserved. The slices are laid in a buttered dish, the eggs broken on top and the bacon fat poured over the eggs.

SERVES TWO

**2 tablespoons butter
4 eggs
Salt and pepper
4 teaspoons melted butter**

Preheat the oven to 350°F (180°C).

Put the butter into two small individual ramekins or ovenproof dishes and melt it in the oven.

Break the eggs carefully into the dishes, season well and pour 1 teaspoon of melted butter over each egg.

Bake for 4 to 6 minutes or until the whites are just set. The eggs will continue to cook in the heat of the dish and it is therefore important to remove them from the oven just before they are done.

Cheese soufflé

The mixture can be baked in one large soufflé dish or four individual ones. Serve the soufflé as soon as it is cooked, before it has time to collapse.

SERVES TWO TO FOUR

**3 tablespoons butter
2 tablespoons flour
1 cup (250 ml) milk
Salt and pepper
Cayenne pepper
4 egg yolks
3 tablespoons grated
    Gruyère cheese
2 tablespoons grated
    Parmesan cheese
5 egg whites**

Preheat the oven to 350°F (180°C) and put a baking sheet on the middle shelf.

Butter an 8-inch (20-cm) straight-sided soufflé dish.

Melt the butter in a saucepan over low heat, stir in the flour and cook for 1 minute. Add the milk gradually, stirring constantly, and bring to a boil.

Take the pan off the heat and season well. Cool the sauce a little, then beat in the egg yolks and cheese. Set the sauce aside to cool completely.

Eggs and dairy products

Beat the egg whites until stiff but not dry. Work a spoonful of the egg whites into the sauce and then fold in the remainder with light, quick strokes.

Pour the mixture into the soufflé dish, put the dish on the baking sheet, and bake for 35 to 45 minutes or until the soufflé is well risen and golden brown.

Serve immediately.

Chocolate soufflé

For a delicious variation stir a teaspoon of grated orange rind or a tablespoon of finely chopped bitter marmalade peel into the chocolate before the whites are incorporated.

SERVES FOUR

6 squares (175 g) semisweet chocolate, broken into pieces
2 tablespoons coffee or rum
4 egg yolks

5 egg whites
1¼ cups (315 ml) cream or sauce sabayon

Put a baking sheet on the middle shelf of the oven and preheat the oven to 400°F (200°C). Butter a 1-quart (1-liter) soufflé dish.

Melt the chocolate in the coffee or rum in a bowl over simmering water. Remove the bowl from the heat, cool for 1 minute and beat in the egg yolks. Let the mixture cool.

Beat the egg whites until stiff. Stir a spoonful of egg white into the chocolate and then quickly fold in the remainder.

Pour the mixture into the soufflé dish, put the dish on the baking sheet, and bake for 15 to 20 minutes or until the soufflé is well risen with a light crust on the surface.

Serve immediately with the cream or sauce.

Baked custard

The milk may be infused with other flavors such as orange rind, crushed coffee beans or chocolate.

SERVES FOUR

2½ cups (625 ml) milk
1 vanilla bean
2 whole eggs plus 2 yolks
1½ tablespoons fine granulated sugar
Nutmeg

Preheat the oven to 325°F (170°C).

Lightly butter a 1-quart (1-liter) baking dish.

Scald the milk in a saucepan and add the vanilla bean. Remove the pan from the heat and let infuse.

Beat the eggs, egg yolks and sugar together and pour on the warm milk. Strain the custard into the baking dish. Dust the top with grated nutmeg, stand the dish in a double-boiler of warm water and cook for 45 to 60 minutes or until a knife inserted into the custard comes out clean.

Remove the baking dish from the oven and serve warm or chilled.

Caramel custard

If you prefer, make the custard in a 1-quart (1-liter) ovenproof dish instead of in the individual custard cups and bake for about 1 hour. For a richer custard use half milk and half cream.

SERVES FOUR

½ cup (125 g) sugar
2 tablespoons water
2 eggs plus 2 egg yolks
½ teaspoon vanilla extract
2½ cups (625 ml) milk

Preheat the oven to 325°F (170°C). Heat the custard cups.

Put 3 tablespoons of the sugar with the water in a small pan. Cook over moderate heat, stirring constantly, until the syrup is a rich brown.

Pour the caramel into the custard cups. Turn them so that the bottom and sides are coated with the caramel.

Beat the eggs, egg yolks and vanilla extract with the remaining sugar. Scald the milk and pour it over the eggs, stirring.

Strain the custard into the custard cups. Stand the cups in a baking dish. Pour in warm

water to come halfway up the sides of the cups. Bake for 30 to 40 minutes or until the custard has set but is still slightly wobbly.

Let cool. When the custard is quite cold, cover and refrigerate. Unmold and serve.

Petits pots de crème au chocolat

Other flavors such as coffee or vanilla may be used instead of the chocolate.

SERVES SIX

4 squares (125 g) semisweet chocolate, broken into pieces
1¼ cups (315 ml) milk
1¼ cups (315 ml) cream
3 egg yolks plus 1 whole egg
1 tablespoon vanilla sugar

Preheat the oven to 325°F (170°C).

Melt the chocolate in the milk and cream. Mix the egg yolks, the whole egg and sugar in a large bowl. Pour in the milk and chocolate mixture and stir to mix. Strain the custard into 6 custard cups, cover with lids or buttered paper and stand in a double boiler of warm water.

Bake for 30 minutes or until a knife inserted into the custard comes out clean. Serve cold.

Meringues

MAKES ABOUT SIXTEEN SHELLS

4 egg whites
1 cup (225 g) plus 2 tablespoons fine granulated sugar, sifted
1¾ cups (425 ml) whipping cream

Preheat the oven to 250°F (130°C). Line two large baking sheets with nonstick paper or lightly oiled waxed paper.

Beat the egg whites in a large bowl with a wire whisk or electric beater. When the egg whites form stiff peaks beat in 2 tablespoons of the sugar. Beat until stiff and glossy. Using a large metal spoon, fold in all but two tablespoons of the remaining sugar.

Spoon the meringue mixture into a pastry tube fitted with a plain nozzle and squeeze out the meringue shells onto the baking sheets or use two large spoons to shape the shells. Dredge the meringues with 2 tablespoons of sugar and let stand for 5 minutes.

Bake for 1½ hours or until the meringues are a pale beige in color and are set on the outside but sticky on the inside. Look at the meringues from time to time to check that they are not coloring too quickly. If they are, turn off the oven and let the meringues cook more slowly.

Gently lift the meringues from the paper, using a spatula. Press the base of each meringue with your fingertips to make a dent for the cream filling.

Return the meringues, on their sides, to the baking sheets and bake for 20 to 30 minutes.

Cool on a wire rack and when cold either fill with whipped cream just before serving or store in a completely airtight container.

Meringue basket

This is a stiffer meringue that will hold its shape well.

MAKES ONE 9-INCH (23-CM)
BASKET

4 egg whites
1¾ cups (225 g) confectioners'
sugar, sifted
Vanilla extract

Line a large baking sheet with waxed paper.

Preheat the oven to 250°F (130°C).

Beat the egg whites with a wire whisk or electric beater until they are frothy but not stiff. Place the bowl over a pan of hot water over low heat and gradually beat in the sugar. Add 2 drops of vanilla extract and continue beating until the meringue is very thick.

Trace several small circles or one 9-inch (23-cm) circle onto the waxed paper.

Using a pastry tube, squeeze out the meringue in concentric circles to form the base. Then squeeze around the edge to make the sides.

Bake for about 1½ hours. Cool on a wire rack and either use at once or store in an airtight container.

Pavlova

SERVES FOUR TO SIX

1 cup (250 ml) whipping
cream
1 tablespoon Cointreau

1 tablespoon brandy
One 9-inch (23-cm)
meringue basket
1 lb (450 g) fresh fruit,
weight after preparation
1 tablespoon sugar

Whip the cream until thick. Beat in the Cointreau and brandy and beat until stiff. Spread the cream on the base of the meringue basket.

Cut large fruit into cubes, remove pits and seeds. Toss the fruit in the sugar and pile decoratively on top of the cream. Serve immediately.

Meringue hazelnut gâteau

SERVES SIX TO EIGHT

6 egg whites
1½ cups (350 g) fine
granulated sugar
2 teaspoons lemon juice
1 cup (175 g) ground
hazelnuts
1¾ cups (425 ml) whipping
cream
1 tablespoon confectioners'
sugar
1 to 2 tablespoons coffee
extract
Hazelnuts or coffee beans

Preheat the oven to 325°F (170°C).

Line 3 baking sheets with waxed paper. Trace three 9-inch (23-cm) circles on the paper, then lightly oil the paper.

Using a wire whisk or beater, beat the egg whites in a bowl until stiff. Add 2 tablespoons of the sugar and the lemon juice and beat for 30 seconds more. Fold in the remaining sugar and the ground hazelnuts.

Spread equal amounts of the meringue mixture onto the traced circles on the baking sheets. Bake for 25 to 30 minutes or until the meringues are lightly colored and firm to the touch. Carefully transfer the meringues to wire racks to cool.

Meanwhile whip the cream with the confectioners' sugar until stiff, adding the coffee extract to taste. Sandwich the meringue layers with half the cream mixture. Spread the remaining cream over the top and sides. Decorate with the hazelnuts or coffee beans. Put the cake in the refrigerator for 30 minutes before serving.

Baked Alaska

The secret of a successful baked Alaska is that the ice cream should be very cold and the oven temperature high enough to color the meringue quickly without melting the ice cream. Use a really good-quality, well-flavored ice cream.

SERVES SIX

1 quart (1 liter) good-
quality chocolate ice
cream
1 angel food cake, 8 inches
(20 cm) in diameter
4 tablespoons rum
4 large egg whites
Pinch cream of tartar
¾ cup (175 g) sugar

Put the ice cream on a sheet of foil and shape it into a round the same size as the cake. Wrap the foil around the ice cream and put it in the freezer to harden.

Preheat the oven to 450°F (230°C).

Put the cake on an ovenproof plate and sprinkle it evenly with the rum. Leave to soak for 30 minutes.

Beat the egg whites with the cream of tartar until stiff. Beat in the sugar, a tablespoonful at a time, until the whites form glossy peaks.

Very quickly, put the ice cream onto the cake and cover both completely with the meringue, leaving no spaces or the ice cream will melt.

Bake the Alaska for 3 to 5 minutes or until the meringue is golden.

Serve at once.

Queen of puddings

Serve this delightful pudding with plenty of cream.

SERVES FOUR

2½ cups (625 ml) milk
2 tablespoons butter
2 tablespoons sugar
Grated rind of 1 lemon
1 cup (125 g) fresh white
bread crumbs
3 eggs, separated
4 tablespoons of jam
(blackberry, apricot,
strawberry or black
currant), warmed
3 tablespoons powdered
sugar

Butter a 2½-pint (1¼-liter) shallow baking dish.

Heat the milk, butter, granulated sugar and lemon rind slowly in a covered saucepan, stirring once as the butter melts. When the milk is just warmed through, turn off the heat but leave the pan on the stove for 10 minutes.

Put the bread crumbs in a large bowl and pour the milk over them. Let soak for at least 20 minutes.

Preheat the oven to 350°F (180°C).

Beat in the egg yolks and pour the mixture into the baking dish.

Bake the pudding for 30 minutes or until lightly set. Remove the pudding from the oven and spread the warm jam evenly over the top.

Beat the egg whites until they are stiff. Beat in 2 tablespoons of the powdered sugar, and when the mixture is glossy fold in the remaining sugar.

Pile the meringue on top of the pudding and bake for 10 minutes or until the top is set and lightly colored.

Serve hot.

Raspberry tart

SERVES FOUR TO SIX

1⅓ cups (225 g) unblanched
almonds, washed and
dried
1 cup (225 g) fine granulated
sugar
4 egg whites
¾ lb (350 g) raspberries
1¼ cups (315 ml) whipping
cream
Flaked almonds, toasted

Preheat the oven to 350°F (180°C). Line the bottom of a shallow 9-inch (23-cm) cake pan with lightly oiled waxed paper.

Grind the almonds in a blender. Put them in a bowl and mix in the sugar. Beat the egg whites in another bowl until stiff. Fold in the almond and sugar mixture. Spread the meringue smoothly in the cake pan. Bake for 35 minutes or until lightly colored and firm to the touch.

Turn the meringue out carefully onto a wire rack to cool.

Just before serving, cover the meringue with the raspberries, reserving a few for decoration. Swirl the cream over the top and decorate with the reserved raspberries and toasted almonds.

The cold table

These specially selected hors d'oeuvre, pâtés, salads, ices and desserts are additional to the cold dishes included earlier in the book to illustrate the various cooking methods.

Hors d'oeuvre

Pan bagna

Other ingredients which may be included in a pan bagna are cooked, diced artichoke hearts, a few sliced gherkins or a small portion of mushrooms à la Grecque. Salami is not a traditional part of this provençal sandwich, but it adds an interesting flavor.

If the loaf is awkward to handle, cut it into two or three pieces after filling it. A round, flat loaf may also be used.

Pan bagna is excellent to take on a picnic.

SERVES FOUR TO SIX

1 long French loaf
4 to 6 tablespoons olive oil
1 garlic clove, cut in half
½ cup (125 g) black olives, pitted and sliced
¼ cup (50 g) capers
¾ lb (350 g) tomatoes, sliced
8 anchovy fillets, cut into small pieces
½ lb (225 g) salami, diced

Cut the loaf in half lengthwise. Remove some of the bread from both halves and put it into a large bowl.

Lay the two halves of the loaf, crust side down, on a dish. Dribble the oil over the insides, rub with the garlic and set aside for about 1 hour.

Add the olives, capers, tomatoes, anchovies and salami to the bread in the bowl. Stir the mixture well, then pile it into the bottom half of the loaf. Cover with the other half of the loaf, then wrap tightly in aluminum foil.

Put a heavy weight on top of the loaf and leave for several hours or overnight.

To serve, remove the foil and cut the loaf into thick slices.

Crudités

Crudités are raw, young vegetables trimmed and washed and eaten dipped in a vinaigrette or garlic mayonnaise. Use whichever vegetables are available.

SERVES FOUR TO SIX

1 cup (250 ml) aioli
1 cauliflower, washed and cut into florets
10 young carrots, scrubbed
6 celery stalks, washed and cut into strips
12 scallions, trimmed
1 head of Belgian endive, separated into leaves
1 green pepper, seeded, cored and cut into strips

Pour the aioli into a bowl, cover it and chill for at least 1 hour.

Arrange the vegetables on a large serving dish. Serve with the aioli.

Stuffed eggs

Serve stuffed eggs on a bed of watercress as a first course, as part of an hors d'oeuvre or as a garnish for a salad.

SERVES FOUR

8 hard-cooked eggs, shelled
2 tablespoons mayonnaise
8 anchovy fillets, diced
16 capers
2 tablespoons chopped fresh parsley
Salt and pepper

Cut the eggs in half. Remove the yolks and put them into a bowl.

Mash the yolks with a fork, then add the mayonnaise, anchovies, capers and parsley. Mix well and season to taste with salt and pepper.

Fill the eggs with the stuffing.

Chill for at least 30 minutes before serving.

Egg mayonnaise

Serve egg mayonnaise with thin slices of brown bread and butter.

SERVES FOUR

1 small lettuce, washed
6 hard-cooked eggs, shelled and cut in half lengthwise
1 cup (250 ml) thick mayonnaise
6 anchovy fillets, diced
1 tablespoon chopped parsley

Divide the lettuce between four plates and lay three egg halves on each plate. Spoon the mayonnaise over the eggs and garnish with the anchovies and parsley. Chill for at least 30 minutes before serving.

Pears with cream cheese

If the pears are not absolutely ripe, prepare them the previous day and let them marinate in the dressing overnight.

SERVES FOUR

Salt and pepper
1 tablespoon lemon juice
3 tablespoons olive oil
4 pears
1 cup (225 g) cream cheese
1 tablespoon chopped fresh parsley

To make the dressing, mix the salt, pepper and lemon juice in a bowl. Add the oil a little at a time and beat gently until it has amalgamated with the lemon juice.

Peel, core and slice the pears and put them immediately into the dressing. Cover the bowl and put it in the refrigerator for at least 2 hours. Baste the pears with the dressing every 30 minutes.

Shape the cheese into small balls. Roll the cheese balls in the chopped parsley and put them in the refrigerator.

To serve, divide the pears between 4 plates and top each portion with the cheese balls.

Seviche

Although the fish is never actually cooked, the lime juice marinade breaks down the fibers, making it deliciously tender. Use any firm-fleshed white fish.

SERVES FOUR

2 cups (500 ml) fresh lime juice
2 onions, thinly sliced
1 red chili, seeded and chopped
1 garlic clove, crushed
1½ teaspoons salt
Black pepper
1½ lb (700 g) fish fillets, cut into ½-inch (1-cm) pieces
Black olives, to garnish

Combine the lime juice, onions, chili, garlic, salt and a sprinkling of pepper in a bowl.

Add the fish and stir to make sure it is well coated with the marinade.

Cover the bowl and refrigerate for at least 24 hours or until the fish is opaque and tender. Serve garnished with black olives.

Rollmops

Rollmops, or raw pickled herring, should be left to marinate for at least a week, or a few days longer, if possible. Serve them with the onion rings and a little of the pickling liquid, which should first be strained.

SERVES FOUR

12 salt herring fillets
2 cups (500 ml) white wine vinegar
1 cup (250 ml) water
2 tablespoons sugar
French mustard
1 tablespoon capers
12 small gherkins
3 medium-sized onions, sliced and pushed out into rings
8 peppercorns
1 tablespoon mustard seeds
6 juniper berries
Finely grated rind of ½ lemon

Soak the herring fillets in cold water for 12 hours. Drain the fillets, rinse them under cold

Use a sharp, pointed knife to cut a tomato in half decoratively.

Cut a cucumber into lengths then scrape out the seeds.

Before serving, cut the stuffed, chilled cucumber into slices.

running water and dry on paper towels.

To make the pickling mixture, put the vinegar, water and sugar into a saucepan. Stir to dissolve over low heat then bring to a boil, stirring constantly. Remove the pan from the heat and set aside.

Lay the fillets skin side down. On each fillet put a little mustard, a few capers and a gherkin. Roll the fillets up and secure each one with a toothpick.

Put alternate layers of onion rings and herring into a large screw-top jar or deep bowl, sprinkling the layers with the peppercorns, mustard seeds, juniper berries and lemon rind.

Pour the pickling liquid into the jar or bowl, cover and refrigerate.

Curried rice salad

This is a luxurious salad that may be served on its own as a first course or as a main dish accompanied by other salads.

Use a good-quality long-grain rice such as Basmati.

SERVES SIX TO EIGHT

6 tablespoons mayonnaise, made with lemon juice
4 tablespoons heavy cream
1 tablespoon curry paste or powder
Salt and freshly ground black pepper
1 tablespoon lemon juice
1 garlic clove, crushed
2 scallions, chopped
1 green pepper, cored, seeded and chopped
2 avocado pears, peeled, pitted and sliced
1½ cups (225 g) fresh pineapple, cut in small pieces
⅓ cup (50 g) blanched almonds, halved
2 cups (225 g) shelled shrimp
2 cups (225 g) diced cooked chicken
1¼ cups (225 g) long-grain rice, washed, soaked, cooked and cooled

Put the mayonnaise, cream, curry paste or powder, seasoning, lemon juice and garlic into a large salad bowl and stir well. Add the remaining ingredients and toss the salad to coat the ingredients with the dressing. Chill in the refrigerator for 1 hour before serving.

Stuffed tomatoes

SERVES FOUR

4 large, firm tomatoes
½ cup (125 ml) mayonnaise
1 tablespoon lemon juice
1 tablespoon heavy cream
2 cups (225 g) cooked white crabmeat
1 green pepper, seeded, cored and finely chopped

Slice the tops off the tomatoes. Scoop out the flesh then turn the empty tomato cases upside down to drain. Reserve the tops.

Mix the mayonnaise with the lemon juice and cream. Stir in the crabmeat and green pepper.

Fill the tomato cases with the crabmeat mixture and replace the tops. Chill before serving.

Avocados stuffed with shrimp

SERVES FOUR

½ cup (125 ml) mayonnaise
2 tablespoons cream
1 tablespoon lemon juice
2 drops Tabasco sauce
2 cups (225 g) cooked, shelled shrimp
2 large, ripe avocados, halved and pitted
½ lemon

Combine the mayonnaise, cream, lemon juice and Tabasco in a bowl. Add the shrimp and stir until they are well coated. Rub the avocados with the lemon.

Spoon the mixture into the avocados and chill for at least 30 minutes before serving.

Stuffed cucumber

SERVES FOUR TO SIX

1 large cucumber, peeled and cut crosswise into pieces
½ cup (125 ml) canned tuna fish
1 tablespoon butter
2 tablespoons cream cheese
1 tablespoon chopped parsley
1 teaspoon fresh thyme
1 teaspoon fresh oregano
1 teaspoon fresh tarragon
1 teaspoon chopped fresh chives
½ teaspoon lemon juice
Salt and pepper

Using a sharp knife or a teaspoon, scoop the pulp and seeds from the center of each piece of cucumber. Pat dry with paper towels.

Drain the tuna fish and put it in a bowl. Add the butter, cheese, herbs and lemon juice and mash well with a fork. Season to taste.

Stuff the cucumber pieces with the tuna fish mixture and put in the refrigerator for at least 1 hour. Before serving, cut each piece of cucumber into slices.

Cheese ring

SERVES SIX

2 teaspoons flavorless cooking oil
½ lb (225 g) dolcelatte cheese
2 cups (225 g) cream cheese
Cayenne pepper
1 tablespoon chopped chives
1 tablespoon gelatin dissolved in 4 tablespoons hot water
¾ cup (175 ml) mayonnaise
½ cup (125 ml) heavy cream
6 radishes, thinly sliced

Grease a 7½-inch (19-cm) ring mold with the oil and set aside.

Push the dolcelatte through a sieve into a bowl. Beat in the cream cheese, a pinch of cayenne pepper and the chives. Mix thoroughly, then add the dissolved gelatin and continue to stir the mixture for a few minutes more.

Fold in the mayonnaise and cream then spoon it into the ring mold. Chill in the refrigerator for 2 hours or until the mixture has set.

To serve, turn the mold out and garnish with radish slices.

Cantaloupe salad

SERVES FOUR

2 cantaloupe melons
½ cucumber, peeled
2 ripe pears, peeled and cored
6 tablespoons vinaigrette
4 tablespoons sour cream
2 tablespoons lemon juice
2 teaspoons sugar
Salt and freshly ground black pepper

Cut the melons in half and remove the seeds. Scoop out the flesh, leaving ¼-inch (½-cm) thick shells. Dice the flesh and put it into a bowl.

Dice the cucumber and pears and mix with the the vinaigrette and set aside refrigerator.

Drain the fruit and pile into the melon

Beat the sour cream with the lemon juice and sugar and season to taste. Spoon the dressing over the salad and serve.

Grapefruit with shrimp

SERVES FOUR

2 grapefruit, chilled
2 cups (225 g) shelled shrimp, chilled
½ cup (125 ml) mayonnaise, chilled
4 mint sprigs

Cut the grapefruit in half. Using a sharp knife, carefully detach the grapefruit segments. Reserve the shells.

Combine the grapefruit segments, shrimp and mayonnaise. Pile the mixture into the grapefruit shells, garnish with the mint sprigs and serve.

Shellfish cocktail

SERVES FOUR

1 lb (450 g) mixed cooked lobster, crabmeat and shelled shrimp
1 tablespoon chopped walnuts
4 tablespoons chopped celery
1 cup (250 ml) well-seasoned mayonnaise
4 tablespoons heavy cream
1 teaspoon tomato paste
Tabasco sauce
½ teaspoon grated horseradish
Lemon juice
4 watercress sprigs

Cut the lobster into small pieces and shred the crabmeat. Put the shellfish into a bowl and mix in the walnuts and celery.

Combine the mayonnaise, cream, tomato paste, a few drops of the Tabasco sauce and the horseradish. Taste the sauce and add a little lemon juice if necessary.

Pour the sauce over the shellfish mixture and toss well to mix. Cover the bowl and refrigerate for at least 30 minutes.

To serve, spoon the mixture into 4 glass bowls. Garnish with the watercress and serve.

atés

Smoked mackerel pâté
SERVES FOUR

1 smoked mackerel
(approximately 1 pound/
450 g), skinned and boned
¼ cup (50 g) sweet butter,
melted
Grated rind and juice of 1
lemon
1 shallot
¼ teaspoon salt
Black pepper
Sliced cucumber

Break up the mackerel fillets
and put them in a blender
with all the other ingredients
except the cucumber. Blend until smooth. Taste and add more
salt, pepper or lemon juice if
necessary. Chill the pâté.

Game pâté

Line the terrine with fat.

Pour away excess liquid.

Spoon over the jellied stock.

Arrange the cucumber slices
overlapping in a circle on a dish.
Spoon the pâté into the middle
and serve.

Danish liver pâté
SERVES FOUR TO SIX

1 lb (450 g) pig's liver
¼ lb (125 g) fatback
5 anchovy fillets
1 cup (250 ml) béchamel
sauce, cooled
1 garlic clove, crushed
½ teaspoon salt
Pepper
¼ teaspoon ground mace
¼ lb (125 g) fatty bacon
slices

Preheat the oven to 350°F
(180°C).

Grind the liver, fatback and
anchovy fillets very finely or put
in a blender a little at a time
and blend until smooth. Put the
mixture into a bowl and beat in
the béchamel sauce, a little at a
time. Mix in the garlic, salt,
pepper and mace.

Line a 1-pint (500-ml) baking
dish or small loaf pan with the
bacon slices. Spoon in the mixture. Cover the top with buttered
waxed paper or foil. Put the
dish in a baking pan half filled
with boiling water. Bake for 1
hour or until the pâté is firm to
the touch.

Take the dish out of the oven
and let cool. When cool, cover
with fresh foil and chill for 12
hours before serving.

Game pâté
SERVES SIX

¼ lb (125 g) fatty bacon or
fatback
2 pheasants, roasted
1½ lb (700 g) pork belly,
ground
½ lb (225 g) pig's liver,
ground
6 tablespoons diced fatback
1 teaspoon grated orange
rind
1 teaspoon dried thyme
1 teaspoon dried marjoram
1 teaspoon salt
1 teaspoon black pepper-
corns, coarsely crushed
4 tablespoons white wine
2 tablespoons brandy
Clarified stock made from
the bird carcasses, and
thoroughly chilled

Line a 1-quart (1-liter) terrine
with the bacon or fatback. Strip
the meat off the game birds and
chop it coarsely. Mix the meat
with all the remaining ingredients except the cold stock. Put
the mixture into the terrine and
set aside for 1 hour.

Preheat the oven to 325°F
(170°C).

Put the terrine into a roasting
pan. Half fill the pan with boiling
water. Bake the pâté for 1½ to 1¾
hours or until the top is brown
and the pâté has shrunk slightly
from the sides.

Remove the terrine from the
oven. Pour out any liquid. Let
cool. Cover the top with foil
and put a weight on top. When
the pâté is cold, pour a thin
layer of the cold stock over the
top and refrigerate until set.

Hare pâté

The meat may be taken from a
roasted or casseroled hare. One
large hare will provide enough
meat for a roast as well as for a
pâté for four people.

SERVES FOUR

1 lb (450 g) cooked, boned
hare, ground
½ lb (225 g) pork, ground
1 lb (450 g) bacon slices
2 garlic cloves, crushed
1½ teaspoons dried basil
1½ teaspoons dried marjoram
½ cup (125 ml) red wine or
brandy
½ teaspoon salt
1 teaspoon black pepper-
corns, coarsely ground
Grated rind of ½ lemon

Preheat the oven to 325°F
(170°C).

Mix the hare and pork together
in a bowl. Chop ½ pound of the
bacon and mix it in. Stir in the
garlic, herbs, wine or brandy,
salt, pepper and lemon rind.

Line a 1-quart (1-liter) terrine
or loaf pan with half the remaining bacon slices. Spoon in the
hare mixture and cover the top
with the remaining bacon.

Put the terrine in a baking pan
half filled with boiling water and
bake for 1¾ hours or until the
sides have shrunk slightly.

Remove the terrine from the
oven and let cool. When cool,
cover with foil and refrigerate
for at least 3 hours before
serving.

Gelée de saumon
SERVES FOUR

1 tablespoon gelatin
½ cup (125 ml) boiling water
2 tablespoons lemon juice
1 small onion, sliced
½ cup (125 ml) mayonnaise
1 teaspoon dried dill weed
1 lb (450 g) cooked salmon,
boned and skinned, or 1 lb
(450 g) canned salmon,
drained
1 cup (250 ml) whipping
cream
1 teaspoon salt

Lightly oil a 1-quart (1-liter)
mold or loaf pan. Dissolve the
gelatin in the water and pour it
into a blender with the lemon
juice and onion. Blend for 40
seconds. Add the mayonnaise,
dill and salmon and blend for a
few seconds. Add the cream one-
third at a time, blending for a
few seconds after each addition.
If necessary add a little salt.
Blend for 30 seconds.

Pour the mixture into the
mold. Cover and chill for at
least 2 hours before turning it
out onto a serving dish.

Veal and ham pâté
SERVES SIX

½ lb (225 g) veal, ground
½ lb (225 g) pork, ground
½ lb (225 g) fatback, ground
¼ lb (125 g) prosciutto ham,
diced
3 tablespoons capers
2 tablespoons pistachio nuts
4 tablespoons dry sherry
1 teaspoon salt
1 teaspoon peppercorns,
coarsely crushed
1 garlic clove, crushed
2 teaspoons chopped basil
¼ lb (125 g) fatty bacon

Mix all the ingredients except
the bacon in a bowl. Spoon the
mixture into a 1-quart (1-liter)
terrine. Lay the bacon over the
top and set aside for 1 hour.

Preheat the oven to 325°F
(170°C).

Put the terrine in a roasting
pan half filled with boiling water
and bake for 1¾ hours.

Remove the terrine from the
oven and let cool. Cover the
top with foil and put a weight on
top.

When completely cold, refrigerate for 12 hours before serving.

Pâté au cognac

Once the pâté has been cooled, it can be covered with a thin coating of meat glaze or melted butter.

SERVES SIX

6 tablespoons butter
2 shallots, finely chopped
½ fresh bay leaf
2 garlic cloves, crushed
1½ lb (700 g) chicken livers, cleaned, trimmed, washed and dried
1 to 2 tablespoons brandy
2 egg yolks

Melt the butter in a medium-sized saucepan over low heat. Add the shallots, bay leaf and garlic and cook, stirring occasionally, until the shallots are soft but not colored. Add the chicken livers and cook them until they are tender. Mash them with a fork and cook for a further 5 minutes, stirring constantly. Remove the pan from the heat.

Preheat the oven to 350°F (180°C). Grease a terrine or medium-sized baking dish and set it aside.

Put the chicken liver mixture into a blender and blend until smooth. Alternatively, rub the mixture twice through a fine strainer. Beat in the brandy and egg yolks and pour the mixture into the baking dish. Place the dish in a baking pan half filled with water and bake for 1 hour, or until the pâté is firm to the touch.

Cool before serving.

Taramasalata

In Greece this delicious pâté is made from the roe of the gray mullet, but it can also be made from smoked cod's roe. Garnish the pâté with black olives and serve with toast or hot pitta.

SERVES SIX TO EIGHT

¾ lb (350 g) smoked cod's roe
4 slices white bread, crusts removed
6 tablespoons milk
2 garlic cloves, crushed
½ cup (125 g) cream or curd cheese
9 tablespoons olive oil
Juice of 1 large lemon
Salt and pepper

Using a teaspoon, scoop the roe out of its skin into a bowl. Soak the bread in the milk. When the bread is soft, squeeze out any excess milk and add the bread to the roe. Beat in the garlic and cheese. Add the oil and lemon juice a spoonful at a time, beating well between each addition.

Put the mixture into a blender a little at a time and blend until smooth. Season to taste and add more lemon juice if necessary.

Meat loaf

SERVES SIX

½ lb (225 g) pork, ground
½ lb (225 g) veal, ground
1 lb (450 g) ham, ground
2 garlic cloves, crushed
1 tablespoon chopped mint
½ teaspoon salt
½ teaspoon coarsely ground black pepper
2 eggs
3 large hard-cooked eggs

Preheat the oven to 350°F (180°C).

Combine all the ingredients except the hard-cooked eggs in a mixing bowl. Stuff the mixture into a straight-sided, wide-mouthed, heatproof jar. Push the eggs in down the center, nose to tail. If a jar is not available, use a 2-pound (1-kg) loaf pan. Put half the mixture in the bottom of the pan, lay the hard-cooked eggs in a row down the center and cover with the rest of the mixture. Cover the pan or jar with foil, stand it in a roasting pan half filled with boiling water and bake for 1¾ hours.

Remove the meat loaf from the oven and let cool. Cover with fresh foil and refrigerate for 4 hours.

Pâté de campagne

SERVES SIX

1 lb (450 g) veal, ground
1 lb (450 g) pork belly, ground
½ lb (225 g) pig's liver, ground
2 garlic cloves, crushed
6 tablespoons diced fatback
½ teaspoon coarsely ground black pepper
1 heaped teaspoon salt
8 juniper berries, lightly crushed
4 tablespoons brandy
¼ lb (125 g) fatty bacon slices, cut in half lengthwise

Mix all the ingredients except the bacon and put into a 1-quart (1-liter) terrine or loaf pan. Lay the bacon over the top and set aside for 1 hour.

Preheat the oven to 325°F (170°C).

Put the terrine in a roasting pan. Pour some water into the pan and bake the pâté for 1¾ hours.

Remove the terrine from the oven and let cool. Cover the top with foil and leave until completely cold. Chill in the refrigerator before serving.

Pork terrine

SERVES SIX TO EIGHT

½ lb (225 g) fatty bacon
1½ lb (700 g) pork fillet, beaten out into thin scallops
1½ lb (700 g) ham, thinly sliced
2 tablespoons chopped parsley
2 tablespoons chopped onion
2 tablespoons sliced stuffed olives
Salt and pepper
½ cup (125 ml) white wine
¼ cup (65 ml) brandy

Preheat the oven to 325°F (170°C).

Line a 2-pound (1-kg) loaf pan or terrine with half the bacon. Layer the pork and ham, sprinkling the layers with the chopped parsley, onion, sliced olives and seasoning.

Mix the wine and brandy together and pour it over the meat. Cover the top with the remaining bacon.

Bake in a roasting pan half filled with water for 2 hours.

Remove the terrine from the oven, cover with foil and put a weight on top. Leave overnight or until completely cold. Chill and serve thinly sliced.

Ham mousse

SERVES FOUR TO SIX

1 tablespoon gelatin
1 cup (250 ml) chicken stock
2 eggs, separated
⅔ cup (150 ml) mayonnaise
½ lb (225 g) cooked ham, cut into pieces
1 tablespoon chopped chives
2 teaspoons Dijon mustard
½ teaspoon paprika
⅔ cup (150 ml) heavy cream

Lightly oil a 1-quart (1-liter) round mold. Dissolve the gelatin in 3 tablespoons of the chicken stock over low heat. Put the gelatin, the remaining stock, egg yolks, mayonnaise, ham, chives, mustard and paprika into a blender and blend until smooth. Pour in the cream and blend for a few seconds. Pour the mixture into a bowl.

Beat the egg whites until stiff but not dry and fold into the ham mixture. Turn the mixture into the mold, cover and chill for at least 2 hours.

Chopped liver

Serve chopped liver with thin slices of buttered toast.

SERVES FOUR TO SIX

1 lb (450 g) chicken livers, carefully cleaned
1 large onion
2 hard-cooked eggs
2 tablespoons butter
Salt and pepper

Preheat the broiler to moderate. Broil the chicken livers for 1 minute on each side.

Chop the onion coarsely in a large wooden chopping bowl. Add the liver and chop until the mixture is fairly smooth.

Add the eggs and chop them coarsely. Mix in the butter and season to taste. Serve immediately or store in the refrigerator.

Avocado and shrimp cream

Serve as a first course with Melba toast. The cream must be eaten very soon after it has been made, as avocados discolor quickly.

SERVES FOUR TO SIX

3 large, very ripe avocados, peeled and pitted
2 garlic cloves, crushed
1 tablespoon lemon juice
¼ teaspoon cayenne pepper
Salt and pepper
⅔ cup (150 ml) sour cream
½ lb (225 g) fresh shrimp, cooked and shelled

Put a strainer over a mixing bowl and rub the avocados through the strainer with the back of a wooden spoon. Clean out the strainer and rub the avocados through again. Beat in the remaining ingredients and spoon the mixture into a serving bowl.

Salads

Celeriac salad
SERVES FOUR

¾ lb (350 g) celeriac root,
peeled
½ cup (125 ml) mayonnaise
made with extra mustard
½ red pepper, cored and
sliced thinly in rings
½ green pepper, cored and
sliced thinly in rings
½ onion, sliced thinly in
rings

Cut the celeriac into slices and
then into strips. Combine the
mayonnaise with the celeriac
strips. Pile the mixture into a
bowl and garnish with the
peppers and onion.

Russian salad
SERVES FOUR

½ lb (225 g) potatoes, cooked
½ lb (225 g) carrots, cooked
½ lb (225 g) green beans,
cooked
¼ lb (125 g) peas, cooked
2 tablespoons chopped
chives
4 tablespoons vinaigrette
½ cup (125 ml) mayonnaise
6 anchovy fillets
2 hard-cooked eggs, cut into
quarters
2 tablespoons capers

Cut the potatoes and carrots into
¼-inch (½-cm) cubes. Cut the
beans into ¼-inch (½-cm) lengths.
Put the vegetables and the chives
into a bowl, pour in the vinaigrette and toss to mix. Leave for
1 hour to marinate.

Drain the vegetables and put
them in another bowl. Pour in
the mayonnaise and toss to mix.

Garnish with the anchovy
fillets, hard-cooked eggs and
capers.
Serve chilled.

Coleslaw
SERVES FOUR

1 small white cabbage,
finely shredded
¾ cup (175 ml) mayonnaise
¼ cup (65 ml) sour cream
2 teaspoons sugar
1 teaspoon prepared
mustard
Juice of ½ lemon
Salt and pepper

Put the cabbage in a bowl. Mix
all the remaining ingredients together and pour over the cabbage. Toss well. Serve well
chilled.

Rice salad
SERVES FOUR

4 cups (450 g) cooked rice
½ cup (125 ml) vinaigrette
2 tablespoons chopped
parsley
¼ cucumber, diced
6 scallions, chopped
⅔ cup (125 g) stuffed olives,
sliced
2 celery stalks, chopped
2 carrots, diced
2 hard-cooked eggs,
quartered
2 tomatoes, quartered

Put the rice, while it is still hot,
into a salad bowl. Mix in the
vinaigrette, parsley, cucumber,
scallions, olives, celery and
carrots. Garnish with the eggs
and tomatoes. Serve chilled.

Spinach and mushroom salad
SERVES FOUR

¼ cup (65 ml) vinaigrette
½ lb (225 g) mushrooms,
cleaned
½ lb (225 g) fresh spinach,
washed and drained
Lemon juice

Put the vinaigrette in a salad
bowl. Slice the mushrooms fairly
thickly and put them in the bowl.

Remove the central vein from
each spinach leaf. If the leaves
are large, tear them into bite-
sized pieces. Put the leaves on
top of the mushrooms. Add a
squeeze of lemon juice and toss.

Eggplant salad
Serve with Greek bread or toast
as an appetizer.
SERVES FOUR TO SIX

4 eggplants
2 garlic cloves, crushed
½ cup (125 ml) olive oil
Juice of 1 lemon
Salt and pepper
4 tablespoons chopped
parsley

Preheat the oven to 350°F
(180°C).

Wrap the eggplants in foil or
oiled waxed paper. Put them
on a baking sheet and bake for
40 minutes.

Remove the eggplants from
the oven and when they are cool
enough to handle, cut them in
half. Scrape out all the flesh into
a bowl. Mix in the garlic. Beat in
the olive oil a few drops at a time
as you would for mayonnaise.
Mix in the lemon juice and

season with salt and pepper to
taste. Mix in the parsley. Chill
before serving.

Mushrooms à la grecque
SERVES FOUR

1½ cups (375 ml) water
2 garlic cloves, crushed
Juice of 2 lemons
4 tablespoons olive oil
6 peppercorns
Salt
1 tarragon sprig
1 parsley sprig
1 lb (450 g) mushrooms,
stalks removed
Chopped parsley

Put the water, garlic, lemon
juice, olive oil, peppercorns and
a large pinch of salt in a saucepan
and bring to a boil. Reduce the
heat and simmer for 10 minutes.
Add the tarragon, parsley sprig
and mushroom caps and simmer
for 10 minutes.

Drain the mushrooms and put
them in a dish. Return the marinade to the pan and boil rapidly
to reduce to ½ cup. Strain the
marinade over the mushrooms.
Cover the dish and refrigerate.
Serve well chilled, garnished
with the parsley.

Green bean salad
SERVES FOUR

1 lb (450 g) green beans,
trimmed and washed
Salt
½ cup (125 ml) vinaigrette
8 anchovy fillets
4 tablespoons thick
mayonnaise
8 black olives, pitted

Drop the beans into salted boiling water. When the water returns to a boil, reduce the heat and simmer for 5 minutes. Drain and refresh the beans under cold running water.

Drain the beans well and put in a bowl. Pour in the vinaigrette and leave for 1 hour.

Arrange the beans neatly in stacks on 4 plates. Slit the anchovy fillets in half lengthwise and lay them across the beans. Spoon the mayonnaise in between the anchovies. Put the olives on top. Serve chilled.

Celery, apple and walnut salad

SERVES FOUR

1 cup (250 ml) yogurt
2 tablespoons honey
1½ teaspoons dried mint
1 head of celery, washed and sliced
2 apples, cored and sliced
⅓ cup (50 g) coarsely chopped walnuts

Whisk the yogurt in a bowl. Add the honey, a little at a time, and continue to beat until the ingredients are well blended. Stir in the mint.

Put the celery, apples and walnuts in a large bowl, pour over the yogurt dressing and serve.

Carrot and apple salad

SERVES FOUR

½ lb (225 g) carrots, coarsely grated
2 well-flavored, unpeeled eating apples, coarsely grated

4 tablespoons golden raisins
2 tablespoons peanuts
½ cup (125 ml) vinaigrette

Mix all the ingredients together in a salad bowl.

Belgian endive, orange and watercress salad

This salad, which may be garnished with black olives, goes particularly well with duck.

SERVES FOUR

1 tablespoon lemon juice
Salt and pepper
½ teaspoon French mustard
1 teaspoon sugar
Tabasco sauce
3 tablespoons olive oil
2 oranges, peeled and sliced
4 heads of Belgian endive, sliced crosswise
1 bunch watercress, washed

Combine the lemon juice, salt and pepper to taste, mustard, sugar and a few drops of Tabasco in a bowl. Add the oil a little at a time, beating constantly, until the dressing is smooth.

In a large salad bowl, put the orange slices, endive and watercress. Pour over the dressing, toss well and serve immediately, or chill for about 30 minutes before serving.

Tomato salad

A simple tomato salad can be made with peeled, sliced tomatoes, sprinkled with salt, black pepper and chopped fresh basil. Dress with a vinaigrette or omit the basil and use the English salad dressing. This variation comes from Greece. If you are unable to buy feta cheese, mozzarella is a good substitute.

SERVES FOUR

¼ lb (125 g) feta cheese, cubed
2 lb (900 g) tomatoes, peeled and sliced
1 green pepper, cored, seeded and sliced
1 small onion, finely chopped
Salt and pepper
1 teaspoon dried mint
1 garlic clove, crushed
1 tablespoon lemon juice
3 tablespoons olive oil
¼ lb (125 g) black olives, pitted

Put the cheese, tomatoes, pepper and onion in a salad bowl.

In another bowl mix the salt, pepper, mint, garlic and lemon juice. Gradually add the olive oil and beat until all the ingredients are blended.

Pour the dressing over the cheese and vegetables and toss well. Scatter the olives over the salad and serve.

Waldorf salad

This salad is excellent served with cold roast chicken.

SERVES FOUR

1 lb (450 g) apples, diced
2 celery stalks, diced
½ lb (225 g) grapes, halved and seeded
½ cup (50 g) walnut or pecan pieces
½ cup (125 ml) mayonnaise

Mix all the ingredients together in a bowl. Chill well before serving.

Green salad with blue cheese dressing

SERVES FOUR

2 tablespoons crumbled blue cheese
2 tablespoons wine vinegar
½ to 1 teaspoon French mustard
Sugar
Salt and pepper
5 tablespoons olive oil
1 head of Belgian endive, sliced crosswise
1 romaine lettuce
1 head of curly endive, coarsely chopped
A few dandelion leaves

To make the dressing mash the cheese in a bowl. Beat in the vinegar, mustard and sugar, salt and pepper to taste. Add the oil a little at a time, beating well.

Put the Belgian endive, lettuce, curly endive and dandelion leaves, if you have them, in a salad bowl. Toss the salad in dressing and serve.

Avocado salad

SERVES FOUR

1 romaine lettuce heart
3 avocados, peeled and sliced lengthwise
2 oranges, peeled and segmented
1 grapefruit, peeled and segmented
½ cup (125 ml) vinaigrette made with lemon juice

Tear the lettuce into pieces and put in a salad bowl with the avocados, oranges and grapefruit. Pour over the dressing and toss. Serve immediately.

Cold desserts

Lemon curd

This recipe is equally delicious made with oranges instead of lemons.

MAKES FOUR CUPS (900 G)

¾ cup (175 g) sweet butter, cut into small pieces
2 cups (450 g) sugar
Thinly pared rind and juice of 4 lemons
4 eggs, beaten

Put the butter, sugar, lemon rind and juice in an ovenproof mixing bowl. Set the bowl over a pan of barely simmering water and cook the mixture, stirring occasionally, until the sugar has dissolved.

Stir in the eggs and cook the lemon curd, stirring frequently, for about 25 minutes or until it has thickened enough to just coat the back of the spoon.

Remove the pan from the heat and lift out the lemon rind with a slotted spoon. Pour the curd into jam jars and let it cool. When it is completely cold, cover with a circle of waxed paper. Then cover each jar with cellophane and fasten with a rubber band. Store in a cool place.

Lemon curd tarts

MAKES TWELVE

2 teaspoons butter
1 recipe pâte sucrée
8 tablespoons lemon curd
½ cup (125 ml) whipping cream, whipped until thick
1 tablespoon finely chopped pistachio nuts (optional)

Preheat the oven to 375°F (190°C). Using the butter, grease twelve 3-inch (8-cm) muffin tins.

Roll the dough out thinly on a lightly floured board and use it to line the muffin tins. Prick the bottoms with a fork and bake for 10 to 12 minutes or until the pastry is crisp and golden. Remove the tins from the oven, let the pastry cool thoroughly and then turn the tarts out of the tins.

Spoon about 2 teaspoonfuls of the lemon curd into each tart. Fill a pastry tube fitted with a star nozzle with the cream and squeeze it over the lemon curd to cover it completely. Sprinkle over the pistachio nuts, if you are using them, and serve.

Apricot tart bourdaloue

SERVES SIX

Almond pastry for a single-crust pie
½ cup (125 g) sugar
1¼ cups (315 ml) water
1½ lb (700 g) apricots, halved and pitted
2½ cups (575 ml) crème pâtissière, flavored with grated orange rind
2 tablespoons flaked almonds, toasted

Preheat the oven to 375°F (190°C).

Press the pastry dough into an 8-inch (20-cm) pie pan to line it. Bake blind for 25 to 30 minutes, uncovering the pastry for the last 10 minutes to brown. Remove from the oven and set aside to cool.

Meanwhile, dissolve the sugar in the water. When the sugar has dissolved, bring the syrup to a boil and boil for 5 minutes. Add the apricots and simmer for 5 minutes or until the apricots are tender but not mushy.

Drain the apricots and return the syrup to the pan. Boil for 5 minutes or until thick.

Put the pastry shell on a plate. Spread the crème pâtissière over the bottom of the shell, rounding it slightly in the center. Cover the crème pâtissière completely with the apricot halves, cut sides down. Brush the apricots with the syrup. Scatter the almonds on top and serve.

Lemon gelatin

For a sparkling fruit mold clarify the gelatin in the same way as for aspic.

SERVES FOUR

1 tablespoon gelatin
1¾ cups (425 ml) water
½ cup (125 g) sugar
⅔ cup (150 ml) lemon juice
Pared rind of 2 lemons

Put the gelatin and 4 tablespoons of the water into a cup and let soften.

Put the remaining water, sugar, lemon juice and rind into a saucepan. Stir to dissolve the sugar over low heat. Leave for 30 minutes. Stir in the gelatin and stir until it has dissolved. Strain the mixture into a wet 1-pint (500-ml) jelly mold. Chill for 4 hours or until set.

Orange gelatin

Make orange gelatin in the same way as lemon gelatin, using 1¾ cups (425 ml) of orange juice, juice of 1 lemon, thinly pared rind of 1 orange, 2 to 3 tablespoons of sugar, 6 tablespoons of water and 1 tablespoon of gelatin.

Syllabub

SERVES FOUR

Finely pared rind and juice of 1 lemon
6 tablespoons sherry
2 tablespoons brandy
3 to 4 tablespoons fine granulated sugar
1¼ cups (315 ml) whipping cream

Put the lemon rind and juice, sherry and brandy into a small bowl. Cover and leave overnight.

Strain the lemon mixture into a bowl and mix in the sugar to taste. Stir in the cream. Then using a wire whisk or electric beater beat until the mixture is thick and will hold its shape. Serve the syllabub in small cups or tall wine glasses.

Lemon snow

SERVES FOUR

Juice and thinly pared rind of 2 lemons
1¼ cups (315 ml) water
3 tablespoons sugar
1 tablespoon gelatin
2 egg whites

Put the lemon rind and water in a saucepan and heat gently. The water must not boil or simmer. Cover the pan and leave for 30 minutes. Strain and mix in the sugar and lemon juice. Stir until the sugar has dissolved.

Meanwhile, dissolve the gelatin in 3 tablespoons of water over low heat. Mix the gelatin with the lemon juice mixture and pour into a bowl. Chill until nearly set.

Beat the egg whites until stiff but not dry and fold them into the lemon gelatin. Put the bowl back into the refrigerator.

Remove from the refrigerator 1 hour before serving.

Pears sabayon

SERVES FOUR

2 eggs, separated
2 tablespoons sugar
3 tablespoons Marsala wine
½ cup (125 ml) whipping cream, whipped
2 large, ripe pears

Beat the egg yolks with the sugar in the top of a double boiler. Add the Marsala and continue beating over barely simmering water until the mixture is smooth and thick.

Remove the pan from the heat and continue beating until the mixture is cool.

Fold in the cream. Beat the egg whites until stiff but not dry and fold them in gently.

Peel, core and slice the pears. Divide the pear slices between 4 serving bowls or glasses. Pour the sabayon over the pears and refrigerate for at least 3 hours before serving.

Lining muffin tins

Roll out the dough. With a biscuit cutter, cut out circles the same size as the muffin tins.

Lift the dough onto the muffin tins. Using your fingertips, ease it into the bottom and sides.

Trifle

If preferred use a fresh fruit purée instead of the jam.

SERVES SIX

1 day-old sponge cake, made with 3 eggs
Strawberry or raspberry jam
6 tablespoons sherry
2 tablespoons brandy
2½ cups (575 ml) cream
1 vanilla bean
2 whole eggs plus 2 egg yolks
3 tablespoons sugar
1 tablespoon cornstarch
1 cup (250 ml) whipping cream
Vanilla extract
Miniature macaroons
Toasted split almonds

Split the sponge cake in half and cut into pieces. Sandwich the pieces of cake with jam and put them in a glass bowl. Mix the sherry and brandy together and pour the mixture over the sponge. Cover the bowl and set it aside for 1 hour.

Meanwhile, make the custard. Put the cream and vanilla bean in a saucepan and bring to just under boiling point. Remove the pan from the heat, leave for 15 minutes and strain.

Beat the eggs and egg yolks with 2 tablespoons of the sugar and the cornstarch in a bowl. Pour in the cream, beating constantly. Put the bowl over a saucepan of barely simmering water and cook, stirring, until the custard is very thick and smooth. Taste it and add more sugar if necessary.

Pour the hot custard over the sponge and let cool. When cool, cover the bowl and put it in the refrigerator until well chilled.

Whip the whipping cream in a bowl with half the remaining sugar. Taste the cream and add the rest of the sugar if necessary. Mix in a few drops of vanilla extract.

Spread the cream over the custard and decorate the top with the macaroons and almonds.

Strawberry cheesecake

If you like, cut the cheesecake across in half and cover the bottom half with a little whipped cream and some sliced strawberries. Replace the top half of the cake and cover with more cream and sliced strawberries.

SERVES FOUR

½ cup (175 g) graham crackers
3 tablespoons butter
1½ cups (350 g) cream cheese
2 eggs
3 tablespoons sugar
1 teaspoon grated lemon rind
½ cup (125 ml) whipping cream, whipped
½ lb (225 g) strawberries, hulled

Preheat the oven to 350°F (180°C). Lightly grease a 7-inch (18-cm) springform cake pan and set it aside.

Put the graham crackers in a plastic bag and knot the end. Beat the bag with a rolling pin until the crackers are reduced to crumbs.

Melt the butter in a saucepan over moderate heat. Remove the pan from the heat and stir in the cracker crumbs to coat them thoroughly with the butter. Press the mixture into the bottom of the cake pan, smoothing it down well with the back of a spoon.

Put the cream cheese into a mixing bowl and beat it with a wooden spoon until is is smooth. Gradually beat in the eggs, being careful to avoid lumps. Beat in 2 tablespoons of the sugar and the lemon rind. Spoon the mixture into the cake pan, smoothing the top down, and bake for 30 to 40 minutes or until the center is firm when lightly pressed. Do not worry if a few small cracks appear on the top.

Remove the cheesecake from the oven and let it cool completely in the pan. Very carefully remove the cooled cheesecake from the pan and slide it onto a serving plate. Spread over the whipped cream and embed the strawberries in the cream. Sprinkle over the remaining sugar and serve.

Strawberry shortcake

SERVES EIGHT

2 cups (225 g) all-purpose flour
1 teaspoon baking powder
Pinch salt
½ cup (125 g) butter
3 tablespoons sugar
1 egg yolk
2 to 3 tablespoons milk

FILLING
1 cup (250 ml) whipping cream
1 tablespoon sugar
1 lb (450 g) strawberries, hulled

Preheat the oven to 375°F (190°C). Lightly grease two baking sheets with butter.

Sift the flour, baking powder and salt into a mixing bowl. Cut in the butter then work it into the flour with your fingertips.

Mix in the sugar. Make a well in the center. Mix in the egg yolk and enough milk to make a soft dough. Turn the dough out onto a lightly floured surface and knead gently.

Divide the dough in half and roll out two 9-inch (23-cm) circles. Score one circle into 8 pieces. Put the circles on the baking sheets and bake for 12 minutes or until the shortcake is just beginning to brown. Transfer the shortcakes carefully to a wire rack to cool.

To make the filling, whip the cream and sugar until stiff. Slice the strawberries, reserving a few for decoration, and fold them into the cream.

Put one shortcake on a serving plate. Spread the cream and strawberry mixture on top and smooth it down evenly. Cut the other shortcake along the score marks. Place the segments on top, decorate with the reserved strawberries and serve.

Chestnut cake

SERVES SIX TO EIGHT

2 lb (900 g) chestnuts, boiled and peeled
Milk
½ cup (125 g) sugar
¾ cup (175 g) butter
6 squares (175 g) semisweet chocolate, broken into pieces
3 tablespoons brandy or rum

Put the chestnuts in a saucepan. Pour in enough milk to cover and bring to a boil. Cover the pan, reduce the heat to low and simmer for 40 to 60 minutes or until the chestnuts are soft.

Drain the chestnuts and purée them in a blender or push them through a sieve. Beat in the sugar and ½ cup of the butter.

Lightly oil a small loaf pan and line the base with waxed paper. Oil the paper.

Spoon the mixture into the pan and smooth it down. Cover the pan with foil and put it in the refrigerator for 12 hours.

Run a knife around the edges of the pan and turn out the chestnut cake onto a plate.

Put the chocolate into a bowl with the brandy or rum and melt it over hot water. The chocolate must have the consistency of thick cream, so add a little water if the mixture is too thick. Remove the bowl from the heat and stir the remaining butter into the chocolate, a piece at a time. When the chocolate is smooth and glossy, spread it over the cake, using a knife dipped in hot water.

Set aside for 30 minutes or until the chocolate has set.

Chocolate torrone

This marvelously rich Italian dessert can be made one or two days in advance and kept in the refrigerator.

SERVES SIX TO EIGHT

8 squares (225 g) semisweet chocolate
4 tablespoons rum
1 cup (225 g) butter
1 tablespoon sugar
2 egg yolks
¼ lb (125 g) hazelnuts, coarsely chopped
4 egg whites
Salt
12 plain, crisp sugar cookies, broken into pieces

Lightly butter a 1-quart (1-liter) bowl.

Melt the chocolate in the rum in an ovenproof bowl over hot water. When the chocolate has melted, remove the bowl from the heat and let the mixture cool.

Cream the butter with the sugar until smooth, then add the egg yolks one at a time. Stir in the nuts and the chocolate.

Beat the egg whites with a pinch of salt until they form stiff peaks. Using a large metal spoon, fold the egg whites into the chocolate mixture. Carefully mix in the cookies.

Pour the torrone into the bowl, cover with aluminum foil and refrigerate for several hours before serving.

Ices

There are two kinds of ices—ice creams and water ices. Ice creams are divided into two main types: egg-mousse-and-cream-based and custard-based. Water ices are made with well-flavored fruit juice, black coffee or wine, mixed with sugar and water.

The best ices are made in a churn—electrically operated models are now available, but the smallest of these has a one-gallon (four-liter) capacity. If you have a refrigerator with a large ice-making compartment or a freezer, you can also obtain excellent results with a sorbetière, a metal box (one quart/one liter capacity) fitted with electrically operated plastic paddles, which stop moving when the ice is the right consistency.

Good ices can also be made in the ice-making compartment of the refrigerator without special equipment that churns or stirs automatically. These "still-frozen" ices take a long time to freeze, however, and must be thoroughly beaten at least twice during the freezing period to avoid ice crystals forming and spoiling the texture.

To still-freeze successfully, set the refrigerator at its coldest temperature one hour in advance, and chill the ingredients and utensils before using them. The ice cream mixture should have a fairly thick consistency before being frozen and water ices should include gelatin or egg white to ensure a smoother result.

When the mixture is ready and well chilled, put it into an ice cube tray or any other suitable container, cover with foil and put it in the ice-making compartment of the refrigerator. After about forty-five minutes the mixture should be firm around the edges. Turn it out into a well-chilled bowl and beat well. An electrically operated hand-held beater is the easiest to use. Return the mixture to its container. Cover and freeze for another thirty minutes, then repeat the process. After another hour the mixture should be frozen through.

Reset the temperature control to its normal setting and leave the ice in the ice-making compartment for at least one hour but preferably for three hours or more.

The general rules for making ices are the same whether they are made in a machine or still-frozen:

Because freezing diminishes flavors it is necessary to flavor and sweeten the mixture well. If you use too little sugar the ice will be hard and unpalatable; if you use too much the ice will not set properly. The maximum amount that may be used for an ice cream flavored only with an extract, vanilla for example, is about one part sugar to four parts custard or cream (volume measure) or one quarter pound (125 g) sugar to one pint (500 ml) custard or cream.

It is best to add sugar in the form of syrup, unless you are making a custard-based ice cream. The syrup is boiled until the temperature reaches 220°F (104°C) on a candy thermometer. If you do not have a thermometer, boil the syrup for 6 minutes. If you are using a liqueur, pour it over the ice just before serving, instead of including it in the mixture.

Containers should be only three-quarters filled with the mixture to allow for expansion during freezing.

Cream-based vanilla ice cream
Use whipping cream if the mixture is to be still-frozen.

SERVES FOUR TO SIX

2 cups (500 ml) light or whipping cream
1 vanilla bean
4 egg yolks
3 tablespoons sugar
½ cup (125 ml) water

Put the cream and vanilla bean into a small saucepan and bring to just under boiling point. Remove the pan from the heat and let stand for 5 minutes. Remove the vanilla bean, pour the cream into a bowl and set aside to cool. When cool, chill thoroughly over ice cubes.

Beat the egg yolks in a heatproof bowl. Dissolve the sugar in the water over low heat. When the sugar has dissolved, increase the heat and boil the syrup until it reaches a temperature of 220°F (104°C). Remove the pan from the heat, wait 30 seconds then pour in a steady stream over the yolks, beating all the time with a beater—a hand-held electrically operated one is easiest to use. Beat until the mixture is thick and mousse-like, then cool.

If you are using whipping cream, beat it until it is thick but not stiff. Fold the cream into the egg and sugar mixture. For still-freezing, chill the mixture then pour into the freezing tray or container and freeze.

Chocolate ice cream
Melt 6 squares (175 g) dark chocolate with 1 tablespoon of rum and fold it into the cooling cream mixture, but halve the sugar.

Black currant ice cream
Put 1 pound (450 g) of black currants, 1 tablespoon of water and 1 tablespoon of sugar in a pan and cook over low heat for 10 minutes. Sieve into the ice cream mixture, taste and add more sugar if necessary.

Strawberry ice cream

Purée 1½ to 2 lb (700 to 900 g) strawberries and combine with the egg mixture before folding in the whipping cream.

Custard-based vanilla ice cream

SERVES FOUR TO SIX

1¼ cups (315 ml) milk
1 vanilla bean
1 teaspoon cornstarch
2 whole eggs
2 egg yolks
3 tablespoons fine sugar
1¼ cups (315 ml) whipping cream

Put the milk and the vanilla bean into a saucepan and bring to just under boiling point. Remove the pan from the heat and let stand for 5 minutes. Remove the vanilla bean.

Beat the cornstarch with the eggs, egg yolks and the sugar until well mixed. Pour in the milk, stirring constantly. Pour the mixture into the top of a double boiler and cook, stirring, over hot water until the custard is smooth and thick.

Strain the custard into a bowl and cool, stirring occasionally.

Put the cream into another bowl and beat until thick but not stiff. Fold the cream into the custard and chill before freezing.

Orange ice cream

Rub 2 oranges all over with 6 sugar cubes. When the sugar has absorbed all the zest, crush the cubes and dissolve them in 1 tablespoon of water.

Make the custard, replacing some of the milk with the orange juice and some of the sugar with the dissolved sugar cubes.

Lemon water ice

The syrup given in this recipe makes 3 cups (750 ml) and can be used for all water ice recipes. You may use 2 teaspoons gelatin dissolved in a little water instead of the egg white or in addition to it. The gelatin helps to prevent ice crystals from forming when the water ice is still-frozen. Three heads of elder-flowers infused in the syrup after it is taken off the heat will give this ice a delicious flavor.

SERVES FOUR

2 cups (500 ml) water
¾ cup (175 g) sugar
Rind and juice of 3 lemons
1 egg white, stiffly beaten

Put the water, sugar and lemon rind in a saucepan and cook over low heat, stirring, until the sugar dissolves. Increase the heat to high and boil the syrup, without stirring, until the temperature reaches 220°F (104°C) on a candy thermometer or for 6 minutes, if you do not have a thermometer. Remove the pan from the heat and add the lemon juice. Cool the mixture and then chill it.

Strain the mixture into an ice cube tray and freeze until it becomes mushy in the middle and hard around the edges.

Turn the mixture into a bowl and beat until it is smooth. Beat in the egg white, return the mixture to the freezer and freeze for 30 minutes. Beat again and then freeze for 1 to 1½ hours or until the water ice is frozen through.

Grapefruit water ice

Use 2 grapefruit and 3 cups (750 ml) of sugar syrup.

Orange water ice

Use 3 oranges, the juice of ½ lemon and 1 tablespoon orange blossom water to 3 cups (750 ml) sugar syrup.

Berry water ice

Make 1 cup (250 ml) fruit purée from any berry fruit—raspberries, black currants, red currants or gooseberries (use double the amount of strawberries). Use 1 cup (250 ml) sugar syrup and 2 egg whites.

Coffee granita

The ice crystals which form during freezing gives coffee granita its delicious texture.

SERVES FOUR

½ lb (225 g) dark roast coffee beans, finely ground
½ cup (125 g) sugar
5 cups (1 liter) boiling water

Put the coffee and sugar into a heatproof glass or ceramic coffee pitcher. Pour the boiling water into the pitcher. Put the pitcher on an asbestos mat on the lowest heat and leave for 1 hour.

Allow the coffee to cool, then strain it through a sieve lined with cheesecloth. Chill before freezing. Beat three times during the freezing process.

Coffee ice cream

If this ice cream is made in a sorbetière or churn, reduce the cornstarch to 1 teaspoon.

SERVES FOUR TO SIX

1 cup (50 g) dark roast coffee beans, bruised
1 cup (250 ml) cream
⅔ cup (150 g) sugar
Salt
1 tablespoon cornstarch
3 tablespoons milk
3 egg yolks
1 cup (250 ml) whipping cream

Put the coffee beans and cream in a saucepan and bring to just under boiling point. Reduce the heat to very low, cover the pan and leave for 1 hour. The cream should remain hot, but not come to a boil. Strain the cream.

Combine the sugar, pinch of salt and cornstarch with the milk. Beat in the egg yolks and gradually stir in the coffee cream. Cook over barely simmering water until the custard thickens.

Remove the custard and set aside to cool. Stir occasionally as it cools to prevent a skin from forming.

Whip the cream until it is thick and fold it into the custard. Chill the mixture before freezing.

Tutti frutti

SERVES FOUR

⅓ cup (50 g) chopped candied cherries
2 tablespoons chopped angelica
⅓ cup (50 g) chopped candied pineapple
⅓ cup (50 g) light raisins
½ cup (125 ml) rum
2 egg whites
½ cup (125 g) sugar
½ cup (125 ml) water
1 teaspoon gelatin dissolved in 2 tablespoons warm water
1 cup (250 ml) whipping cream
½ teaspoon vanilla extract

Put the fruit in a bowl. Pour over the rum. Cover the bowl and set aside for 1 hour.

Have the egg whites ready in a heatproof bowl.

Put the sugar and water in a saucepan and stir to dissolve over low heat. Increase the heat and boil the syrup for 6 minutes or until the temperature reaches 220°F (104°F) on a candy thermometer.

Using an electric beater, beat the egg whites until stiff but not dry. Pour the syrup over the egg whites in a steady stream, beating constantly. Pour in the gelatin and beat until thick.

Beat the cream and vanilla extract until thick but not stiff. Fold the cream into the egg white mixture and freeze, beating twice. Drain the fruit and add it after the final beating.

Pistachio ice cream

SERVES FOUR TO SIX

¼ lb (125 g) shelled pistachio nuts
1 cup (250 ml) light cream
3 tablespoons sugar
½ cup (125 ml) water
4 egg yolks
Almond extract
Green food coloring
1 cup (250 ml) whipping cream
4 egg whites

Put the nuts in a blender with just enough of the cream to prevent the machine clogging and blend until smooth.

Put the sugar and water in a saucepan and stir to dissolve over low heat. When the sugar has dissolved, boil rapidly for 6 minutes or until the temperature reaches 220°F (104°C) on a candy thermometer. Remove the pan from the heat.

Using a beater, beat the egg yolks in a bowl. Pour in the syrup in a steady stream beating steadily until the mixture is thick and fluffy. Mix in the pistachio cream, the remaining light cream, a few drops of almond extract and 1 to 2 drops of food coloring.

Beat the whipping cream until thick but not stiff and mix it into the custard. Chill the mixture.

Beat the egg whites until stiff. Fold into the mixture and freeze.

Glossary

Acidulated water. Water to which lemon juice or vinegar has been added. Cut fruit and vegetables are dropped into acidulated water to prevent them from discoloring. Add 1 tablespoon of lemon juice or vinegar to 2 cups (500 ml) of water.

Aspic. Clear jelly made from meat, chicken or fish stock, used to coat food or chopped and used to garnish a cold dish.

Au bleu. A method of cooking live freshwater fish. The fish is stunned and put in a pan. It is then sprinkled with vinegar and cooked in a court bouillon.

Au gratin. Food which is covered with a sauce, bread crumbs and/or grated cheese and then baked or broiled.

Bain-marie. A large pan (a roasting or baking pan or dish may be used) filled with hot water in which smaller pans or pots can be placed. It is used to cook or heat custards and sauces that are too delicate to be put over direct heat.

Baking blind. Baking pastry shells without a filling.

Barding. Covering large pieces of lean meat and the breasts of poultry or game birds with strips of fatback or fat bacon, to prevent them from drying out during roasting.

Basting. Moistening meat, game, poultry or fish with fat, stock or other liquids.

Beurre manié. A paste made from equal quantities of flour and butter kneaded together. It is used to thicken soups, sauces and stews.

Blanching. Plunging food—fruit, vegetables, nuts or meat—briefly into boiling water, or putting them in cold water, bringing them to a boil and, sometimes, boiling them for a few minutes. This is done to loosen the skin prior to peeling; to reduce strong flavors, saltiness or bitterness; or to set the color and prepare food for freezing.

Blending. Mixing ingredients together with a spoon or in an electric blender until thoroughly combined and smooth.

Bouquet garni. Various herbs, including parsley, bay leaf and thyme, sometimes contained in a cheesecloth bag. It is used to flavor soups, stews and sauces.

Braising. Cooking meat, game, fish or vegetables first on top of the stove and then with very little liquid in a slow oven.

Clarified butter. Butter melted, cooked gently and strained to eliminate salt, milk solids and moisture. This gives a clear fat that can be heated to a higher temperature than butter without burning.

Compound butters. Butter to which various savory flavorings have been added. They are always chilled and served with hot food.

Court bouillon. A seasoned, acidic liquid for poaching fish.

Croustade. A fried or baked bread case.

Croutons. Small cubes of bread which are fried or toasted and used to garnish soups and some salads. The term also applies to larger pieces of fried or toasted bread used as a base for steaks or small birds.

Deglazing. Dissolving the sediment left in a pan after frying or roasting. A little liquid is poured in, stirred and mixed with the sediment, then brought to a boil and used as gravy.

Degorging. A process used to draw out the juices and bitterness from such vegetables as zucchini or cucumbers before they are cooked. The vegetables are sliced, sprinkled with salt and left to drain, weighted down with a plate, for 30 minutes.

Degreasing. Removing the grease from a cooked liquid, such as stock. The liquid is cooled. When the grease rises to the surface it is skimmed off.

Dice. To cut food into small cubes.

Drippings. Fat that has dripped into the pan from meat or poultry during roasting.

Duxelles. A paste made from finely chopped mushrooms and/or mushroom stalks that is used to flavor soups, stews and various other dishes. It can be stored in a screw-top jar in the refrigerator for 1 month and in the freezer for 3 months.

En croûte. A term used to describe meat that is cooked wrapped in pastry or bread dough. The pastry is not eaten.

En papillote. A term used to describe food that is cooked and served wrapped in paper.

Fatback. Pork fat used for larding or barding; also used in the making of pâtés.

Flambé. To pour alcohol over food and set it alight. The food and the alcohol must be warm before being ignited.

Fondue. Pieces of bread or other food speared on long-handled forks and dipped into a cheese or chocolate sauce or hot oil.

Folding in. Carefully mixing an ingredient into a mixture with a large metal spoon, without stirring or beating.

Giblets. Edible entrails, such as the liver, heart and gizzard, which are removed from poultry or game birds.

Glaze. A glossy finish given to food by coating it with egg, water, syrup, puréed jam or concentrated stock.

Jam glaze. Jam heated with a little water and lemon juice, then strained.

Julienne. A term used to describe any food that is cut into narrow strips.

Lard. Pork fat that is melted down, clarified and used as a cooking fat.

Larding. Threading pieces of fatback through large pieces of lean meat that are to be roasted.

Liaison. The thickening agent —for example a roux, egg yolks and cream, or blood—used to bind sauces.

Marinade. An acidulated or seasoned liquid, often a mixture of oil and wine or vinegar, spices and herbs, which is used to tenderize and give flavor to food. Yogurt is used as a marinade in many Eastern countries.

Marinate. To soak food in a marinade.

Mask. To coat food completely with a sauce or aspic.

Meat glaze. Brown stock, degreased and boiled until it is reduced to a clear, dark brown, syrupy glaze. Four to 6 cups (1 to 1½ liters) of stock will make ½ cup (125 ml) of glaze. It is used to enrich gravies, sauces and stocks.

Mirepoix. Diced or sliced root vegetables and, sometimes, diced bacon, cooked in butter until tender and used to enhance the flavor of fish, poultry and meat.

Oeufs mollets. Eggs boiled for 4½ to 5 minutes or until the yolks are soft but the whites firm.

Panade. A thick paste made either with flour, butter and water or milk, or with bread crumbs soaked in milk or water, and used to bind and thicken quenelles and forcemeat.

Paper collar. A strip of paper tied around a soufflé dish to support a hot soufflé as it rises and a cold soufflé or mousse until it sets.

Parboiling. Cooking food in boiling water for a short time before continuing to cook it by another method, such as baking.

Pickling onions. Small button or pearl onions used whole for pickling and in stews and sautés.

Reducing. Boiling liquid rapidly until it has reduced in volume and strengthened in flavor.

Rendering fat. The process of slowly melting down fat from its solid to its liquid state.

Roux. A base for sauces, composed of flour mixed with hot fat (usually butter).

Sautéing. From the French verb *sauter*, to jump. Cooking food briskly in a little fat until it is brown on all sides. Often, after a preliminary sautéing, a little liquid is added, the pan covered and the food cooked gently until it is tender.

Scalding. Heating liquid to just under boiling point.

Scoring. Making incisions in fish or meat.

Seasoned flour. Flour seasoned with salt and pepper and sometimes cayenne pepper or herbs, and used to coat food for frying.

Stir-frying. A method of frying used by the Chinese. Meat, poultry, fish or vegetables are cut into small pieces of equal size and fried quickly in hot oil. The food must be stirred constantly to prevent burning and to insure that it is cooked evenly.

Trussing. Tying up a bird with trussing string so that the legs and wings are kept neatly in place during cooking.

Vanilla sugar. Sugar that has been put in a jar with a vanilla bean so that it absorbs the vanilla flavor.

Wok. A large frying pan with a rounded base, used in Chinese cooking.

Zest. The colored part of orange or lemon skin, which can be thinly pared with a potato peeler. The word zest is also used to mean the oil that can be extracted from the skin if a cube of sugar is rubbed over it.

Recipe titles and page numbers are in bold type. Illustrations are denoted by italic numerals.

A

Aioli 68
Ajja 162
Almond/s
  curried 91
  deviled 155
  macaroons 192
  preparation 46, 46, 47, 47
  salted 155
Almond cookies 190
Almond filling, Danish pastries 192
Almond pastry 48
American doughnuts 158
Anchovies, preparation 20
Anchovy butter 129
Anchovy sauce, steamed fish mold recipe with 79
Androuët, M. 12
Anisette, grapefruit 134
Apple/s
  baked 184
  cake, Danish 96
  carrot and, salad 213
  crumble 185
  flan, French 184
  fried, and bacon 155
  fritters, special 154
  guinea hen with 172
  pommes aux fruits glacés 96
  pork and 114
  preparation 46, 46
  red cabbage with 120
  storing 11
  walnut and celery and, salad 213
Apple dumplings 184, 186–7
Apple filling, Danish pastries 192
Apple fritters 154, 155
  special 154
Apple sauce 69
Apple strudel 184, 184–5
Apples with Calvados 155
Apricot/s 46
  ham with 133
  in vanilla syrup 94
  roast duck with 170
Apricot fritters 154
Apricot soup 63
Apricot tart bourdaloue 214
Artichoke/s
  buying 10
  preparation 42, 42
  tray-frozen 14
Artichokes, Jerusalem, cream of, soup 62
Artichokes with shrimp and mushroom mayonnaise 90, 91
Asparagus
  boiling and steaming 92
  buying 10
  cream of, soup 61
  preparation 42, 42
  steam-boiled 72
  velouté with 62
Aspic 58
  coating fish with 76, 76
Au bleu 75
Austrian chocolate pudding 103
Avocado/s (pear/s)
  baked spiced 183, 183
  buying and ripening 10
  cream of, soup 62
  freezing 15
  preparation 47, 47
Avocado and shrimp cream 211
Avocado salad 213
Avocados stuffed with shrimp 209

B

Bacon
  bananas and, broiled 124
  broiling 124
  eggs and 163
  fried apples and 155
  preparation 36, 36
  sautéed liver and 149
  slices, cooking time 146
Bacon rolls 36, 36
Baked Alaska 205
Baked chicken pancakes 189
Baked custard 203, 204

Baked eggs 203
Baked fish with olives 166
Baked ham 178
Baked mackerel 166
Baked pasta with seafood 188
Baked potatoes 180
Baked scallops 169
Baked spiced avocados 183, 183
Baked stuffed onions 183, 183
Baked tomatoes 182, 182
Baking, roasting and 164–5
  blind 185, 185
  equipment 9, 9, 50, 50
Bamboo shoots, stir-fried 153
Banana/s
  baked 184
  broiled 124
  buying 11
  freezing 15
  preparation 46, 46
  sautéed 154–5
Banana and bacon fritters 154
Banana fritters 154
Barbecuing 124
Barley 122
Barley and vegetable casserole 123, 123
Basic bread dough 52, 52
Basic pasta dough 50
Basic pie pastry 48, 48
Basic sponge cake 193
Bass 18
  baked 166
  roast stuffed 167
  see also Sea bass
Bass à la provençale 138
Batter, fritter 156
Bavarois 102, 102
Bean/s
  buying 10
  preparation 43, 43
  see also specific bean e.g. Lima
Bean sprouts
  steaming 92
  stir-fried 153
Bean sprouts and shrimp Chinese style 141
Bean sprouts with omelet shreds 162
Béarnaise sauce 64, 67
  curdling and 65
Béchamel sauce 64, 66
Beef
  boiling and steaming 86, 86–7, 88, 88
  broiling 132
  buying 13
  freezer storage life 14
  frying and sautéing 146, 146–7, 148–9
  pickling 86
  preparation 32, 32
  roasting and baking 174, 175, 177, 177, 179, 179
  stewing and casseroling 114–16, 114–15
Beef olives 116
Beef stroganoff 146
Beef Wellington 174, 177, 177, 179, 179
Beet salad 92
Beets
  boiling and steaming 93
  chilled Borscht and 59
  preparation 41
Beignets soufflés 158
Belgian endive
  boiled 91, 92
  buttered 120
  preparation 44
Belgian endive au gratin 181
Belgian endive, orange and watercress salad 213
Belgian fish stew 108
Berries
  buying 11
  freezing 14
Berry water ice 217
Besan 152
Beurre manié 64
Beurre noir 68
Bing cherries, flan with 185
Biryani 123
Bisques (soups) 59
Bivalve mollusks 22
Black currant/s 46
  crumble 185
  water ice 217

Black currant ice cream 216
Black currant kissel 96
Black currant mousse 96
Black Forest cherry cake 194–5, 195
Blackberry/blackberries 46
  summer pudding 96
Blanching, vegetables 14
Blanquette de veau 116–17
Blinis 157
Boeuf à la Bourguignonne 114, 115
Boeuf à la mode 114, 115
Boeuf en daube 115
Boiled Belgian endive 91
Boiled chicken, English 83
Boiled (corned) beef and dumplings 86, 87
Boiled fennel 92
Boiled frosting 197
Boiled ham with lentils 88
Boiled shoulder of mutton 88
Boiling and steaming 72–3
  cereals 97, 97–9, 98–9
  eggs and dairy products 100, 100–3, 101–3
  fish 74–5, 74–5, 76–9, 76, 78–9
  fruit 94–6, 94–5
  meat 86, 86, 86–7, 88–9, 88–9
  poultry 82, 83, 82–3, 84–5, 85
  shellfish 80–1, 80–1
  vegetables 90, 90–1, 91–3
Bone stock 56
Borscht 59
Boston baked beans 180
Boston scrod
  bouillabaisse 106
Boston steamed bread 99, 180
Bouillabaisse 104, 106, 106–7
Bouquet garni 45, 45
Bourride 78
Brains, preparation 38, 39, 39
Braised chestnuts with Chinese cabbage 120
Braised kidneys 117
Braised lettuce 120
Braised onions 120
Braised venison with juniper berries and sour cream 119
Braising 104
Brandy butter 69
Brandy snaps 190–1
Brassicas, preparation 41, 41
Brazil nut 46
  preparation 47, 47
Bread 198–201, 198–201
  freezing and storage life 15
  fried 156, 158
  preparation 51–2, 52
Bread and butter pudding 189
Bread cases 52, 52
Bread sauce 69
Bread crumbs 52
  frying fish in 141, 141
Bride's cake 194–5, 196
Brill 19, 21
Brisket 30
Broccoli
  au gratin 181
  boiling and steaming 92
  buying 10
  preparation 41, 41
  steam-boiled 72
Broiled chicken livers 130
Broiled grapefruit 134, 134–5
Broiled halibut steaks with orange sauce 127
Broiled lobster 127
Broiled mushrooms 134
Broiled oysters 128
Broiled partridge à la diable 130–1
Broiled pineapple with rum 134
Broiled pork chops 133
Broiled quail with orange and sage 131
Broiled Roquefort 135
Broiled salmon steaks 127
Broiled tomatoes 134, 134–5
Broiling 124–5
  fish and shellfish 126–8, 126–7
  meat and game 132–3
  poultry and game birds 130–1, 130–1
  vegetables fruit and dairy products 134–5, 134–5
Brownies 190, 190
Brussels sprouts

  boiling 92
  bubble and squeak 152
  buying 10
  preparation 41, 41
  tray-frozen 14
Brussels sprouts with chestnuts 91
Brussels sprouts with curried almonds 91
Bubble and squeak 152
Buck rabbit 135
Buckwheat 122
Bulghur pilaff 122
Butter/s
  clarified 53
  compound 129, 129
  freezing 15
  storing 12
Butter cookies 191
Butter cream 197
Buttered Belgian endive 120
Butterscotch sauce 69
Buying and storing food 10–13

C

Cabbage 10
  boiling and steaming 92
  bubble and squeak 152
  coleslaw 212
  preparation 41, 41
  sauerkraut 121
  steamed stuffed 91
Cabbage dolmas 87, 89
Cake/s (including cookies and pastries) 190–7, 190–1, 192, 194–5, 205
  fillings and icing 197, 197
  freezing and storage life 15
Calf elk 13
Cannelloni, pasta and 50
Cannelloni di spinace 188, 188–9
Canteloupe salad 209
Caponata 121
Caramel custard 202, 204
Caramelized pineapple 155, 155
Caraway sauce, squash in 92
Carbonated drinks, freezing and 15
Carbonnade de boeuf à la flamande 114
Cardoons, preparation 42
Carp
  Belgian fish stew 108
  gefilte fish 78
  roast 168
Carrot/s
  boiling and steaming 93
  buying and storing 10
  cream of, soup 62
  glazed 91
  preparation 40, 41, 41
Carrot and apple salad 213
Carrot and parsnip purée 91
Carving
  beef and lamb 176, 176
  poultry 173, 173
Cassata alla Siciliana 194–5, 196
Casseroled celery 120
Casseroled pheasant with cranberries and cream 113
Cassoulet 117, 118, 119
Cauliflower
  boiling and steaming 92
  buying 10
  cream of, soup 61, 62
  preparation 41, 41
  steam-boiled 72
Cauliflower cheese fritters 152
Cauliflower salad 91
Celeriac
  boiling and steaming 93
  cream of, soup 62
  preparation 41, 41
  sautéed 152
Celeriac salad 212
Celery
  au gratin 181
  buying 10
  boiling 92
  casseroled 120
  cream of, soup 61
  freezing 15
  guinea hen and 113
  pheasant with 172–3
  preparation 42, 42
Celery, apple and walnut salad 213

Cereals
baking **188–201**, 190, *190–2, 194–5,
198, 198–9, 200–1*
boiling and steaming 97, **97–9**, *97,
98–9*
frying and sautéing 156, **156–8**, *159*
preparation 48–9, *48–9*
stewing and casseroling 122, **122–3**,
122–3
Charlotte russe 101, *101*
Cheese
bread making and 51
broiling 134–5, *134–5*
buying and storing 12
freezing 15
fried mozzarella **162**
ravioli filling **97**
tarte au Gruyère **203**
Cheese and walnut fingers 135
Cheese fritters, cauliflower **152**
Cheese omelet 160
Cheese ring 209
Cheese sandwiches, fried **162**
Cheese soufflé *202–3*, **203–4**
Cheese toast 134–5, *134–5*
Cheesecake
Italian ricotta **194**
strawberry **215**
Chelsea buns *199*, **200–1**
**Cherries jubilee with vanilla ice
cream** *94*, **95**
Cherry/cherries *46*
buying 11
clafoutis **186**
duck with *110–11*, **112**
fritters 154
preparation 47, *47*
Cherry cake, Black Forest 194–5
Cherry flan 185
Chestnut/s
brussels sprouts with **91**
preparation 46, *46, 47, 47*
Chestnut cake 215
Chestnut stuffing 172
Chicken
boiling and steaming 82, *82–3*, **83–5**
broiling 130, 131, *131*
buying 13
carving 173, *173*
cream of, soup 61
frying and sautéing **142–5**, *142–4*
preparation 26, *27*
roasting and baking 170, *171*, **173**
roasting time 172
scrambled eggs with **162**
stewing and casseroling 110, *110*
Chicken à la king 82, *83*, **84**
Chicken and mushroom velouté 62
Chicken and pineapple salad 82, *83*,
84
Chicken brochettes 130, *130–1*
Chicken chaud-froid 82, *83*, **85**
Chicken florentine 85
Chicken fricassee 84
Chicken galantine **85**
Chicken in cider 110
Chicken kiev 142, *142–3*, **144**, *144*
Chicken kromeski 144–5
Chicken lemon sauté 144
Chicken liver sauté 145
Chicken livers
broiled **130**
scrambled eggs with **162**
Chicken maryland 142, *143, 143*
Chicken pie, country **173**
Chicken poached in wine 84
Chicken salad **84**
Chicken sauté à la bordelaise 142,
142–3
Chicken sauté a l'italienne 142
Chicken sauté paprika 145
Chicken stock 56
Chicken with almonds 145
Chicken with spicy mayonnaise 84
Chick-pea flour 152
Chilies, preparation 45, *45*
Chinese cabbage
chestnuts with **120**
preparation 41, *41*
stir-fried **153**
Chinese omelet **161**
Chips, potato 40, *40*, **150**
Chive/s
egg and, butter **129**
herb butter **129**

soup garnish 59
Chocolate
brownies **190**
flavored bavarois **102**
pudding, Austrian **103**
Chocolate cake 193
Chocolate chip cookies 191
Chocolate frosting 197
Chocolate ice cream 216
Chocolate mousse 101
Chocolate sauce 69
Chocolate soufflé 204
Chocolate torrone 215
Chopped liver 211
Choux pastry 48, **50**, *50*
consommé aux profiteroles and 59
puffs, soup garnish 59
Christmas cake *194–5*, **196**
Christmas pudding 98
Cioppino 109
Clafoutis 186
Clam/s
buying 13
cioppino **109**
freezing 14
preparation 23, *23*
Clam bisque 63
Clam chowder 61
Clam fritters 140
Clams with Gruyère sauce 128
Clarified butter 53
Clarifying, stock 58, *58–9, 59*
Clafoutis 186 *(sic)*
Coconut, preparation 46, *47, 47*
Cod *18*
cioppino **109**
cream of fish soup **61**
dried salt 20
fish casserole with peppers **108**
kebabs 124
poaching method and 74
Portuguese salt **108**
preparation 20
quenelles 79
roe *see* Taramasalata
Spanish stewed fish **106**
Cod rarebit 127
Coffee and walnut cake 193
Coffee éclairs 192
Coffee-flavored bavarois **102**
Coffee granita 217
Coffee ice cream 217
Cold desserts **214–15**
Cold pressed tongue 89, *89*
Cold sauce/s 64, **68–9**
Cold table **206–17**
Coleslaw **212**
Compotes, fruit **94**
Compound butters **129**, *129*
Confit d'oie, cassoulet with **117**
Conger eel
bouillabaisse **106**
matelote **109**
Consommé/s 58, *59*, 59
Consommé aux profiteroles 59
Consommé madrilène 59
Cookies **190–2**
freezing and storage life 15
Coq au vin 110, *110*
Coquilles St. Jacques 80, *80–1*
Corn 10
boiling 93
Corned beef **86**
Corn fritters 153
Corn on the cob
blanching 14
boiling 93
preparation 43, *43*
Cornish hens 13
Cornish pasty 179, *179*
Cornmeal
Boston steamed bread **99**
polenta **98**
Cottage cheese, cheesecake with **194**
Cottage fries **151**
Country chicken pie 173
Court bouillon 58
Couscous, steaming 72
Crab
boiling 74
buying 13
dressed 80, *80*
freezing 14
preparation 24, *24–5*
shellfish cocktail **209**
Crab au gratin 168

Crab soufflé 168–9
Cracked wheat 122
pilaff 122
Crackling, pork 36, *36*
Cranberry/cranberries *46*
casseroled pheasant with **113**
Danish dessert **96**
Cranberry and orange sauce 69
Crayfish, preparation 24, *24, 25, 25*
Crayfish with butter sauce 80–1
Cream
buying and storing 12
freezing 15
preparation 53
sauces and 15, *64*
soups and 15, 59
whipped, curdling and use of 65
Cream-based vanilla ice cream 216
Cream cheese pastry 50
Cream of asparagus soup 61
Cream of avocado soup 62
Cream of cauliflower soup 62
Cream of fish soup Normandy 61
Cream of watercress soup 61
Cream sauce 66
Creamed rice pudding 99
Crème brulée 102
Crème Crécy 59, *62*
Crème pâtissière 197
Crème vichyssoise 62–3
Creole jambalaya 122
Crêpe/s *78*, 156, *156*
Crêpe pan
how to season 8
Crêpes Suzette 156, *156*, **157**, *159*
Croissants 201, *201*
Croquettes, potato **151**
Crostata di ricotta *190–1*, **194**
Croustades (bread cases) 52, *52*
Croutons 52, 59, *158*
Crown loaf 200, *200*
Crown roast 30, 34, *34*, **176**
Crudités 208
Crumble, rhubarb 185, *187*
Crusty noodles 158
Cucumber/s
boiling and steaming 93
buying 10
chicken and, velouté 62
freezing 15
preparation 40, 45
wilted **100**
Cumberland sauce 69
Curly endive
preparation 44
Curried almonds, Brussels sprouts with
91
Curried eggs 101
Curried rice salad 209
Custard
baked 203
freezing 15
Jamaican rum **103**
Custard-based vanilla ice cream 216
Custard cream filling 197
Custard filling, Danish pastries 192
Custard sauce 69

D

Dab *19*
Dairy products 12
baking **203–5**, *202–3*
boiling and steaming **100–3**, *101–3*
broiling 134–5, *134–5*
freezing and storage life 15
frying **162**
preparation 53
Danish apple cake 96
Danish liver pâté 210
Danish pastries 191, *192*, **192–3**
Date and walnut loaf 191, *193–4*
Date bars 186
Deep-fat frying 136
Deep-fried chicken 144
Deep-fried mushrooms 152
Deep-fried onions 152
Deep-fried parsley 153
Demi-glace, brown sauce **66**
Dessert sauces 64, **69**
Deviled almonds 155
Deviled herring 126
Deviled turkey legs 130, *130–1*
Dods, Margaret 55

Dogfish *18*
Dolmas
Cabbage 87, **89**
grape leaves **182**, *182*
Doughnuts **157–8**
Dover sole *19*
preparation 21, *21*
Drawing poultry/game 26, 28
Dressed crab 80, *80*
Dried
beans
boiling 92
preparation 43
fish 20
fruit
bread making with 51
compote **94**
pork and 114
Drippings 65
Drop scones 157
Duck
buying 13
carving 173, *173*
preparation 26, *27*
roast with apricots **170**
roasting time 172
wild, à la Seville **145**
Duck galantine 85, *85*
Duck with cherries *111*, **112**
Duck with olives 112
Duck with turnips 112
Dumplings 59, *87*
corned beef and **86**
Duxelles 152

E

Eel/s *18*
fried **140**
jellied **79**
preparation 20, 21, *21*
Eel pie 169
Eels stewed in white wine **108**
Egg/s
baking 203, **203–5**
boiling and steaming 100, **100–3**,
101–3
buying and storing 12
freezing 15
frying 160, **160–2**, *161–3*
preparation 53
sauces and dressings made with 64,
65, **67–9**
yolks, thickening sauces and 64
Egg and chive butter 129
Egg fu-yung 161
Egg mayonnaise 208
Eggplant
broiled 124, 134
buying 10
degorged 45
moussaka **181**
preparation 40, 45, *45*
sautéed *152–3*
Eggplant à la nîmoise 180–1
Eggplant fritters *150–1*, **153**
Eggplant salad 212
Eggs florentine with ham 100, *103*
Eggs in aspic 100
Eggs in crispy rolls 100
Elk 13
Endive
See Belgian and curly endive
English apple pie 184
English boiled chicken 83
English crumpets 156, *157*
English doughnuts 157–8
English flaky pastry 49, *49*
English muffins 157, *159*
English roast chicken 170, *170–1*
English salad dressing 68–9
English steak and kidney pudding
86, *87, 88*, **88**
Entrecôte à la viennoise 146–7
Entrecôte au poivre verte *147*, **149**
Equipment, kitchen 8–9, *8–9*, 50, *50*, 53,
53
Espagnole, brown sauce 64, **66**

F

Fat/s 15
Feet, pig's 38, 39, *39*
Fennel, Florence
au gratin **181**

boiled 92, **92**
cream of, soup **62**
preparation 42
Fern shoots, preparation 42
Figs, buying 11
Filets de sole meunière 140
Fillets of haddock dieppoise 106
Fillets of sole à la panetière 140
Fillets of sole florentine 78
Finnan haddie crêpes 78
Finnan haddie flan 169
Finnan haddie potatoes 180
Fish
boiling and steaming 74–5, **76–9**, *78–9*
braising 104
broiling 126, **126–8**, *126–7*
buying and storing 12
coating with aspic 76, *76*
freezing 14
frying 138, **138**, *138–9*, **140–1**, *141*
gelée de saumon **210**
kebabs 124
preparation 18, *18–19*, 20–1, *20–1*
roasting and baking 166, **166–9**, *166–7*
rollmops **208–9**
seviche **208**
smoked mackerel pâté **210**
stewing and casseroling 106, **106**, *106–7*, **108–9**
stock 56, **58**
taramasalata **211**
Fish cakes 138
Fish casserole with peppers 108
Fish mold, steamed **79**
Fish pie 169
Flan pastry, French (pâte sucrée) 48, **49**, *49*
Florence fennel *see* Fennel
Florentines *190*, **191**
Flounder *19*, 21
cooking time 75
fish stock and **58**
matelote 104
poaching method 75
preparation 20, 21
Fondue, Swiss **101**, *102*
Fondue bourguignonne 148
Freezing 14–15
French apple flan 184
French dressing 68
French flan pastry (pâte sucrée) 48, **49**, *49*
French fries 150
French fritters **158**
French omelet 160
French onion soup 60
French roast chicken 170
French toast **158**
Fresh fruit compote 94
Fresh green pea and lettuce soup 63
Fresh peaches in vanilla syrup 94
Fricassee, chicken **84**
Fried
eggs and bacon *163*
foods, freezing and 15
Fried apples and bacon 155
Fried bread 158
Fried eels 140
Fried eggs 160
Fried fish 138
Fried mozzarella cheese 162
Fried mushrooms 152
Fried onions 152
Fried rice 158
Fried scampi 141
Fried whitebait 138
Fritter/s
beignets soufflés **158**
clam **140**
fruit 154, **154**, *155*
vegetable 150–1, **152–3**
Fritter batter 156
Fritto misto di mare 138, *139*
Frogs' legs, sautéed **141**
Frosting **197**
Fruit
baking 184, **184–7**, *184*, *186–7*
boiling and steaming 94–6, *94–5*
broiling 134, **134**, *135*
buying 10–11
cold desserts, additional **214–15**
freezing 14–15
frying and sautéing 154, **154–5**, *154–5*
hors d'oeuvre, additional **208–9**
ices **216–17**

meat and 114
preparation 46–7, *46–7*
salads with **213**
Fruit loaf 198
Fruit pie/s 184, **184–5**, *186*
freezer storage life 15
Fruit sauce 69
Fruit soup/s 59, **63**
Frying and sautéing 136–7
cereals 156, **156–8**, *156*, *159*
eggs and dairy products 160, **160–2**, *161–3*
fish and shellfish 138, **138**, *138–9*, **140–1**, *141*
fruit 154, **154–5**, *154–5*
meat and game 146, **146–9**, *146–7*, *148*
poultry and game birds 142, **142**, *142–3*, **144–5**, *144*
vegetables 150, **150–3**, *150–1*

G

Galantine/s
duck 85, *85*
veal 89
Game 13, 30
frying 148
preparation 37, *37*
roasting 178
roasting time 174
stewing and casseroling **118–19**
Game birds 82
broiling **130–1**
buying and preparing 13
frying and sautéing 142, **145**
preparation 26, *26–9*, *28–9*
roasting and baking **172–3**
roasting times 172
stewing and casseroling 110, *110–11*, **112–13**
stock 56
Game consommé 59
Game pâté 210, *210*
Game pie *170–1*, **173**
Garlic 11
preparation 43, *43*
Garlic bread 189
Garlic butter 129
mussels with **128**
Garlic mashed potatoes 180
Garlic mayonnaise 68
Gazpacho 63
Gefilte fish 78
Gelée de saumon 210
Génoise sponge 193
Ginger root, preparation 41, *41*
Ginger sponge pudding 99
Glacé icing 197
Glazed carrots 91
Globe artichoke/s 10
boiling 92
preparation 42, *42*
Gnocchi di semolina 98
Goose
buying 13
preparation 26, *27*
preserved, cassoulet with **117**
roasting 170
roasting time 172
Goose with sauerkraut 172
Gooseberries *46*
crumble **185**
Goulash **115**, 118, *119*
Gram flour 152
Granary bread 198
Granary flour, bread and 51
Grape/s
buying and storing 11
preparation 46, *46*, 47
Grapefruit *46*
broiled 124, **134**, *134–5*
buying and storing 11
Grapefruit anisette 134
Grapefruit water ice 217
Grapefruit with shrimp 209
Gravy/gravies 64, 65
Greek fish stew 108
Green bean/s
boiling and steaming 92
buying 10
preparation 43, *43*
Green bean salad 212–13
Green peppers, broiled **134**
Gremolata 116

Ground meat 32
Grouse
buying 13
preparation 26, *26*, *27*
roasting time 172
Grouse casserole 112
Grouse en cocotte 112–13
Grunt
bouillabaisse 106
Guard of honour, lamb 34, *34*
Guinea hen
buying 13
preparation 26, *27*
roasting time 172
Guinea hen and celery casserole 113
Guinea hen with apples **172**
Guinea hen with juniper berries 145

H

Haddock
cioppino **109**
cream of fish soup **61**
fillets of **106**
fish casserole with peppers **108**
Indonesian baked fish **168**
kebabs 124, **127**
Haddock kebabs 127
Hake *18*
cioppino **109**
Halibut 21
broiled **127**
kebabs 124
Halibut with lemon sauce 168
Ham
baked **178**
boiled, lentils with **88**
broiling 124
honey-glazed **178**
preparation 36, *36*
steamed stuffed cabbage with **91**
veal and, pâté **210**
Ham boiled in cider 86
Ham mousse 211
Ham with apricots 133
Hamburgers 132
freezing 14
Ham-stuffed potatoes 180
Hanging, poultry and game birds 26
Hare 30
freezer storage life 14
jugged, **118**
preparation 13, 37, *37*
stew **119**
Hare pâté 210
Haunch of venison 178
Hazelnuts
chocolate torrone **215**
macaroons **192**
meringue gateau **205**
preparation 34, *46*, 47, *47*
Head cheese 38, *39*
Heart, preparation 38, *39*, *39*
Herb/s
bread making with 51
buying and storing 11
casserole of mushroom and **121**
freezing 14, 15
preparation 45, *45*
Herb butter 129
Herb stuffing 176
Herring 12, *18*
broiling **126**
deviled **126**
frying 138
Indonesian baked fish recipe **168**
preparation 20, *20*
rollmops **208–9**
soused 77, *78*, *78–9*
Herring in oatmeal 140
Herring with mustard sauce 126
Hollandaise sauce 64, 65, **67**
Hominy 122
Honey-glazed ham 178
Hors d'oeuvre additional recipes **208–9**
Hot pot, Lancashire **117–18**, *118*
Hot water crust 48, **50**
Household stock 56
Huevos rancheros 162
Hungarian goulash 115, 118, *119*

I

Ices **216–17**
Icing 197, **197**, *197*

Indonesian baked fish 168
Inkfish, fritto misto di mare **138**, *138–9*
Italian sauce **142**

J

Jamaican rum custard 103
Jambalaya, Creole **122**
Jellied eels 79
Jelly/jellies, freezing 15
Jelly roll 193
Jerusalem artichoke
boiling 93
cream of, soup **62**
preparation 40, *40*
Jugged hare 118
Julienne strips 41, *41*

K

Kale
boiling 92
preparation 41
Kasha 122
Kebabs 124
Lebanese **132**
Kedgeree 140
Kidney/s
broiled 124
broiling times 132
frying 146
mixed grill **132**
preparation 38, *38*
Kidney bean salad 93
Kidneys braised in red wine 117
Kipper 20
Kipper pâté 79
Kitchen equipment 8–9, *8–9*, 50, *50*, 53, *53*
Kohlrabi
boiling 93
preparation 41, *41*
Kuku sabsi 161
Kulibyaka 169

L

Lamb
broiling times 132
buying 13
carving 176, *176*
freezer storage life 14
frying 148
ground, **89**, **181**, **182**
kebabs 124
kidneys 38
mixed grill **132**
preparation 34–5, *34–5*
roasting 176
roasting time 174
stewing and casseroling **117–18**, *118*
Lancashire hot pot 117–18, *118*
Larding 32, *32*, 37, 170
Lardy cake *198*, **200**
Lasagne 189
Lebanese kebabs 132
Leek/s
boiling and steaming 93
buying and storing 11
crème vichyssoise **62–3**
potage bonne femme **60**
preparation 43, *43*
soup normande **63**
Leeks provençal 120
Lemon butter 129
Lemon curd 214
Lemon curd tarts 214
Lemon gelatin 214
Lemon meringue pie 185, *186*
Lemon mousse 101
Lemon snow 214
Lemon water ice 217
Lentil/s
boiled ham with **88**
boiling 92
preparation 43
purée of, soup **62**
Lentil salad 90, 93
Lettuce
braised **120**
cream of, soup **61**
freezing 15
fresh green pea soup **63**
preparation 44
Lima bean/s 14

Lima bean and mackerel salad 93
Lima beans with garlic 93
Liver
  broiling 124
  chicken, recipes **130**, **145**, **162**, **211**
  frying time 146
  pâtés with **210–11**
  preparation 38, *38*
Liver and bacon, sautéed **149**
Lobster
  bouillabaisse **106**
  broiled 126, **127**
  buying 13
  cioppino **109**
  freezing 14
  preparation 24–5, *24–5*
  shellfish cocktail **209**
Lobster à l'américaine 108–9
Lobster bisque 63
Lobster mayonnaise 81, *81*
Lobster thermidor 128
Lyonnaise potatoes 151

M

Macaroons 192
Macaroni cheese 188
Mackerel *18*
  baked **166**, *167*
  broiling 124, 126
  Indonesian baked fish **168**
  Lima bean and, salad 93
  preparation 20
Madeira or red wine sauce 66
Maître d'hôtel butter 129
Maize (hominy) 122
Mallard, preparation 26, *26*, *27*
Malt, bread and 51
Malt loaf 200
Mango, preparation 47, *47*
Marrow bones, stock with 56.
Marzipan 197
Marzipan roll *194*, **196**
Mashed potatoes 93
Matelote 109
Mayonnaise sauce 64, 65, **68**
  freezing 15, 64
Meat
  boiling and steaming 86, **86–9**, *86–9*
  broiling 132, **132–3**
  buying 13
  freezing 14
  frying and sautéing 146, **146–9**, *146–8*
  pâté recipes **210–11**
  preparation 30–9, *30–9*
  roasting and baking 174, **174**, *175*, **176–9**, *176–7*, *179*
  stewing and caseroling 114, **114–18**, *114–15*, *118–19*
  stock 56
Meat loaf 211
Meat pies, raised 174, 177, *177*, **178–9**
Meatballs with sweet and sour sauce 149
Melons *46*
  buying and storing 11
  hors d'oeuvre **209**
  preparation 47, *47*
Meringue baskets 205
Meringue hazelnut gateau 205
Meringues 204–5
Milk
  buying and storing 12
  freezing 15
Millet 122
Mincemeat 184
Mince pies 184
Minestrone 60
Mint chutney 152
Mint sauce 69
Minute steaks 132
Mirepoix 104
Mixed grill 132
Mollusks
  buying 13
  freezer storage life 14
  preparation 22–3, *22–3*
Moose 13
Moules marinières 80, 81, *81*
Moussaka 181
Mousse
  black currant **96**
  chocolate **101**
  ham **211**
  lemon **101**

  raspberry **96**
  salmon **78**
  strawberry **96**
Mozzarella cheese
  fried **162**
  tomato salad **213**
Mozzarella in carrozza 162
Muffin/s, English 156, **157**, *159*
Muffin tins, lining 214, *214*
Mulberries, summer pudding **96**
Mullet
  broiling 124
  fritto misto di mare **138**, *138–9*
  gray, roe of, pâté from **211**
  red, *18*, **127**, *166*
Mushroom/s
  broiled 124, **134**
  buying 10–11
  cream of, soup **61**
  duxelles **152**
  fried **152**
  preparation 40, 44, *44*
  scrambled eggs with **160**
  spinach salad with **212**
  steaming 93
  thin soup **60**
  vegetable fritters *150–1*
Mushrooms à la grecque 212
Mushroom and herb casserole 121
Mushroom omelet 160
Mushroom sauce 66–7
Mushroom vol-au-vents 181
Mussel/s
  baked pasta with **188**
  bisque **63**
  buying 13
  frying **138**
  matelote **109**
  moules marinières 80, *81*
  paella **123**
  pizza con cozze **188**
  preparation 22, *22*, *23*
  seafood en brochette **128**
  sole with *167*
  Spanish stewed fish **106**
Mussel stew 109
Mussels with garlic butter 128
Mustard butter 129
Mutton
  boiled shoulder of **88**
  Lancashire hot pot **117–18**, *118*
  navarin printanier **118**
  neck of, Scotch broth with **60**
  preparation 34–5, *34–5*
  roasting time 174

N

Navarin printanier 118
Nectarines, buying 11
New England fried scallops 140
Noisettes of lamb 34, *34*
Noisettes of lamb with stuffed tomatoes 148
Noodles
  crusty **158**
  fried **156**
Noodles alfredo 97
Nut/s, preparation 46–7, *46–7*

O

Oatmeal, porridge **99**
  herring in **138**, *140*
Oatmeal and apple pudding 189
Octopus, preparation 22, *23*
Oeufs à la neige 103
Oeufs mollets 100
Oeufs sur le plat 203
Okra, stews and 114
Omelet/s **160–1**, *161*, *161*
Omelet Arnold Bennett 160–1
Omelet au Grand Marnier 161
Omelet fines herbes 160
Omelet flambé 161
Omelet pan 160
  how to season 8, *8*
Onion/s
  baked stuffed **183**, *183*
  boiling and steaming 93
  braised **120**
  broiling 124
  buying 11
  fried **152**
  preparation 43, *43*

  soup, French **60**
Orange/s *46*
  Belgian endive, watercress and, salad **213**
  buying and storing 11
  cranberry and, sauce **69**
  preparation 47, *47*
Orange butter 129
Orange curd 214
Orange-flavored bavarois **102**
Orange fritters **154**
Orange ice cream 217
Orange gelatin 214
Orange sponge pudding 98, **99**
Orange Victoria cake 193
Orange water ice 217
Oranges in caramel 95, *95*
Oxtail
  pot au feu **57**
  preparation 38, 39, *39*
Oxtail stew 116
Oyster/s *23*
  broiled **128**
  buying 13
  cioppino **109**
  freezing 14
  preparation 22, *22*
Oyster bisque **63**
Oysters on skewers 128

P

Paella Valenciana *122–3*, **123**
Pakoras with mint chutney 152
Pancakes (crêpes) **156**, *156*
  crêpes Suzette 156, *156*, **157**
  finnan haddie crêpes **78**
  spinach purée with 92
Papillotes
  to make 148, *148*
  trout **167**
  veal chops **148**
Parisienne potatoes 151
Parsley
  deep-fried **153**
  preparation 45, *45*
Parsnip/s
  boiling and steaming 93
  buying 10
  carrot purée and **91**
  preparation 41, *41*
  sautéed **152**
Partridge
  broiled **130–1**
  preparation 26, *26*
  roast **173**
  roasting time 172
  sautéed **145**
Pasta
  basic dough **50**
  boiling 97
  recipes **97**, **158**, **188–9**
Pastries **192–3**, *192*
Pastry, preparation **48–50**, *48–50*
  freezing and storage life 14, 15
Pasty, Cornish **179**, *179*
Pâté 79, **210–11**, *210*
Pâté au cognac 211
Pâté de campagne 211
Pâté sucrée 48, **49**, *49*
Pavlova 205
Pea/s
  blanching 14
  boiling 93
  buying 10
  lettuce soup and **63**
  petit pois à la française **91**
  preparation 43, *43*
  split
    boiling 92
    soups with **62**
Peach/peaches
  broiled 124
  buying 11
  fresh, in vanilla syrup **94**
  fritters **154**
  preparation 46
  sauce with **69**
Peaches with wine 134
Peanut sauce **133**
Pear/s *46*
  baking 184
  broiling 124

  fritters **154**
  storing 11
Pear tart 186
Pears in red wine 94–5, *94–5*
Pears sabayon 214
Pears with cream cheese 208
Peperonata 121
Pepper/s (vegetable fruit)
  broiled 124, **134**
  buying 10
  fish casserole with **108**
  preparation 45, *45*
  stuffed **121**
Periwinkles, preparing 22, 23, *23*
Pesto 98, *98*
  spaghetti with **97**
Petits pois à la française 91
Petits pots de crème au chocolat 204
Pheasant/s
  buying 13
  casseroled **113**
  game consommé and 59
  game pâté **210**
  preparation 26, *26*
  roasting time 172
Pheasant with Calvados *111*, **113**
Pheasant with celery 172–3
Pie/s
  chicken **173**
  fish **169**
  freezing 14, 15
  fruit **184–5**, *186*
  game *171*, **173**
  meat *177*, **178–9**
Pig/s
  feet, preparation 38, 39, *39*
  suckling, preparation 36, *36*
Pigeon/s
  game consommé and 59
  roasting time 172
  See also Squab
Pike *18*
  Belgian fish stew **108**
  gefilte fish with walleyed **78**
  quenelles **79**
Pilaff/s
  bulghur **122**
  long grain rice for 97
Pineapple/s *46*
  broiled 124, **134**
  buying and ripening 11
  caramelized *154–5*, **155**
  chicken salad with **84–5**
  ham with **133**
  preparation 47, *47*
Pineapple fritters **154**
Pineapple upside-down cake 186–7
Pinwheels, Danish pastries 193
Pipérade 153
Pistachio/s, preparation 46
Pistachio ice cream 217
Pitta, preparation 51
Pizza alla Francescana 188
Pizza con cozze 188
Pizza dough 188
Pizza Napoletana 188
Plucking 26, 28, *28*
Plum/s 11, *46*
Plum cake *194–5*, **196**
Polenta 98
Pommes aux fruits glacés 96
Porgy, bouillabaisse **106**
Pork
  broiling 132, **133**
  broiling times 132
  buying 13
  freezer storage life 14
  ground, meatballs **149**
  kebabs 124
  meat loaf **211**
  preparation 36, *36*
  red-cooked **117**
  roasting and baking **176–7**, *177*, **178**, *179*
  roasting times 174
  shoulder, cassoulet with **117**
Pork pie 177, *177*, **178–9**, *179*
Pork saté 133
Pork spareribs 177
Pork terrine 211
Porridge 99
Portuguese salt cod 108
Pot au feu 57, *59*, 86
Pot roast with prunes 116

Pot roasting
  meat 114
  method 104
  poultry 110
Potage bonne femme 60
Potato/potatoes
  boiling 93
  bubble and squeak 152
  buying and storing 10
  freezing 15
  frying and sautéing 150–2
  mashed 93
  preparation 40
  roasting and baking 180
Potato chips 40, *40*, **150**
Potato croquettes 151
Potato flour, thickening sauces 64
Potato salad 93
Potato scones 152
Potatoes à la dauphinoise 180
Potted shrimp 81
Poulet sauté chasseur 144
Poultry
  boiling and steaming 82, *82–3*, **83–5**, *85*
  broiling 124, 130, **130–1**, *130–1*
  buying 13
  carcasses for stock 56
  freezing 14
  frying and sautéing 142, **142**, *142–3*, **144–5**, *144*
  preparation 26, *26–7*, **28–9**, *28–9*
  roasting and baking 170, **170**, *170–1*, *172–3*, *173*
  stewing and casseroling 110, **110**, *110–11*, **112–13**
Poussins with lemon butter 130, *131*
Pressed tongue, cold **89**, *89*
Prune/s
  pot roast with **116**
  squab with port and **113**
Prune fritters 154
Psari plaki 108
Pudding/s
  Austrian chocolate **103**
  bread and butter **189**
  Christmas **98**
  ginger sponge **99**
  oatmeal and apple **189**
  orange sponge **99**
  queen of **205**
  rice **189**
  rice, creamed **99**
  steak and kidney, English **87**, **88**, *88*
  syrup sponge **99**
  Yorkshire **174**
Puff pastry 48, **49**, *49*
Pumpkin, preparation 45, *45*
Purée of lentil soup 62
Purée Saint Germain 62

Q

Quail
  broiling 124, 130, **131**
  consommé and 59
  preparation 26, *26*
  roast **173**
  roasting time 172
Queen of puddings 205
Quenelles 79
Quiche Lorraine *202*, **203**
Quince, apple pie with **184**

R

Rabbit/s 30
  freezer storage life 14
  preparation 13, 37, *37*
  white stew and 104
Rabbit stew 119
Radish, preparation 44
Raisin filling, Danish pastries **192–3**
Raspberry/raspberries
  Danish dessert **96**
  mousse **96**
  preparation 46, *46*
  sauce **69**
  summer pudding **96**
  water ice **217**
Raspberry tart 205
Ratatouille 120, **121**
Ravioli 97, *97*, *99*
  pasta and 50
Red berry delight 96

Red cabbage
  boiling 92
  preparation 41
Red cabbage with apples 120
Red-cooked pork 117
Red currants 46, *46*
  crumble **185**
  Danish dessert **96**
  sauce **69**
  summer pudding **96**
  water ice **217**
Redfish *18*
Red mullet *18*
  baked **166**
  fritto misto di mare **138**, *138–9*
Red mullet with dill butter 127
Red snapper
  bouillabaisse **106**
  sweet-sour pungent fish **77**
Red wine sauce 66, 68
Rhubarb *46*
Rhubarb crumble 185, *187*
Rhubarb fool 95
Rice
  boiled **97**
  fried 156, **158**
  mold **122**
  savory **122–3**
Rice pudding 189
  creamed **99**
Rice salad 212
  curried **209**
Rich pie pastry 48
Risotto alla Milanese 122
Roast breast of veal with sour cream and tarragon 174
Roast carp with julienne vegetables 168
Roast chicken **170**, *171*
Roast duck with apricots 170
Roast guinea hen with apples 172
Roast partridge (or quail) with vine leaves 173
Roast pork 176–7
Roast ribs of beef with Yorkshire pudding 174, *175*
Roast shoulder of lamb with herb stuffing 176
Roast stuffed bass 167
Roast suckling pig 178
Roast turkey 172
Roasting and baking 164–5
  cereals (including pasta, bread, cakes, pastries and cookies) **188–201**, 190, *190–1*, *192*, **194–5**, 198, *198–9*, 200, 201
  eggs and dairy products 202–3, 203, *203–5*
  fish and shellfish 166, **166–9**, *166–7*
  fruit 184, **184–7**, *184*, *186–7*
  meat and game 174, **174**, *175*, **176–9**, *176*, *177*, *179*
  poultry and game birds 170, **170**, *171*, *172–3*, *173*
  vegetables 180, **180–3**, *182–3*
Roasting times
  meat and game 174
  poultry and game birds 172
Rollmops 208–9
Romaine lettuce
  braised **120**
  preparation 44
Rösti 151
Roquefort cheese, broiled **135**
Roux, sauces and 64, 66
Royal icing 197, *197*
Rum babas 194, **196**
Rum butter 69
Russian salad 212
Rutabaga/s *40*
  boiling 93
  buying 10

S

Salad/s, additional **212–13**
  chicken **84**
  curried rice **209**
  melon **209**
  vegetable **91–3**
Salad dressing 68–9
Salad niçoise 92
Salad vegetables
  freezing 15
  greens 10
  preparation 44, *44*

Salmon *19*
  broiled **127**
  coating with aspic 76, *76*
  kulibyaka **169**
  mold **210**
  poached **76**
Salmon baked in foil 166
Salmon mousse 78
Salmon trout *19*
  baked in foil **166**
  in aspic **77**
  poached **76–7**
Salsify
  boiling and steaming 93
  preparation 41
  sautéed **152**
Salt cod, Portuguese **108**
Salted almonds 155
Saltimbocca 148
Sardines *18*
  preparation 20
Saté, pork **133**
Sauce à la diable 130–1
Sauce bâtarde 67
Sauce béarnaise 67
Sauce béchamel 66
Sauce bigarade 66
Sauce bordelaise 66
Sauce demi-glace 66
Sauce espagnole 66
Sauce hollandaise 67
Sauce maltaise 67
Sauce mayonnaise 68
Sauce mornay 66
Sauce mousseline 67
Sauce normande 67
Sauce poulette 67
Sauce ravigote 67
Sauce Robert 66
Sauce sabayon 69
Sauce suprême 67
Sauce tartar 68
Sauce velouté 67
Sauce verte 68
Sauce vinaigrette 68
Sauces **64–9**, *66–9*
  freezing 14, 15, 64
  stock for 56, 58, 64
Sauerkraut 121
  goose with **172**
Sausage/s
  broiling time 132
  freezer storage life 14
  frying time 146
Sautéed eggplants 152–3
Sautéed bananas 154–5, *155*
Sautéed frogs' legs à la niçoise 141
Sautéed liver and bacon 149
Sautéed partridge jubilee 145
Sautéed soft roes 138
Sautéed sweetbreads Saint Médard 149
Sautéed venison steaks 148
Sautéing *see* Frying and sautéing
Scallop/s
  baked **169**
  buying 13
  coquilles St. Jacques **80**
  frying **138**
  freezing 14
  New England fried **140**
  preparation 23, *23*
Scallop brochettes 128
Scallops à la provençale 80
Scampi
  fried **141**
  frying **138**
Scones 190
Scorzonera
  boiling and steaming 93
  preparation 41
Scotch broth 60
Scotch eggs 161
Scotch woodcock 160
Scrambled eggs 160
Scrambled eggs with cheese 160
Scrambled eggs with chicken 162
Scrambled eggs with chicken livers 162
Scrambled eggs with mushrooms 160
Scrambled eggs with smoked salmon 162
Sea bass
  squirrel fish **141**
  steamed **77**

Sea bass with herbs flambé *126*, **127**
Seafood en brochettes 128
Seed cake 193
Semolina, gnocchi **98**
Seviche 208
Shad, Indonesian baked fish **168**
Shallot/s, preparation 43
Shallot butter 129
Shell beans
  boiling and steaming 92
Shellfish
  boiling and steaming **80–1**, *80–1*
  broiling 126, **127**, **128**
  buying **12–13**
  freezer storage life 14
  frying **138**, *138*, *138–9*, **140–1**
  preparation **22–5**, *22–5*
  roasting and baking 166, **168–9**
  stewing and casseroling 106, **106**, *106–7*, **108–9**
Shellfish cocktail 209
Shoestring potatoes 150
Shortbread 190
Shortcake, strawberry **215**
Shrimp
  artichokes with **91**
  baked pasta with **188**
  bean sprouts and **141**
  bouillabaisse **106**
  buying 13
  cioppino **109**
  freezing 14
  fritto misto di mare **138**, *138–9*
  hors d'oeuvre **209**
  jambalaya **122**
  potted **81**
  preparation 24, *24*, *25*, *25*
  scampi **141**
  seafood en brochette **128**
  sole with **167**
  Spanish stewed fish **106**
  stir-fried giant **140–1**
Shrimp butter 129
Shrimp cream, avocado and **211**
Skate *18*
  edibility of 21
  poaching method 74
Smelts, preparation 20
Snail/s, preparation 22, *22*
Snails à la bourguignonne 81, *81*
Snipe
  preparation 26, *26*
  roasting time 172
Snow peas
  boiling and steaming 93
  preparation 43, *43*
  stir-fried **153**
Soda bread 201
Soft roes, sautéed **138**
Sole *19*
  broiling 124
  fillets of **78**, **140**
  Greek fish stew **108**
  poached **75**
  preparation 20, *21* *21*
Sole florentine 78
Sole Ormondville 167
Sole Véronique 77
Sorbetière **216**
Sorbets **216**
Sorrel, cream of, soup **62**
Soufflé/s **203**
  cheese *202–3*, **203–4**
  chocolate **204**
  preparing dish **101**, *101*
Soufflé omelet **160**
Soufflé potatoes 150
Soups **59**, *59–63*, *58–9*
  freezing and storage life **14–15**
Soup normande 63
Soupe à la bière 63
Sour cream pastry 50
Soused herring 77, 78, *78–9*
Spaghetti 98, *98–9*
Spaghetti with pesto 97, *98–9*
Spanish omelet 161
Spareribs, pork **177**
Spatchcock chicken 130
Special apple fritters 154
Spice cake 193
Spinach
  boiling 92
  buying 10
  cream of, soup **61**, **62**
Spinach and mushroom salad 212

Spinach purée 92
Spiny lobster
  broiling 126
  preparation 24, 25
  See also Lobster
Split peas
  boiling 92
  preparation 43
Sponge cake, basic **193**
  génoise **193**
Sponge pudding, orange *98*, **99**
Squab/s
  preparation 26, *26*
  roasting time 172
Squabs with prunes and port 113
Squash
  boiling and steaming 93
  buying 10
  freezing 15
  preparation 45, *45*
  stuffed baked **181**
Squash in caraway sauce 92
Squid
  fritto misto di mare **138**, *138–9*
  preparation 22, *22*, 23, *23*
  Spanish stewed fish **106**
Squid casserole 109
Squirrel fish 141
Steak and kidney pie 179
Steak and kidney pudding, English *86*, *87*, *88*, **88**
Steak au poivre 146
Steak Diane 146
Steamed fish mold with anchovy sauce 79
Steamed sea bass 77
Steamed stuffed cabbage *90*, **91**
Stewing and casseroling 104–5
  cereals 122, **122–3**, *122–3*
  fish and shellfish 106, **106**, *106–7*, **108–9**
  meat and game 114, **114–19**, *114–15*, *118–19*
  poultry and game birds 110, **110**, **112–13**, *110–11*
  vegetables 120, **120–1**
Stir-fried bean sprouts 153
Stir-fried chicken and mushrooms 145
Stir-fried giant shrimp 140–1
Stir-frying 136
Stock/s 55, 56–7, **56–7**
  aspic **58**
  clarifying **58**
  court bouillon **58**
  freezing and storage life 14, 15
Strawberry/strawberries
  Danish dessert 96
  fritters **154**
  preparation 46, *46*, 47, *47*
  rum babas **196**
  sauce **69**
  water ice **217**
Strawberry cheesecake 215
Strawberry ice cream 217
Strawberry mousse 96
Strawberry shortcake 215
String beans
  boiling and steaming 92
  preparation 43, *43*
Strudel pastry 48, 50
Stuffed baked squash 181
Stuffed cucumber *208*, **209**
Stuffed eggs 208
Stuffed grape leaves 182, *182*
Stuffed loin of pork 177
Stuffed peppers 121
Stuffed pork chops 133
Stuffed tomatoes 209
Stuffing
  chestnut **172**
  herb **176**
  jugged hare with **118**
  roast bass with **167**
Suckling pig
  preparation 36, *36*
  roast **178**
Suet crust 48, 50
Summer pudding 96
Sweet and sour meatballs *147*, **149**
Sweet potato
  preparation 40
  sautéed **152**
Sweet potato soufflé 180
Sweet-sour pungent fish 77

Sweet white bread 198
Sweetbreads
  preparation 38, 39, *39*
  sautéed **149**
Sweetbread vol-au-vents 89
Swiss fondue 101, *102–3*
Syllabub 214
Syrup sponge pudding **99**

T

Tajine 114
Tangerine *46*
Taramasalata 211
Taramasalata eggs 100
Tarte au Gruyère 203
Teal, preparation of 26, *27*
Terrine, pork **211**
Thin mushroom soup 60
Thousand island dressing 68
Toast
  French **158**
  melba **81**
Tomato/tomatoes
  baked *182*, **182–3**
  broiling 124, **134**, *134–5*
  buying 10
  consommé madrilène and **59**
  freezing 15
  gazpacho **63**
  noisettes of lamb with, stuffed **148**
  peperonata **121**
  preparation 45, *45*
  ratatouille **121**
  stews and 114
Tomato butter 129
Tomato rice 122
Tomato salad 213
Tomato sauce 69
Tomato soup 62
Tongue 30, 38
  cold pressed **89**, *89*
  corned **86**
  pickled **86**
Torrone, chocolate **215**
Tournedos, preparation 32, *32*
Tournedos au vin rouge 149
Tournedos Rossini 132
Tray freezing 14, 15
Triangles, Danish pastries **193**
Trifle **215**
Tripe, preparation 38, 39, *39*
Trout *19*
  au bleu 75
  baked in foil **166**, *166*
Trout in cider 77
Trout with almonds 140
Truites en papillotes 167
Tuna *18*
Turbot *19*, *21*
  baked in foil **166**
  Greek fish stew **108**
  poaching 74
Turkey
  boiling 82
  broiling **130**
  buying 13
  carving 173, *173*
  deviled legs **130**, *130–1*
  preparation 26, *27*
  roast **172**
  roasting times 172
Turnip/s
  boiling and steaming 93
  buying and storing 10
  cream of, soup **62**
  duck with **112**
  preparation 41
Tutti frutti 217

U

Univalve mollusks 22, *22–3*
  preparation 23, *23*

V

Vanilla ice cream **216**, *217*
  cherries jubilee with **95**
Variety meats
  freezer storage life 14
  preparation 38–9, *38–9*
  see also Specific meat
Veal
  boiling and steaming **89**

buying 13
  freezer storage life 14
  frying and sautéing 146, **147–9**, *147*, *148*
  meat loaf **211**
  pâté de campagne **211**
  preparation 32–3, *32–3*
  ravioli filling **97**
  roasting and baking **174**
  roasting time 174
  stewing and casseroling **116–17**
  stock 56, 60
Veal and ham pâté 210
Veal chops en papillotes 148, *148*
Veal cutlets Milanese style 147
Veal scallops, cooking time 146
Veal galantine 89
Veal Marsala 148
Veal Zürich style 147
Vegetable/s
  boiling and steaming 90, *90–1*, **91–3**
  broiling **134**, *135*
  buying 10–11
  freezing 14, 15
  frying and sautéing 150, **150–3**, *150–1*
  preparation 40–5, *40–5*
  roasting and baking 180, **180–3**, *182–3*
  stewing and casseroling 120, **120–1**
  stock 56–7
Velouté sauce 64, 66, **67**
Venison
  braised with juniper berries and sour cream **119**
  buying 13
  freezer storage life 14
  haunch of **178**
  marinade 114
  preparation 37
  roasting time 174
  sautéed **148**
Victoria layer cake *193*
Vinaigrette 64, **68**, 75
Vol-au-vent/s
  cases **181**, *181*
  mushroom **181**
  sweetbread **89**

W

Waffles 156, **157**, *159*
Waldorf salad 213
Walnut/s *46*
  butterscotch sauce 69
  cheese and, fingers **135**
  date loaf with *191*, **193–4**
  macaroons **135**
  preparation 47, *47*
Walnut, apple and celery salad 213
Water melon *46*
Watercress
  Belgian endive, orange and, salad **213**
  cream of, soup **61**
  preparation 44
Water ices 216, **217**
Welsh rabbit 135
White beans
  baked **180**
  cassoulet **117**
  minestrone soup **60**
  purée of, soup **62**
White Christmas cake *194–5*, **196**
Whitebait *18*
  deep-frying temperature 136
  fried **138**
Whitefish
  gefilte fish **78**
Whiting *19*
  bouillabaisse **106**
  broiling 124
  cream of fish soup **61**
  fish mold **79**
  fish stock and **58**
  gefilte fish **78**
  Indonesian baked fish **168**
  matelote **109**
  poached 75
  quenelles **79**
Wholewheat bread 198–9
Wiener schnitzel *147*, **149**
Wild duck
  roasting time 172
Wild duck à la Seville 145
Wilted cucumber **100**

Winter fritters 154
Wok 136
Woodcock
  preparation 26, *26*
  roasting time 172

Y

Yam, preparation 40
Yeast 51–2, *52*
Yeast dough, freezer preparation 15
Yogurt
  buying and storing 12
  freezing 15
  marinade and 114
  meatballs with **149**
Yorkshire pudding 174, *175*

Z

Zabaglione 102
Zabaglione à la creole **102**
Zarzuela de pescado 106
Zucchini
  boiling and steaming 93
  buying 10
  fritters **150–1**, **153**
  preparation 45, *45*
Zucchini salad 92